African Entrepreneurship

African Entrepreneurship

Theory and Reality

◇◇◇◇◇◇◇◇◇◇◇◇

Edited by Anita Spring and Barbara E. McDade

University Press of Florida

Gainesville Tallahassee Tampa Boca Raton
Pensacola Orlando Miami Jacksonville

03 02 01 00 99 98 6 5 4 3 2 1

Library of Congress Cataloging-in-Publication Data

African entrepreneurship: theory and reality /
edited by Anita Spring and Barbara E. McDade
p. cm.
Includes bibliographical references and index.
ISBN 0-8130-1563-4 (alk. paper)
1. Entrepreneurship—Africa, Sub-Saharan. 2. Business enterprises—Africa, Sub-Saharan.
3. Small business—Africa, Sub-Saharan. I. Spring, Anita. II. McDade, Barbara E.
HC800.A5676 1998
338'.04'0967—dc21 97-24237

The University Press of Florida is the scholarly publishing agency for the State University
System of Florida, comprised of Florida A&M University, Florida Atlantic University,
Florida International University, Florida State University, University of Central Florida,
University of Florida, University of North Florida, University of South Florida, and
University of West Florida.

University Press of Florida
15 Northwest 15th Street
Gainesville, FL 32611
http://nersp.nerdc.ufl.edu/~upf

Contents

Tables

Preface

This book grew out of a conference of scholars from around the world who came to the University of Florida in Gainesville to present their cutting edge research on African entrepreneurship. Presenters from the United States, Africa, Europe, and Japan assembled to define, decipher, and delineate the dynamics of entrepreneurship—a topic that has come to be regarded as central to economic development in Africa. The occasion was the convening of the Ninth Annual Carter Lecture Series symposium. The chapters here, revised and coordinated, are a selection of the materials presented.

The Carter Lecture Series provides a national forum for the discussion of issues important to Africa. The series is co-sponsored annually by the University of Florida's Center for African Studies and was organized in 1988 to honor internationally renowned author Dr. Gwendolen Carter. It has produced five edited books that have become significant additions to the literature in African Studies. The editors of this volume welcome the opportunity to present selected papers from the symposium contributors, some of whom are already prominent in their fields and others who are beginning to make their contributions known.

The authors in this book approach the subject in a variety of ways. However, the prevailing theme is that entrepreneurship in Africa is a reality. The discussions, therefore, bridge the theoretical with the actual, propelling the actual toward the ideal. This book is intended for scholars and students of both African Studies and development studies. The various authors present the hands-on experiences of entrepreneurs in Africa and evaluate how entrepreneurship is expressed in the daily lives of its players and in the societies where they operate.

The book is comprehensive in including various dimensions of this many-faceted process, from finance and trade to cultural analysis of the economics of popular music. Each chapter also presents data and detailed analysis from authors whose expertise includes the disciplines of anthropology, economics, gender studies, geography, history, and political science.

Each of the geographical regions in Africa is represented (except, unfortunately, the Horn). The areas stretch from Ghana in West Africa to Kenya in East Africa, and from Cameroon, Nigeria, and Congo (Zaire) in the central region to South Africa and Zimbabwe in the southern region. The discussions range from traditional informal microenterprises to large, formal sector manufacturing operations.

The potential for entrepreneurship in Africa is in the capacity to transform the ingenuity and resourcefulness of individuals into powerful agents of progress for the whole of their societies. There are no simple or simplistic solutions to the problems and crises that confront Africa, but most likely, the energy of entrepreneurs will be the fuel that drives the continent forward into the future.

Preparation of this volume was a "treat, not a treatment," in that the editors and the authors worked in harmony and support. Funding for the symposium and secretarial assistance for the volume came from the University of Florida's Center for African Studies under interim director Goran Hyden and the Office of Research, Technology, and Graduate Education under Vice-president Karen Holbrook, as well as from the Florida/West Africa Linkage Institute, Barnett Bank, and Gainesville/Alachua Black Business Association. Graduate students Victoria Michener, Dierdre Williams, and Holly Blumenthal helped to type the manuscript. Linda Kahila, of the Center, assisted with the funding logistics. Meredith Morris-Babb and Kenneth Scott, editor-in-chief and director, respectively, at the University Press of Florida, provided enthusiastic support for the project. Reviewers and colleagues gave feedback on the introductory chapter and on others, but the authors take full responsibility for the content.

Anita Spring
Barbara E. McDade

1. Entrepreneurship in Africa: Traditional and Contemporary Paradigms

Anita Spring and Barbara E. McDade

Although the literature on entrepreneurship is vast, this book reviews those issues particularly relevant to entrepreneurship in Africa. Much of the early literature on entrepreneurship has roots in Europe and other Western cultures. Therefore, there is considerable interest in whether or not it has similar expressions in Africa. One of the major questions this book addresses is what form this subject has taken in Africa both at the present time and during its development. Are there some problems that are common to all entrepreneurs, and others that are unique to various parts of Africa? This volume provides some answers to questions about individual entrepreneurs and the process of entrepreneurship within the context of Africa's many social and economic environments.

The authors here examine the expressions of entrepreneurship in the formal and informal sectors, as public and private enterprises, and along class and gender lines. They evaluate entrepreneurial activities with respect to practice, policy, and access to resources. A range of entrepreneurial activities is presented—from microenterprises in Cameroon, Ghana, and Zambia to large industrial manufacturers in Nigeria, South Africa, and Zimbabwe.

Entrepreneurship is an essential component of the economic development process. In his book *The Theory of Economic Development*, originally published in 1911, Joseph Schumpeter was one of the first twentieth-century scholars to describe entrepreneurship as the process of creating new combinations of factors to produce economic growth (Schumpeter 1934). The entrepreneur introduces change, said to be pivotal to economic growth, into an economic system, and that results in increased production. Entrepreneurship conveys the notion of something special happening, something that adds more to the production function than is obtained by simply managing it. The Schumpeterian entrepreneurs are individuals who "possess, in more than an ordinary degree, the ability to visualize profit possibilities in unproved commodities, organizations, methods, and markets, and to overcome the obstacles that may stand in the way of getting new things done" (Clemence and Doody 1950:9). Entrepreneurial talent is not thought to be a rare commodity, and Schumpeter believed that, to some degree, it is common in most populations.

Defining Entrepreneurship

In order to determine if entrepreneurship as a process is similar or different in Africa, various standard and derived definitions are examined. Partly, the dilemma of knowing when and where to apply the label *entrepreneur* results from the inability of theorists and practitioners alike to reach a consensus on what entrepreneurship actually is, how to measure it, and how to derive universal specifications for identifying the entrepreneur. Kilby's (1971) reference to the illusionary animal the "Humpelumpf" reified this enigma. Entrepreneurship looks different to different people. No one has been able to capture the "beast," but everyone imagines what it looks like.

In order to define entrepreneurship, the view taken here is that a broad and inclusive approach must be used. Various authors in this book take on the conundrum and give their own specificity to the definition of entrepreneurship. Most do so by developing a checklist of attributes and conditions that identify the entrepreneur as a distinctive actor in an economic system. Based on their own empirical studies, observations, and fieldwork, the authors contribute to an understanding of how the entrepreneurial process is expressed in various African countries within a spectrum of circumstances. The merit of this approach lies in the fact that the resultant themes and theoretical explanations derive from concrete examples and never stray too far from the realities of the circumstances upon which they are based.

Schumpeter made the entrepreneur "the focal point and key to the dynamic of economic development and growth" (Greenfield and Strickon 1986:5). It is entrepreneurs who put together new combinations, and whose actions have consequences on the basis of their organizational skills, their creativity as decision makers, and the distinctive "opportunity structures (the settings, circumstances or situations within which the decisions and choices are made)" (ibid.: 11). Says Schumpeter, "The entrepreneur is the decision maker in a particular cultural context [who commands a] range of behaviors [that exploits] the opportunities" (ibid.: 15). Schumpeter's idea that the entrepreneur functions primarily as a creator of innovations in the production process has influenced much of the literature on entrepreneurship in developed economies. Alternative explanations of the entrepreneurial role have focused more on the entrepreneur's ability to organize rather than to create.

Many authors consider innovation to be the main characteristic of entrepreneurship, which they define as introducing new products, implementing new production techniques, finding new sources of raw materials, and discovering new markets (Marsh and Mannari 1986; Chileshe 1992; Gray et al. 1996). As innovators, entrepreneurs provide "new supplies in response to observed demand," Chileshe points out, and they create demand with new products and processes, with materials and markets, and with distribution channels (1992:101).

Entrepreneurs may not always be innovators, but they have to be coordinators. Even Schumpeter remarks that innovations of entrepreneurs need not be the products of brand-new ideas; they may be reconfigurations. Geertz observes that "the major innovational problems that the entrepreneur faces are organizational rather than technical" (quoted in Acheson 1986:47). The creation of a market (for example, creating a market for ethnic fashions that are custom designed by wealthy Zambian women, as discussed by Kasengele in this volume) may not represent a new idea; it may simply be a different approach for the particular industry.

In addition, the many decisions and actions in which business owners engage daily to maintain or expand their operations may include normal actions that can be considered "unheralded" innovations. In one Kenyan example, these range from developing a market strategy to improving product quality (Gray et al. 1996). And in some cases, the old may be more valuable to budding entrepreneurs than the new. Knowledge of methods used by experienced business owners can be helpful to those just starting out. Entrepreneurs may learn by observation or inspiration from others. They need not reinvent the wheel, and, since "novelty of innovation provides the most important competitive edge . . . innovation can be something as simple as courtesy, friendliness, and helpfulness" to potential customers (ibid.: 107).

The element of risk taking is also an aspect of entrepreneurship. Chileshe, writing on Zambia, argues that an entrepreneur "is a person with certain unique characteristics, capable of organizing and managing commercial undertakings that involve considerable risks" (1992:96). In this way, "they become the main pillars on which the internalizing of a country's economy using its natural resource endowment can be based" (ibid.). Entrepreneurs can control the means of production, and they have the ability to act as intermediaries between supply and demand. In the public arena, entrepreneurs can act as brokers between the masses and elites. These "political entrepreneurs" may bridge the gap between the public and the governing elite, and they can "transform social relationships, patronage, and dependency into political power, and in some cases . . . economic wealth" (Barnes 1986:225).

Entrepreneurs "exhibit at the most opportune moments, the necessary capability by initiating, conceptualizing and managing the required changes where others have not [yet] been able to do so" (Chileshe 1992:97). They provide an essential element to socioeconomic progress, and they are often described as "adventurous, innovative, risk-taking and . . . very tight fisted" (ibid.: 100). Individual entrepreneurs create considerable collective impact for the society as a whole. According to Landa, "entrepreneurs make choices, and larger patterns of change are reflected as the aggregates of those choices" (1991:141).

The interest in entrepreneurship and the attention now being accorded the entrepreneur derive from the fact that entrepreneurial activities help to achieve the principal objectives of economic development: creating jobs, increasing household incomes, and improving the quality of life. This has led to a closer examination of the entrepreneurial function in developing countries. The discourse in this book addresses the manifestation of this phenomenon in Africa.

Entrepreneurship and Economic Growth

Although entrepreneurship as an element of economic growth was postulated in the 1700s, it was largely absent from the mainstream of economic development thinking throughout the nineteenth century, which focused on two factors: capital accumulation and labor (Tyagarajan 1959; Wilken 1979). In the twentieth century, Schumpeter reintroduced the concept that entrepreneurship is a primary factor in economic development and growth. Nevertheless, the prevailing neoclassical premise is still that economic growth occurs during the process of achieving and maintaining a state of economic equilibrium with the proper combination of capital and labor. Schumpeter countered this by postulating that economic growth occurs only when the existing equilibrium of production inputs is destroyed. He describes this process as "creative destruction" and proposes entrepreneurship as the causative factor in this process.

Subsequent studies help affirm the concept of entrepreneurship as one of the primary factors in economic growth (for example, Glade 1967; Katzin

1964; Kilby 1971; Stevenson and Sahlman 1986). While entrepreneurship alone is not a sufficient condition in the process, economic development will not occur without entrepreneurial activity (Brinks and Vale 1990). Peter Drucker, in a discourse on business development, describes the entrepreneur as someone who seeks and welcomes change that can be exploited as an opportunity. Drucker derides the romantic notion that an entrepreneur is a rare and exceptional person and dismisses the fascination with the "entrepreneurial mystique" (Richman 1985:35). Entrepreneurship, he says, is not an activity confined to geniuses or a special class of people. Drucker's definition of an entrepreneur is "somebody who endows resources with new wealth producing capacity" (ibid.:35).

According to Acheson (1986), entrepreneurs' organizational skills reduce the transaction costs in firms. The type of firm that entrepreneurs can establish depends on organizational skills in combination with the efficiency of final and intermediate product markets.

Any useful explanation of entrepreneurial activity must be referenced within its overall socioeconomic environment, because "business activity does not take place in a vacuum but is set within a socioeconomic system" (Kennedy 1980:2). The circumstances that favor entrepreneurship may vary considerably from one society to the next. Its form of expression differs according to historical stages of the society's development and whether the economic system is precapitalist, early or late capitalist, socialist, or other.

Psycho-Sociological Theories and Characteristics of Entrepreneurs

Entrepreneurship and economic development are linked with innate personality traits of individuals based on indoctrination in specific cultural values, according to McClelland (1961). He isolates a critical ingredient in the psychological makeup of the entrepreneur and calls it the "need for achievement," or "nAch." This drives a person to strive for success, and entrepreneurship is the vehicle through which the success is attained. However, emphasis on the psychologically constructed "need for achievement" is criticized because it attempts to explain a complex process on the basis of a single variable. The emphasis on the psychological factors relegates economic factors to rather insignificant roles in the development process, and, hence, conclusions about the prevalence of entrepreneurial characteristics in certain societies (usually those with a Western European background) do not stand up to evidence from other culturally diverse countries (Kallon 1990).[1]

Others suggest that entrepreneurial activity emerges within certain

groups of people who have been affected by a series of identifiable historical events (Hagen 1962; Chileshe 1992). Hagen, observing the differences
in the incidence of entrepreneurial behavior in various ethnic groups within
the same society, concludes that entrepreneurship comes about when one
or more specific groups are discriminated against by the majority. Those
ethnic groups who are denied the normal opportunities for advancement
have lower status and command less respect. Consequently, they compen-
sate for their lower personal, social, and economic position by seeking avenues for success outside the normal means.[2] Hagen's thesis is that the
need to achieve status and success is the motivating factor behind a particular group's entrepreneurial expression, but this entrepreneurial behavior is "deviant"—at odds with the norms of the society in which it occurs.

Contrasting with the emphasis on individual or ethnic attributes as the
motivating force in entrepreneurial activity is a more holistic analysis, a
broader but ambiguous view. In this context, "cultural resources of a particular group or society [are] less relevant in producing economically rational behavior than [is] the gradual accumulation of experiences" based
on day-to-day decision making and problem solving (Kennedy 1980:7;
1988). Some authors suggest that entrepreneurial behaviors are responses
to circumstances in which individuals make decisions based on several
choices and parlay them into economic, social, and political advantages
(Glade 1967; Greenfield and Strickon 1986). Those who successfully exploit the advantages created within the opportunity structure, Glade concludes, are called entrepreneurs. As economist Hirschman points out, "enterprise is seldom found wanting in a society where it can be favorably
exercised" (1958:3).

Entrepreneurship in Africa

Are these experiences attributable (along with others) to entrepreneurship
and its expression? What are the constraints? And where does the potential lie? How will entrepreneurship promote sustained growth? Does African entrepreneurship follow the same or different paths from those of entrepreneurial activities in other parts of the world?

For scholars, with regards to the fact that much of the earlier literature
on entrepreneurship has its roots in Europe, are these concepts and theories universally applicable? Cummings (1995) asks a number of questions
along these lines. How have past economic patterns and entrepreneurial
practices changed? How have they been replaced or modified, and what
new ones have been added? How far is it necessary to go beyond the stan-

dard Western models to construct paradigms more relevant to African conditions?

It may not be appropriate or desirable for developing countries to import entrepreneurial techniques wholesale from developed countries. For example, a recent study of African businesses concludes that entrepreneurs in the United States and in other developed countries can learn from the experiences of entrepreneurs in West Africa (Diomande 1990). Those in West Africa often plunge into business with a bare minimum of capital or resources, and some are quite successful despite these austere starts. Diomande believes that the "sheer availability of abundant resources" encourages the entrepreneur in rich countries to "oversource and wastefully use resources that are not really needed" (1990:191). For example, African entrepreneurs usually cannot select their workers from a large skilled labor force, so they secure and train personnel through apprenticeships, tutelage arrangements, family members, and acquaintances. They raise startup and operating capital from community resources such as rotating credit systems involving social groups. Operating several businesses simultaneously is criticized by Western observers as evidence of a lack of commitment to develop a single enterprise fully. But African entrepreneurs choose to diversify their investments, believing that owning several types of businesses guards against risks that are common in the economic climates of many African countries. Diversification of economic activities, particularly in the rural areas, is regarded as a rational investment strategy.

The visible evidence of entrepreneurship is not the same in Silicon Valley, California, as it is in Sekondi-Takoradi, Ghana, but the functions of the entrepreneur, which are to coordinate resources and increase economic output, are the same. Much of the attention in industrialized countries is accorded to entrepreneurial activity in high-technology industries and to the introduction of high-tech products. However, entrepreneurs all over the world are involved in other economic sectors, such as trade, real estate, and agriculture. The establishment of cash cropping in certain areas and the ubiquitous trading and transport operations of local people are, indeed, entrepreneurial activities (Meier and Seers 1984:31).

Hirschman observes that people in traditional cultures make changes in their lifestyles and behavior when they believe the changes to be beneficial. He notes that "when economic opportunity is perceived, consumption-savings and work-leisure patterns are drastically readjusted" (1958:3). Early scholars in Africa of such behavior include Polly Hill (1963), who identified entrepreneurship among Ghanaian cocoa farmers in the 1960s, and Odufalu (1971), who studied indigenous enterprise in Nigerian manu-facturing. Subsequent studies of both modern and traditional business-men in Zambia (Beveridge and Oberschall 1979), Ghana (Kennedy 1980, 1988), Sierra Leone (Kallon 1990), and other countries in Africa (see, among others, Berman and Leys 1994) supply ample evidence of the dynamics of entrepreneurship in Africa.

This book provides some new models for studying entrepreneurs and their environments. Many of these models have been derived from entre-preneurial methods that evolved in response to colonialism, to post-inde-pendence systems, and to the increasingly global environment. One ques-tion that may be specific to Africa is why so few of the indigenous African entrepreneurial enterprises grow into large-scale organizations. Several of the studies in this volume (Blewett and Farley, Daniels, Fafchamps, and MacGaffey) provide some answers to this question. Years ago it was noted that "it seems paradoxical that in Ghana and Nigeria, where trading is almost a universal occupation, there are comparatively few large African trading firms. . . . [There] are numerous craftspersons . . . [but] few large African manufacturing firms" (Herskovits 1964:194). Scarcity of capital for investment has been propounded as a major constraint to the expansion of small firms into large corporations. The process of capital accumulation is discussed in the following section.

Capital Accumulation in Africa

Capitalist penetration in Africa is incomplete and "coexists with other non-capitalist modes of production" (MacGaffey 1987:15). Africa has little in-dustrial capitalism, a legacy of the colonial institutions that used Africa as a source of raw materials and new markets but not as a place to invest. Africa has "plugged" into capitalism rather late in the history of world capitalism, rather than developing it locally. Under colonialism, commerce in the formal sector was restricted and was often structured to bypass Af-ricans (see also Himbara, this volume, who presents a rebuttal of this premise). Since independence, many African governments have established and encouraged the rise of public enterprises such as parastatals that also impede indigenous private-sector development (Grosh and Mukandala 1994).

Both the legacy of colonial exploitation by foreign governments and the experience of foreign capital that benefits a small percentage of the local population influence leaders of many independent countries to es-chew capitalism in favor of what they hope will be more equitable eco-nomic systems. For example, in the early 1960s, the governments of Ghana and Tanzania implemented economic policies to discourage the emergence of "African capitalism" (Elkan 1988:21). After independence, most African governments decided that industrial and commercial development should be managed by the state. One reason for this strategy is the belief that economic development for the masses should not be left in the hands of a few individuals in the private business sector.

However, in three of Africa's best economic success cases (Ivory Coast, Kenya, and Nigeria), there is a critical debate "on the degree of autonomy possible for indigenous accumulators under the external structural constraints imposed by the capitalist world economy and state system" (Lubeck 1987:3). Because of the colonial legacy, and because of African modes of production, the ways in which capital is accumulated in these countries are uneven, often "joined and articulated with the pre-capitalist social relations and strata from which they emerged" (ibid.:7). In these cases, indigenous institutions have been mobilized for accumulation, with examples that include subsidizing wage labor with household production, using traditional labor owed to chiefs and lineage heads, and forming alliances with aristocrats and merchants.

The development of an African, capital-endowed, entrepreneurial class may require alliances between the state and private interests. For example, in the Côte d'Ivoire a tripartite political alliance is developing that consists of the Ivorian bourgeoisie ruling class with the political support of the Ivorian peasantry and the external support of foreign capital. The state here assists indigenous entrepreneurs, especially in the formal sector, by providing a favorable environment for capital accumulation (Rapley 1993).

The African bourgeoisie can serve as an indigenous source of dynamism in economic development if this class can influence the state to implement economic policies that are favorable to indigenous capital accumulation and entrepreneurship (Rapley 1993). Compared with foreign capitalists, local entrepreneurs may have less capital, but they have better connections to their country's institutions and people. They may be more likely to produce for local arenas, to buy local inputs, and to hire local people to run their firms (Chileshe 1992; Rapley 1993). They may spend or reinvest salaries and profits locally, thereby causing a greater multiplier effect than do foreign firms that typically take salaries and profits out of the local arena. Domestic entrepreneurs may perhaps adapt technology to local conditions, as has been the case in the Côte d'Ivoire. Such reasoning explains why indigenous entrepreneurial development may contribute to sustainable economic growth and development.

State intervention in the national economy may be necessary to promote the accumulation of capital to finance African indigenous industry and entrepreneurship, but many interventionist states are detrimental to such development. Neoclassical economic theory argues that when the state intervenes in the economy, it stifles the initiatives of the private sector. However, the models of the successful newly industrializing countries in Asia show that the development of indigenous industry financed by local entrepreneurs can be promoted by state policy protectionism that shields the nascent enterprises against foreign competition resulting from liberalized trade regimes.

The Informal Sector: Survival Strategies in Micro and Small Enterprises

African economies, often considered to be composed of two sectors—the formal and the informal—pose dilemmas for both policy and growth. The formal sector, given official recognition, with recorded and measured indicators of gross domestic product (GDP), contrasts with the informal sector, with its lack of official recognition and unregulated and unmeasured components. The informal sector is sometimes considered undesirable, a "retarded" sector with low productivity, a drag on economic growth (Juma, Torori, and Kirima 1993). However, others see it as a productive sector, providing employment, services, and goods (Hart 1973; Cornia, van der Hoeven, and Mkandawire 1992). As a result, the International Labour Organization (ILO) and some African governments are developing polices and projects to promote employment and income generation in this sector. Hence comes the notion that there is no need to subsume the people and their activities into the regulated formal sector. Nevertheless, some still regard informal sector activities as poor substitutes for formal sector dynamism. In this view, informal activities are a consequence of the inability of the formal sector to provide employment opportunities for the increasing labor force.

Much of the productive entrepreneurial activity in developing countries in Africa and elsewhere is in the informal sector (de Soto 1989), but Grosh and Somolekae note that "there are as many definitions of the informal sector as there are people studying it" (1996:1879). It is identified by such characteristics as ease of entry, unregulated and competitive markets, reliance on indigenous resources, family ownership, small-scale operation, labor-intensive adoptive technology, and skills acquired outside of the formal education system (ILO 1985; Thomas 1992).[3] Size of business (based on numbers of employees, assets, and revenues) is another criterion (Juma, Torori, and Kirima 1993). The informal sector and micro and small enterprises (MSEs) are sometimes regarded as synonymous. Legal definitions differentiate between registered (formal) and non-registered (informal) enterprises (Grosh and Somolekae 1996).

The informal sector provides the training ground for entrepreneurial development and management, similar to other systems of apprenticeship in Africa (Chileshe 1992:107). Entrepreneurs tend to come from families with entrepreneurial parents (Grosh and Somolekae 1996); one advantage of this arrangement is that family involvement in business allows for ownership succession and continuation of businesses for more than one generation.

The informal sector also encompasses the irregular sector (for example, legal goods illegally distributed), as well as the criminal sector (Thomas 1992). MacGaffey (1987 and this volume) uses the term *second economy*, referring to "economic activities that are unmeasured and unrecorded. Some . . . are illegal, others are not illegal . . . but are carried out in a manner that avoids taxation or in some way deprives the state of revenue" (1987:23). The "second economy" is as much a political as an economic designation, in that it denotes a class struggle—the second economy deals not only with economic exigency, but also with the indifference of some African governments to the needs of business.

An important problem with most informal-formal distinctions is that they place all of the activities involved in the informal sector "under one basic rubric with little concern for their diversity" (Murphy 1990:161). In an example from Latin America, mobile retail produce vendors in the Dominican Republic defy many of the characteristics used to define informal sector activity. Entry into the occupation is not so easy; it is limited by occupation-specific knowledge and the ability to establish contacts that can facilitate access to capital, loans, and storage garages. Earnings are superior to those in the formal sector, and most participants choose (rather than gravitate to) this occupation. Nevertheless, even while decrying the dual-sector approach, most analysts continue to use this analytical frame.

Informal sector MSEs present problems to policy makers both within the government and in the private sector, as in the case of Tanzania (Sokoni 1991). There, the unemployed and the underemployed find work and provide cheap goods and services. However, entrepreneurs also defy and confound regulatory intrusions upon their nonstandard business practices and unauthorized locations. They often do not have the means or the inclination to pay for any infrastructure and social and business services, thereby presenting policy makers with a challenge to keep systems ongoing. Sokoni notes that policy makers see MSEs' positive contribution, "but have done little to facilitate it," and that tolerating and assisting them "is [merely] a way of sympathizing with and assisting those in poverty" (Sokoni 1991:1).

The informal sector may be characterized as having limited access to modern facilities and support services—such as electricity, credit, and government services—as well as having differential access to technology, as in the case of Kenya (Gray et al. 1996). Most of the entrepreneurs lack formal education and business training (see Naudé, this volume), which disadvantages them in terms of successfully expanding their business productivity and profitability. However, levels of skills vary within the informal sector, as, for example, among furniture industry entrepreneurs in Kisumu, Kenya, who are better educated now than they were twenty years ago. This can be attributed to a fall in real wages (which has forced more highly educated persons to enter self-employed small-scale manufacturing) and to increased competition (which has compelled artisans to improve the quality of their products).

Factors limiting growth of small enterprises include lack of access to capital for expansion, lack of business training of the owners, and poor facilities (Grosh and Somolekae 1996). Financial programs that specifically target MSEs may help a few firms, but what is usually needed is reform of macroeconomics policies that both limit capital access by maintaining high interest rates and place restrictions on obtaining loans. Policy revisions could help to create a business climate that would increase returns on savings and investments, which in turn would help enterprises to accumulate capital. Daniels (this volume) notes that in Zimbabwe, tens of thousands of MSEs remain untouched by any such assistance. Capital accumulation is inhibited by the dearth of financial institutions to provide security for savings and availability of deposits for business expenses.

The informal sector serves as an employment incubator for jobs that help to reduce income disparity and increase domestic consumption capacity. A rise in the level of consumption creates additional demand for products and services, and this in turn stimulates the start-up or expansion of indigenous enterprises. Within the appropriate economic climate, this process becomes an engine of economic energy that creates additional jobs and the production of more goods and services. Much of the growth of the informal sector is spontaneous and has taken place largely in spite of government policies or programs.

For example, the Kenyan government finally recognized the important role of its informal sector, and, as a result, outlined specific measures to assist the sector in the Sixth Development Plan of 1989–93 (Juma, Torori, and Kirima 1993). Other African governments are beginning to institute similar measures. However, legal requirements and regulations for establishing and operating formal sector businesses work against the expansion of firms ranging in size from micro-informal to more visible small industries and medium size businesses. Many entrepreneurs consider it more efficient to diversify into another microenterprise rather than expanding or upgrading their existing business.

All societies have informal components, and there is tension between the formal and the informal. The informal is not necessarily traditional; instead, it "may represent the newest economic form or . . . set of adaptations" (Halperin and Sturdevant 1990:334). Minimizing the divisions between the formal and informal sectors may be an effective way to improve the productivity of both. Despite the dualistic analysis, the sectors are already linked in many ways. For example, a study in Ghana found that most of the trained masters in informal sector automotive shops came from the formal sector (ILO 1985). In addition, many of these automobile shops are financed with savings from earnings in formal sector employment (backward linkages). Strong forward linkages are indicated by the fact that 80 percent of the master mechanics' business is with auto owners in the formal sector. The author of the 1985 study suggests (ibid.:76) that "the best way to improve the productivity of the informal sector would be by increasing its backward and forward linkages with the formal sector."

Formal Sector: Public and Private Enterprises, Large and Small Industries

The African formal sector includes both public and private enterprises. Public enterprises (PEs) include not only government institutions such as hospitals, universities, and administrative agencies, but also "quasi-independent entities that African governments have created to do what they feel their private sectors and bureaucracies cannot do" (Nellis 1994:3). These public enterprises, sometimes referred to as parastatals or state-owned-enterprises (SOEs), "are supposed to earn their revenues from the sale of goods and services, are self-accounting, and have a separate legal identity" (Shirley, quoted in Nellis 1994:3). During the 1970s, public enterprises in sub-Saharan Africa increased to number more than 3,000. PEs account for an average 10 percent of the GDP in countries worldwide, and the share of PEs in the GDP of African countries ranges considerably. In Guinea, Senegal, Sudan, and Zambia, PEs accounted for 20 to 40 percent of the share of the GDP during the 1970s. During this same period, the PE share of the GDP for Botswana, Kenya, Liberia, and Sierra Leone was less than 10 percent.

Structural adjustment programs adopted throughout Africa during the mid-1980s to the 1990s mandate reduction of the public sector and the divestiture of state-owned enterprises. The objective is to allow more resources to be invested in the private sector, considered to be a more efficient provider of goods and services because of its market-oriented production and distribution systems. However, Grosh and Mukandala maintain that an efficiently functioning public enterprise sector performs "essential functions that enabled the private sector in Kenya to be one of the most dynamic ones in Africa" (1994:43). These authors conclude that in Africa, the relationship between the public and the private enterprise sectors has been one of "interdependence and mutual reinforcement" (ibid.:43).

The formal private sector in Africa consists of a range of enterprises, from small to large in size. Small-scale enterprises (SSEs), small and medium enterprises (SMEs), and small industries (SIs) represent intermediate stages between microenterprises and large firms. Young (1994:31) notes that the SIs are primarily engaged in light manufacturing, have ten or more employees, operate away from home in urbanized locations, and deal with modern commodities (such as baked goods, furniture and woodwork, and metal products). Although small in production scale, most SIs and SMEs are formal sector businesses that do not originate from within the informal microenterprise sector.

In attempting to provide quantitative definitions of small industries, the number of employees—rather than such factors as capital investment, profit, and value added—is the focus (Hansohm 1992). But this number varies considerably: it has been up to 100 employees (Fafchamps, this volume), up to 50 (Daniels, this volume), and up to 10 (for example, McDade defines 0–3 as micro and 4–9 as small-scale).

SIs are a training ground for entrepreneurs: they learn firsthand the challenges of sustaining a business in a developing economy. They need to mobilize local resources efficiently, produce for the low-income population, and establish linkages to other sectors in the economic system. Some also pursue new approaches in attempts to improve their operations.

The SI sector has been targeted for assistance from Structural Adjustment Programs (SAPs), but many of these programs tend to be biased in favor of the larger, upper range of SIs in the urban areas (Hansohm 1992:9). They often are oriented toward the few small firms that produce for export, rather than toward the many that supply the domestic market. Consequently, tariff structures, trade liberalization programs, and foreign exchange policies instituted under SAPs may actually penalize small firms. For example, for a small clothing manufacturer, imported sewing machines are capital equipment for use in the clothing production process. However, sewing machines are usually classified as consumer goods and are assessed at higher import tax rates than the intermediate goods and capital equipment imported by large-scale manufacturers.

African economies need to foster linkages among small, medium, and large-scale enterprises to develop an integrated economic system. A major advantage of efficiently run large enterprises is that they raise productivity levels by achieving economies of scale in their operations. Manufacturing productivity among some small enterprises has been constrained because of their size, which "precludes gains from economies of scale" (African Development Bank 1994a:16). Therefore, industrialization programs in many African countries target both small- and large-scale enterprises. When linked with other firms in the domestic economy, large-scale enterprises can provide a market for intermediate production goods from smaller industrial firms. Especially in industries such as agro-processing, large-scale operations may improve the profitability of small-scale enterprises by supplying them with cheaper, locally produced inputs. Currently, weak or nonexistent linkages to the domestic economy and uncertain markets in the international arena reduce the overall output for certain large-scale manufacturing industries to less than 25 percent of capacity.

The African Development Bank in cooperation with its member countries seeks to address this deficiency. The bank provides funding for agro-based industries that process both industrial and agricultural raw materials (African Development Bank 1994b). Large-scale private companies are increasingly used (rather than SOEs) to build the infrastructure needed for development—including highways, railways, and telecommunications facilities.

Gender and Entrepreneurial Activities

Entrepreneurial activities are engendered in terms of access, control, and remuneration. More men than women tend to be in the more lucrative enterprises, especially in the formal sector, as owners and managers of large firms and small industries. Many (but not all) women tend to be in the smallest informal sector microenterprises. Both sexes share the middle ground of higher profit informal sector activities. MSEs as income-generating activities are the norm for many women from all parts of Africa (Spring 1995), providing small-scale remuneration, and, it often seems, handicapping enterprise expansion. Women may not be able to accumulate sufficient capital to expand their operations and upgrade their management skills; their networks may be restricted to other micro and small-scale enterprises. However, they pursue entrepreneurial activities and acquire assets increasingly as the decline of the "administrative apparatus of the state and the expansion of the (informal) economy have weakened the mechanism of male control over women" (MacGaffey 1987:166). Women's associations and specific women's projects are making some progress in achieving female solidarity to address these and other issues. But class distinctions, as well as ethnic and socioeconomic differences, may prove divisive in terms of achieving common goals.

There is a substantial literature, especially for West Africa, on women traders and entrepreneurs, mostly in the informal sector (see Spring and Trager 1989; Clark 1994; and references cited in chapters by Horn, Krieger, and Robertson). Such roles, discussed by various authors in this book (Daniels, Horn, Iheduru, MacGaffey, Osirim, and Robertson), are somewhat newer in central, eastern, and southern Africa. Men and women traders may specialize in different commodities altogether (MacGaffey 1987; Robertson 1997) and may employ different strategies (Kasengele, this volume). Women generally have less education to qualify for formal sector employment, loans, or programs. Thus they are more likely to be informal sector traders and vendors. Women's lack of formal education and their use of African rather than European languages are not barriers to business transactions in the informal sector, and there is no need to secure licenses, keep accounting records, or apply for bank loans. However, the informal sector is not an ideal environment for doing business, both because of limitations placed on it and because of its lack of official support and methods of capital accumulation (MacGaffey 1987; Women's Bureau 1993).

The prominence of African women in many of the chapters of this book reflects the significance of their contributions to economic development. Despite this significance, and although their entrepreneurial activities are essential to the functioning of their societies, they are often marginalized during the creation and implementation of public and private sector development strategies. For example, as entrepreneurs, women are involved in supplying most of the food to people in large cities such as Harare, Kinshasa, and Nairobi (see the chapters by Horn, MacGaffey, and Robertson), as well as in provisioning their local village and household units (Krieger, this volume). Women rarely receive formal recognition or assistance in these largely unheralded roles. In fact, women's enterprises are often proscribed by municipal regulations, and they may be subjected to harassment by local authorities.

But African women are not a homogeneous group, and not all women entrepreneurs in Africa have the same problems. Middle- and upper-class women often succeed in both the formal and the informal sectors in arenas from which poor women are excluded because of their lack of education, networks, and capital (see the chapters by Iheduru, Kasengele, and Osirim).

Themes and Realities of African Entrepreneurship

The chapters in this book elucidate a variety of specific themes and present detailed studies of a wide range of entrepreneurial expressions: small, medium, and large; legal and illegal; formal and informal. The geographical area covered spans the continent and includes Cameroon, Ghana, Kenya, Nigeria, South Africa, Zaire (now the Democratic Republic of the Congo), Zambia, and Zimbabwe. The chapters have been grouped into the following sections: entry into entrepreneurship, entrepreneurs as provisioners of the city and household, state policy toward entrepreneurial development, finance and credit for enterprises, and structural adjustment and African entrepreneurs. These divisions represent the major themes in entrepreneurial research as presented by the contributors.

Interpretations presented in these chapters may prompt the reconsideration of previous dictums or assert the applicability of new theorems. Factors that determine whether entrepreneurship falters or flourishes can be quite specific to a particular country. While recognizing the specificity of circumstances that may exist in each situation, the chapters are organized to present, as an aggregate, general requisites—some causal, others associative—for sustaining entrepreneurship.

Entry into Entrepreneurship

This section explores the reasons why men and women become entrepreneurs and explains much about the nature of entrepreneurial activities. Is entry driven by the needs of the participants or by the marketplace? In Zaire, MacGaffey shows that the lack of state support for business activities forces survival strategies to new heights as entrepreneurs provide missing infrastructure, use substitute currencies, and pursue unusual trade networks to maintain "the second economy" in the absence of the first. The scope of these entrepreneurial enterprises encompasses large and small firms, mostly in the informal sector, because there is precious little left of the formal sector.

Daniels argues that surplus labor in Zimbabwe is the entry reason for the multitude of low-profit MSEs, while market demand is the reason for entry into high-profit industries. It is useful in this case to disaggregate the types of firms that constitute the informal sector, because a classification that lumps them together would overlook their basic differences. This is an example of the previously noted misconceptions that result when the informal sector is analyzed as a single homogeneous category.

Ethnicity and group barriers affect entry into entrepreneurial activities in examples from South Africa and Zambia. According to Iheduru, black African businesses are few on the Johannesburg Stock Exchange, but millions find entry points in the informal sector MSEs. Kasengele presents evidence showing the barriers that Zambian men encounter as they attempt to enter the formal sector clothing and textile industries dominated by Asians. However, upper-income Zambian women have been able to penetrate certain areas of the formal sector retail clothing industry and establish their own niche and clientele.

To summarize each chapter separately, in chapter 2 Janet MacGaffey borrows from Schumpeter's definition that entrepreneurs "have not accumulated any kind of goods, they have created no original means of production, but have employed existing means of production differently, more appropriately, more advantageously" (Schumpeter 1934:132). Entrepreneurs in Zaire function outside the defunct official economy using creativity and ingenuity, in the face of "insurmountable obstacles." These include the collapse of the official banking and transportation systems, the unavailability of foreign exchange, the decline in public services and administration, the collapse of supply systems, and the harassment, extortion, and arrest of entrepreneurs.

Zairian entrepreneurs import goods from other countries and travel the globe (including, most recently, to South Africa) to obtain commodities. Because of a lack of foreign currency, they use gold, diamonds, cobalt, malachite, coffee, ivory, and drugs for exchange purposes. They employ networks of kin, friends, and ethnic groups for overseas assistance with visas, supplies, and accommodations during buying trips. Within Zaire, entrepreneurs may have to repair roads and bridges, invest in transportation systems, and keep the second economy alive so that fuel and other scarce commodities are available. Entrepreneurs fill in the functions of a government that has failed to supply the infrastructure that is conducive to business.

Lisa Daniels in chapter 3 presents the variables and models that drive the small-scale sector in Zimbabwe, questioning whether the labor supply hypothesis (surplus labor with limited skills and access to capital) or the market demand hypothesis (entry influenced by consumer demands for micro and small enterprises) holds. She shows that both influence entry into commerce, but the labor supply hypothesis is supported by evidence from low-profit MSEs in which people turn to these informal sector enterprises as alternative income sources in a declining economy. In contrast, the high-profit entry model is not driven by excess supply of labor, nor is it affected by changes in the GDP: these entrepreneurs have some access to capital, as well as greater business experience. Still, there are entry barriers to high-profit entrepreneurial activities, and these include capital, experience, and government regulations. High-profit industries (such as auto works, carpentry, electrical repair, and the retail sale of garments) and low-profit activities (tailoring, vending foods and farm products, knitting, and wood carving, among others) represent 19 percent and 81 percent respectively of the MSEs in a sample of more than 12,000. Expansion for high-profit industries is related to decreases in formal sector wage rates. The MSE sector is heterogeneous, and if both low- and high-profit industries were aggregated, the significant differences in the barriers, or entry-inducing factors, would be overlooked.

In chapter 4, Okechukwu Iheduru looks at the past and present situation of black entrepreneurs in post-apartheid South Africa and discusses two opposing strategies for black economic empowerment. The top-down, formal sector approach includes the few black firms (condescendingly referred to as "black chips") on the Johannesburg Stock Exchange (JSE), potential JSE companies, portfolio investment trusts, and professional investors. The bottom-up approach, which Okechukwu believes has a greater chance for success, includes the MSEs, encompassing registered but unlisted firms and informal sector vendors. MSEs and the informal sector (estimated to be 6.8 million mostly black operators) contribute 45 percent of the GDP. Sixty-two percent of the informal entrepreneurs are women. The sector lacks access to financing and faces extremely competitive market conditions.

Some black entrepreneurs have been successful, but their capacity for economic empowerment is greatly limited. This is because the formal structure is closed to outsiders, and also because there is a tendency to concentrate directorships in the hands of a few people—previously whites, and now blacks.

Although economic reforms and the deregulation of black entrepreneurship result in increased income and buying power, black businesses are not faring particularly well. Some large conglomerates are "unbundling," which is a way to share ownership and receive funds from a large segment of the black population. More than 5 million blacks now own shares in the stock market, including a group called the Women's Investment Portfolio, which has bought shares in both black- and white-owned companies.

Chapter 5, by Mwango Kasengele, analyzes the structure of Lusaka's clothing industry in terms of the entrepreneurs and their market. The industry is split into formal sector domestic clothing factories, dominated by Asian entrepreneurs; "boutique" garments fabricated by middle- and upper-class Zambian women (for both the formal and informal sectors); and informal sector local Zambian male tailors. Wealthy Zambian male entrepreneurs are unsuccessful in competing in the Asian market, but Zambian female entrepreneurs concentrate on producing high-quality fashion garments for higher income clients who wear cosmopolitan, international clothing. These upper-income women, however, encounter constraints to their business expansion. For example, as with many entrepreneurs, these women also have domestic responsibilities that limit the time they can devote to business. In addition, the increase in imports of second-hand clothing from Europe and North America looms as a major threat to all the local clothing industries.

Entrepreneurs as Provisioners of the City and Household

Several chapters document how small-scale entrepreneurs, especially women, supply the essential foodstuffs to some of Africa's largest cities. The importance of women's forward and backward linkages to the rural areas, to commercial growers, and to local producers is the theme of chapters by Robertson, Horn, and Krieger in this section, and by Osirim in a later one. Geographical aspects of development are emphasized in the spatial allocation of natural and constructed resources within rural and urban areas. Allocation and control of commercial spaces determines the layout of markets and the zoning of selling areas. This in turn affects the scale of operation, the profits, and the capacity for the expansion of MSEs.

In terms of provisioning large urban areas, Claire Robertson (chapter 6) analyzes the efforts of urban and peri-urban Kikuyu and Kamba women and men who provide foodstuffs to Nairobi, a city of 2 million. Male traders tend to be young, often landowners and wage job seekers with few or no dependents, while female traders are older, often landless, and have families. Women lack formal education and have domestic responsibilities that contribute to their relative disadvantage in the marketplace. Like women in other African countries (Clark 1994; Spring 1995; chapters in this volume by Horn, Osirim, and Daniels), female entrepreneurs in Kenya have less start-up and operating capital. Their profits on average tend to be less than men's, who are usually better financed and buy and sell higher priced commodities. Domestic obligations reduce women's selling hours and contribute to their withdrawing capital from the business for family needs. Poor women tend to sell in areas that may not be zoned for commercial activities, whereas men can afford to locate their operations in legal areas with better access to customers, thereby ensuring higher profits. Women spend more total years in entrepreneurial activities, but men's individual businesses last longer.

Women entrepreneurs in Harare, Zimbabwe, described by Nancy Horn in chapter 7, are the city's main distributors of produce emanating from mostly white-owned, large commercial farms and sold to informal sector wholesalers. Here again, women entrepreneurs meet domestic responsibilities, deal with reduced profits because of large numbers of competitors, and provide foodstuffs for their families (often to augment husbands' inadequate wages). Yet they are viewed neither as serious provisioners of the city nor as income earners.

The current marketing situation is exacerbated by the country's structural adjustment program, in which transportation is more expensive; sources for wholesale stocks are diminished; and market sites are now located away from pedestrian traffic. Trade liberalization policies under SAP allow more produce to be imported, thereby depressing domestic markets.

Women's commercial agricultural production is also constrained because of the labor they must perform on subsistence food crops as well as because of household chores, lack of access to land and credit, lack of water for irrigation, and lack of extension information. SAP policies that reduce employment in the formal sector increase the number of traders in the informal sector. Some fresh-produce trading is now being taken over by men.

Horn's chapter concludes with "ten tenets of women's entrepreneurship" that seem applicable to many African countries:

(1) Entrepreneurship is a gendered activity.
(2) Market women take risks.
(3) They diversify income-earning activities.
(4) They create microenterprise niches.
(5) They do not have access to formal capital opportunities but rely on spouses, kin, money lenders, and savings.
(6) Entrepreneurship requires market intelligence and reliable wholesalers, as well as knowledge of clients and their preferences.
(7) Women apprentice themselves to experienced vendors to learn entrepreneurial skills.

(8) They adapt trading techniques to available locales and spaces.
(9) Women strategize in terms of ways to make a profit and devote much time to their business.
(10) Some women find freedom from domestic chores by engaging in entrepreneurial activities.

Judith Krieger (chapter 8) compares entrepreneurial and non-entrepreneurial households in Cameroon in terms of demographic characteristics, dietary items, and expenditures. She relates these to children's health using growth indicators (weight and height for age, weight for height). She finds that the children of women entrepreneurs weigh significantly more for their height, indicating a greater food intake over an extended period, than do the children of collaborative households where husbands and wives farm together. Entrepreneurial women have a larger variety of food items in their pantries, as well as a greater quantity of food available. Women's entrepreneurial activities vary widely in scale and range, from buying and reselling small quantities of rice on the local market to large-scale operations producing commodities for export. There are a number of reasons why entrepreneurial women's families do better, including small but steady incomes, the ability to conceal income from spouses and other relatives, and the use of commodities to feed their children.

Entrepreneurial Management Styles and Characteristics

The chapters in this section examine the diversity of management styles in organizing enterprises. Traditional networks, ethnicity, and a display of wealth (to be interpreted as evidence of business acumen) are used by entrepreneurs in precolonial Cameroonian commerce, as discussed by Yvette Monga. In modern-day Nigeria, by contrast, Ukaegbu shows that owners of large formal sector firms balance the traditional custom of employing family members with contemporary business administration practices of hiring management based on expertise. This is a delicate balance when the business owner must deal with relatives who rely on traditional notions of patronage and clientelism for employment. Ghanaian artisans employ a variety of methods—networking, apprenticeship or otherwise learning skills—in what is usually considered a traditional crafts industry. Artisans consider themselves business owners rather than craftspersons, and McDade evaluates behavioral characteristics that are associated with business success in these enterprises.

In Yvette Monga's study (chapter 9) of the Duala entrepreneurs of precolonial Cameroon, she challenges the Weberian view that the Protestant-type value system is the requisite for entrepreneurial development and the presumption that savings and economic frugality outweigh other cultural characteristics in achieving capital accumulation. Another approach was used with considerable success, that of conspicuous consumption and copious spending on social and familial obligations (such as bride wealth, weddings, and status occasions) to "advertise" the affluence of Duala entrepreneurs.

This served as a confirmation of their business competence and helped to attract the attention of potential customers and future business partners. Both German and French colonial administrations attempted to obstruct or constrain indigenous entrepreneurship, but Duala entrepreneurs successfully manipulated their schemes, primarily through reliable social networks. Social networking, critical in precolonial Duala society, formed an economic basis for commerce and trade in Cameroon that persisted until the twentieth century and that is also important to the success of business enterprises in many places (see McDade and Malecki 1997).

As noted, chapter 10, by Christian Ukaegbu, examines the contentions that arise when wealthy Nigerian entrepreneurs with limited formal education seek highly educated managers to run their enterprises. These wealthy men (and occasionally women) may have accumulated considerable savings from trade, lending, or in the informal sector. Realizing their lack of formal education and modern management training, they hire managers with B.A. and M.B.A. degrees from prestigious schools.

However, vestiges of the traditional system of placing relatives in top positions in one's business complicate the relationship between owners/entrepreneurs and managers. Relatives who are invariably given positions within the firms may avail themselves of company funds, vote as a block, and otherwise undermine the "modern managers." These managers often find themselves in unenviable positions between contentious relatives and the patriarch owner. Their own positions are at risk if they make decisions that might raise the ire of the owner's relatives. Managers are impressed with the owners'/entrepreneurs' skill in accumulating capital and ability to take the necessary risks to establish complex enterprises, then realizing their own limitations and seeking competent administrators to manage their large businesses.

Nevertheless, managers complain that entrepreneurs can be secretive about their finances and about other business transactions, and that they may withhold essential information from managers. The managers need this information, for example, to negotiate with competitors or to be aware of the value of the firm's total capital assets and reserves. Such information may be withheld from the relatives as well, often leading to the demise of the firm if patriarchs die without grooming successors.

Barbara McDade, in chapter 11, delineates characteristics associated with the business success of Ghanaian cane- and rattan-weaving artisans. A quantitative analysis using business success (indicated by sales revenues) as the dependent variable shows that business success for both rural and urban artisans results from decisions taken and actions performed. It is not statistically related to personal characteristics, as postulated by McClelland (1961).

For rural artisans, the most significant characteristics are related to innovation (improving products and production processes), opportunity seeking, and traveling to other rural locations. For urban artisans, the most significant characteristics have to do with organizing the business—deciding whether it is to be a full-time or part-time operation and what is to be its location, in addition to considerations such as the owner's investment plans, source of start-up or operating capital, number of employees, previous experience in business, and product innovations. McDade observes that innovation and change are not rare among these so-called traditional crafts entrepreneurs.

Public Policy and Private Initiatives in Entrepreneurial Development

Entrepreneurial activities are highly affected by public policies and their level of enforcement, as the chapters in this section attest. Whether the climate for business is favorable or restrictive helps or hinders business success. It has already been noted that the informal sector frequently suffers from harassment by officials (see chapters by Daniels, Robertson, Horn, Osirim, and Himbara) through campaigns to "clean up" street and informal market vendors, as well as through requirements for licensing, attempts at taxation, and the like. Even within the formal sector in Africa, private enterprises often do not find a conducive environment for obtaining loans and tax credits (Fafchamps), reducing tariff restrictions, providing adequate infrastructure (Himbara), producing educated skilled labor (also see Naudé, next section), ensuring access to technology, and creating markets (Blewett and Farley).

Availability of credit for conducting commerce may vary according to group affiliation, even in private financial networks in the formal sector. Fafchamps reveals that "trade credits" between buyer and seller help ease cash flow and liquidity problems, but they are more likely to be offered to white than to black Zimbabwean business owners. For Kenya, Blewett and Farley show that ethnic affiliation influences business transactions. Ethnic affiliations among Asians within the popular music industry provide advantages through international purchasing and marketing networks. This proves to be a definite advantage for them over the locally oriented Kikuyu, who do not have extensive networks outside the country.

Specifically focusing on policy, David Himbara (chapter 12) departs from conventional interpretations (compare with Monga, this volume) that hold that colonial governments used restrictive policies to impede the development of indigenous African enterprises and to restrict them to a few types of industries. He maintains that such interpretations are myths and argues that instead of impeding or obstructing African entrepreneurs, British colonial policy in Kenya fostered an indigenous entrepreneurial class by promoting MSEs in the informal sector as the base from which an indigenous capitalism could develop.

However, the postindependence Kenyan government supports the practice of placing Kenyan Africans directly into the mainstream economy dominated by ethnic Asians and foreign business interests. Government policy encourages Kenyan Africans to establish medium- and large-scale businesses in commerce and industry, but, Himbara argues, most Kenyan Africans are not yet ready for this step. He therefore attributes the stagnation in the private enterprise sector to policies that impose "capitalism from above." These policies primarily benefit reigning politicians and high-level civil servants rather than indigenous private sector business persons.

The misunderstood colonial approach was vindicated in the 1980s, when the government began to integrate the small-scale and informal sectors into its overall policy regime. However, the government's "preoccupation" with loans, offices, business sites, and so on, rather than with more "decisive factors such as business skills, technical know-how, organizational competence, and establishing relationships with mainstream commerce and industry," says Himbara, do not aid the informal sector (also see Iheduru and Robertson, this volume).

Robert Blewett and Michael Farley (chapter 13) consider the effects of national economic policies on entrepreneurial enterprises by evaluating what went wrong with Kenya's popular music industry following that country's independence. Using the booming popular music industry in Zaire in the 1960s and 1970s for comparison, the authors (like Himbara above) cite government policy to "Africanize" the economy as a primary reason for the decline of Kenya's music industry. Noneconomic factors such as social networks, trust, reputation, and personal relations are shown to be essential to the viability of this industry.

The Kikuyu Kenyans took control of the industry from the Asian Kenyans, but the Kikuyu apparently do not have credibility within the international business community. They also lack experience in international music networks, and they fail to see the popular music industry as one that is continuously changing and innovating. Their own ethnocentrism contributes to their narrowing the scope of the music produced to predominantly Kikuyu ethnic music, which does not have the mass appeal necessary to create successful popular music. Furthermore, macroeconomics policies (such as government controls on licensing and imports, and foreign-exchange restrictions) inhibit the music trade.

Marcel Fafchamps argues in chapter 14 that bank credit is not the primary source of external finance for most African firms. Rather, trade credit (credit offered by suppliers) is most widely used and is of primary significance in the majority of commercial transactions. In a study encompassing more than two hundred Zimbabwean firms (ranging from small to large) and various ethnic groups (African, Asian, and European) in manufacturing and nonmanufacturing sectors, examples of trade credit included cash discounts and tolerance of delayed payments. The implicit consensus among large firms is that the cost of trade credit is cheaper than finance from banks or other formal financial lending institutions, because trade credit can be obtained more quickly and easily. Some smaller black-owned firms do not accept credit because they prefer to pay in cash, finding this more convenient than keeping track of outstanding loan accounts. White-owned firms, however, are more likely to buy on credit, finding these transactions more convenient and safer than carrying large amounts of cash.

In considering the offer of trade credit, clients are evaluated for credit worthiness through a combination of methods. These range from formal screening using published credit reports (similar to those in developed economies) to "social capital methods" that take into account the personal qualities of the potential creditor, such as reputation and social relationships. These informal methods tend to work against black business owners, whose enterprises are smaller and less well known in the formal banking and business communities.

Structural Adjustment and African Entrepreneurs

No study of development in the present period would be complete without addressing the global allocation of resources. Discussions here focus on the impact of externally induced policies, such as Structural Adjustment Programs and foreign assistance and control. How entrepreneurs react to these external pressures, and how these programs affect the ability of African entrepreneurs to compete in their own domestic markets and succeed in the international marketplace, is considered in the final chapters.

How do Structural Adjustment Programs affect entrepreneurs? Mary Osirim argues in chapter 15 that entrepreneurs in the informal sector are particularly affected, in part because of their already disadvantaged status in obtaining capital, credit, and training, and in part because of the increased competition from those who have lost formal sector jobs and enter the informal sector. Women microentrepreneurs in particular face declining profits, increased competition from men (especially retrenched male workers), loss of customers, increased input costs, rising transportation costs, and inadequate workspaces. Women also face double jeopardy in terms of feeding the family as food costs increase, with spouses losing jobs and social services such as health care being cut.

Zimbabwean women are largely restricted to entering MSEs because of their low educational levels, traditional gender notions of the division of labor, and domestic responsibilities. Even their MSEs are limited to trade in foodstuffs, food processing, and household goods. They are limited as well to certain occupational categories: domestic service, beer brewing, hairdressing, sewing, knitting, crocheting, and pottery and craft making.

Many of the recent policy measures taken to remedy the problems of African economies have prescribed market liberalization, which requires resources such as labor and capital to be allocated by private sector entrepreneurs for tradable goods. In chapter 16, Willem Naudé, writing on South Africa, argues that the positive impact of liberalization can be obstructed when investors and entrepreneurs begin to doubt that it can correct economic ills, especially if they do not understand the importance of their own roles in making it work.

Liberalization programs may initially cause increases in unemployment and resource scarcity, as the economy tightens into a more efficient system. Entrepreneurs may interpret this as the failures of liberalization rather than the transitory effects that will be corrected, and there may be private sector demands to discontinue such liberalization programs.

Naudé recalls that in South Africa, entrepreneurs began to lobby for trade protection and more government intervention when they felt they were being hurt by liberalization, thereby turning the situation into a self-fulfilling prophecy. In a case such as this, liberalization measures fail because they are not given sufficient time to effect reform. The ability of African entrepreneurs to maximize their returns from such reforms can be enhanced if they develop their technical, managerial, accounting, marketing, and sales skills in order to respond more effectively to the new incentives and opportunities. Education programs that teach skills that enhance international competitiveness are needed to build a more capable entrepreneurial sector that can more effectively compete in the international market.

Conclusion

In summary, this volume looks at how African societies are working out the answers and solutions to economic development through the experiences of their entrepreneurs. Its prevailing theme is that the concept of entrepreneurship, in both theory and practice, must be expansive and inclusive enough to account for the multitude of entrepreneurial dimensions. Entrepreneurship finds expression in a variety of contexts that include innovation, but it is not defined by this single component. What may be new in some situations may be African versions or adaptations of phenomena already established elsewhere. Entrepreneurship in Africa encompasses both innovators and business owners.

Within the African context, there is a merger of traditional business methods (such as utilization of kinship-based networks, patronage and clientelism, and combining household and business activities) and global business practices (hiring managers with advanced degrees, employing trade credit, using computerized systems, and so on). The ways in which capital is accumulated reflect a syncretism of these methods, from lending based on ethnicity to standard bank financing.

This book necessarily gives emphasis to the importance of women entrepreneurs, who are as diverse as are their male counterparts and who carry out entrepreneurial activities at several levels. They range from the ubiquitous, well-recognized market traders and informal sector provisioners locally and in big cities to the fewer large-scale international traders and formal sector owners of firms.

The chapters in this book present a realm of variations on the theme of entrepreneurship. The authors expound on a diversity of expressions among countries and conditions in Africa that are somehow unified under the goals of economic growth. The task of providing cohesion is complex, because entrepreneurial experiences are heterogeneous. Entrepreneurs range from the woman in an open-air market selling dried beans and earning sixty-one cents a day to the M.B.A.-schooled manager of a large firm that has revenues of millions of dollars annually.

Can or should there be a general theory for this entire realm? The explanations offered here are attempts to come to terms with these issues. For example, as African entrepreneurs reformulate political and economic paradigms from their own historical and cultural perspectives, it may be inaccurate (or irrelevant) to define them strictly as "capitalists" (see Berman and Leys 1994).

This volume contributes to the process of answering questions while at the same time posing additional ones for future consideration, as part of a continuing debate about development. These studies describe and analyze enterprises that vary in size from manufacturing firms with 100 or more employees to handicraft enterprises with one employee. In addition to enterprise or firm size, the continuum of formal and informal sectors and private and public (to a lesser extent) enterprises is considered. In all, these studies show that entrepreneurship is not a missing commodity in Africa.

But some questions remain. A primary one is whether entrepreneurs will be the engine for economic development. Will each category of entrepreneurial enterprise (MSEs, SSEs, SIs, and large firms) have to change or evolve from smaller to larger and from local to global in its methods and strategies? Will the enterprises have to move from nonstandard to so-called standard business practices, from low to high levels of capitalization, and so on, to be the catalysts of development and change? Will distinctly African patterns of entrepreneurship emerge?

For example, the consolidation of small businesses and farms into increasingly larger firms characterizes the U.S. economy. By contrast, Italy, the fifth largest economy in Europe, supports a mix of small entrepreneurs and large firms. Will African governments create optimal business climates in the private sector, in particular those governments with formerly socialist backgrounds and centralized public enterprises? Will governments fund the necessary educational and business-skills training programs, endow financial institutions to become business financiers, protect infant industries, retrench on harassment of informal sector MSEs, enhance market development both financially and spatially, and modify tariff and trade restrictions? Will gender divisions be maintained that relegate the bulk of women entrepreneurs to MSEs and only a few to formal sector industries?

The answers to these and other questions are not yet known. While the social organization and economic systems resulting from Africa's past contribute to its present dilemma, the future will be constructed from the efforts of its entrepreneurs as they work within the evolving systems. But entrepreneurs cannot maximize their efforts in isolation. A supportive socioeconomic milieu, as well as appropriate government policies, will play critical roles in their success or failure.

How distinctly African patterns will combine with global ones remains to be seen. Also as yet unknown is how African countries will cope with the impact of entrepreneurial efforts promulgated by international agencies, foreign governments, and multinational corporations. Development will depend on how these countries harness the entrepreneurial drive and energy into a consistently potent force for progress.

Notes

1. A study of the lifetime experiences of 1,259 entrepreneurs and 111 managers in the United States finds little evidence to support the idea that a singular lifetime experience or characteristic distinguishes entrepreneurs from "ordinary" managers (Kent et al. 1982). Brockhaus and Horwitz's study (1986) of the psychology of the entrepreneur concludes that a causal link between small business ownership and high need for achievement is unclear.

2. Within the African context, certain ethnic groups have come to be associated with entrepreneurial prowess, as for example, the Bamileke in Cameroon, the Gurage in Ethiopia, the Ibo and Ibibio in Nigeria, and the Chagga in Tanzania (Chileshe 1992). Locally their success is frequently attributed to personal characteristics, but location vis-à-vis trading arenas and business opportunities have been factors as well.

3. Thomas (1992) divides informal economic activities into four sectors: the household, with its absence of market sector activities; the informal sector, where small-scale producers and their employees provide goods and services; the irregular sector, with its legal goods and services but production and distribution that involves some illegalities, such as tax evasion and avoidance of regulation; and the criminal sector, with its illegal output of goods and services.

References

Acheson, James. 1986. Constraints on Entrepreneurship: Transaction Costs and Market Efficiency. In *Entrepreneurship and Social Change,* edited by Sidney Greenfield and Arnold Strickon. Lanham, Md.: University Press of America, 45–53.

African Development Bank. 1994a. *Operations in Ghana.* Abidjan: ADB Communications Unit.

———. 1994b. *African Development Report.* Abidjan: Development Research and Policy Department (CDEP).

Barnes, Sandra. 1986. Political Entrepreneurs in a West African City. In *Entrepreneurship and Social Change,* edited by Sidney Greenfield and Arnold Strickon. Lanham, Md: University Press of America, 224–61.

Berger, Brigitte. 1991. *The Culture of Entrepreneurship*. San Francisco: Institute for Contemporary Studies Press.

Berman, Bruce, and Colin Leys. 1994. *African Capitalists in African Development*. Boulder, Colo.: Lynne Rienner Publishers.

Beveridge, Andrew, and Anthony Oberschall. 1979. *African Businessmen and Development in Zambia*. Princeton, N.J.: Princeton University Press.

Brinks, Martin, and Philip Vale. 1990. *Entrepreneurship and Economic Change*. London: McGraw-Hill.

Brockhaus, R. H., and P. S. Horwitz. 1986. The Psychology of the Entrepreneurs. In *The Art and Science of Entrepreneurship*, edited by D. Sexton and R. W. Smilor. Cambridge, Mass.: Ballinger Publishing Company.

Chileshe, Jonathan. 1992 (2d edition). *Nothing Wrong with Africa, Except . . .* New Delhi: Viokas Publishing House.

Clark, Gracia. 1994. *Onions Are My Husband: Survival and Accumulation by West African Market Women*. Chicago: University of Chicago Press.

Clemence, R. V., and F. S. Doody. 1950. *The Schumpeterian System*. Cambridge: Addison-Wesley Press.

Cornia, Giovanni, Rolph van der Hoeven, and Thandika Mkandawire, eds. 1992. *Africa's Recovery in the 1990s*. New York: St. Martin's Press.

Cummings, Robert. 1995. African Entrepreneurship: Past, Present, and Future. Paper presented at the Carter Lecture Series Symposium, Gainesville, Fla.

de Soto, Hernando. 1989. *The Other Path*. New York: Harper and Row.

Diomande, Mamadou. 1990. Business Creation with Minimal Resources: Some Lessons from the African Experience. *Journal of Business Venturing* 5: 191–200.

Elkan, Walter. 1988. Entrepreneurs and Entrepreneurship in Africa. *Finance and Development* 25 (20): 41–42.

Glade, William. 1967. Approaches to a Theory of Entrepreneurial Formation. *Explorations in Entrepreneurial History* (2d series) 4: 245–49.

Gray, Kenneth, William Cooley, Jesse Lutabingwa, Bertha Mutai-Haimenyi, and L. Oyugi. 1996. *Entrepreneurship in Micro-Enterprises*. Lanham, Md.: University Press of America.

Greenfield, Sidney, and Arnold Strickon, eds. 1986. Introduction. In *Entrepreneurship and Social Change*. Lanham, Md.: University Press of America.

Grosh, Barbara, and Gloria Somolekae. 1996. Mighty Oaks from Little Acorns: Can Microenterprise Serve As the Seedbed of Industrialization? *World Development* 24: 1879–90.

Grosh, Barbara, and Rwekaza Mukandala, eds. 1994. *State-Owned Enterprises in Africa*. Boulder, Colo.: Lynne Rienner Publishers.

Hagen, Everett. 1962. *On the Theory of Social Change: How Economic Growth Begins*. Homewood, Ill.: Dorsey Press.

Halperin, Rhoda, and Sara Sturdevant. 1990. A Cross-Cultural Treatment of the Informal Economy. In *Perspectives on the Informal Economy*, edited by M. Estellie Smith. Lanham, Md.: University Press of America, 321–39.

Hansohm, Dirk. 1992. *Small Industry Development in Africa: Lessons from Sudan.* Munster and Hamburg: Lit Verlag.

Hart, Keith. 1973. Informal Income Opportunities and Urban Employment in Ghana. *Journal of Modern African Studies* 11: 61–89.

———. 1975. Swindler or Public Benefactor? The Entrepreneur in His Community. In *Changing Social Structure in Ghana,* edited by Jack Goody. London: International African Institute.

Herskovits, Melville, and M. Harwitz, eds. 1964. *Economic Transition in Africa.* Evanston, Ill.: Northwestern University Press.

Hill, Polly. 1963. *The Migrant Cocoa Farmers of Ghana: Study of Rural Capitalism.* Cambridge: Cambridge University Press.

Hirschman, Albert. 1958. *The Strategy of Economic Development.* New Haven: Yale University Press.

International Labour Organization (ILO). 1985. Informal Sector in Africa. Addis Ababa: Jobs and Skills Programme for Africa.

Juma, Calestous, Cleophas Torori, and C. Kirima. 1993. *The Adaptive Economy: Economic Crisis and Technological Innovation.* Nairobi: Africa Centre for Technology Studies Press.

Kallon, Kelfala. 1990. *The Economics of Sierra Leonean Entrepreneurship.* Lanham, Md.: University Press of America.

Katzin, Margaret. 1964. The Role of the Small Entrepreneur. In *Economic Transition in Africa,* edited by M. Herskovits and M. Harwitz. Evanston, Ill.: Northwestern University Press.

Kennedy, Paul. 1980. *Ghanaian Businessmen.* London: Weltforum Verlag.

———. 1988. *African Capitalism: The Struggle for Ascendancy.* Cambridge: Cambridge University Press.

Kent, Calvin, Donald Sexton, and Karl Vesper. 1982. *Encyclopedia of Entrepreneurship.* Englewood Cliffs, N.J.: Prentice-Hall.

Kilby, Peter. 1965. *African Enterprise: The Nigerian Bread Industry.* Stanford: Hoover Institution.

———. 1971. *Entrepreneurship and Economic Development.* New York: Free Press.

Landa, Janet. 1991. Culture and Entrepreneurship in Less-Developed Countries. In *The Culture of Entrepreneurship,* edited by Brigitte Berger. San Francisco: Institute for Contemporary Studies Press.

Lubeck, Paul, ed. 1987. *The African Bourgeoisie: Capitalist Development in Nigeria, Kenya, and the Ivory Coast.* Boulder, Colo.: Lynne Rienner Publishers.

MacGaffey, Janet. 1987. *Entrepreneurs and Parasites: The Struggle for Indigenous Capitalism in Zaire.* Cambridge: Cambridge University Press.

Marsden, Keith. 1990. African Entrepreneurs: Pioneers of Development. International Finance Corporation Discussion Paper 19. Washington, D.C.: World Bank.

Marsh, Robert, and Hiroshi Mannari. 1986. Entrepreneurship in Medium- and Large-Scale Japanese Firms. In *Entrepreneurship and Social Change,* edited by Sidney

Greenfield and Arnold Strickon. Lanham, Md.: University Press of America, 19–44.

McClelland, David. 1961. *The Achieving Society.* Princeton, N.J.: Van Nostrand.

McDade, Barbara E., and Edward Malecki. 1997. Entrepreneurial Networking: Industrial Estates in Ghana. *Tijdschrift voor Economische en Sociale Geografie* 88:262–72.

Meier, Gerald, and Dudley Seers, eds. 1984. *Pioneers in Development.* New York: Oxford University Press.

Murphy, Martin. 1990. The Need for a Re-evaluation of the Concept 'Informal Sector.' In *Perspectives on the Informal Economy,* edited by M. Estellie Smith. Lanham, Md.: University Press of America.

Nafziger, E. Wayne. 1977. *African Capitalism: A Case Study in Nigerian Entrepreneurship.* Stanford: Hoover Institution.

Nellis, John. 1994. Public Enterprises in Sub-Saharan Africa. In *State-Owned Enterprises in Africa,* edited by Barbara Grosh and Rwekaza Mukandala. Boulder, Colo.: Lynne Rienner Publishers, 30–24.

Odufalu, J. O. 1971. Indigenous Enterprise in Nigerian Manufacturing. *Journal of Modern African Studies* 9: 593–607.

Oyejide, T. Ademola. 1991. Entrepreneurship and Growth in Sub-Saharan Africa: Evidence and Policy Implications. In *Economic Reform in Sub-Saharan Africa,* edited by Ajay Chhibber and Stanley Fischer. Washington, D.C.: World Bank.

Rapley, John. 1993. *Ivoirien Capitalism: African Entrepreneurs in Côte d'Ivoire.* Boulder, Colo.: Lynne Rienner Publishers.

Richman, Tom. 1985. The Entrepreneurial Mystique. Interview with Peter Drucker. *Inc.* 7: 34–38.

Robertson, Claire. 1997. *Trouble Showed the Way: Women, Men and Trade in the Nairobi Area, 1890–1990.* Bloomington: Indiana University Press.

Schumpeter, Joseph. [1934] 1961. *The Theory of Economic Development.* New York: Oxford University Press.

Sokoni, Cosmos. 1991. Distribution of Small Manufacturing Enterprises in Morogoro Town, Tanzania: Some Implications to Urban Development. Unpublished paper, Geography Department, University of Dar Es Salaam, Tanzania.

Spring, Anita. 1995. *Agricultural Development and Gender Issues in Malawi.* Lanham, Md. and London: University Press of America.

Spring, Anita, and Lillian Trager. 1989. Gender Issues in Rural-Urban Marketing Networks. Sub-Saharan Africa Conference on Market Towns and Rural Growth: Economic and Social Linkages. Yamoussoukro, Côte d'Ivoire: USAID Office of Housing and Rural Programs.

Stevenson, Howard, and William Sahlman. 1986. Importance of Entrepreneurship in Economic Development. In *Entrepreneurship, Intrapreneurship, and Venture Capital,* edited by Robert Hisrich. Lexington, Mass.: Lexington Books.

Thomas, J. J. 1992. *Informal Economic Activity.* Ann Arbor: University of Michigan Press.

Tyagarajan, M. 1959. Development of the Theory of Entrepreneurship. *Indian Economic Review* 4: 135–50.

Wilken, Paul. 1979. *Entrepreneurship: A Comparative and Historical Study.* Norwood, N.J.: Ablex Publishing Company.

Women's Bureau. 1993. *Employment and Earnings in the Formal and Informal Sectors: A Gender Analysis.* Nairobi: Ministry of Culture and Social Services.

Young, Robert. 1994. *Enterprise Scale, Economic Policy, and Development.* San Francisco: Institute for Contemporary Studies Press.

PART I

Entry into Entrepreneurship

❖❖❖❖❖❖❖❖❖❖❖❖

2. Creatively Coping with Crisis: Entrepreneurs in the Second Economy of Zaire (the Democratic Republic of the Congo)

Janet MacGaffey

Innovate, innovate all the time. Every single day a resident [of Kinshasa] innovates, invents. . . . Life has become a permanent struggle. One can only escape by fending for oneself, that in itself is a tribute to a continually renewed and permanent creativity. . . . Instead of falling into the flood one takes matters into one's own hands.

(*La Référence Plus*, 15 February 1993; author's translation)

Zaire in the 1990s exists in a chronic state of economic crisis and political impasse: it does not seem to be an encouraging place from which to report on African entrepreneurship. Yet, if the political and economic situation were to improve, an encouraging prospect for business could be seen in the astonishing creativity, ingenuity, and talent of Zairian entrepreneurs in finding ways to cope with a situation so inimical for enterprises. This chapter details some of the versatility Zairians have shown in confronting the seemingly insurmountable problems with which they are faced. In addition, it shows some of the diverse ways in which they have managed to find opportunity in the chronic state of crisis of their country. While official economic activity is almost at a standstill, the unofficial activities of the second economy, by which the population survives, proliferate. This account has relevance not only for Zaire's future, but also for assessing the entrepreneurial potential that exists in other African countries in similar states of economic and political crisis.[1]

The term *entrepreneur* implies innovation of some sort in commercial activity. Joseph Schumpeter's definition specifies that entrepreneurs "have not accumulated any kind of goods, they have created no original means of production, but have employed existing means of production differently, more appropriately, more advantageously" (Schumpeter 1934:132).

"Economic development in our sense," he continues, "is only accomplished in the form of carrying out new combinations of existing goods" (139). For Schumpeter, the entrepreneur is the vehicle for reorganization of the economic system and for change in the composition of the upper levels of society (156).[2] For the Zairian traders discussed here, the distinguishing characteristics seem to be innovation and bold decision making to take advantage of opportunities that arise.

In Zaire, a vast expansion of the second economy has accompanied the decline of the official economy. The second economy consists of unrecorded activities that are not reported in the national accounts and evade state taxes and regulations. The second and official economies do not form distinct sectors of the total, or "real," economy, but they intermingle in complex ways: the same individuals operate in both; a single commodity may pass from one to the other in the course of successive transactions (MacGaffey et al. 1991). The entrepreneurs of this study operate both within and outside of the legally regulated official economy, but most of their activity takes place in the second economy.

This chapter focuses on men and women trading across Zaire's borders and in other continents. It documents the changing flows of trade from Europe to South Africa, details gender differences among traders dealing in certain commodities, and shows the entrepreneurial talent, creativity, and extraordinary persistence and ingenuity of traders.

Zaire's Political and Economic Crisis

Zaire's immense natural resources make it potentially one of Africa's wealthiest countries, yet it has a per capita income that is among the lowest in the world. The economy has been in a spiraling decline since the mid-1970s, a decline that intensified drastically at the end of the 1980s (Young and Turner 1985; Leslie 1987; Schatzberg 1988; Willame 1992).

The decline in government revenues that resulted from this situation caused a devastating deterioration of the economic and transportation infrastructure, widespread food shortages, the virtual disappearance of public health and education, and the collapse of the administrative capacity of the state. Beginning in 1982, the World Bank and the International Monetary Fund (IMF) imposed draconian austerity measures as a condition for continuing their aid, the IMF undertaking one of their most comprehensive Structural Adjustment Programs in Africa (Leslie 1987:66). But the expected increased investment from donor countries did not materialize. Business owners found themselves in dire straits and many closed their enterprises; some multinationals moved their operations elsewhere; unemployment expanded.

By 1994, GECAMINES, the copper mining company that had been Zaire's principal exporter, was barely producing.[3] Artisanal mining of gold and diamonds, however, enormously increased in the 1980s following liberalization in 1983, and it expanded again with the discovery of new diamond beds in the northeast in 1989–90. By 1994, diamonds were the principal source of Zaire's foreign exchange earnings. But the huge scale of diamond smuggling and fraudulent export has deprived the state of the revenues it should be receiving from this immense resource.[4]

This collapse of the official economy has been accompanied by a political crisis equally inimical to the business climate, centering on the stormy and violent efforts to establish multiparty democracy. This struggle began in 1990, when President Mobutu Sese Seko dissolved the single party, the Mouvement Populaire de la Révolution (MPR). In September 1991, polity and economy almost totally collapsed in a popular explosion of protest against hunger and desperate living conditions, the huge rise in prices resulting from a 48 percent devaluation of the zaire, the clearly perceived exploitation by Mobutu and the ruling class, and the ineffectiveness of the National Conference. Underpaid soldiers and large numbers of the population looted and destroyed stores, businesses, and homes throughout the country, as well as the headquarters of the MPR. As the Zairian press makes clear, particular targets were foreigners and the more arrogant members of the ruling class. At least two hundred people died in the violence. Major urban centers were devastated and infrastructure destroyed, 20,000 foreigners were evacuated, businesses were abandoned, and Chevron and other big foreign companies pulled out (Willame 1991; de Villars 1992:121–55). Major outbreaks of pillage also occurred in 1992 and 1993.

By 1995, after a succession of governments, Mobutu appeared to have regained the control that had seemed to be finally slipping away from him in the early 1990s. His "illusory peace, founded on institutionalized violence, systematic repression and fear" (Braeckman 1992:101), was reestablished. The years 1991 to 1995 have seen drastic intensification of the long economic decline. Inflation that had hovered from about 50 percent to 100 percent in 1990 rose to dizzying levels by 1994.[5]

Desperate to curb inflation and find banknotes to pay the regular army, the government introduced a new currency in October 1993: one new zaire was worth three million old ones. In some parts of the country, however, people refused to use it to show their opposition to the regime. More outbreaks of looting and violence resulted from this measure.

These political and economic problems have had many consequences
that have severely affected entrepreneurs: shortages of supplies and goods
of all sorts; the collapse of the banking system, which has meant that with-
drawals of only very limited amounts have been possible, seriously ham-
pering business; the unavailability of foreign exchange through the banks
and the worthlessness of the zaire internationally; uncontrollable prices;
the collapse of the transportation system as roads, railways, and ferries
have decayed and fuel and vehicles have become almost impossible to
obtain through official economic channels; the virtual disappearance of
public services and of functioning legal and administrative systems; and
continual harassment, extortion of money, and arbitrary arrests by the authorities. Supplying and operating a business and marketing products in
such conditions presents enormous problems, and many businesses failed
in the 1980s and early 1990s.

But as these larger concerns have diminished, smaller ones have cropped
up: Zairians have been quick to take advantage of opportunities that have
arisen alongside the problems of economic crisis. In 1992, one observer of
Zaire noted that although at a general level the economy was devastated,
small initiatives were burgeoning as people fended for themselves (*se
débrouillaient*) with a renewed spirit of creativity and resourcefulness. Small
enterprises, workshops, and garages were proliferating and sold all kinds
of things. Small-scale producers rivaled the declining operations of multinationals: people made soap and competed in selling it with the wholesale
importer Marsavco; shoemakers produced shoes and sandals to outcompete
Bata (Ciervide 1992:224).

Zaire's crippling shortages of goods and materials are being relieved
by traders who import the consumer goods, vehicles, construction materials, pharmaceuticals, foodstuffs, and other things that the country so badly
needs. Such import trade is the most profitable form of enterprise. A previous study of large-scale entrepreneurs in Kisangani showed that taking
advantage of the opportunities that came with crisis was, in some cases,
the basis for the initial capital accumulation that led to growth and expansion into large-scale enterprises (MacGaffey 1987).

Responses of Entrepreneurs to the Crisis

Given the shortage of goods, raw materials, and foreign exchange, entrepreneurs take it upon themselves to go on trading trips to other countries
to import the goods that the country needs. Zairian traders go all over the
world to obtain commodities they can sell profitably: they travel to other
African countries, to Europe, to the United States, to the Middle East, and

to the Far East. Which country they go to depends on ease of entry or the stringency of visa regulations at any particular time, and on the opportunities traders can find for making such trips possible. The direction of trade shifts rapidly as conditions open up or close down with changing government attitudes and demand for—and availability of—particular commodities.

Zairian traders must first confront the problem that their national currency has collapsed and is valueless beyond their borders. They must find ways, within the law or outside it, to obtain currency or commodities that are in demand internationally. In Zaire, such commodities in the transit trade to Europe are gold, diamonds, cobalt, malachite carvings, jewelry, coffee, ivory tusks (before the wholesale destruction of the elephant population), and, increasingly, drugs (Fottorino 1991:31–32). Traders buy hard currency on Kinshasa's parallel money market. Very large sums of money are changed daily for almost any foreign currency on this market.

These money changing operations are dominated by women and carried out openly on the streets, especially at *le Beach*. Some of the women work on commission for highly placed male relatives in the political hierarchy; others work on their own account. These money changers often get currency from the diamond traders who make massive purchases of U.S. dollars with their diamonds at the airline Scibe Zaire's Bureau de Change (*La Référence Plus,* 31 March 1993). Traders also obtain gold or diamonds from artisanal miners in Zaire, or they barter goods for diamonds in Angola and sell the gold or diamonds for hard currency. They sell goods for CFA (Coopération Financière en Afrique) francs across the river in Congo–Brazzaville and use them to buy other currencies in Kinshasa (Makwala 1991),[6] or they smuggle, fraudulently export, or directly barter cobalt, malachite, coffee, ivory, or other goods according to supply and demand (Rukarangira and Schoepf 1991; Vwakyanakazi 1991).

At the end of the 1980s, an important trade flow between Zaire and neighboring African countries emerged with the expansion of the trade to Angola into a vigorous and flourishing commerce. Travel in this trade is difficult and sometimes dangerous because of land mines, risky crossings of the Zaire River from Boma by canoe (the danger coming not only from the river but also from thieves overturning canoes and taking goods), and ambushes by frontier guards who beat up the traders and take their goods. If these problems are not encountered, the trade is profitable.

Some traders barter, others pay cash. They take beer, plastic products, and wax-print cloth through Soyo and import clothes and fuel for Banana, Boma, and Matadi on the Zaire estuary; they bring a wide range of goods to sell at the Mariano market in Kinshasa. This market flourished from 1988 to 1993. Two-thirds of its goods came from Angola, and they cost less than local ones, so they competed favorably with the Kinshasa supermarkets.[7] The goods principally sold by entrepreneurs in this market included cigarettes, soap, powdered milk, salt fish, margarine, cereals, whiskey and champagne, rice (imported from Europe), cooking oil and canned goods, glassware, and children's toys. A whole section concentrated on selling fuel from Cabinda. Women dominated the market: out of five hundred sellers in July 1992, only ten were men (*Le Soft du Finance*, 20 July 1992; *La Référence Plus*, 2 August 1993).

Through Tembo in Southern Bandundu, traders take radios, clothes, liquor, and jewelry to Angola to barter with diggers or traders for diamonds. They also take beer, locally very scarce, which they sell or barter for goods. Truckloads of passengers from Kinshasa were arriving daily in Tembo in 1993 (*Le Soft de Finance*, 6 May 1993).

This trade fluctuated according to changes in government and the course of the Angolan civil war. An abundance of goods in the Mariano market indicated that Savimbi, leader of UNITA, had increased his control. However, when UNITA captured Soyo, the traders in Mariano "went into mourning" because a profitable trading link that they had established disappeared: Kinshasa traders had established connections with the foreign workers of the big oil companies (ELF, Shell, and so on) in Soyo, and these workers served as intermediaries to Portugal, Belgium, and Spain, supplying products such as second-hand clothing and electrical appliances in exchange for African art and diamonds. Some women resorted to prostitution to get start-up capital to enter this trade, which could earn them large profits in Kinshasa. Some Zairian students at European universities earned their tuition and living expenses during their long vacations practicing this trade; others established permanent partnerships with traders, while yet others participated in the trade by long-distance air travel. But when Savimbi occupied Soyo, the foreigners left and the Kinshasa residents stopped going there. The Zaire-Angola trade then took a new direction: through Namibia by rail to Windhoek and Johannesburg. It was part of the expanding trade to South Africa described below (*La Semaine*, 1 January–4 February 1993).

The extensive trade between East Africa and Zaire in the 1980s has also been documented (Vwakyanakazi 1991; MacGaffey 1987:143–64). Recent information indicates its continuing expansion, and in 1991, despite unrepaired roads, 1.7 tons of merchandise were imported daily from East

Africa into North Kivu, as estimated from the daily arrival of eight truck-loads of goods. In the absence of any official allocation of foreign exchange, these goods were mostly paid for in gold (BEAU 1991:11). In 1994, an extensive trade was reportedly carried out across the border to Rwanda or Uganda by boat from Bukavu, with high-value imported goods being sent by air from Goma to Kinshasa.

Among imports from West Africa, wax-print cloth is especially important, as are clothing, shoes, and pharmaceuticals. Research in Kinshasa in 1988 showed the importance of women ("the real international traders") in supplying the town with imported Dutch wax-print cloth, shoes and accessories, gold jewelry, and electrical appliances. These women traders make long journeys to Europe, West Africa, and the United States to get supplies and to bring them to Kinshasa and sell them to retailers, including Lebanese and Asians. They constitute *une bourgeoisie commerçante* based on the wholesale trade (Kanene-Mpali 1992:185–86).

Traders buy goods in Europe to export to Zaire. Research in 1994 showed that this trade, though still continuing, was in decline in the 1990s because of many European governments hostile to immigration and the consequent tightening of their visa regulations.

Men and women traders each specialize in different goods in this trade. Women especially import to Zaire wax-print cloth, jewelry, blouses and other clothing, beauty products, foods (canned goods, salt, sugar, and onions), and shoes. Men primarily specialize in importing second-hand cars, trucks and spare parts, office equipment (photocopiers, computers, and printers), and pharmaceuticals. However, with the exception of cloth, some men also trade in the commodities traded by women, and some wealthy women traders invest their profits in buying and exporting second-hand cars from Europe to Zaire. Both men and women import televisions, VCRs, radios, and household appliances such as refrigerators and freezers.

Traders ship their goods from Europe to Zaire by sea and also take them in their baggage allowance by air. By way of promotion to try to increase their diminishing business, the Belgian airline Sabena and two Zairian airlines, Shabair and Scibe, have increased their free baggage allowance from 30 kilograms to 60, and it is said to be easy to get by with 66 kilos.

Traders were quick to react to increasing entry restrictions to European countries—they found new and more profitable opportunities elsewhere. South Africa, faced with anti-apartheid trade restrictions, increased its trade with African countries. Starting in 1990, three flights a week from Kinshasa to Johannesburg brought a flood of Zairians; others too poor to buy airplane tickets arrived by land through Zambia, Zimbabwe, or Botswana. Numbers increased after the outbreaks of pillage and looting in Zaire in September 1991 and January 1993.

Until March 1992, under the terms of an agreement between the two countries, Zairians were issued a two-week visa and a three-month temporary residence permit at the South African border. If they found a job, they could become permanent residents. For the year 1992, Zairians were estimated to constitute about half of the immigrants arriving in South Africa, numbering about 4,500 (Fidani 1993:52–53). After 1993, when the South African authorities began to get worried about this influx, the residence permit was no longer issued, the fifteen-day visa was not renewable, and Zairians traveling to South Africa had to give a security deposit of U.S.$1,000 to the South African representative in Kinshasa. But at the end of the fifteen days, migrants simply went underground to avoid being sent home, living with the help of networks of compatriots who had come to South Africa within the previous five years. The flood of immigrants included business persons, traders, ambulant vendors, students, and smugglers. They lived in the suburbs of Johannesburg. Ponte City, a fifty-one floor luxury apartment tower, was two-thirds occupied by Zairian families (*Le Monde*, 15 April 1994).

Informants in Brussels, where traders were finding that they sometimes had to wait six months for a thirty-day visa for Belgium, said that the attraction of South Africa, aside from ease of entry, was that the same goods were cheaper there than in Europe. Since 1989, South Africans living in Zaire have imported frozen foods and other goods. But as political and economic circumstances have changed, Zairians have gone themselves to find the goods they have wanted and have traded them in many African countries (Fidani 1993:54). For some years, planes have flown daily from Zaire to South Africa carrying diamonds, coffee, gold, and cobalt, bringing back fresh meat to be sold at very high prices in Kinshasa (Braeckman 1992:208). There is now an expansion of small airline services from Shaba to South Africa as the trade from that region of Zaire intensifies.[8]

Trade to the Far East includes exports of malachite and formerly of ivory to Hong Kong. Wax-prints have been imported from China since 1989, and since 1992 they have outcompeted the local product because of their lower prices (37,500,000–40,000,000 zaires compared with 43,900,000–48,300,000 zaires) and their superior quality.[9] These prices are possible because production is subsidized by the Chinese government, which is anxious to get foreign exchange. The cloth is often bought directly with smuggled gold (*La Semaine*, 23–26 July 1993).

Traders have solved the problem of lack of goods and of foreign exchange in these multiple and diverse ways. They have also initiated for themselves efforts to solve transport problems. In some areas, local businessmen pay for the upkeep of roads and the repair of bridges (Goossens and Tollens, in Bruneau 1989). Commonly, the profits of trade are used to import second-hand trucks, cars (to run taxi services), and spare parts. Small-scale entrepreneurs have found another solution: trucks belonging to public companies and supposedly making the journey from Kinshasa to Matadi empty are in fact used by traders to Angola, who pay a fee to the driver (Rapoport 1993:708).

A shortage of fuel resulted in distribution by quota to privileged groups who paid the official price; by 1992, only in Kinshasa and Lower Zaire was there any permanent service at gas pumps. Through entrepreneurial initiative, however, it was widely accessible through the parallel market—at five times or more than the official price (Alliez 1992). Unofficial fuel importers—as well as theft from big companies, from the military, from government personnel, and from others to whom it has been officially allocated—have supplied the "Kadhafi," the unofficial sellers of fuel who have proliferated throughout the country (Omasombo 1992).

Strategies for Organizing Unofficial Trade

The extraordinary responsiveness and flexibility that traders exhibit as they respond to opportunities immediately raises the question: How is it possible for them suddenly to travel to a strange country to find, purchase, and ship desired commodities, cope with an unknown language, and find a place to stay while so doing? These problems are solved because this trade, largely carried on outside the law, is organized by means of personal connections based on ethnicity or nationality, kinship, friendship from neighborhood or workplace, and religion.

Traders rely on such ties for hospitality and shelter and for help in finding their way around; for locating goods at cheap prices and learning how best to purchase, ship, and get through customs; for assistance with language problems; and for finding means to evade visa regulations. Traders will stay with kin, friends, chance acquaintances who are members of their ethnic group, or sometimes just any Zairians. In return, they will give Zairian foodstuffs they bring with them, or other gifts or favors. These contacts will guide traders to appropriate wholesalers or marketplaces and show them the ropes so that they can continue on their own. If customs fees are paid, it makes the goods very expensive, so fees are evaded as often as possible. Traders either do not declare their goods (risking confiscation), send them with flight attendants, or rely on personal connections to customs officials to evade or get dues reduced. In order to get visas to enter different European countries, traders may borrow the residence papers of an immigrant to whom they have a personal connection and who lives in France or Belgium.

New Problems

As entrepreneurs cope with some of the problems they confront, new ones are generated. For example, Mahagi, a town in Upper Zaire, was expanding into a modern city under the impetus of the flourishing commerce of fish and goods imported from East Africa, with buyers coming from all over Zaire as well as from Uganda. But then fish gradually became scarce because of thieves stealing the nets, and because of rising prices. In addition, corrupt authorities and officials bent on harassment fastened on the perceived opportunity of this new commerce, and their depredations gradually killed the trade (*Elima,* 28–29 May 1992).

The state lacks revenues to pay its personnel, who survive by extortion, of which entrepreneurs are often the victims. One newspaper reporter commented on the way police and the army harass traders—demanding money, setting up roadblocks, and levying tolls or confiscating goods—and illustrated with the example of a trader who gave up commerce because the gendarmes at the roadblocks were becoming rich while he earned nothing because of their extortion and the high price of fuel (*Umoja,* 23 October 1992).

Zairian entrepreneurs organizing their business interests in other countries sometimes face serious hostility and even violence from local people. In 1993 in Luanda, Angola, there was a pogrom against Zairians. For three days, armed bands in the city's markets pillaged Zairian shops and stalls and raped women. The police were conspicuous by their absence. The Zairian embassy gave a figure of sixty-five dead; many Zairians fled (*Jeune Afrique,* 4–10 March 1993).

In South Africa, Zairians are not well integrated into local society. They have access to a lifestyle denied to most black South Africans and speak none of the local African languages. They are often regarded with considerable hostility (Fidani 1993). In Europe, Zairians must deal with racism and discrimination that sometimes lead to violent confrontations.

Foreign business communities have at various times constituted formidable competitive blocks for indigenous entrepreneurs, who do not unite and cooperate to give one another interest-free credit and exchange of information, as do Greeks, Portuguese, Asians, and "Sénégalais" (non-Zairian

Africans). These foreigners have dominated in different forms of import-export trade (MacGaffey 1987:74–79). Most recently, the Lebanese have dominated some sectors of the economy and are fiercely disliked.

"The Lebanese are strangling us," say the retailers of second-hand clothing who buy bales of such clothes from the Lebanese importers. The Lebanese counter that prices increase because the zaire loses value weekly and because they are harassed by the authorities (*Le Potentiel*, 30 April 1991). Lebanese fortunes have waxed and waned and their degree of economic domination has fluctuated, producing abrupt changes in the economic environment of Zairian entrepreneurs.

Conclusion

The extraordinary degree of resilience shown by the Zairian entrepreneurs described here is necessary to cope with the extreme unpredictability and uncertainty of the economic and political situation in Zaire. These entrepreneurs are also subject to the economic repercussions of other peoples' political changes, such as the civil wars in Lebanon and Angola, the political gains of the European right wing with its anti-immigration stance, and the crumbling of apartheid in South Africa. Such changes both constrict and open up opportunities; entrepreneurs need to be innovative, bold, and quickly responsive. The enterprises they can build may only be ephemeral; success lies in moving on to build others. The investment of profits into a business, followed by its expansion and then the move to manufacturing concerns that builds economic development are all severely constrained by present circumstances.

What are the prospects of political and economic stabilization at the national and global levels? Are they going to improve, or does it seem likely they will continue as they are at present? If the foreseeable future promises more of the same, Zairian entrepreneurs are certainly developing the skills needed to function in such circumstances and are doing extremely well. Zaire is dependent upon them to provide whatever goods—and even services—are available.

Notes

1. Current conditions in Zaire make research on activities that are marginal to or outside the law virtually impossible. This research is based on Zairian newspapers in Brussels, interviews with Zairians in Belgium and Holland in March 1994, and five months' fieldwork in Paris on traders from Zaire and the Congo. I am grateful for a grant from the Joint Committee on African Studies of the Social Science Research Council and the American Council of Learned Societies with funds pro-

vided by the National Endowment for the Humanities and the Ford Foundation. I thank my informants and the directors and librarian of CEDAF (Centre d'étude et de documentation Africaines) in Brussels for their cooperation and assistance. Thanks are also due to my research assistant, Lisa Toccafondi.

This chapter was written before Laurent Kabila overthrew Mobutu and took over as president in May 1997. He renamed the country the Democratic Republic of the Congo.

2. Yves-André Fauré gives a balanced and nuanced discussion of the meaning of *entrepreneur* and the relevance of its usage in Africa (1994:66–70).

3. Copper production was estimated at 485,000 tons in 1985, 134,300 tons in 1992, and only 29,949 tons in 1994 (De Boeck 1996).

4. According to an estimate by Hugues LeClerqc, more than U.S.$666 million worth of gold and diamonds was smuggled out of the country in 1992 (personal communication). In 1993, an estimate given in one of Zaire's newspapers was that 80 percent of the country's gold and diamond production was smuggled (*La Semaine* 16–17 July 1993).

5. In 1995, one observer reported that the government of Prime Minister Kengo wa Dondo had succeeded in controlling inflation only to have it destabilized once more by Mobutu's distribution of money to calm the population during the Ebola virus scare. This resulted in prices escalating again (Walter Zinzen, personal communication, July 1995).

6. In 1992, traders selling goods in Brazzaville that had cost them five million zaires could realize ten to twenty million zaires upon their return to Kinshasa, by selling the CFA they had received (*Le Soft du Finance*, 26 March 1992). Several trips often provided the means to finance moving into more profitable trading in other countries.

7. One woman trader, age twenty-eight, with a diploma in business management, sold laundry soap at 70,000 zaires a cake, as compared with 130,000 zaires for local soap (*Le Soft du Finance*, 20 July 1992).

8. Although GECAMINES production has dwindled drastically, some cobalt is produced and is still smuggled to South Africa (*Umoja*, 25 August 1993). In 1992, a ton of cobalt realized U.S.$45,000 (*Le Monde*, 15 April 1994).

9. In November 1993, the rate of exchange was 8 million zaires to one U.S. dollar. After the devaluation, the new zaire was worth 3 million old zaires.

References

Alliez, Jean-Luc. 1992. Reflexions sur l'approvisionnement en carburants au Zaire (Reflections on fuel supply in Zaire). *Zaire-Afrique* 261:19–27.

BEAU. 1991. *Les villes secondaires* (Secondary towns). Kinshasa.

Braeckman, Colette. 1992. *Le Dinosaure: le Zaire de Mobutu* (The dinosaur: Zaire under Mobutu). Paris: Fayard.

Bruneau, J. C. 1989. Pauvreté urbaine et initiatives populaires au pays du cuivre du Zaire méridional (Urban poverty and initiatives of the people in the copper regions of southern Zaire). In *Pauvreté et développement dans les pays tropicaux* (Poverty and development in tropical countries). Centre d'Etudes de Géographie Tropicale.

Ciervide, Joaquin. 1992. Zaire, 1990–1992, éveil du peuple (Zaire, 1990–1992, the awakening of the people). *Zaire-Afrique* 264:219–26.

de Villars, Gauthier. 1992. *Zaire 1990–1991: Faits et dits de la société d'après le regard de la presse* (Zaire, 1990–1991: actions and words of society according to the press). Brussels: CEDAF.

Devisch, René. 1995. Frenzy, Violence, and Ethical Renewal in Kinshasa. *Public Culture* 7 (3):593–629.

Fauré, Yves-André. 1994. *Petits entrepreneurs de Côte-d'Ivoire* (Small-scale entrepreneurs in the Ivory Coast). Paris: Karthala.

Fidani, Geneviève. 1993. Les Zairois à l'assaut de Johannesburg (Zairian migrants besiege Johannesburg). *Jeune Afrique* 1690:52–54.

Fottorino, Eric. 1991. *La Piste blanche: L'Afrique sous l'emprise de la drogue* (The white trail: Africa in the grip of drugs). Paris: Balland.

Kanene-Mpali, S. 1992. L'Espace commercial de Kinshasa (Commercial space in Kinshasa). *Bulletin géographique de Kinshasa* 3 (2):179–215.

Leslie, Winsome J. *The World Bank and Structural Transformation in Developing Countries: The Case of Zaire*. Boulder, Colo.: Lynne Rienner.

MacGaffey, Janet. 1987. *Entrepreneurs and Parasites*. Cambridge: Cambridge University Press.

MacGaffey, Janet, with Vwakyanakazi Mukohya, Rukarangira wa Nkera, Brooke G. Schoepf, Makwala ma Mavambu ye Beda, and Walu Engundu. 1991. *The Real Economy of Zaire*. London and Philadelphia: James Currey and the University of Pennsylvania Press.

Makwala ma Mavambu ye Beda. 1991. The Trade in Food Crops, Manufactured Goods, and Mineral Products in the Frontier Zone of Luozi, Lower Zaire. In *The Real Economy of Zaire*, edited by MacGaffey et al., q.v.

Omasombo, Jean Tshonda, Murhega Mashanda, Nagif Deamo, and Shabanza Kazadi. 1992. Les kadhafi: revendeurs non officiels de carburant (The Kadhafis: unofficial fuel sellers). In *Economie populaire et phenomènes informels au Zaire et en Afrique*, edited by Gauthier de Villars. Les Cahiers du CEDAF. Brussels: Centre d'Etude et de Documentation Africaines.

Pabanel, Jean-Pierre. 1993. Conflits locaux et stratégie de tension Nord-Kivu (local conflicts and North-Kivu rivalries strategy). *Politique Africaine* 52:132–34.

Rapoport, Hillel. 1993. L'approvisionnement vivrier de Kinshasa (Zaire): Stratégies d'adaptation à la crise du système alimentaire (Kinshasa's [Zaire] food supply: adaptive strategies for the food-system crisis). *Cahiers Sciences Humaine* 29 (4):695–711.

Rukarangira wa Nkera and Brooke Grundfest Schoepf. 1991. Unrecorded Trade in Southeast Shaba and Across Zaire's Southern Border. In *The Real Economy of Zaire*, edited by MacGaffey et al., q.v.

Schatzberg, Michael G. 1988. *The Dialectics of Oppression in Zaire*. Bloomington: Indiana University Press.

Schumpeter, Joseph. 1934 [1961]. *The Theory of Economic Development*. Cambridge: Harvard University Press.

Vwakyanakazi, Mokohya. 1991. Import and Export in the Second Economy in North Kivu. In *The Real Economy of Zaire*, edited by MacGaffey et al., q.v.

Willame, Jean-Claude. 1991. L'Automne d'une monarchie (The end of a monarchy). *Politique Africaine* 41:10–21.

———. 1992. *L'Automne d'un despotisme: Pouvoir, argent, et obéissance dans le Zaire des années quatre-vingt* (The end of despotism: power, money, and obedience in Zaire in the 1980s). Paris: Karthala.

Young, Crawford, and Thomas Turner. 1985. *The Rise and Decline of the Zairian State*. Madison: University of Wisconsin Press.

3. What Drives the Small-Scale Enterprise Sector in Zimbabwe: Surplus Labor or Market Demand?

Lisa Daniels

Limited opportunities in the formal sector and high unemployment rates in many African countries have led to increased attention on the micro-sized and small enterprise (MSE) sector in recent years. This is not surprising, given the relatively high proportion of the population that is engaged in MSEs in many countries. For example, the MSE sector employs 22 percent on average of the adult population in five southern African countries, compared with only 15 percent of the adult population employed in the formal sector.[1] Mead (1993) reports that over 40 percent of the increase in the labor force in the 1980s was absorbed by the MSE sector in five countries in southern and eastern Africa.

Acknowledging MSE contribution to income and employment, many donor and government organizations have tried to assist the MSE sector through increased access to credit and technical training. But the number of MSEs that can be assisted by these programs is limited in comparison with the size of the MSE sector. In Zimbabwe, for instance, only 0.4 percent of all MSEs had received assistance from nine of the largest MSE assistance programs in 1993 (Daniels 1994).

Given the small size of assistance programs compared with the large number of MSEs, it is important to allocate existing resources carefully. This allocation may require a choice between short-term poverty alleviation and long-term economic growth. Short-term poverty alleviation is often necessary to help poor households survive. This type of assistance may focus on low-profit MSEs that will not necessarily expand or survive. This chapter shows that this may not be the best use of resources. If long-term economic growth is the goal, then profit levels as well as sustainability of employment must be considered.

One way to address the sustainability of MSE employment is to examine the factors that drive entry. For example, are MSEs driven by surplus labor? Do people turn to the MSE sector as a means of survival under poor economic conditions? Alternatively, are MSEs driven by consumer demand for MSE products?

Little information is available about MSE entry in developing countries. Liedholm (1990) estimated entry based on existing MSEs for a one-year period in Sierra Leone. Because the estimates did not include firms that opened and folded during the period under examination, the estimates had a downward bias. Cortes, Berry, and Ishaq (1987) estimated entry rates based on government statistics for two cities in Colombia. These rates also had a downward bias, however, because they did not include small plants and may not have included firms that opened and closed within the period. Although both studies provide entry rates, they do not explore the factors that influence entry.

The lack of information on entry arises from methodological limitations of previous studies. For example, many studies have focused on a set of firms at one point in time. While these studies provide valuable information on existing MSEs, they do not examine entry and exit, nor do they take into consideration the turnover of MSEs. Furthermore, the relationship between economic growth and changes in the MSE sector cannot be documented by these types of studies. Studies that follow a set of firms over time improve the ability to examine changes within firms, but they cannot explore entry of new MSEs due to methodological limitations.

This chapter attempts to address the issue of sustainability by examining the factors that drive entry among high- and low-profit MSE industries in Zimbabwe.[2] It begins by reviewing hypotheses about MSE entry and then describes the data collection, model specification, and the expected relationship between entry and each variable in the model based on previous literature, as well as on some factors that are unique to Zimbabwe. By using information from a nationwide survey of more than 11,500 enterprise sites and two surveys covering 1,800 enterprises that closed in Zimbabwe, the limitations mentioned above can be addressed.[3] First, a more accurate measure of entry is estimated based on existing and closed MSEs. Second, the determinants of entry are explored using industrial organization theory as a conceptual framework. While this framework has been used frequently to examine entry in industrialized countries, the determinants of entry have not been systematically explored in developing countries. Because industrial organization theory focuses on determinants of entry within an industry, entrepreneurial choice theory is also used in this study to examine proprietor alternatives outside of the MSE sector, such as farming or working for someone else. Finally, this study measures the relationship between MSE entry and economic growth.

Based on an error components model, the results suggest that both labor surplus and market demand play a role in firm entry. Among low-profit industries, entry appears to be driven by surplus labor. This is supported by the negative relationship between economic growth and entry rates. Furthermore, there is a lack of barriers to entry in low-profit industries, suggesting that these industries provide an alternative source of income for unskilled labor with limited access to capital. In contrast, entry in high-profit industries is characterized by significant barriers to entry, including physical capital, human capital (proprietor skills), and licensing requirements. Although entry into high-profit industries is unrelated to economic growth, it does not appear to be driven by surplus labor.

Hypotheses Related to MSE Entry

Micro-sized and small enterprise industries comprise a range of skills, profits, and access to capital in Zimbabwe. This range may help explain two conflicting hypotheses about the forces that drive firm entry: the market-demand hypothesis and the labor-supply hypothesis. The market-demand hypothesis assumes that firm entry is primarily driven by consumer demand. This implies that most firms would be profitable and may require high capital and skill levels. The market-demand hypothesis has been supported by several studies that have shown that the demand for MSE products increases as rural household income increases (King and Byerlee 1978; Hazell and Roell 1983; Deb and Hossain 1984).

Alternatively, the labor-supply hypothesis assumes that firm entry is driven by an excess supply of labor. In this case, people enter MSE industries in search of alternative income sources regardless of demand. Firms in this category would be characterized by low profits and low costs of entry. Although the labor-supply hypothesis has not been empirically supported, Daniels (1994) shows that the majority of MSEs in Zimbabwe are in low-profit industries.

Rather than assuming that only one hypothesis is correct, both the market demand and labor supply hypotheses may play a role in driving firm entry. For example, high-profit industries with corresponding high levels of skills and capital are most likely driven by market demand forces. Alternatively, low-profit industries may be driven by an excess supply of labor. If both are true, then the factors that influence entry should be different in the two types of industries. In addition, the relationship between gross domestic product (GDP) and entry should differ between the two types of industries. If the labor-supply hypothesis is correct, entry should be inversely related to GDP. As GDP declines, people lose jobs and turn to the MSE sector as a means of survival. Among high-profit industries, entry should be positively related to GDP. As GDP rises, demand for MSE products increases and people turn to the MSE sector to earn higher incomes. These hypotheses can be tested by estimating an entry model separately for high- and low-profit industries.

The Model Using Zimbabwean Data

The data for this study were collected by two nationwide surveys of MSEs in Zimbabwe funded by the United States Agency for International Development (Daniels 1994; McPherson 1991). An MSE was defined as any business activity that employed fifty or fewer employees and marketed at least 50 percent of its product. Although fifty employees is high for a definition of micro and small enterprises, only 1.6 percent of all enterprises had more than ten employees.

The results of the model primarily reflect, therefore, the situation in smaller enterprises with ten or fewer employees. Information on both existing MSEs and those that had collapsed or folded prior to the survey was collected during both studies in 1991 and 1993. A total of 10,940 existing MSEs and 1,807 folded MSEs were interviewed. The data used for this study, however, include only information on the 5,365 existing MSEs from the 1993 survey and all of the 1,807 folded MSEs from both surveys.[4]

An error components model using a linear functional form was used to estimate an entry model of MSEs in Zimbabwe. This model was selected because of the nature of the data. In this case, the data represent a set of firms that are followed over time, called a panel data set. Ordinary least squares should not be used to analyze a panel data set since the assumptions of homoskedasticity and independent errors are likely to be violated. This would lead to inefficient estimates and invalid statistical tests. To avoid this, the error components model uses generalized least squares (GLS) to estimate the model. GLS uses assumptions about the regression disturbance that are not restrictive. The appropriateness of the error components model compared with ordinary least squares without group effects is tested with Breusch and Pagan's (1980) lagrange multiplier statistic.

Entry in twenty-one industries that have a four-digit standard industrial classification from 1986 to 1993 was examined.[5] The industries were divided into high- and low-profit categories using the minimum taxable income of 4,801 Zimbabwean dollars as the dividing point.[6] As illustrated by table 3.1, ten industries fall into the high-profit category, while the remaining ones are in low-profit industries. Among the MSEs within these industries, 81 percent are in low-profit and 19 percent are in high-profit industries.

Table 3.2 shows the breakdown by gender within the industries. Sixty percent of all proprietors in high-profit industries are men while only 37 percent are women. Table 3.3 shows that 91 percent of all women in the MSE sector are located in low-profit industries, while 52 percent of all men are in low-profit industries.

The dependent variable, annual gross entry rate, is measured as the number of new firms established in year t, industry i, divided by the num-

Table 3.1. Profits and start-up costs by type of MSE industry

Sector	Avg. annual profits (Zimbabwe $)	Avg. cost of entry (Zimbabwe $)
High-profit industries		
Retail garments	97,630	1,102
Auto works	71,388	8,930
General trader	28,970	42,336
Grocery	13,817	1,344
Construction	9,126	1,643
Welding	8,619	1,643
Hairdresser/barber	7,078	3,688
Vending garments	6,027	149
Carpentry	5,560	242
Electrical repair	5,512	6,220
Low-profit industries		
Dressmaking	4,233	600
Tailoring	3,817	366
Shoework	3,813	278
Other textile	3,709	43
Vending foods	2,674	54
Knitting	2,417	4
Grass/cane	1,355	43
Crocheting	1,355	43
Vending farm products	1,142	28
Traditional healer	1,003	*
Wood carving	607	28

Source: 1993 survey data
Note: U.S.$1.00 = Z$6.70
* Not available

ber of firms in existence at the beginning of year *t*, in industry *i*. It shows the number of new enterprises in a given year as a percentage of the enterprises that were alive at the beginning of that year for a particular industry. This measure combines information from an existing enterprise questionnaire with a questionnaire on enterprises that folded.

Table 3.4 shows the names, definitions, and expected signs of the independent variables. There are two types of independent variables listed on the table that are common to the industrial organization literature: barriers to entry and entry-inducing factors. Barriers to entry are expected to be negatively correlated with entry. When they exist, entry barriers allow firms to maintain higher profit levels, since competition is limited. In a perfectly competitive industry without barriers to entry, firms will enter an industry until economic profits are driven to zero.

Although there is no empirical evidence from developing countries, significant barriers to entry from the U.S., Canadian, and European literature include market concentration, advertising, economies of scale, capital expenditures, human capital requirements, and government policies (Mans-

Table 3.2. Proportion of men and women in high- and low-profit industries (column percentages)

	High-profit industries	Low-profit industries
Women	37	83
Men	60	15
Mixed[a]	3	2
Total	100	100

Source: 1993 survey data
a. Mixed refers to MSEs owned jointly by men and women.

Table 3.3. Proportion of men and women in high- and low-profit industries (row percentages)

Proprietors	High-profit industries	Low-profit industries	Total
Women	9	91	100
Men	48	52	100
Mixed[a]	35	65	100

Source: 1993 survey data
a. Mixed refers to MSEs owned jointly by men and women.

Table 3.4. Barriers to entry and entry-inducing factors by expected sign for high- and low-profit MSE industries

Variable name	Definition	Expected sign	
		High-profit	Low-profit
Barrier to entry variables			
CAPITAL	Average expenditure in hundreds of Zimbabwe dollars on equipment and building to start a business in industry i	Neg	NS
SQCAPITAL	Square of Capital	Pos	NS
WORKCAP	Average value of expenditures on variable costs during the week prior to the survey in industry i in hundreds of Zimbabwe dollars	Neg	NS
YRSEXP	Average number of years that proprietors have operated in industry i	Neg	NS
LICENSE	Percentage of firms that have licenses in industry i during period t	Neg	NS
Entry-inducing variables			
PAIDEMPL	Average number of paid employees added or subtracted since the start of the business in industry i	Pos	NS
UNPEMPGR	Average number of unpaid employees added or subtracted since the start of the business in industry i	NS	NS
WAGE	Domestic worker's salary in 1990 Zimbabwe dollars per month	Neg	Neg
SQWAGE	Square of Wage	Pos	Pos
GDP	Percentage change in GDP in period t expressed in constant 1980 dollars using 1990 weights	Pos	Neg
MAIZE	Average kilograms of maize harvested by proprietors in industry i from 1991 to 1993 in thousands of kilograms	Neg	Neg
URBAN	Percentage of firms in industry i during period t located in urban areas	Pos	Pos

Source: Daniels (1995)
Pos = positive sign
Neg = negative sign
NS = These variables are expected to be not significant.

field 1962; Orr 1974; Duetsch 1975, 1985; Gorecki 1975; Hause and Du Rietz 1984; Hamilton 1985; Khemani and Shapiro 1986; MacDonald 1986; Acs and Audretsch 1989). Several of these barriers to entry would not be relevant in Zimbabwe. For example, market concentration, advertising, and economies of scale are practically nonexistent in the MSE sector in Zimbabwe for the following reasons.

First, MSEs are too numerous to allow market concentration. In 1995, there were 942,000 MSEs in Zimbabwe. Within the twenty-one industries examined in this study, the average number of MSEs was 32,240. Second, while some limited advertising may occur, it may only be within a small geographic area such as a town. This type of advertising would not block firms from entering the industry throughout the rest of the country. Third, most MSEs are small and do not exhibit economies of scale. For example, 78 percent of all firms were owned and operated by the proprietor alone. Ninety-six percent of all MSEs had only one to four workers.

Other barriers to entry from the industrial organization literature, such as capital expenditures, human capital, and government policies, are expected to have an impact on MSEs in Zimbabwe. The impact of these variables should vary depending on whether firms are driven by market demand or by surplus labor. Assuming that firms driven by market demand are in high-profit industries with barriers to entry, start-up capital (CAPITAL), working capital (WORKCAP), and human capital (YRSEXP) are expected to be significant barriers to entry.[7] Government policies such as licensing requirements (LICENSES) are also frequently cited as impediments to MSEs and should be negatively correlated with entry in high-profit industries (Waterhouse 1986; Jassat and Jirira 1987; Konrad Adenauer Foundation 1988; UNIDO 1988; ILO/SATEP 1990; ENDA 1990; IMANI 1990; Saito and Van Dijk 1990; Robinson 1991; Harbin 1993; Hess 1993).

Assuming that firms driven by surplus labor are in low-profit industries with low barriers to entry, start-up capital, working capital, and human capital should not be significant barriers to entry. Table 3.5 illustrates the large differences in the mean of these barriers to entry among high- and low-profit industries. Licensing may also not be a barrier to entry in low-profit industries. This may be partly due to the large numbers of MSEs in low-profit industries, making licensing more difficult to enforce. For example, the average number of firms in a high-profit industry is 12,895, compared with 49,826 in a low-profit industry.

Entry-inducing factors are typically represented by industry employment growth. Economic theory predicts that MSEs will be attracted to industries with high profits that may be reflected in employment growth.

Table 3.5. Values of barriers to entry variables for high- and low-profit industries

	High-profit industries	Low-profit industries
Capital (mean value)	Z$8,522*	Z$152*
Workcap (mean value)	Z$477*	Z$19*
Yrsexp (mean value)	11 years*	7 years*
License (% of MSEs with licenses)	30.7 %	9.7%

Source: 1993 survey data
Note: U.S.$1.00 = Z$6.70
* significant difference at the a = .001 level.

Among high-profit industries, individuals with access to capital and greater experience may have choices regarding which type of industry to enter. Employment growth is therefore included in the model. Unlike manufacturing industries in industrialized countries, however, MSEs in Zimbabwe employ both paid and unpaid employees. Unpaid employees are usually immediate family members or relatives who may not have other employment opportunities. Because this type of employment may not represent industry growth or positive profits, unpaid employment growth (UNPEMPGR) is measured separately from paid employment growth (PAIDEMPL) to test this hypothesis. Daniels (1995) shows, for example, that profits are not significantly correlated with unpaid employment growth using firm-level data.

In low-profit industries, profits are also the ultimate goal of proprietors. The constraints faced by most proprietors in low-profit industries, however, may severely limit their choice of industries. Table 3.5 illustrates that the start-up capital required in low-profit industries was more than fifty times lower than the capital required for high-profit industries. The experience of proprietors in low-profit industries was also 1.6 times lower than that of proprietors in high-profit industries. Proprietors who choose low-profit industries may therefore consider more favorably industries that require low skills and little capital or industries that can be started within their towns or in their homes.

In addition to growth within the industry, proprietors may compare the expected income of operating an MSE to the alternatives of working for someone else, being unemployed, or turning to agriculture on a full-time basis as a source of income. Wages (WAGE and SQWAGE) outside of the MSE sector and agricultural alternatives (MAIZE) are, therefore, included in the model.

Wages in the formal sector are used to represent what the worker could have made outside of the MSE sector, i.e., the opportunity cost. This is defined as the real minimum wage in time period t as measured by the monthly salary of domestic workers in Zimbabwean dollars of the year 1990. This wage was chosen because it was the minimum wage of all industries monitored by the government.

Although entrepreneurs in high-profit industries may find higher paying jobs outside of the MSE sector, many entrepreneurs in low- and high-profit industries may not have the skills or experience necessary to acquire these jobs. It is hypothesized that as the real minimum wage decreases, entry increases as individuals search for higher incomes.

The opportunity cost of working full time in the MSE sector rather than farming will be measured by the average kilograms of maize harvested by firm owners in industry i from 1991 to 1993, in thousands of kilograms. It is included to test the hypothesis that industries characterized by proprietors who are also engaged in agriculture will experience lower entry rates. This is because agriculture may provide a source of income and subsequently reduce the search for alternative income sources in the MSE sector. In industries where proprietors are not also engaged in agriculture, entry rates may be much higher.

The GDP is included as a measure of the performance of the economy. Over the eight-year period examined in this study, the GDP growth rate fluctuated from a high of +8.3 percent in 1988 to a low of -6.6 percent in 1992. This variation reflects several factors. Specifically, the Economic Structural Adjustment Program (ESAP) was implemented in 1991. Also, Zimbabwe faced the worst drought of the century in the 1991–92 agricultural season. Agricultural output decreased by 35 percent compared with that of the previous year, while maize production decreased by 80 percent. Based on these shortages, high interest rates, and reduced consumer demand, the real GDP fell by 6.6 percent in 1992.

These changes in the GDP should have an impact on the MSE sector. In particular, more individuals may turn to the MSE sector as an alternative source of income as the GDP declines, particularly in low-profit industries. Among high-profit industries, as the GDP rises, entry should also rise if MSEs are driven by market demand for MSE products. These possibilities are tested in the model and discussed below.

Finally, the regional location of the proprietor should be controlled for in the analysis of entry. As mentioned above, proprietors are constrained by their locations. They may not have the option of moving to new locations where the market demand is greater. The regional location (URBAN) is therefore included as the proportion of all exiting MSEs in industry i during period t that are located in urban areas. This is expected to be positively correlated with entry in low-profit industries, because more people may turn to MSEs in urban areas where formal sector jobs are limited and agriculture may not be a viable alternative. In high-profit industries, more people may also turn to the MSE sector in urban areas where a larger market exists for their products.

Results

Table 3.6 presents the results of the entry model for low-profit industries, high-profit industries, and all industries combined. As predicted, the forces that drive entry are different for the low- and high-profit industries.

Beginning with the first barrier to entry in table 3.6, capital is not a significant determinant of entry to low-profit industries; however, it is a significant barrier to entry to high-profit industries. These results reflect the large difference in the average costs of entry between high- and low-profit industries (table 3.5).[8] Combining high- and low-profit industries in the last column in table 3.6, capital is a significant barrier to entry. These results show that it is misleading to consider the MSE sector as a whole, since the MSE sector is not homogeneous. Capital is a significant barrier to entry only to high-profit industries, which represent only 19 percent of all MSEs in the sample.

The second barrier to entry in table 3.6, working capital, is also different for the two types of industries. Low-profit industries are not affected by working-capital requirements, whereas entry into high-profit industries is positively correlated with working-capital requirements. This positive relationship could reflect the correlation between profits and working capital. Since working capital is positively correlated with profits, entry driven by profits may be higher in industries characterized by greater working-capital requirements.[9]

Experience was not a significant determinant of entry in low-profit industries. Again, this supports the labor-supply hypothesis that proprietors are driven into low-skill industries due to an excess supply of labor and limited options. Experience is a barrier to entry, however, in high-profit industries, where more technical and marketing skills may be necessary.

Licensing, used here as a proxy for government regulations, is a significant barrier to entry in high-profit but not in low-profit industries. Although licenses are required by both high- and low-profit industries, the difference may reflect a higher level of enforcement within highly visible high-profit industries.

Entry-inducing factors were represented by growth in paid and unpaid employment. Growth in paid employment was negatively correlated with entry in low-profit industries. Again, growth in paid employment should be positively correlated with entry if proprietors enter an industry because of potential profits. Among high-profit industries and all industries combined, growth in paid employment was not significant. Unpaid employment growth, as predicted, was not significantly related to entry in any of

Table 3.6. Entry model results of high- and low-profit industries

Dependent variable: gross entry rate			
	Low-profit industries	High-profit industries	All industries combined
Variable	Coefficient (t-statistic)	Coefficient (t-statistic)	Coefficient (t-statistic)
Capital	-6.23	-0.56**	-0.40**
	(-1.01)	(-2.72)	(-2.60)
Sqcapital	.001	0.12E-04**	0.76E-05**
	(0.92)	(2.52)	(2.31)
Workcap	18.30	1.93**	1.08**
	(0.21)	(2.26)	(1.74)
Yrsexp	-2.54	-1.83**	-1.56**
	(-1.55)	(-3.44)	(-4.88)
License	-0.21	-0.41**	-0.13**
	(-1.16)	(-3.02)	(-1.93)
Unpempgr	-77.53	17.26	102.5**
	(-0.47)	(0.27)	(3.73)
Poidempl	-594.54*	-1.84	-0.41
	(-1.63)	(-0.36)	(3.81)
Wage	-1.61	-4.39**	-3.04**
	(-1.39)	(-2.88)	(-2.89)
Sqwage	0.71E-02*	0.02**	0.14E-01**
GDP	-0.63**	-0.38	-0.60**
Maize	-1.57	-1.42**	-0,60*
	(-1.18)	(-2.40)	(-1.67)
Urban	0.59**	0.31**	0.21**
Constant	135.19**	275.38**	182.71**
	(2.08)	(3.46)	(3.35)
No. of observations	88	80	168
R-square	.39	.43	.29
Lagrange Multiplier Test	2.96*	4.27**	2.88*

Source: 1993 survey data
* = significant at the a = 0.10 level
** = significant at the a = 0.05 level

the models. This is reasonable, since unpaid employment growth is not tied to positive profits, as mentioned previously.

Wage rates were not significant among low-profit industries. Among high-profit industries and all industries combined, however, wage rates were negatively correlated with entry. But there is a turning point within the observed range of real wage rates. Initially, MSE entry decreases as formal sector wage rates rise, suggesting that people turn to the formal sector. After wages reach a certain level, however, formal wage rates are positively correlated with MSE entry. This positive relationship could reflect higher demand for MSE products as wages rise, or lower demand for labor in the formal sector as wages rise.

The growth rate of the GDP was negatively related to entry in low-profit industries. Again, this supports the labor-supply hypothesis. With slow or negative economic growth, more people turn to self-employment in low-profit industries as an alternative source of income. In the high-profit industries, the GDP was not a significant determinant of entry. This is surprising, since the market-demand hypothesis suggests that higher levels of income should lead to an increase in demand for MSE products. Entry in high-profit industries would, therefore, be expected to be positively related to the GDP growth. Nonetheless, the fact that the GDP is not significant suggests that people do not turn to self-employment in high-profit industries as an alternative source of income when the economy declines.

The level of maize production within proprietor households is not significant in low-profit industries; however, it is inversely related to entry in high-profit industries. Higher levels of maize production within high-profit industries lead to lower entry rates. This suggests that farming may provide an alternative or an additional income source that leads to lower entry rates within high-profit industries.

Industries that are predominantly located in urban areas tend to have higher entry rates in both low- and high-profit industries, when other factors are held constant. Although a larger number of MSEs in urban areas is typically explained by greater market opportunities, this may not be the case for low-profit industries. Instead, higher entry in low-profit industries could reflect higher population growth due to urban migration.

Conclusion

The labor-supply hypothesis suggests that entry is driven by surplus labor with limited skills and limited access to capital. Alternatively, the market-demand hypothesis suggests that entry is influenced by consumer demand for MSE products. The results from this study suggest that both the labor-supply and market-demand hypotheses influence entry.

The labor-supply hypothesis appears to be supported by the results of the low-profit entry model. The insignificance of capital expenditures and experience indicate that proprietors with low capital and limited skills can easily enter these industries as an alternative source of income. The hypothesis is further supported by the inverse relationship between the GDP and the entry rate. As economic growth declines, more people turn to these industries as an alternative source of income. As the economy grows, the entry rate in low-profit industries declines.

The results of the high-profit entry model suggest that capital, experience, and government regulations are barriers to entry. Furthermore, entry into these industries is not affected by changes in the GDP, as is the case in low-profit industries. Although these results do not necessarily support the market-demand hypothesis for high-profit industries, they do not coincide with the labor-supply hypothesis. Firms within these industries do not appear to be driven by an excess supply of labor.

Based on government priorities, policies and assistance programs can be developed using these results. If economic growth is a priority, then policies and assistance programs should be directed toward high-profit industries or proprietors who exhibit the potential to succeed, based on past performance. This could be achieved by reducing government regulations such as licensing, and by providing technical and financial support to reduce the financial and human capital barriers to entry identified in the model.

If poverty alleviation is a priority, then government could focus on low-profit industries where proprietors may depend on MSE income to survive, and where start-up capital, experience, and licensing are not barriers to entry. Different strategies for proprietors in low-profit industries are therefore necessary. First, concerning start-up capital, the results showed that low-profit industries on average require only 152 Zimbabwean dollars. Credit programs that are designed to provide start-up capital for new MSEs in low-profit industries may not, therefore, have a sustainable impact. Although proprietors may use the credit for other short-term household needs, the business may not survive and provide a steady income over time.

Second, experience is not a significant barrier to entry among low-profit industries. Programs designed to provide technical training for low-profit industries may, therefore, represent a misallocation of scarce resources. Furthermore, most low-profit industries are saturated. Skills training and credit would be wasted without effective market demand for MSE products.

Combining the results regarding start-up capital and experience, poverty alleviation strategies may have better success by moving proprietors from low-profit into high-profit industries. For example, skills training in jobs that are related to high-profit industries could be provided for proprietors who are currently in low-profit industries. Combined with new skills, credit could then be provided as start-up capital for proprietors who are entering new higher profit industries.

Poverty alleviation strategies may also address gender issues. As described earlier, over 90 percent of all women in the MSE sector are located in low-profit industries. Helping women move into higher profit industries may assist the goals of poverty alleviation. Even a move within the low-profit industries from crocheting to dressmaking, for example, has the potential to more than double profits.

Third, licensing requirements are not a barrier to entry for low-profit industries, but they are for high-profit industries. Again, moving proprietors out of low-profit industries into higher profit industries could be facilitated by removing or reducing the licensing constraint.

A final conclusion from this model is that the MSE sector is heterogeneous. Examining barriers to entry and entry-inducing factors for all industries combined would have provided misleading results. For example, capital and experience are barriers to entry for all industries as a group. But a breakdown by high- and low-profit industries reveals that start-up capital and experience are not barriers to entry to low-profit industries, but they are barriers to entry to high-profit industries. Credit and training programs that target all types of MSE industries may not, therefore, be appropriately allocated. Instead, assistance programs should carefully consider specific groups within the MSE sector. Sustainable economic growth in the MSE sector may be best served by traditional credit and training programs for proprietors in high-profit industries, while poverty alleviation may have greater success by moving proprietors from low- into high-profit industries.

Notes

1. For purposes of a cross-country comparative survey, an MSE is defined as a business activity that employs fifty or fewer workers and markets at least 50 percent of its output. The adult population is defined as fifteen years or older. The five countries include Zimbabwe (Daniels 1994), Botswana (Daniels and Fisseha 1992), Malawi (Daniels and Ngwira 1992), Lesotho (Fisseha 1991), and Swaziland (Fisseha and McPherson 1991).

2. An industry is defined as "the set of firms that produce products that are

viewed as close substitutes by consumers" (Varian 1987). In particular, industries within the MSE sector will be categorized by the standard industrial classification four-digit codes.

3. A complete description of the methodology used to collect these data can be found in McPherson (1991) and Daniels (1994).

4. Although information on existing MSEs from the two data sets could have been combined, only information on the 1993 existing MSEs was used in order to maintain consistency in the data set. For the folded MSEs, it was necessary and preferable to use both data sets. The 1991 data set covered folded MSEs up to 1990. The 1993 data set covered those that folded from 1991 to 1993.

5. These twenty-one industries represented almost three-quarters of all existing MSEs in 1993 and had at least thirty observations in the sample. The remaining 25 percent of MSEs comprised fifty-six coded four-digit industries. Because each of these industries had fewer than thirty observations in the sample, their entry rates were sporadic and could not be calculated in years when there were no existing enterprises for that industry. They were therefore excluded from the model.

6. Although the determination of high versus low profit is subjective, the minimum taxable income rule is an attempt to use an objective measure established by the government of Zimbabwe. In this case, the government does not consider anything below 4,801 Zimbabwean dollars a high enough income to be taxed.

7. The square of capital is included to allow for a nonlinear relationship between entry and the capital expenditures. As the cost of capital rises, for example, entry may decline, but at a decreasing rate.

8. The square of capital is also significant, suggesting that as capital increases, entry decreases at a decreasing rate within the relevant range.

9. The correlation coefficient between working capital and profits is .482 and is significant at the .001 level.

References

Acs, Zoltan, and David Audretsch. 1989. Small-Firm Entry in U.S. Manufacturing. *Economica* 56 (222) (May):255–66.

Breusch, Trevor, and Adrian Rodney Pagan. 1980. The Lagrange Multiplier Test and Its Applications to Model Specification in Econometrics. *Review of Economic Studies* 47:239–53.

Cortes, Mariluz, Albert Berry, and Ashfaq Ishaq. 1987. *Success in Small and Medium-Scale Enterprises: The Evidence from Colombia.* New York: Oxford University Press.

Daniels, Lisa. 1994. Changes in the Small-Scale Enterprise Sector from 1991 to 1993: Results of a Second Nationwide Survey in Zimbabwe. GEMINI Technical Report No. 71. Bethesda, Md.: Development Alternatives.

———. 1995. Entry, Exit, and Growth among Small-Scale Enterprises in Zimbabwe. Ph.D. dissertation. Michigan State University.

Daniels, Lisa, and Yacob Fisseha. 1992. Micro- and Small-Scale Enterprises in Botswana: Results of a Nationwide Survey. GEMINI Technical Report No. 46. Bethesda, Md.: Development Alternatives.

Daniels, Lisa, and Austin Ngwira. 1992. Results of a Nationwide Survey on Micro, Small, and Medium Enterprises in Malawi. GEMINI Technical Report No. 53. Bethesda, Md.: Development Alternatives.

Deb, Nibaran Chandra, and Mahabub Hossain. 1984. Demand for Rural Industries Products in Bangladesh. *The Bangladesh Development Studies* 12 (182) (March–June):81–99.

Duetsch, Larry. 1975. Structure, Performance, and the Net Role of Entry into Manufacturing Industries. *Southern Economic Journal* 41 (January):450–56.

———. 1984. Entry and the Extent of Multiplant Operations. *Journal of Industrial Economics* 32 (June):477–87.

Environmental and Developmental Activities (ENDA). 1990. Women in the Informal Sector: A Zimbabwean Study. Harare: ENDA.

Fisseha, Yacob. 1991. Small-Scale Enterprises in Lesotho: Summary of a Countrywide Survey. GEMINI Technical Report No. 14. Bethesda, Md.: Development Alternatives.

Fisseha, Yacob, and Michael McPherson. 1991. A Countrywide Study of Small-Scale Enterprises in Swaziland. GEMINI Technical Report No. 24. Bethesda, Md.: Development Alternatives.

Gorecki, Paul. 1975. The Determinants of Entry by New and Diversifying Enterprises in the U.K. Manufacturing Sector, 1958–1963: Some Tentative Results. *Applied Economics* 7:139–47.

Hamilton, R. T. 1985. Interindustry Variation in Gross Entry Rates of "Independent" and "Dependent" Businesses. *Applied Economics* 17:271–80.

Harbin, Nancy. 1993. Government Regulations and the Costs of Compliance for Small-Scale Metal-Working Enterprises in Zimbabwe. Draft report. Harare: ENDA.

Hause, John C., and Gunnar Du Rietz. 1984. Entry, Industry Growth, and the Microdynamics of Industry Supply. *Journal of Political Economy* 92 (4):733–57.

Hazell, Peter, and Alisa Roell. 1983. Rural Growth Linkages: Household Expenditure Patterns in Malaysia and Nigeria. International Food Policy Research Institute Research Report 41. Washington, D.C.: IFPRI.

Hess, Richard. 1983. Cost of Business Compliance. Small-Scale Garment and Textile Sector. Paper presented at the Conference on Deregulation, 16–18 May 1993, Nyanga, Zimbabwe.

ILO/SATEP. 1989. The Promotion of Economic Development and Equity in Zimbabwe. Report to the Government of Zimbabwe. Harare: ILO.

IMANI Development. 1990. Impediments Confronting the Informal-Sector Enterprise In Zimbabwe. Harare: IMANI.

Jassat, E. M., and K. O. Jirira. 1987. Industrial Development in Zimbabwe: The Case of Women in Manufacturing Activities. Harare: Zimbabwe Institute of Development Studies (mimeo).

Khemani, R. Shyam, and Daniel Shapiro. 1986. The Determinants of New Plant Entry in Canada. *Applied Economics* 18 (November):1243–57.

King, Robert P., and Derek Byerlee. 1978. Factor Intensities and Locational Linkages of Rural Consumption Patterns in Sierra Leone. *American Journal of Agricultural Economics* 60 (2):197–206.

Konrad Adenauer Foundation. 1988. Small-Scale Enterprise Development: An Assessment of Progress and Strategies for Growth. National Seminar Series, 26–29 July, Ranche House College, Harare, Zimbabwe.

Liedholm, Carl. 1990. The Dynamics of Small-Scale Industry in Africa and the Role of Policy. GEMINI Working Paper No. 2. Bethesda, Md.: Development Alternatives.

MacDonald, James M. 1986. Entry and Exit on the Competitive Fringe. *Southern Economic Journal* 52:640–52.

Mansfield, Edwin. 1962. Entry, Gibrat's Law, Innovation, and the Growth of Firms. *American Economic Review* 52 (5):1023–50.

McPherson, Michael. 1991. Micro and Small-Scale Enterprises in Zimbabwe: Results of a Countrywide Survey. GEMINI Technical Report 25. Bethesda, Md.: Development Alternatives.

Mead, Donald. 1994. The Contribution of Small Enterprises to Employment Growth in Southern Africa and Eastern Africa. *World Development* 22 (12):1881–94.

Orr, Dale. 1974. The Determinants of Entry: A Study of the Canadian Manufacturing Industries. *Review of Economics and Statistics* 56 (1974):58–67.

Price Waterhouse. 1986. African Investment Corporation International (AIC): An Assessment of the Private Sector in Zimbabwe. Harare: Price Waterhouse (mimeo).

Robinson, Peter. 1991. Small-Scale Industry in the Context of Structural Adjustment. Notes for a meeting of researchers and donor agencies. Harare: Zimconsult (mimeo).

Saito, Katrine, and Meine Pieter Van Dijk. 1990. The Informal Sector in Zimbabwe: The Role of Women. *Environmental and Development Activities.* Harare: ENDA.

UNIDO. 1988. Human Resources in Zimbabwe's Development: The Current and Prospective Contribution of Women. Harare: UNIDO.

Varian, Hal. 1987. *Intermediate Microeconomics: A Modern Approach.* New York: W. W. Norton and Company.

4. Black Entrepreneurs in Post-Apartheid South Africa

Okechukwu C. Iheduru

The official dismantling of apartheid since 1990 and the establishment of a black-led Government of National Unity (GNU) on 10 May 1994 have resulted in unprecedented changes in the political, economic, and social arenas in South Africa. One aspect of this change is the growing number of black entrepreneurs in various sectors of the economy, sectors from which they were previously excluded by law and by social conventions. These nascent black enterprises fall into seven categories: holding/listed companies, or what white stockbrokers derogatorily refer to as "black chips"; potential listed companies; portfolio investment trusts; professional women investors; micro and small enterprises (MSEs), ranging from registered unlisted companies to "closed corporations" to sole proprietorships and partnerships; the informal sector, where a majority of black entrepreneurs operate; and the political "business" entrepreneurs.[1] The most prominent entrepreneurs (in terms of the publicity they receive) tend to be represented by the companies listed on the Johannesburg Stock Exchange (JSE), but the bulk of black entrepreneurs are in MSEs and informal sector businesses. Whereas there were only eight black-owned businesses on the JSE as of July 1997, there were more than 1 million MSEs and a further 2.5 million informal "survival" enterprises in South Africa, with the majority of the latter being owned by blacks.

Several important studies of these businesses have been conducted since 1990; most of them focus on the MSEs (Riley 1993; Manning and Mashigo 1994; Coetzee and Visagie 1995; Randall 1996). This chapter attempts to unify the ongoing study by highlighting the structure and activities of all seven types of black entrepreneurs in the post-apartheid era.[2] The central argument is that although these entrepreneurs have achieved tremendous success under very trying circumstances, their capacity to bring about black economic empowerment is severely limited without a deliberate state policy to balance growth with equity. The reason for this is that the South African economy is not only oligopolistic, it also has a closed business culture that tends to keep "outsiders" out of the mainstream.

The second proposition is that among the black entrepreneurs, the category that is most likely to widen the scope of—or democratize—effective black economic empowerment seems to be the MSEs, simply because only a negligible percentage of blacks will eventually be able to join the ranks of investors on the JSE. Indeed, only a handful are likely to earn any profits from such investments. In addition, South Africa cannot buck the global trend in which formal sector jobs are increasingly being created by MSEs, while the giant corporations are literally outbidding each other in employee layoffs and corporate downsizing and are relying increasingly on government incentives to survive.

Black economic empowerment here refers to the process by which the black majority becomes part of the mainstream of the South African economy, reflecting its newly acquired political status and its numerical strength as consumers. It is a process that seeks first to correct and balance current disparities in income and wealth between whites and blacks and then to close the gap between the two groups in terms of their control of income-producing assets in relation to the direction of the economy (Sethi and Voorhes 1995:5).

Up to mid-1997, the GNU has not enacted any national policies geared toward helping black entrepreneurs in general or MSEs in particular, but has relied on the promised trickle-down effects of market forces as the optimal corrective for the economic inequities of the apartheid era. While the benefits of a top-down economic growth could theoretically filter down to blacks, this concept operates under the assumption that South Africa is a normal free-enterprise economy, but it is not. The history of South Africa suggests that economic improvements for blacks have not occurred in times of high economic growth in the general economy, but only during those times when external forces, or blacks themselves, have forced change on the captains of industry and commerce.

This chapter first provides an overview of black entrepreneurial experience in South Africa, then describes the nature and characteristics of the seven categories of black entrepreneurs operating today. Finally, an analysis of the constraints confronting these entrepreneurs and the policy implications of a top-down versus a bottom-up approach to black economic empowerment are discussed.

Black Entrepreneurship in Historical Perspective

Accounts of black entrepreneurial activities in South Africa often suggest a "lack of community status for business" and "lack of business socialization" among Africans. Some even point to traditional sanctions against wealth accumulation in the rural areas as the reason for the paucity of black entrepreneurs (Godsell 1991:92). Little is written on black economic activities between the period of the first European intrusion in 1652 and the late nineteenth century, when mining began to transform the economy. Early examples of a culture of entrepreneurship among blacks occur in farm production from 1800 to 1900, with frequent friction between blacks and poor Afrikaner farmers (Motsuenyane 1989:5; Beinart 1994:57).

The use of the poll-tax system, pass laws, segregated housing, job reservation, and influx control laws to force blacks to work for pay with the advent of the mining economy did not dampen their entrepreneurial drive, especially as more blacks migrated to the urban centers. Urbanization created opportunities to provide ox wagons and horse carts—replaced later by taxis and buses—to transport workers from the newly established black townships to the towns.

Entrepreneurship also flourished in such trades as small restaurants, retail shops, tailoring, carpentry, motor mechanic workshops, bicycle shops, and funeral parlors. Many blacks were also involved in the sale of all types of homemade drinks (for example, the infamous *shebeens*) and in the entertainment business. Success for many involved adapting to apartheid by circumventing the law, living in the informal economy, or acquiring a powerful patron—a chief or a white person. Others found a niche in the formal economy as teachers, nurses, or industrial workers. These ceased to be marginal, and they formed the nucleus of an African middle class and an African working class.

But even these businesses were prevented from developing to any size before the 1980s, and they competed with state monopolies, especially in alcohol sales. It had been a principle of the administration of black townships since colonial times that no expense should fall upon the white rate payers. The municipal and later state monopoly of alcohol sales provided the minimal revenues required to administer the townships.

With the rise to power of the National Party in 1948, laws were enacted that continued until the mid-1970s to inhibit black participation in the economy. Table 4.1 summarizes some of the major pieces of legislation at the central government level. It has been noted that there were more than 500 laws and regulations that in one way or another impeded the involvement of the black community in the economy as owners and managers (Motsuenyane 1989).

Table 4.1. Major laws inhibiting black entrepreneurship, 1910–1975

Legislation	Provisions
Master and Servant Act (1911)	Decreed conditions under which black labor must be made available to whites; criminalized breach of contract because of white farmers' fear of the corrupting influences of towns. Amended in 1974 to facilitate labor mobility.
Mines and Works Act (1911)	Prohibited black engagement in certain skilled or semiskilled occupations in the mines exclusively reserved for whites.
Native's Land Act (1913)	Prohibited Africans from purchasing or leasing land outside the reserves; prohibited sharecropping in the Orange Free State. Listed 22 million acres (7% of the country) as the reserves. Native's Trust and Land Act of 1936 raised it to about 13%.
Native Urban Areas Act of 1923; replaced by Native (Urban Areas) Consolidation Act, No. 25 of 1945	Entrenched social and residential segregation, instituted pass laws and the influx control system. Curtailed freedom of movement by blacks (i.e., blacks defined as temporary sojourners in South African urban areas). Permitted black business in the townships to sell daily essentials of living, such as milk, bread, and vegetables. Barred blacks from owning and operating dry cleaners, book shops, garages, and pharmacies.
Group Areas Act (1950)	Prohibited different racial groups from trading or residing in areas not specifically earmarked for their groups. The Group Areas Development Act (after 1966 the Community Development Act) provided a mechanism for expropriation and land development.
Natives' Resettlement Act (1945)	Provided the mechanisms required to remove blacks (and their businesses) from inner black areas.
Regulations Governing Black Business in Urban Areas (1962)	Prohibited all black businesses not catering to basic necessities of life in black townships. Only 25 types of licenses could be issued to black business operating in urban areas. The informal sector was totally banned.

Another inhibition to black entrepreneurship was the difficulty in obtaining business permits and the fact that one had to be "if not corrupt in an economic sense, then certainly politically corrupt and in cahoots with the white administrative bureaucracy of the township" in order to receive such services (Godsell 1991:92). Additionally, the black entrepreneur in the township was probably the only businessman in South Africa to be the target of community and family contempt and hostility, especially by the youth, who defined him first as a businessman and second as a black man. He was therefore a legitimate target of theft and attacks, along with white entrepreneurs, policemen, and community councilors (Bank 1994:75–99).

Although the *stokvels* (revolving financial and credit associations and other helping networks such as burial societies and women's church organizations) blossomed in the townships during this period, they were generally not oriented to helping small businesses or to generating start-up capital. Few family businesses existed and survived. School graduates tended to join the industrial and civil service sector, where there were fewer raids and intimidation by the police and few if any attacks by the radical youth for collaborating with "the system" (Bank 1994).

These factors explain the "lack of community status" and "lack of business socialization" among blacks in South Africa. Their exclusion from the economy continued unabated until the mid-1970s, when both the government and the private sector began to introduce reforms that resulted in genuine growth and advancement of black entrepreneurs, especially in the rural areas, by late 1989. The homeland governments, despite all their failings, were instrumental in creating a sizable class of entrepreneurs, since the Group Areas Act and other apartheid laws prohibited white businesses (except financial institutions) from operating in black enclaves (Beinart 1994:208–11). Pretoria funneled large quantities of money into the homelands, emphasizing emerging social differentiation and diverting the ambition of the African educated classes from major cities so that they would help to guide the journey toward separate development. The strategy was to build a large black middle class that would become a willing ally of the apartheid state and that would eventually overshadow the radicalized urban political and youth leadership.

Specifically, the state revamped the Bantu Investment Corporation (BIC), created in 1959 to finance black businesses *only in the homelands,* in consonance with its theory of "separate development." A number of legal and / or administrative changes were also made after 1976, such as the extension of property and ownership rights to urban blacks for a ninety-nine-year period in 1978; the right of blacks to register trade unions in 1979; and the abolition of the Bantu Education Act of 1953 in 1979, allowing blacks to hold apprenticeships and jobs in certain areas previously reserved for whites under the Industrial Conciliation Act of 1956. The state also amended harsh regulations that forbade company formation by blacks, and it enlarged the range of areas of permissible black business activities from only twenty-five in 1963 to fifty-two. All restrictions on business ownership by blacks were eventually lifted in the 1980s (Beinart 1994:222–31; Motsuenyane 1989:9–10). Further relaxation of restrictions followed the creation of the Small Business Development Corporation (SBDC) in 1980 to finance all small businesses on a nonracial basis. The repeal of the Influx Control Act in 1986 and the privatization and commercialization of state assets from 1988 also made the deregulation of black businesses imperative. The Group Areas Act was amended to allow blacks access to the central business districts of the major urban areas in about ten cities as residents and property owners.

The climax came in 1991, when President F. W. de Klerk repealed the remaining "pillars of apartheid" and most of the more visible laws that inhibited black entrepreneurship, with the passage of the Abolition of Racially Based Measures Act (1991). The Business Act (1991) eliminated many of the remaining regulatory burdens on black entrepreneurs by denying municipalities the right to declare certain areas off-limits to street trading, a practice common in many South African towns.

However, not all of the five hundred regulations noted earlier were abolished; neither did the institutionalized and behavioral forms of inhibition against black entrepreneurship disappear with the official dismantling of apartheid. For instance, the force of the restrictions against municipal governments in the Business Act was mitigated by another provision empowering municipal authorities to apply to the provincial administrator for permission to close areas to street trading. Municipal regulations, health, safety and labor codes, and taxation administration related to the value-added tax continue to affect small businesses (Riley 1993:7).

The private sector, out of sheer self-interest, created the Urban Foundation, dedicated to improving the quality of life for urban blacks. The foundation initiated and supported housing, education, business, and welfare projects in many black townships. By the late 1980s it began to encourage the government to hasten or bring about desirable sociopolitical adjustments. It agreed to fund the SBDC by 50 percent (the other half to be provided by the state), and many white companies began to participate in the National African Federated Chamber of Commerce (NAFCOC) as associate members. In addition to paying higher membership dues, they also donated generously to various NAFCOC services aimed at assisting black entrepreneurs (Motsuenyane 1989:9–10). Some big companies also started to recruit blacks and train them for future private employment, while some, like Standard Bank, pioneered the creation of small business development initiatives to help finance many black entrepreneurs.

These economic reforms and the deregulation of black entrepreneurship during the last twenty years have had tremendous consequences in the economy. An enlarged black middle class has been created, fundamentally shaking up the system. In the 1980s, the regime touted its rising number of black millionaires as an indication that things were not so bad for the black majority when compared with their counterparts in black-ruled Africa (Burton 1988:56–57; Jones 1989:47).

Some examples of the transformative effects of the reforms are telling. In 1985, whites accounted for 56 percent of personal disposable income, while Africans accounted for 32 percent, coloreds for 9 percent, and Indians for 4 percent. According to the estimates of the Bureau for Market Research at the University of South Africa, whites' share of disposable income is expected to decline to 43 percent by the year 2000, while that of blacks will increase to 41 percent. Blacks account for over 40 percent of all retail purchases, a figure that could increase to 50 percent by the year 2000.

At the entrepreneurial level, blacks dominated the transport services in the townships, partially relieving transport difficulties with the proliferation of microbus taxis. Between 1970 and 1989, the number of these buses increased from 24,000 to 174,000; an estimated 80,000 of them operated without licenses. This phenomenal rise in the availability of automobiles reduced workplace travel time dramatically to 2.5 hours per day in 1995 and opened up new markets in the townships and in the rural areas. Taxis, which carried few black passengers in the 1970s, carried 30 percent of commuters in 1989 and over 40 percent by 1992. Bustling taxi ranks became a new feature of most urban centers, as did conflicts over custom and routes. The black operators were eventually organized into an economically and politically important union called the Southern African Bus and Taxi Association, whose membership had reached 45,000 by late 1989 (Beinart 1994:202–3; Khosa 1990).

Other small businesses and informal sector activities also helped give some blacks a share in the economy. The informal sector alone is currently estimated to contribute between 20 percent and 30 percent to South Africa's gross domestic product (GDP), while the SBDC counts about 1 million MSEs generating sales of 15 billion to 20 billion rands annually.

By 1990, many blacks expected more rapid improvements to complement their improved economic position. Unfortunately, five years after the unraveling of apartheid, their aspirations have not yet been realized. A mere 3 percent of blacks are currently involved in entrepreneurial activity, as opposed to 13 percent of whites. The average income in the informal sector was 500 rands a month in 1989, as against 830 rands a month for blacks in the nonprimary modern sector. Moreover, the distribution of income in the informal sector is highly skewed, with 27 percent of people earning less than 150 rands per month and 44 percent less than 250 rands per month. Overall, black business accounted for less than 2 percent of the country's GDP in 1995. Of the 3 million households in poverty in the country (about 38 percent of all households), blacks made up 94 percent of the total; moreover, 64 percent of them lived in rural areas or in small towns (Nyandeni 1995:49–50; *SouthScan* 1995d:272).[3]

Characteristics of Black Entrepreneurs in the Post-Apartheid Era

Black entrepreneurship since 1990 can be divided into seven categories: listed/holding companies; potential listed/holding companies; portfolio investment trusts; professional women investors; the MSEs; the informal sector; and the political "business" entrepreneurs. The first four constitute the top-down strategy, while the last three represent the bottom-up approach to black economic empowerment.

Listed/Holding Companies

There are seven trail-blazing black companies listed on the JSE. Referred to derogatorily by white stockbrokers as "black chips," they resulted from the hiving off of the assets or operations of the giant white-controlled holding companies that were later sold to and controlled by blacks. Fearing an antitrust legislation, some of these conglomerates adopted a so-called "unbundling" strategy as their own form of affirmative action and as their perceived appropriate route for blacks to achieve economic empowerment.[4] Others (mainly top white financial institutions) have established an enterprise capital fund to channel millions of rands to emerging black businesses, providing finance for suitable undertakings, arranging partners where necessary, and monitoring the recipients' activities.

Some of the listed companies were subsidiaries of large conglomerates that were not doing particularly well before their unbundling. They are led mostly by activists turned business tycoons, some of whom had worked for or been friendly with the parent companies. Often they are perceived as black faces in the white man's club (Shilowa 1994). Like their white counterparts, they have quickly become clubbish, gone on acquisition sprees, and taken over or acquired shares in dozens of existing white and black businesses—from banking, insurance, and other financial services to transportation, construction, engineering, print and electronic media, tourism, health care, and manufacturing. This has given them a pyramidal structure of ownership. Some have attempted to broaden their share ownership by mopping up funds from a large segment of blacks, ranging from private businesses to trade unions, employee-benefit associations, insurance and provident-fund investors, churches, the National Stokvels Association, and some grassroots organizations. Some have also sold shares to prominent African-American diplomats, politicians, sports and entertainment superstars, business people, and legal luminaries. Reportedly, more than 5 million blacks have so far been afforded opportunities, directly or indirectly, to own shares in the stock market for the first time (Smith 1995b:62–65; *SouthScan* 1995a:100–102). The current market capitalization of these companies ranges from 300 million to 2 billion rands, with net asset values of more than 7 billion rands.[5] By mid-1997, 8 percent of equities listed on the JSE were owned by black shareholders, compared to only 0.3 percent two years earlier (Koch 1997).

A subcategory of the "black chip" companies consists of those businesses under black management that, though unlisted on the stock market, were created from scratch to achieve the same unbundling objective, that is, to deflect criticisms from the black majority and forestall any interventionist actions by the new government. A good example is the Community Bank, which began operations in June 1994 with initial capital of 200 million rands generated in the form of loans from a group of eight top white financial institutions. The bank was established explicitly to cater to the savings and borrowing needs of lower income urban and rural communities, in response to the difficulty blacks (lacking collateral) encountered when trying to secure loans and venture capital.

Potential Listed/Holding Enterprises

This second category includes horizontally integrated large black enterprises that exhibit the potential, or have declared their intention, to seek listing on the JSE.[6] Their interests span a wide spectrum—from financial services, tourism and aviation, entertainment and leisure to industrial holdings in catering services, computers, educational publishing, properties, and printing (*SouthScan* 1995b:181). Founded mostly since 1990, these companies are the fastest-growing black holding companies. Several of their founders and/or managers and directors are ex-guerrillas, anti-apartheid activists, and former top officials of black political parties.

Some of them (for example, Thebe Investments) have taken over completely or acquired shares in major white businesses and have entered into joint-venture arrangements with white companies and with foreign investors wishing to reenter the South African market. Some of the partnerships with African-American investors recruit mainly black managers and have plans to broaden their ownership and eventually transfer majority shareholding to black South Africans through employee share schemes and other empowerment programs (Faison 1994). Additionally, these JSE-bound companies generally have a broad range of black shareholders, including sports officials, church leaders, and professionals, with others coming from civic organizations and labor groups. These companies also include some of the very few investment trusts in which there is a large contingent of black women professionals (for example, New Age Beverages).

Portfolio Investment Trusts

Black investment trusts generally pool funds from major trade unions and civic associations and their memberships and often invest them in "socially responsible" white firms that may or may not be listed on the JSE. They act increasingly as facilitators of economic empowerment for a large number of individuals who otherwise would be locked out of the stock market. One pioneer is the Community Growth Fund (CGF), founded in 1992 as a portfolio investment belonging to several trade-union groups; a few years ago, these trade unions staunchly advocated "a socialist South Africa." By June 1994, CGF was worth 120 million rands and reportedly paid a handsome return of 46 percent as dividends to its members (CBM 1993:39–40). By 1997, practically every major trade union, especially the Socialist-inclined ones like the National Union of Mineworkers and the South African Clothing and Textile Workers Union, had an investment trust through which they invested millions of rands in the stock markets, large corporations, and other businesses in many sectors of the economy (Copelyn 1997; Golding 1997; Koch 1997; Naidoo 1997).

Another trailblazer is Kagiso Trusts, an aid organization worth 520 million rands (in March 1995) and funded by the European Union. It provides funds for bursaries and literacy programs and enables communities to own companies so they can participate in the mainstream economy. It has become a model of black economic empowerment and is keenly studied by international aid organizations and donor countries (*SouthScan* 1995a:101). Investment trusts have also been established by community development associations, civic associations, major black businesses, pension funds, and groups of private individuals. They have begun to buy up or invest in a variety of businesses, thereby enlarging ownership of property and participation in the mainstream economy by blacks.

Black Professional Women Investors

Ordinarily these investors should be part of the Investment Trusts group, but their uniqueness in the history of women's entrepreneurship and empowerment in Africa requires that they be given more prominence. Women have traditionally engaged in entrepreneurial activities in South Africa, usually at the most basic level of operations. Since the 1990s, however, a new breed of professional black women has taken the lead in ensuring that gender differences and constraints of patriarchy are taken into consideration in the debate about economic empowerment. These women point to the potential economic power of black women, if only they could be mobilized and organized. For them, economic empowerment can only happen if women themselves control resources as independent actors, rather than as wives or daughters. According to one activist, "the long political struggle [will] not have been worthwhile if [women] cannot all reap the economic benefits of democratization and transition from apartheid" (Smith 1995a:73). Their program pools funds and purchases shares in both black- and white-owned businesses on behalf of women, a strategy that could have wider implications if it were fully developed and applied in other settings.

The Women Investment Portfolio (WIP), which has already bought shares in a number of black- and white-owned companies since its inception in 1994, typifies this strategy. This consortium of black women professionals does not allow individual members to join; rather, it uses group structures to their greatest advantage. By the first quarter of 1995, it had more than fifty block members representing more than 30,000 women. Its ultimate goal is to achieve a membership of 5 million to utilize women's purchasing power as leverage for equity participation. It invests mostly in agro-business in rural areas and in tourism, if such investments represent sustainable opportunities with a real profit motive (Smith 1995d:73).

Other prominent pioneers include the Professional Women's Leadership and Development Organization (PWLDO), which facilitates the empowerment of women in employment and business. Bridging the Gap, a human resources consulting firm, is a founding member of PWLDO.

The Small, Medium, and Microenterprises

MSEs are of two types: the "integrationist" partnerships and the "parallelist" models. The integrationist model of MSEs involves close interaction or alliances between Africans and non-Africans in the business scene that developed largely in the post-apartheid era. Its advocates claim that this is "the most appropriate strategy for an intensive entrepreneurial learning process" for blacks, while some black entrepreneurs resent it as a humiliating and paternalistic way to do business. Its proponents see such arguments as a reminder "of the way Afrikaners during the early decades of this century felt humiliated and exploited by English, Jewish, and other 'foreign business interests,' yet learned from them and eventually grew into equally powerful partners" (Thomas 1994:376).

The "parallelist" model, on the other hand, has been typical of black entrepreneurial enterprises since the creation of the apartheid state, during which black contacts and competition with non-black business was discouraged (Thomas 1994:377). There are about 1 million formal business entities in South Africa in the small and medium enterprises sector, all contributing an estimated 30 percent of the GDP. They employ approximately 2.5 million people, that is, 17 percent of the total 14.3 million people classified as "economically active." About 200,000 of these businesses are "closed corporations"; another 430,000 of them are sole proprietorships (Vosloo 1994:163, 169). Black entrepreneurs in the small and medium enterprises subcategory (those employing ten to two hundred employees) tend to have more education than the average microentrepreneur—ten years rather than the average six. They also generally have prior business or employment experience, earn more than other black owners of MSEs, and, at age forty to forty-five, are about ten years older (Riley 1993:xii).

Most black businesses in this subcategory were launched during the apartheid period, the average age of the firm being nine years. A few of them functioned as virtual monopolies in the townships, while others established in the homelands were effectively supported by training, access to finance, and subsidized inputs by the government. Overall, they have higher levels of turnover and profitability than microenterprises, although employment remains low, even among the most dynamic of them (Riley 1993:xii).

The largest and most well-established black entrepreneurs in the MSE categories are found in the retail, taxi, construction, and garment manufacturing subsectors. About 20 percent of them can be defined as dynamic (that is, in terms of growth in turnover, profitability, employment, and assets). Another 20 percent are potentially dynamic but kept from growing by various internal and external constraints, while the remaining 60 percent—though better off than the average microenterprise—function at the survival level (Riley 1993:xii).

The Informal Sector

The informal-sector microenterprises constitute a significant part of the business of entrepreneurship, with an estimated 6.8 million South African operators, mostly black. Together with MSEs, they contribute at least 45 percent of the GDP. It is an important haven for self-employment in rural areas, for the newly urbanized, for unemployed or retrenched people, for housewives looking for an additional source of income, for recent immigrants and, naturally, for a large number of embryonic entrepreneurs. Some participants are "survival" or "fall-back" operators; others are initiators of "planned and well-contemplated" business. Vosloo (1994) notes the extraordinary range, the large number of people involved, the low capital cost per job, the often zero skills required, and the low cost of on-the-job training in the informal sector. "Not only does the sector help newly urbanized people in their search for an income base, but it also plays a catalytic, as well as a selective role in creating entrepreneurship . . . it serves as a damper on wage inflation, as well as a mobilizer of capital at the grassroots level" (164).

This sector is also particularly important because the economically disenfranchised black majority constitutes more than 80 percent of its participants, while black women account for more than 62 percent of all informal sector entrepreneurs. They deal in livestock, basket making, egg production, fish culture, home crafts, market gardens, weaving, food preparation and sales, and other commercially viable activities. According to the SBDC, 62 percent of all (800,000) small businesses are owned by women, and according to the 1991 census, 51 percent of the total South African population is female, projected to reach 54 percent by 1999 because of gender-differential mortality patterns.

The most important constraints faced by informal sector entrepreneurs include lack of access to financing, competitive market conditions (such as lack of customers, the increasing number of competitors as over 4 million immigrants flood into the country, and rising cost of inputs and supplies), and inadequate premises from which to operate their businesses. The deregulation measures discussed earlier have effectively removed regulations as the primary constraints on the establishment and growth of black business, although microentrepreneurs continue to be constrained by the legacy of apartheid, which limited the ability of blacks to gain skilled employment, establish businesses, and receive a good education.

The Political "Business" Entrepreneurs

Entrepreneurs in this category have generally entered into partnerships with foreign investors. Some tend to be political operatives, such as middle-level black political party officials or comrades turned business people through whom local and foreign partners seek joint ventures, exclusive licenses, and other similar arrangements. The local partner seldom brings any expertise into the particular business and is essentially viewed as selling influence. The most important entry qualification seems to be jail time served in some of South Africa's notorious prisons with the present black ruling class (Randall 1996:668, 669, 671). These businesses include lesser known franchisers, technical contractors, and small business promoters. Curiously, this type of entrepreneurship has received funding and technical support from development aid agencies such as the United States Agency for International Development (USAID) and the Danish government.[7]

Constraints on Black Entrepreneurs after Apartheid

Despite the spectacular inroads they have made, black entrepreneurs' capacity to empower the black majority economically is still limited by a number of internal, external, and structural factors. First, black entrepreneurs, especially those with small enterprises, have developed several organizations in the townships and rural areas but lack the confidence and strong leadership to initiate or join the debate about economic empowerment at a higher level. Many of these organizations are still managed and/ or controlled by the so-called liberal whites who have yet to develop more proactive programs such as lobbying. The division among black entrepreneurs contrasts with the superior organization and clout of white businesses and political groups, which have more access to black members of parliament and to ministers (Malala 1995:24).

The history of black political struggles and contemporary black politics have also contributed to both the division and the powerlessness of black entrepreneurs and their organizations. It appears that the government has virtually surrendered empowerment programs to white businesses in a desperate attempt to win their confidence. Many white businesses have already suspended their affirmative action and empowerment programs, since it seems unlikely that the government will force them to implement the programs fully (Malunga 1995:10). Yet few, if any, black business organizations or prominent business people have openly challenged the African National Congress (ANC)–led government to deliver on its promises.

Another issue that has both advantages and disadvantages is the wave of immigrants (currently estimated at about 4 million) coming into South Africa, especially from West Africa, Zambia, the Democratic Republic of Congo (Zaire), and Zimbabwe. Most of them cannot find paid employment and have flooded the informal sector, thereby giving their hosts serious competition. They have the potential to disturb tolerable patterns of social relations within the country, as well as to transform this sector of the economy and become better off than their hosts, since they tend to be more educated than South Africans. Also, while most black South African youth are now beginning to learn the rudiments of capitalism, most of the immigrants are already schooled in the art of MSEs, especially trading, and have brought with them the legendary survival skills, determination, and industry of first-generation immigrants that had such transformative powers in places like the United States, Canada, Western Europe, and Malaysia.

In addition to these largely organizational difficulties, all categories of black entrepreneurs face certain unique constraints, such as institutional bias in favor of the larger firms; distrust of carryover apartheid institutions; too much reliance on nongovernmental organizations; and the racially exclusive character of the culture of business networks (Manning and Mashigo 1994:30–36).

Imperatives of Black Empowerment and Policy Implications

These and other firm-specific constraints and the apparent inability of black entrepreneurs to transcend them are at the root of the ongoing controversy over the appropriate and quickest approach to achieve black economic empowerment. The debate mainly is between advocates of a top-down strategy and supporters of a bottom-up approach.

The Top-Down Strategy

The question here is whether joining the JSE through partnerships and stakes in unbundled corporations is the proper path to economic empowerment, or whether this process should focus on empowering a small section of the black elite, some of whom also benefited from the homelands policies of the apartheid era (Malala 1995:25; Malunga 1995:13). According to Dr. Nthato Motlana, one of the best-known advocates of the top-down approach, "only through entrepreneurship, leadership and hard work will blacks inherit the economic kingdom. We do not want guilt offerings or hand-outs. . . . We cannot wait decades to participate fully and effectively in the economic future of South Africa" (Smith 1995b:65). In principle, this strategy "gives black business more flexibility; access to capital; allows it to operate in an open and transparent manner; and gives it the opportunity of competing in the mainstream economy" (quoted in Smith 1995c:66). The refrain for many proponents of this strategy is "Don't give blacks a small business because they will fail; give them a big business and see them excel" (Nthato Motlana, quoted in Malunga 1995:11–12).

One argument against this top-down approach is the increasing concentration of access and wealth in the hands of a select few black men and women as owners, directors, and managers of the giant corporations. In 1991, blacks occupied only 30 (less than 2 percent) of the approximately 2,550 directorships available in the top 100 companies listed on the JSE. By May 1995, black men held 276 directorships, a jump from 120 in 1993. However, "The same black faces have begun to crop up time after time on the boards of the big white companies, mimicking the clubbishness of the white corporate world" (Pedder 1995:19).[8]

The consequences of this strategy have already started to attract negative attention. For instance, the minister for public works stated that, "In 1991, the bottom 40 percent of the African population received 6.4 percent of the total African income, while the top 10 percent . . . received 46.6 percent of the total African income. This means that the poor are getting poorer and the rich richer" (quoted in African Communist 1995:2). Unbundling as a means of redressing racial economic imbalances is also deeply suspect because it is being perceived as a strategy to create and enrich a new (and narrow) black business elite. According to one critic, "If, at the end of five years, blacks in South Africa own a larger slice of the economy, this will be largely irrelevant if the change is simply the statistical result of a few Nthato Motlanas having become multi-millionaires" (ibid.). On 3 March 1997, deputy president Thabo Mbeki warned the new black elite to clean up its image of "a parasitic class that can thrive only on pillaging state resources" (quoted in SouthScan 1997b:65). Other critics allege that these empowerment businesses have already become pyramid schemes that have enriched their founders and managers (Koch 1997).

The black-owned companies that are now listed on the JSE will also find it difficult to compete with white-owned businesses due to the dearth of an experienced black professional and managerial class to run them. In 1994, for instance, there were only 65 black chartered accountants versus 14,000 whites. Current estimates also suggest that there are less than 300,000 blacks employed in the professional, administrative, and technical capacities, and they are found mostly in the lower rungs of the occupational ladder, or in sinecure affirmative action positions. In the 100 largest South African companies, 98 percent of managers are still white and 93 percent are men (Sethi and Voorhes 1995:7–8). Consequently, a top-down strategy will have to continue the paradoxical practice of relying on white professionals to run companies that are supposed to be empowering blacks.

Among most of the nascent black entrepreneurs, the issue of lack of management experience suitable to a listed company has rarely been thoroughly discussed. This is especially important because most of the spinoff or joint venture companies have managed to generate funds from black grassroots, labor, and religious organizations whose members have courageously invested their meager savings in these untested businesses. There is always the fear that these companies—most of which have gone on an acquisition-spree and have expanded quickly—could collapse, despite their published audited accounts showing them in good financial standing.[9]

Additionally, South Africa's corporate culture is characterized by the concentration of much wealth in a few white hands. Prevented by foreign exchange controls from investing abroad, the industrial giants have for years been incestuously buying into one another's companies, creating a formidable tangle of cross-holdings. These holding companies exist in a maze of shared ownership and cross-directorships, which in turn has produced a myriad of subsidiaries with interests in every facet of the South African economy—from precious metal mining to life insurance and the export-import business.[10] These companies operate in a costly, protected, and oligopolistic market paid for by the consumers.

For example, two suppliers together have a 75 percent share of the sugar market; three jointly control 75 percent of the fertilizer market; and three among them divide up 90 percent of the market in chemical fibers used to weave textiles. Firms seldom compete; until now, they have had no need to (Pedder 1995a:10).[11] Despite all the fanfare about "going the listing route," black entrepreneurs allied with these same giants do not seem capable of upstaging this market.

Another constraint is that blacks would not be the primary beneficiaries of unbundling, because of the difficulty of their financing the takeover of some of the more lucrative offshoots of the unbundling white corporations.[12] In South Africa since 1990, the formal sector has stagnated, shedding more than 238,000 jobs in six years. On the other hand, the microenterprises sector, in which half of the firms are less than six years old, has grown dramatically, with employment among "surviving firms" growing an estimated 24 percent a year. Additionally, the sector as a bloc contributes more than half of the household income of those engaged in it.

Putting too much faith in the top-down strategy is tantamount to ignoring the tidal wave of globalization and the burst of entrepreneurial energy that has already been unleashed by the dismantling of apartheid. South African blacks cannot afford to be called upon years from now to subsidize or bail out the prematurely bloated listed companies because they might relocate to other countries or collapse due to their inability to compete against much trimmer and more profitable firms within the country and internationally.

The Bottom-Up Approach

Arguments for the bottom-up approach are based on the notion of economic democracy, in which the economic benefits of the transition are made available to all participants in the economy. Some obvious beneficiaries of this strategy would be women, whose economic marginalization has continued under a black-led government. According to one observer, South Africa "is still a very chauvinistic, male-dominated society. . . . Although white men hold the great majority of executive positions, black South African men are just as chauvinistic, if not more so" (Hayes 1995:73).

It is, therefore, not surprising that very few women have benefited from unbundling or from the various joint ventures and partnerships described in this chapter. Yet, women constitute 41 percent of the total economically active work force. It is not enough to argue the worn-out trickle-down economic theory or to suggest that men who invest in the big corporations will share the benefits with their families. In fact, nearly half of all marriages in the country end in divorce, and 60 percent of households, due to death, divorce, and abandonment, are female-headed, meaning that these women will lose out as wealth is concentrated beyond their means. Already black women make up a large percentage of the work force that labors throughout life with no retirement (Hirsch 1995:65). A top-down strategy will further exacerbate their economic marginalization, despite the laudable efforts of groups such as WIP to highlight gender inequalities.

The bottom-up approach promotes a culture of enterprise, rather than one of entitlement. Although they reject any such label, some of those who vigorously advocate the top-down approach see empowerment largely as an entitlement, with quotas to be attained at specified dates.[13] Their programs tend to reflect the elitist frame of mind of the advocates. Often little is said about the millions of blacks who would not qualify for or be able to avail themselves of the opportunities that would be created by a top-down strategy. The only way the objectives such as those advocated by NAFCOC will be realized is if whites are willing to give them to blacks as an entitlement. A sustainable culture of entrepreneurship that would spur growth and democratize access to wealth for blacks is more likely to develop through encouraging serious and prosperous MSEs, as well as through capacitating millions in the informal sector with sustainable institutional arrangements.

This requires a proactive role by the state. The continued reliance of the GNU and the ANC on the market system to democratize the economy for the benefit of blacks is suspect, because the South African economy is not an open economy with a level playing field for all participants. Neither is the exclusive emphasis on a top-down strategy a wise choice.

The government's stance may dash the black majority's expectations with serious political consequences. It also deviates from the country's history of massive state assistance that the Afrikaner elite gave to Afrikaner businesses during the last seventy years. The government spent 112 million pounds on agriculture alone between 1911 and 1936, in the form of direct assistance and subsidies, tariff protection, research, administration, and the dissemination of information, mostly to the Afrikaners.[14] It may no longer be feasible to recreate the business condition of apartheid; however, a selective adoption and implementation of similar policies and programs would boost black businesses and advance their overall goal of economic empowerment.

Conclusion

The history of black enterprises in South Africa shows a deliberate attempt by the apartheid regime to deny the majority of its population the right of full participation in the economy as individuals who could freely introduce new goods or improve existing goods, develop new methods of production, open new markets, find new sources of supply, and create new forms of business organization.[15] The economic reforms and deregulation of black business activities from 1976 to 1990 helped to create an emergent black middle class and entrepreneurs. New entrants have joined this class since 1990, giving rise to the seven categories of entrepreneurships discussed.

Although each category has made some inroads into the mainstream economy, black entrepreneurs still face enormous internal, external, and structural constraints. No one group—or collection of them—is capable of surmounting these difficulties alone, nor can it be accomplished through reliance on white big businesses that created and thrived on the perpetuation of some of these hurdles in the first place. Hence, this chapter has suggested that the state should design policies and programs for black businesses similar to those that provided state support for Afrikaner businesses.

Two contending strategies of black economic empowerment—the top-down and bottom-up approaches—are part of the debate. Evidence suggests that the most effective approach to economic empowerment for blacks and for democratization of the South African economy is through a bottom-up strategy built around small firms and the informal sector. These require institutionalized arrangements to help them graduate from lower levels of entrepreneurship to more sophisticated ones. Most black entrepreneurs operate MSEs; starting from this level is consistent with the global trend toward job creation at a much faster rate by small firms, while the giant corporations are laying off thousands of employees despite the enormous subsidies and incentives they receive from the state and society. In addition, more than 64 percent of MSE operators are women who have borne the brunt of apartheid and patriarchal policies. Providing them with self-employment and broadening the spirit of entrepreneurship may not guarantee blacks access to the "commanding heights" of the economy, but it certainly has the potential to democratize the economy and to take up the slack left by the large corporations in this era of corporate downsizing.

Notes

1. These categories were intentionally chosen because they are useful in capturing the uniqueness of different black entrepreneurs in the post-apartheid era.

2. Although there is some overlap between the origins, structures, and activities of black businesses discussed in Randall (1996) and in this chapter, the two studies differ significantly. For example, the former is limited to the top-down approaches to black empowerment while its central question is whether black South Africans can develop true capitalist roots instead of the rent-seeking entrepreneurships that emerged in much of Africa shortly after independence.

3. In the southern African context, some observers believe that black South Africans have not done badly. For instance, in Zimbabwe after fifteen years of independence and despite having the second most developed economy in the region, blacks own less than 1 percent of all enterprises. Multinational corporations there own two-thirds of all enterprises, while the state owns around 4 percent (*SouthScan* 1995c:100).

4. In 1992, the national team of the Consultative Business Movement warned that "a new government may well consider imposing race and gender quotas . . . as a means of satisfying the demand by the electorate for greater participation in the economy. The extent to which business is pro-active will have a bearing on the need, nature and extent of state intervention after the transition from apartheid" (CBM 1993:43).

5. The first spinoff agreement occurred in 1993 between a black consortium, Methold, and Sankorp, Sanlam's investment arm, in which Methold acquired a 10

percent stake in South Africa's seventh largest life insurer, Metropolitan Life (a Sanlam subsidiary) and created a new company called New Africa Investments, Ltd., or NAIL. Other entrants into the stock market include Corporate Africa, which has a controlling stake in NAIL; Kilimanjaro, a bottling group led by a Sowetan businessman; Umbono Investments Ltd., set up in 1995 by American-based Acacia Mutual Life Assurance Company—a subsidiary of the Calvert Group—and South African shareholders such as the RCB Trust New Africa; Johnnic Ltd., acquired in August 1996 by the National Empowerment Consortium led by the directors of NAIL and about 300,000 other shareholders; and Citizen's Bank, formerly a building society acquired in 1993 by Thebe Investments and FirstCorp Merchant Bank, with 1,200 shareholders and a client base of 40,000 investors. If Metropolitan Life and African Life are added, the number of listed black companies is 8 out of more than 700 listed on the JSE. On average, the shares of these listed companies have fared well since their listing. Consequently, the initial negative reaction of white stockbrokers, such as avoiding them and dubbing them "black chips," has been replaced by favorable market reactions.

6. They include Thebe Investments, New Age Beverages, AfricOil, and National Sorghum Breweries (the largest black-owned manufacturing holding company, with 10,000 black shareholders). These are companies that currently boast annual turnovers of up to 200 million rands and assets estimated at more than 500 million rands.

7. A number of better-known multinational corporations such as Digital Equipment, Macmillan Publishing, and Nike have also used variants of this approach by aligning themselves with "facilitating organizations" or distributing small amounts of equity to prominent local black leaders.

8. Former KaNgwane homeland chief minister, Enos Mabuza, topped the list with fourteen directorships in 1996, followed by Dr. Nthato Motlana with twelve, the latter being the best known name in the black economic empowerment debate, even before the political transition in 1994. Other sought-after blacks were Professor Wiseman Nkulu and Don Mkhwanazi, who had seven directorships, respectively; Dikgang Moseneke (six), Dr. Sam Motsuenyane, and Mr. Cyril Ramaphosa (six). Mr. Israel Skosana of Thebe Investments and Ms. Wendy Luhabe of Bridging the Gap Foundation had at least five directorships apiece (*SouthScan* 1997a:23). The percentage of black managers at middle and senior levels has equally risen since the early 1990s.

9. The collapse of African Bank in mid-September 1995, despite its glowing audited accounts and accolades and patronage from prominent blacks (including President Nelson Mandela), is a reminder of the disaster that the advocates of top-down economic empowerment are courting (*SouthScan* 1995d:272–73).

10. According to Robin McGregor (1993), the four biggest companies—Anglo American, Sanlam, Rembrandt, and South Africa Mutual—control a staggering 76 percent of the JSE market, with a capitalization value of more than $260 billion. In the pre-Mandela JSE, six holding companies controlled approximately 87 percent of the stock exchange, distributed as follows: Anglo-American, 43 percent control

of the listed companies; Rembrandt Group, 13 percent; Sanlam, 10 percent; South Africa Mutual, 10 percent; Liberty Group, 7 percent; and Anglovaal Group, 4 percent. Of the 654 companies listed on the exchange, only about 7 percent actively trade; hence, the lack of liquidity in the market (Mack 1995:80).

11. The difficulty of breaking up these conglomerates was highlighted in the recent war of words between the ANC and the Anglo American and De Beers Corporations. While the ANC referred to them as "a problem not only for the economy but for the entire democratic movement," Anglo American defiantly said it would not be "cowed by populist rhetoric," and De Beers sharply criticized the ANC for wanting forcibly to unbundle the conglomerates (AC 1995:1).

12. It took New Africa Investments Ltd. (NAIL) and other black investors more than a year to form the National Empowerment Consortium (NEC) that eventually enabled them to put together the initial capital to acquire 35 percent controlling shares in Johnnic Ltd., in August 1996, in the biggest empowerment deal. However, NEC, owned by more than 300,000 black shareholders, is unlikely to survive unless Johnnic achieves a compound earnings growth of 12 to 14 percent over the next five years. Yet many of the parties who used institutional funding to finance their participation in the deal could be forced to transfer ownership of Johnnic shares to the white financial institutions to repay loans, thereby hindering long-term empowerment of black investors (see High Growth Catch to Black Empowerment Deal, *SouthScan*, 24 January 1997, 22; Not Entirely Black and White, *Economist*, 19 October 1996, 72).

13. For example, the Gauteng branch of NAFCOC in 1992 initiated a four-point program to promote black economic empowerment, so that by the year 2000, "30 percent of seats of boards of companies quoted on the JSE should be occupied by blacks; 40 percent of equity should be held by blacks; 50 percent of inputs should be sourced from black enterprise; and 60 percent of managerial posts should be held by blacks." These targets would ensure that black business would be contributing not less than 10 percent of South Africa's GDP in ten years' time (Mortimer 1995:69; Sethi 1991:8–11).

14. For a detailed analysis of different aspects of this policy, see Heribert Adam and Hermann Giliomee, *Ethnic Power Mobilized: Can South Africa Change?* (New Haven: Yale University Press, 1979); Nancy Clark, "South African State Corporations: 'The Death Knell of Economic Colonialism,' *Journal of Southern African Studies* 14 (October 1987):99–122; Ben Fine and Zav Rustomjee, "The Political Economy of South Africa in the Interwar Period," *Social Dynamics* 18 (2) (1992):26–54; T. Cross, "Afrikaner Nationalism, Anglo American, and Iscor: The Formation of the Highveld Steel and Vanadium Corporation, 1960–1970," *Business History* 36 (3) (1994):81–99; and Nancy Clark, *Manufacturing Apartheid: State Corporations in South Africa* (New Haven: Yale University Press, 1994).

15. This is a paraphrasing of Joseph A. Schumpeter's definition of an entrepreneur, in *The Theory of Economic Development* (New York: Oxford University Press, 1934 [1961]), 65–67.

References Cited

AC (Africa Confidential). 1995. South Africa I: Unbundling Time. *Africa Confidential*, 8 September, 1–2.

African Communist. 1995. No to Mindless Privatisation! *The African Communist* (second quarter):1–2.

Bank, Leslie. 1994. Between Traders and Tribalists: Implosion and the Politics of Disjuncture in a South African Homeland. *African Affairs* 93 (370):75–99.

Beinart, William. 1994. *Twentieth-Century South Africa*. New York: Oxford University Press.

Burton, Sandra. 1988. The New Black Middle Class: With Drive and Talent, an Affluent Elite Shakes Up the Old Order. *Time*, 29 February, 56–57.

CBM (Consultative Business Movement National Team). 1993. *Managing Change: A Guide to the Role of Business in Transition*. Johannesburg: Ravan Press.

Coetzee, A., and J. C. Visagie. 1995. SME Challenges in Reconstructing South Africa. *South African Journal of Entrepreneurship and Small Business* (May):37–50.

Copelyn, John. 1997. Seizing the Moment: Union Investment Companies. *South African Labour Bulletin* 21 (2):74–78.

Faison, Seth. 1994. Pepsi Sets a Return to South Africa; Black Americans Invest in Post-Apartheid Venture in Soft Drinks. *New York Times*, 4 October, C2, D5.

Godsell, Gillian. 1991. Entrepreneurs Embattled: Barriers to Entrepreneurship in South Africa. In *The Culture of Entrepreneurship*, edited by B. Berger. San Francisco: ICS Press.

Golding, Marcel. 1997. Pioneers or Sellouts? Exploring New Lands. *South African Labour Bulletin* 21 (3):85–90.

Hayes, Cassandra. 1995. Can a New Frontier Boost Your Career? *Black Enterprise*, May, 73.

Hirsch, Bryan. 1995. Women Must Provide for Themselves. *Enterprise* (Houghton, South Africa), May, 65.

Jones, Jim. 1989. A Free-Market Cure for Apartheid Ills: From Grocery Stores to Street Stalls, Small Businesses Are Buying Blacks a Stake in South Africa's White-Run Economy. *U.S. News and World Report*, 7 August, 47.

Khosa, M. 1990. The Black Taxi Revolution. In *The Political Economy of South Africa*, edited by N. Nattrass and E. Ardington. Cape Town: Oxford University Press.

Koch, Eddie. 1997. From Shop Floor to Trading Floor. *Mail & Guardian*, 16 May.

Mack, Gracian. 1995. Getting In on the Ground Floor. *Black Enterprise*, May, 80.

Malala, Justice. 1995. Apartheid in Democracy. *The Black Leader* (Houghton, South Africa), April, 24.

Malunga, Mzimkulu. 1995. Black Business in South Africa. *African Business* (London), June, 10–13.

Manning, Claudia, and Angela P. Mashigo. 1994. Manufacturing in South African Microenterprises. *IDS Bulletin* 25 (1):30–36.

McCoy, Frank. 1995. Doing Business in South Africa. *Black Enterprise*, May, 60.

McGregor, Robin, ed. 1993. *McGregor's Who Owns Whom*. Cape Town: Juta.

Mortimer, Bev. 1995. SA Economy Needs to be Reborn. *Enterprise*, May, 12, 69.

Motsuenyane, A. 1989. *The Development of Black Entrepreneurship in South Africa.* Lagos: Nigerian Institute of International Affairs.

Naidoo, Ravi. 1997. Union Investment: Can It Drive Transformation? *South African Labour Bulletin* 21 (3):80–84.

Nyandeni, Reginald. 1995. Black Business Needs a Lift. *Enterprise*, April, 49–50.

Pedder, Sophie. 1995a. A Giant for Africa. *Economist*, 20 May, 10.

———. 1995b. The Darkening of White South Africa. *Economist*, 20 May, 19.

Preece, Howard. 1995. Black on Track: The Unbundling of JCI Could Be of Huge Importance to Black Economic Empowerment. *Southern African Decisions* (1995):49–53.

Randall, Duncan J. 1996. Prospects for the Development of a Black Business Class in South Africa. *Journal of Modern African Studies* 34 (4):661–86.

Riley, Thyra A. 1993. Characteristics of and Constraints Facing Black Businesses in South Africa: Survey Results. Informal Discussion Papers on Aspects of the Economy of South Africa, no. 5. Washington, D.C.: World Bank.

Sethi, Prakash S. 1991. Operational Models for Multinational Corporations in Post-Apartheid South Africa: A Proposal for a Code of Affirmative Action in the Marketplace. *Journal of Business Ethics* 12 (1):1–12.

Sethi, Prakash, and Meg Voorhes. 1995. Economic Prospects of a Democratic South Africa: The Potential Role of U.S. Multinational Corporations. Manuscript.

Smith, Lee-Anne. 1995a. Economic Empowerment in Action. *Enterprise*, April, 17–19.

———. 1995b. NAIL Goes from Strength to Strength. *Enterprise*, April, 62–65.

———. 1995c. The Role of the Merchant Banker. *Enterprise*, April, 66.

———. 1995d. Women Help Make It Happen. *Enterprise*, April, 73.

SouthScan. 1995a. Black Business Makes Its Stock-Exchange Debut, 31 March, 100–102.

———. 1995b. Thebe to Set Up Black Bank, 16 June, 181.

———. 1995c. New Study Shows Little Economic Improvement for Blacks, 22 September, 272.

———. 1995d. Recrimination as Black-Empowerment Bank Fails, 22 September, 272–73.

———. 1997a. Mabuza Leads Black Directorships, 24 January, 23.

———. 1997b. Mbeki Warns New Black Elite to Avoid 'Parasite' Image, 7 March, 65.

Thomas, W. H. 1994. Promoting Entrepreneurship among Black South Africans. In *Entrepreneurship and Economic Growth,* edited by W. B. Vosloo. Pretoria: HSRC Publishers for the Small Business Development Corporation.

Vosloo, W. B. 1994. The Small Firm As a Vehicle for Entrepreneurship. In *Entrepreneurship and Economic Growth,* edited by W. B. Vosloo. Pretoria: HSRC Publishers for the Small Business Development Corporation.

5. Differentiation among Small-Scale Enterprises: The Zambian Clothing Industry in Lusaka

Mwango Kasengele

In the past three decades, there have been a number of studies of the informal sector in Africa. Studies in Ghana (Hart 1973) and Kenya (ILO 1977) have characterized the informal sector as consisting of those economic activities that share features such as small-scale operation, labor-intensive techniques, low technology, and indigenous ownership. Sometimes the term *small-scale industry* (SSI) is used synonymously with *informal sector*, but at other times the designation SSI includes formal sector enterprises up to a certain number of workers.

The danger in lumping all small or informal enterprises together in a single category is that the circumstances of individual businesses may not be recognized (see also Daniels, this volume). This can be a particular problem when policies and programs to assist these enterprises do not differentiate between them according to their specific needs (SATEP 1982). Therefore, it is necessary to look at the heterogeneity of this sector to understand its potential for income and for employment generation (Frankman 1973). Among other issues, differentiation reveals the wide variations among smaller enterprises in their capacity to provide opportunities for self-employment for the owner, as well as salaried employment for local workers. The capacity to create jobs for someone other than the owner or her/his family members is important. This occurs when a small-scale enterprise is able to expand its production beyond the household level to create additional jobs, which contributes to meeting one of the primary goals of economic development.

This chapter looks at the small-scale clothing industry in Zambia. In the analysis for this study, the businesses have been classified in three categories according to their ownership: members of the Asian community;

Zambian women; and Zambian men. The reason ownership is chosen as the distinguishing criterion is that differences in descriptive characteristics among the businesses (such as average revenues, product mix, production techniques, number of employees, and markets) are primarily a function of an owner's access to resources.

In Zambia, the clothing industry is dominated by Asian entrepreneurs. This study examines how resources and services are accessed and utilized by the three above groups in the capital city of Lusaka. It also examines the impact of imports from other countries on the Zambian clothing industry, and how this globalization of trade is affecting the local demand for domestically produced clothing.

Methodology

The research for this study was carried out in Lusaka from June to September 1995. Fieldwork observation of business activities and interviews with the business owners and employees were used to collect information.

One hundred and fifty businesses are included, divided equally among the three groups. This does not necessarily represent their quantitative proportion in the business population, but it allows for a more comprehensive assessment of the strategies used for sustaining a business in this industry. Interviews were conducted in English, as well as in two Zambian languages, Bemba and Nyanja.

The Lusaka Clothing Industry: Background

Despite the fact that manufacturing of clothing lends itself well to small-scale, labor-intensive production, its development in pre-independent Zambia was slow due to severe competition from foreign imports (Young 1973). The market for locally produced goods increased substantially after independence, partly as a result of a rapidly growing urban population with increased purchasing power, and partly because of the imposition of import restrictions by the Zambian government on goods coming from the regimes in Southern Rhodesia (currently Zimbabwe) and South Africa.

The Asians residing in Zambia were in the best position to exploit this new market. Already involved in the retailing of clothing, they invested rapidly in the mass production of simple garments for the urban working population. By 1972 there were officially twenty-six clothing factories in Lusaka, nearly all with less than fifty employees, and owned and operated by Asians. The dominance of the Asian community in this industry has continued to the present, with certain areas in Lusaka specifically demarcated for Asian enterprises.

Indigenous Zambian entrepreneurs moved into the industry in the mid-1970s, and small factories appeared that were fully in Zambian hands. In 1981, one study listed forty-six factories in Lusaka, eighteen of which were owned by Zambians, mostly women (Hoppers 1981). These tended to be small establishments, with the number of employees between five and eighteen. The following sections look at the Zambian clothing industry from the perspectives of the three groups listed above.

The Asian Community in the Clothing Industry

Asians own the larger, more established factories in the Zambian clothing industry. Some of these businesses have moved into the specialist production of knitwear or of uniforms and protective clothing. However, the majority of them manufacture a variety of simple, low-cost men's and/or children's wear. They supply a number of private stores as well as a network of Asian-owned retail outlets in Lusaka's commercial center and in other parts of Zambia. The Asian shops also supplied government-owned department stores before these were privatized in 1991–94 under Structural Adjustment Programs designed to promote a market exchange economy.

The Asian factories usually employ male tailors aged thirty to forty years. A number of them were interviewed in this study. Most have little or no formal education. They usually have no written conditions of service and, in almost all cases, they remain with the same employer for a long time (Kapferer 1972). Women workers are few and only serve as general workers, doing such jobs as sweeping the premises and washing linen. If vacancies arise and candidates with some factory experience are not available, chances are given to unskilled "cotton boys" who clean the garments. It is clear from the Asian employers who were interviewed that such "boys" have to demonstrate reliability, obedience, and quickness in learning about techniques before they are employed in the production process.

Wages are low, in comparison with other industries, rarely reaching more than 30,000 Zambian kwacha (U.S.$5.00) per month for experienced tailors in 1995. Yet these wages are still higher than those of some government employees, for instance drivers, typists, clerks, and receptionists, who earn 25,000 Zambian kwacha, or about U.S.$4.00 (*Times* 1995). This situation of such low salaries undermines the hope among tailors working for Asians that they will be able to start their own workshops and become self-reliant. Asked why they show loyalty to their employers and remain with them despite low wages and poor working conditions, many of them reply with a question: Where else can I go?

However, the issue of low wages in the Zambian clothing industry is part of the larger issue of inadequate salaries for lower level employees throughout the country and the failure of the current economic system to increase income levels.

Zambian Men and Women in the Industry

An important factor affecting the indigenous Zambian business sector is that it developed in a period when the national economy was experiencing serious problems. These included escalating costs of imported raw materials and equipment, shortage of foreign exchange due to the high exchange rate of the Zambian kwacha to the U.S. dollar, and diminishing domestic purchasing power, especially among the lower income groups. The response to this situation by male and female Zambians has differed substantially. Some of the men have tried to compete with the Asian factories by producing similar clothing for the same market. Most of these efforts have not been successful due to controlled markets, and the Zambian men do not have business ties with wholesale suppliers.

By contrast, a certain group of women has concentrated on a different line: producing high-quality fashion garments for higher income clients who prefer imported clothing from London, Paris, or New York over what they have perceived as the "cheap" local wear (Kasengele 1995). These operations involve a relatively high input of capital and foreign exchange. Such constraints have been eased because the women involved in these activities are well off, usually married to wealthy men. This enables them to travel abroad to take design and fashion courses. Through their husbands' connections and their own travel, they have developed a network of personal contacts that enables them to gain access to financing and entry into the upscale fashion markets. So far, they have not had much competition from the Asian entrepreneurs because of the uncertainties inherent in this rather new and emerging market.

The majority of these women have been formally educated. Some of them are university graduates who gave up their jobs to become self-employed or took early retirement from formal sector jobs. They are well equipped to enter the Zambian business sector because of professional experience from their previous jobs in government, parastatal, and private sectors (Finnegan 1994). Furthermore, these women come from a variety of Zambian ethnic groups as a result of extensive social and commercial interaction among people of various ethnic groups, particularly in the urban areas of Lusaka and the Copperbelt provinces. They reside in good residential areas, not in the numerous shanty compounds where most of the Lusaka population is found. Many of them are successful enough in their businesses to be able to build their own houses. These women entrepreneurs are able to establish successful production units with boutique-style outlets along Lusaka's prestigious Cairo Road, and they are now spreading to some other prestigious locations such as Cha Cha Cha and Kalambo Roads with famous shops such as Simson and Cariouse (Kasengele 1995).

Unlike these upper income women, the majority of women in the clothing industry are struggling small-scale producers in the poor and lower income groups. They cite their major problems as limited markets, domestic responsibilities, the need for the husband's permission to do business, and cultural attitudes toward women. Men are considered the household heads, and women in this group are restricted by various traditional expectations from fully participating in the business world. For example, it is still not easy for a woman to contravene tradition and undertake business activities such as negotiating for loans. Most poor and lower income Zambian women, particularly married women, are isolated from men other than their husbands and relatives. As a result, they are constrained from fully participating in business networks, as well as from dealing with financial institutions and other lending agencies. Even when a married woman is able to seek a credit arrangement and is judged eligible for a loan, administrative practice is influenced by tradition and dictates that she must produce evidence of her husband's consent (ZARD 1985).

Zambian businessmen play limited roles in the clothing industry due to lack of investment capital. In addition, they have characteristics that are a result of the Asian system, which has left them with few savings and a narrow skill base—they have no experience in designing, cutting, or other important skills. However, some have been fortunate enough to secure funding to set up a few factories similar to those owned by Asians close to Lusaka's city center. Their profits are low and barely sufficient to cover labor and overhead (Kasengele 1995). With high operating costs and no secure market at this level, they lack the basic conditions for expanding or improving their enterprises.

Workshop Tailors: A Challenge to the Asian Dominance of the Clothing Industry

The main challenge to the Asian dominance of the production of low-cost clothing comes from tailors who have established themselves in the numerous small workshops located near the big markets of the high-density townships. They have formed a business entity relying on a network of customers who order regularly enough to allow the tailors to have a dependable production schedule with reliable anticipation of sales to these customers. These workshops are usually one-person enterprises, but some generate enough consistent business to hire one or two employees or to take on apprentices.

Unlike the Zambian men who have attempted to set themselves up in factory style production, the workshop tailors are able to compete to some extent with the Asian producers. This is primarily because their production operations require a very small capital outlay, they generally have no employees or wages to pay, and they have a reliable customer base of personal clients. Many of them locate close to the residences of their actual or potential clients, and they gain favor with their customers by their widespread practice of extending credit instead of demanding cash. Profits fluctuate widely. Certain factors make a difference, such as a shop's location in the market area, a decision to produce a certain quantity of garments in anticipation of the demand for school uniforms at the term's start, or the handling of slow-paying customers.

Not all of these workshop tailors are doing well in their businesses; there are still those who feel that they are just one step above bankruptcy. Those that do well attribute their success to extraordinary personal efforts and being able to adjust to and withstand difficult conditions. But even among those tailors who claim to be doing well, expansion of their customer base seems to come from luring away customers of other workshop tailors rather than from finding new customers or attracting clients away from the Asian shops (Kasengele 1995).

The "Veranda" Tailors

The problems faced by the workshop tailors are intensified at the lowest levels of the clothing production industry. Here the tailors do not even have small workshops. Instead, they work outdoors, around their residences, or on the veranda of a store. Their capital base is much smaller, and the absence of even a semblance of a workshop, together with the lack of working capital, forces them to concentrate on repair services for a tiny circle of poorer clients in the immediate neighborhood vicinity. They do not have a steady stream of orders, so they are often without work; theirs is basically a subsistence activity.

These subsistence or veranda producers have a number of similarities with the workshop tailors. The starting capital, for example, usually comes from wage employment that they undertake after retirement. In both cases, skills are acquired from training in factories or from colleagues. Their operations are significantly smaller in scale, and they differ in work motivation, a finding that seems to be linked to age. The veranda producers tend to be older men for whom the activity is a form of retirement, constituting a more acceptable alternative than returning to their home villages after retirement. By contrast, most of the workshop tailors are in their late twenties and early thirties and have opted for self-employment as a means of escape from the drudgery of the factory and in order to earn higher incomes as independent entrepreneurs.

However, several younger males—under the age of twenty—are also working without shops at the subsistence level of production. They have obtained sewing machines through relatives and regard this self-employment as a better means of acquiring some investment money than the casual jobs they previously had to accept. The increasing numbers of those who leave school at this level (also observed in other trades) may be a sign of things to come; it may demonstrate their inability to obtain other forms of employment. High youth unemployment has prompted the Zambian government to negotiate for a loan from the American-based African Development Foundation with the aim of promoting entrepreneurship and business ownership among youth in the towns of Lusaka, Kitwe, and Livingstone (*Post* 1995a).

Petty Producers: Toward Evolution or Involution?

Because of the small size of most Zambian clothing producers, virtually all of them could be considered small-scale enterprises, regardless of ownership. But the industry is diverse in its production capacities, particular problems, and prospects for development. A consideration of the types of production operations provides an understanding of the dynamics of all of these small enterprises within the clothing industry. Production in this industry varies according to whether operations occur in factories, workshops, or outdoors. The factory is characterized by the capitalist nature of the production process, involving the separation of ownership, control, and production, as well as a high degree of rationalization in using the forces of production to generate surplus value (Bienefeld 1975). In the workshops and in outdoor production units, there is little, if any, differentiation between owner, manager, and worker. These artisans control their means of production with a very small capital base, usually receiving little or no assistance from formal sector agencies.

It would be optimistic to regard the different forms of production as part of a continuum along which an artisan could move and that in time would carry her or him into large-scale production. Unfortunately, the evidence suggests that the prospects for accumulation and expansion among the petty producers are limited (Hoppers 1983). When accumulation does occur among the petty producers, it only allows for expansion within the same mode of production, rather than allowing an entrepreneur to make the transition to a higher level and a more profitable mode. All of the petty producers interviewed have been at their current scale of production since they first got involved in manufacturing clothing. The greatest obstacle seems to be between the more advanced form of petty production (the workshops) and the small capitalist production (the factories). In the case of the entrepreneurs who reach the ceiling of expansion within their mode, further growth is only likely to take place laterally, by establishing additional workshops, rather than vertically, by establishing a small factory.

The critical point is that such a transition does not merely involve a further expansion of the existing unit (for example, by employing wage workers or purchasing additional sewing machines). Transition requires the transformation of a person's commercial relations, usually symbolized by a physical move to upgraded premises. At each step, inputs such as equipment, type of labor, and technical and managerial skills need to be of a different kind, or, as with raw materials, need to come from different sources.

Similarly, a producer needs a different relationship with the market; for example, a clothing factory requires a steady and reliable flow of orders. In the absence of a retail outlet, this can be secured by building up a network of institutional customers. The nature of this transformation is such that it requires a major change to occur in an entrepreneur's resource base. The rare occurrence of such an event is emphasized by the fact that the few examples of transition that were traced occurred in the late 1960s, when tailors who started at home could still cross the then relatively small barrier between outdoor and workshop production. The other example is the situation involving the higher status women, who, because of their privileged access to resources and markets, have been able to expand the operation of a workshop at home into a prosperous business in the city center.

Apart from the low purchasing power of most of the urban population, the major problem of the petty producers is their disadvantage within the competitive arena in available markets. The petty nature of their activities is perpetuated through the control exerted by the formal capitalist sector over scarce resources. Within the clothing industry, the petty tailors are still fairly autonomous in their ability to make decisions that involve their business ventures. Contractual relationships between capitalist and petty producers do not exist at present, as Asian entrepreneurs prefer to have direct control over all production, and, in view of prevailing low wages, they would not gain financially by subcontracting.

It is clear that the Asian producers create the broader conditions in which the petty producers are allowed to operate. The Asians have a near monopoly on the market for institutional clothing, a portion of which would no doubt enable some petty producers and tailors to make a transition into small capitalist production. The big producers dominate the market for low-cost clothing despite the fact that this market is accessible to the petty producers due to their closer contact with poorer and lower income customers. But even here, they are at a competitive disadvantage. Low labor costs, preferential access to sources of raw materials and capital, and more efficient production methods all enable the factories to keep their customers' prices down.

The petty producers often must purchase their inputs at retail prices from Asian shops. They cannot afford to hire skilled labor, and they spend a lot of time searching for materials and seeking customers (Bardouille 1982). In such a situation, production costs are high; most of these producers rely on the labor of relatives or must pay low wages to workers. Such exploitative labor conditions are bolstered by the ever growing numbers of unemployed youth. The petty producers are unable to accumulate resources to increase their production capacity, so they reinforce the very conditions from which most of them are trying to escape.

The Effect of *Salaula* on the Lusaka Clothing Industry

A study of current developments in the clothing industry in Zambia—in Lusaka in particular—must include a discussion of the impact of *salaula*. This term refers to the buying and selling of used or second-hand clothing imported from western Europe, North America, and Japan. Some of it is donated by nongovernmental organizations in Zambia and is not intended for commercial resale. However, unscrupulous dealers manage to subvert the charitable intentions. Articles of second-hand clothing have become popular among consumers in Zambia, primarily because they are cheap and many people can afford to buy them.

Salaula is dominated by the Asian community. A chain of shops now exists in Lusaka's Kamwala township where used garments are sold in bulk soon after their arrival. All of the shops, as well as the residences in the Kamwala area, are owned by Asians (Kasengele 1995). Most of the Zambians who sell second-hand clothing work for the Asian entrepreneurs. They are paid on commission and are primarily young boys and girls who have left school at the ninth-grade level, at an average age of fourteen years. They come from poor families where their parents encourage them to find jobs, and they live in Lusaka's shanty compounds such as Misisi, Mutendere, Kalingalinga, Kanyama, Bauleni, and Mandefu, not far from the big city-center market.

During the time I spent there talking with many of them, in 1995 my observation was that they seemed to be reasonably satisfied with their work. Most of them described the terms of their commissions as fair. They felt that the salaula trade provided them with an opportunity for employment that they otherwise would not have had.

However, salaula has had a severe impact on the Zambian clothing industry. This impact has both immediate and potentially long-reaching effects. Salaula has been blamed for the demise of many small indigenous tailoring and textile production enterprises (Finnegan 1994). Even some of the clothing shops and traders have begun to buy used clothing to resell because it is cheaper than new clothing. Of course, this results in declining purchases and revenues for the local tailors and textile producers.

A visit to the markets at Kamwala, Soweto, and the city center shows how extensively salaula has impacted the clothing industry in Lusaka. A random survey conducted among visitors to these markets shows who the salaula customers are. Those surveyed represent a cross section of Lusaka residents and a variety of occupations. There are teachers, doctors, nurses, clerks, secretaries, as well as people not employed in the formal sector. A majority of those questioned (64 percent) welcomed the coming of salaula to Zambia, because it has made available a wider variety of cheap clothing. A substantial proportion (74 percent) said they had bought at least one such item within the past two years. Among these items were ties, belts, T-shirts, shorts, shirts, trousers, stockings, shoes, jackets, blouses, and dresses.

Under the current policy of economic liberalization in Zambia, there are few restrictions on the quantity of salaula goods imported into the country. The high volume of these imports has already had an impact at the national level and has led to increasing difficulties in the textile industries at Kafue, Mulunguishi, and Livingstone. The output of these factories is more expensive than salaula goods, and it is beyond the purchasing power of most ordinary Zambians. Many of the factories are now operating at a loss as parastatals. Three of them have been put up for sale to the private sector by the Zambia Privatization Board (*Post* 1995b).

The general consensus of Zambian consumers is that government policy is at fault for allowing salaula to reach the point where it is a threat to the country's indigenous clothing industry. Some of those interviewed say that the government should do something to limit the import of used clothing and to curb the salaula trade. However, the Zambian government defends its policies and says that it should not interfere with the operation of a free market.

Policy Reforms to Support the Clothing Industry

To enable small-scale enterprises to make a transition upward along the scale of production, services such as credit, marketing, and management support are needed. These service providers could focus their attention on indigenous enterprises that show promise of developing into larger, modern businesses. In addition to providing some support for petty producers, it may be particularly productive to assist higher level businesses to expand even more. (As previously noted, most Zambian private sector clothing manufacturers can be classified as small.)

Such support would be particularly well placed among the women producers discussed earlier, who have found a niche in the high-quality fashion segment. They use the *chitenge* fabrics (gaily printed cotton) to make dresses, skirts, trousers, and suits. These garments are lightweight and more suitable for African climates than Western-type clothing. Zambian-made chitenge garments are less expensive than those imported from Zaire and West Africa; they are even less expensive than those imported from Pakistan and Indonesia. Promoting the chitenge industry would have multiplier effects in the other sectors of the clothing industry. In addition to directly increasing jobs in these enterprises, it could also stimulate the development of related enterprises. Such enterprises might include manufacturers of natural and synthetic fabrics, as well as artisanal enterprises such as embroidery, tie-dye, makers of ornaments and accessories, and so on.

However, the chitenge producers represent only a small sector of the Zambian clothing industry. Most of the industry is populated by petty producers whose customers are lower income or poor. The low purchasing power of the masses of Zambian people is an impediment to these entrepreneurs' ability to expand and develop their businesses. Reinforcing their ability to compete with the Asians and to supply goods for middle-income consumers may be a more immediate way to help these enterprises generate revenue. This may entail intervention in the entrepreneurs' structural relations with their sources of supply and with formal sector producers. It could involve giving the producers some form of preferential access to certain suppliers and markets, for example uniforms and other goods purchased by government agencies.

Assistance to producers should focus on increasing credit flows and the accessibility to raw materials and other resources. In addition, improvements in the quantity and quality of local materials must be encouraged. Marketing efforts should be expanded to enlarge the customer base for these goods. It is important to intensify campaigns to stimulate demand for good quality Zambian-made garments.

The main thrust of assistance aimed directly at individual producers should be geared to upgrade the scale of production. This could be accomplished by building the capacity of small operators who have the interest and potential to move to bigger workshops. Such operators could be provided with technical assistance aimed at higher efficiency, they could be helped to upgrade the technology of their equipment, and they could be helped to increase their knowledge.

Individual enterprises could expand their capacity by collaborating with other enterprises. Despite the emphasis in Zambian culture on maintaining strong interpersonal relationships, cooperative associations in the business sector have not been very effective. However, there are ways to collaborate while maintaining autonomy and identity as a separate enterprise. These include joining together to purchase materials and supplies in bulk, thus reducing the cost; jointly procuring certain types of equipment; subcontracting together to fill large orders; and establishing industrial districts to network and exchange information and technology, as is done in many industrialized countries. Such actions could increase the scale of production and elevate the level of operations of the petty producers. Of course, some of the microenterprises and less-capable owners would falter or remain at the same levels regardless of whatever programs or support services were provided.

Conclusion

The Zambian clothing industry is quite heterogeneous, as this study has shown. It consists of a diversity of operations—the sole proprietor working on infrequent small orders for tailored garments, tiny workshops, small factories, larger factories dominated in the private sector by Asians, and public sector parastatals. There are also new and emerging specialty segments, such as that developed by educated, upper-middle-class women whose products cater to a high fashion clientele. Some areas of the industry are being threatened by the salaula trade: the resale of used clothing imported from industrialized countries.

The clothing industry is a major employer of urban workers, in both the formal and informal sectors. Those who cannot find work can make work for themselves in this industry. Workers include fabric cutters and garment sewers who hire out at exploitatively low wages, as well as young people who leave middle school and find employment by peddling used clothing on commission. Policies that seek to promote economic development and job creation must address the diversity of this industry. Lower end petty producers need support to expand their scale of operations, to attract a larger share of the consumer market, and to make the transition upward along the production scale. Both small and large textile and clothing manufacturers face a threat from imported used clothing. If the industry is to remain viable in the long run, a counterstrategy of some protective measures is required. If Zambia is to resolve the critical problems facing this important and diverse industry, all of these considerations must be addressed through initiatives from both the public and private sectors.

References Cited

Bardouille, Raj. 1982. Men's and Women's Work and Opportunities in the Urban Informal Sector: The Case of Some Urban Areas in Lusaka. *Manpower Research Unit Report* (University of Zambia) 10:35–41.

Bienefeld, Manfred. 1975. The Informal Sector and Peripheral Capitalism: The Case of Tanzania. *IDS Bulletin* 67:4–11.

Finnegan, Gerry. 1994. *Marketing in Zambia: A Practical Guide.* Dublin: Irish Printing Resources.

Frankman, Myron. 1973. Employment in the Service Sector in Sub-Saharan Africa. *Journal of Modern African Studies* 11:201–10.

GRZ (Government of the Republic of Zambia). 1990. *Guidelines on the Minimum Wage in the Manufacturing Industry.* Lusaka: Government Printers.

Hart, Keith. 1973. Informal Income Opportunities and Urban Employment in Ghana. *Journal of Modern African Studies* 11:61–89.

Hoppers, Wim. 1981. Out-of-School Youth and the Urban Labour Market: A Case Study of Selected Lusaka Industries. *Urban Community Research Report* 4:11–33.

———. 1983. Youth Apprenticeship and Petty Production in Lusaka. *International Journal for Education and Development* 1:6–10.

ILO (International Labour Organization). 1977. *Narrowing the Gaps: Planning for Basic Needs and Productive Employment in Zambia.* Addis Ababa: Economic Commission for Africa.

Kapferer, Bruce. 1972. *Strategy and Transaction in an African Factory: African Workers and Indian Management.* Manchester, England: Manchester University Press.

Kasengele, Mwango. 1995. A Study of the Clothing Industry in Urban Lusaka. Unpublished report, ODA (Office of Development Assistance).

The Post (newspaper). 1995a. American Assistance for Enterprise Development. 7 July.

———. 1995b. The Decline of the Clothing Industry: Salaula Takes Over. 9 October.

SATEP (Southern Africa Team for Employment Promotion). 1982. *The Urban Informal Sector in Zambia: A Programme for Action.* Geneva: ILO.

Times of Zambia (newspaper). 1995. Civil Servants Demand More Pay. 15 June 1995.

Young, Andrew. 1973. *Industrial Diversification in Zambia.* New York: Praeger.

ZARD (Zambia Association for Research and Development). 1985. *An Annotated Bibliography of Research on Zambian Women.* Lusaka: Printing Services.

PART II

Entrepreneurs as Provisioners of the City and the Household

◇◇◇◇◇◇◇◇◇◇◇◇

6. Women Entrepreneurs? Trade and the Gender Division of Labor in Nairobi

Claire C. Robertson

For urban and peri-urban Kikuyu and Kamba women and men in the Nairobi area of Kenya, market trade is an increasingly important means of earning a living. But the living earned is not equal for men and women. This chapter explores the substantial differences between women and men small entrepreneurs, differences that are rooted in varying degrees of access to critical resources according to gender, as well as in the "domestic" gender division of labor. Using data collected in seventeen Nairobi-area markets in 1987–88 from both men and women, the study demonstrates close connections between the so-called private aspects of traders' lives and their public achievements. The data show that policy makers concerned with improving opportunities for small entrepreneurs cannot hope to ameliorate and equalize conditions among traders without dealing holistically with many aspects of their lives.[1] For women in Africa, separating the "public" from the "private" sphere has never been and is not now a viable approach, either for analysis or for practice.

The history of Kikuyu and Kamba women's trade goes back at least as far as the mid-nineteenth century. Kikuyu women conducted both local and long-distance trade chiefly in agricultural produce and especially in dried staples (Robertson 1996). In the nineteenth century, they supplied Swahili- and European-led caravans from the coast with sufficient supplies to cross the dry area on their way to Lake Victoria Nyanza. Today, the dried-staples trade forms a base from which many women traders begin and then expand into more profitable commodities. Kenyan women farmers supply most of the food for Nairobi and for Kenya as a whole, and women traders convey the food to market. With the increase in landlessness and divorce, women are becoming full-time urban-resident traders in ever larger numbers.

Nairobi itself has reached approximately 2 million in population; feeding it is a labor-absorptive enterprise at every level. Although the growing importance of such trade networks is evident, relatively little scholarly energy has been devoted to analyzing their nature and how the lives of the participants are affected by the context in which they operate. In sub-Saharan Africa, much local trade is dominated by women traders; in coastal West Africa, the stereotypical woman is a small-scale trader. There are, relatively speaking, numerous studies of their activities.[2] Men rarely sell in markets in West Africa. By contrast, in East Africa the stereotypical woman is a farmer, although there are many women in East African markets. My book, *Trouble Showed the Way: Women, Men, and Trade in the Nairobi Area, 1890–1990*, is the first monograph on the subject of women's trade in East Africa that documents the expansion of women's trade in the Nairobi area into a system for supplying all of Kenya with dried staples.

In the Nairobi area, the presence of substantial numbers of men as sellers in markets allows for a direct assessment of the gender differences affecting trade, an opportunity not presented by most studies of West African market traders. These differences include both substantial inequities in access to critical resources such as land and education, and a gender division of labor that assigns to women exclusive responsibility for child rearing and its attendant household tasks (cooking, laundry), as well as more of the routine time-absorptive farming tasks, such as weeding. Data concerning these differences are scarce, and they have largely been ignored by policy makers and academics alike, who often persist in viewing women's unpaid labor as invisible and/or valueless, and the gender division of labor as an unproblematized "traditional" artifact, ignoring the historical changes that have to a large extent withdrawn men's labor from agriculture in many areas.

The data for this study are derived from a large body of archival, survey, and oral history data collected in 1987–88 in the Nairobi area, including urban and suburban markets and those in one rural area, Kiambu, that borders Nairobi. A census of seventeen markets was conducted that includes more than 6,000 male and female traders. Most of these traders came from rural areas near Nairobi: Kiambu, Ukambani, or Murang'a (only 4 percent were born in Nairobi). In this chapter, the data in the tables come mainly from a sample survey of 1,018 traders selected randomly in the censused markets. In the urban markets, men slightly outnumber women sellers, while in rural markets, women predominate by a large margin; overall, two-thirds of the traders are women. Rural women traders are often also farmers, but urban women traders also often spend part of their time in rural areas farming, especially if they have land.

Gender Differences in Access to Critical Resources

What are the differences among traders? In the survey, differences between men and women traders are startling and pervasive. These differences are evident in everything from reasons for entering trade to capital invested and income derived from trade. In terms of entering trade, men traders are more likely to have had a wage job that allowed them to save start-up capital, whereas women are more likely to begin by selling their own produce. Men are more likely to be permanent Nairobi residents, which is reflected in their lower participation in farming. Men are, in fact, 41 percent of the traders in urban markets, compared with only 19 percent in rural markets and 28 percent in suburban markets. They are more often wage-job seekers with few or no dependents, generally younger than women at an average age of 33.6 years compared with 39.6 years for women. Women enter trade at a later age than men—at an average of 30.6 years compared with 25.1 years for men. They chose trade from among limited options in order to meet family needs, often in response to a crisis, rather than as a career selected in preference to others.

Women suffer from lack of the two most critical resources for generating capital: land and education. Landlessness is an increasing problem that deprives individuals of the possibilities of both cash-crop (a category that now includes many food crops) income and of help in feeding their families. For the 272 women in the sample who have access to land, those aged seventy and over averaged 7.5 acres each, compared with 1.8 acres for those aged twenty to twenty-nine, with steadily diminishing amounts in intermediate age groups.

The pattern is just the opposite for the forty-two men in the sample who had access to land, with more landlessness in older age groups and steadily increasing amounts for younger men who have access to land. These figures for men are surprising; the expectation was that older men would be able to purchase or inherit more land, but inheritance patterns and the scramble for land in areas surrounding Nairobi have created the pattern observed. A large wave of landless men who came to Nairobi in the 1960s are now in their fifties and sixties or older. Many became traders; those who could not purchase land remained in Nairobi. Some may have lost their land due to their absence from home, as chronicled by several women traders, victims of rapacious husbands' relatives who forced them off the land.

The next wave, especially in the 1970s, found it more feasible to "straddle," as Cowen and Kinyanjui (1977) put it, that is, they left their wives to farm their land while they continued to trade and even purchased more land. There are not many in this group, however. Table 6.1 shows the severity of the land access problem for men and women traders that pushes them into trade.

Only 1.9 percent of women and 3.6 percent of men traders own land. Altogether, 43.5 percent of women traders have access to land in some fashion, mainly through their husbands, while men are more likely to have acquired land through purchase or inheritance, with ownership that can be converted into collateral for acquiring loans. However, for both men and women, land ownership is minuscule (2.5 percent); 65.6 percent of all traders have no access to land in any manner.[3] The number of women claiming land-use rights through their husbands is equivalent to less than half of the women who were married at the time of the survey, indicating substantial landlessness among their husbands. Women's strategies for survival often include growing their own food on small plots of rented land on which they sometimes build shacks to house their families. The high proportion of young landless men in the market is indicative of the high degree of absolute landlessness.

Table 6.2 shows that the best way for women to secure more land is to purchase it. Marriage is the most common method for women to get access to land, but purchase is the better method for securing more land. Women doing business or living in Nairobi acquired more land than either rural or suburban women. None of the women who sold in rural markets had bought land, although five who lived in a rural area but did not sell there had purchased land.

Men's best access to land is through inheritance, a finding also supported in studies by Stamp (1991) and MacKenzie (1990a; 1990b) that show

Table 6.1. Percentage of traders with access to land, by gender and landownership, 1987–1988

	% of women traders (N=685)	% of men traders (N=331)	% of all (N=1016)
Owner of land			
Self	1.9	3.6	2.5
Spouse	24.8	0	16.7
Father	3.5	3.0	3.3
Landlord	3.8	0.6	2.7
Other	2.2	0.3	1.7
Unknown	7.3	8.1	7.5
Total	43.5	15.7	34.4

how male reinterpretation of customary law is being used to deprive women of access to land by inheritance. MacKenzie argues—and it is borne out here—that women's land-use rights have now become dependent on individual male action rather than on corporate kin, a more fragile position.[4] These women told numerous stories of landlessness caused by husbands or sons selling land or husbands' relatives seizing it sublegally (see also Davison 1989:172).

The sum total of this landholding evidence indicates both the vulnerability of women traders (most of whom would farm if they could) to landlessness and the differentiation among traders themselves. The few who do own land have substantially more than the average landholding in Kiambu and Murang'a (less than one acre per household). However, this is partly because of the proportion of Kamba women in this sample. Land scarcity is not as prevalent in Ukambani, and the thirty-three Kamba women with access to land had an average of 6.5 acres each, compared with two acres each for Kikuyu women with access (there was only one Kamba man in the sample, so the male comparison is not valid). Even when ethnicity is taken into account, traders with land had more than the average household's landholding. But when the amount of land is divided among all traders including the landless, the average is only .78 acres—below average household landholding for Murang'a, Kiambu, and Ukambani.[5]

In general, men traders with any involvement in farming were able to secure more land. They had three acres on the average, compared with 2.6 for women who farm. A comparison of several more prosperous urban groups of traders confirms this. A group of eight Nyamakima male store owners aged forty-eight and over had an average of 9.9 acres of land, all of it worked by their wives and most of it purchased. A comparable group of seven Shauri Moyo women stall holders aged forty-five and over were not farming themselves and owned no land, except for one woman who had access to thirty-five acres owned by her deceased husband and worked by her wife, acquired through woman-marriage, an uncommon practice in

Table 6.2. Mean average acreage by gender and source of access, 1987–1988

Source of access	Women	Men
Purchase	4.6	3.6
Marriage	2.0	0
Inheritance	2.4	5.2
Rental	1.1	1.8

which a relatively prosperous widow might pay bridewealth for a younger woman whose children (fathered by a lover) became the heirs to perpetuate the dead husband's lineage.

Hence, even women who were relatively prosperous, with a long trading history, were not usually able to buy land. Moreover, most of their spouses were not farming (five out of seven were not), so they could not supplement their earnings with food produced in the rural area. Conversely, these women were more likely to be sending food to rural areas. The Nyamakima men, in contrast, were often getting income from cash crops sold by their wives. The diminishing amount of land available to women is probably the single most crucial factor increasing their involvement in trade; it also helps to explain their lack of capital for beginning in trade, as shown in table 6.4.

Another factor furthering women's involvement in trade is their lesser access to Western-type education, which has become a critical resource for Kenyans. Table 6.3 compares the level of education among women and men traders. The most significant difference lies in the number of traders with no formal education, who are mostly older women. Fewer men in the sample are in this category. The largest expansion in provision of primary education for Kenyan girls came in the 1970s (Robertson 1986). This differential access to education carries over into the level of education attained by those in the sample who did go to school: 64 percent of the 465 women who had attended school had primary education only, compared with 56 percent of the men. Only 24 percent of all of the women traders reached Standard 6 or 7 in primary school, compared with 33 percent of the men.

To set these statistics in the context of those for the population of Nairobi, 27 percent of the women traders in the sample completed Form 1 or higher, compared with 38 percent of the women aged fifteen and over in Nairobi

Table 6.3. Level of education for Nairobi area traders by gender, 1987–1988 (in percentages)

	Women (N=685)	Men (N=331)
Level of education		
None	29.3	3.0
Primary (standards 1–7)	43.4	44.9
Middle (forms 1–4)	24.9	50.5
Secondary (forms 5–6)	0.1	0.3
Postsecondary (teacher training, vocational)	2.3	0.6

in 1979. For men, 51 percent of the traders completed Form 1 or higher, compared with 44 percent of men fifteen and over in Nairobi.[6] The case is apparently quite different for men and women traders. Women simply lacked education as a result of a number of factors, such as age, fewer available school places, lower quality schools or curricula, pregnancy terminating school attendance, parental reluctance to send them to school because of their labor value, and poverty forcing that parental choice.[7] In contrast, the chief difficulty facing men is not access to schooling—male traders had above-average access—but finding a job commensurate with that schooling.

Therefore, there are good reasons for the increasing intensity and scope of women's involvement in trade. They have fewer choices than men in terms of occupation and training, and they are more vulnerable to landlessness in that they rarely own land and have less land than men when they are farming. Marriage is becoming more fragile, thus weakening women's most common method of access to land and forcing more dependence on trade for a living.

Gender differentiation among traders is also very evident in profits and in the amount of start-up capital. Table 6.4 shows the average amount of start-up capital and gross profits (on a good day), according to whether the selling location is a periodic or a daily market.[8] The mobility and scale of women's trade does not make a significant difference for their gross profits, which averaged about a third to a half of men's profits. Gender differentiation is always far more significant than either of these characteristics. Profit levels do not differ much between women trading in daily markets and those trading in periodic markets, but start-up capital does.

Gender differences are even more evident in the short- versus long-distance trade results concerning profits. Men who live and sell in the same areas make significantly lower profits on good days than those who sell in different areas from where they live: an average of 262.95 Kenyan shillings

Table 6.4. Mean average amounts of start-up capital and profits per day by gender and market type, 1987–1988 (in Kenyan shillings)

| Market type | Start-up capital | | Profits | |
| | Women | Men | Women | Men |
	(N=835)		(N=1012)	
Daily	1004.13	2542.16	135.9	301.5
Periodic	523.8	1931.2	126.8	386.8

per day versus 341.98 shillings. For women, there is no significant differ-ence; those who live and sell in the same area make 138.88 shillings on an average good day, versus 134.47 shillings for those who leave their resi-dential areas to sell. The gender differences here distinguish men who sell imported goods in rural areas from poor rural women who turn to Nairobi trade due to landlessness and lack of capital; many are hawkers but some are wholesalers. Greater mobility does not bring a significant upward shift in profits for most women, nor does involvement in wholesaling.

Nor does selling in a legal location make a significant difference for women. Women who sold in enclosed premises with a roof constructed of permanent materials made 138.88 shillings on an average good day, com-pared with 131.38 shillings for those selling legally outdoors, and 131.05 shillings for those selling on illegal premises with no permanent infrastruc-ture. Men paid more for selling space (either building legal or renting ille-gal ones) because they can afford more. More than half of the women were selling with no infrastructure, compared with less than a quarter of the men. The number of men selling in enclosed legal market space is about equal to the number with no infrastructure.

Unlike women, men show significant differences according to the legal status and infrastructure of the selling space. Those who sold in legal, per-manent, enclosed premises made an average of 221.96 shillings on a good day. Those who sold legally in outdoor markets made 328.65 shillings, while those selling from illegal premises made 380.27 shillings (a result strongly affected by the high profits in the illegal used-clothing trade). For men, then, there was a strong disincentive to sell in legal premises that also af-fected women when the cost of selling space is considered.

The cheapest method of obtaining selling space was to sell in rural, out-door, periodic markets for a fee calculated according to the number of bags of produce brought to sell. Next in cost was illegal space, subject in some areas to rents or initial fees charged by market committees who use the proceeds to hire watchmen and carry out sanitary measures such as rat killing. Highest in cost by far, at two or three times the cost of illegal space, was the rent charged for permanent selling premises in legal markets. How-ever, those working in spaces often need to construct their premises them-selves; the building expenses usually raise the price of the illegal space so that it costs more, in the end, than the legal space, which often comes with a stall included. Table 6.5 shows the cumulative initial costs of selling space according to gender and according to the legal status of the market space.

Table 6.6 shows the mean average differences, according to age and gender, in profits made on good and bad days of selling (N = 835 for a

Table 6.5. Mean average costs of selling space by legal status and gender, 1987–1988 (in Kenyan shillings)

	Legal Enclosed		Legal Outdoor		Illegal	
	Women	Men	Women	Men	Women	Men
Acquisition cost	141.02	243.34	15.09	25.38	69.85	73.29
Building cost	85.87	166.87	20.47	60.02	140.78	191.92
Total cost	226.89	410.21	35.56	85.40	210.63	265.01

good day and 828 for a bad day). On both good and bad days, men's average profits are more than twice those of women. The reasons for men's greater profits include their higher start-up capital, which allowed them to deal in commodities with a high unit value, such as imported goods, and on a larger scale, and their lesser domestic work obligations that allowed them to work longer hours.

Family obligations weigh heavily on women, not only in reducing their selling hours, but also in withdrawing capital from their business. Table 6.6 shows that women's earnings dropped sharply when they reach their forties, mainly because they withdrew capital from businesses to pay school fees that increase as children get older.[9] Women's profits also diminished after age sixty. For men the indicators are less certain because of the high incidence of missing data in older, usually more successful age groups.

The relationship of land-use rights to profit levels among traders ties together this section and makes a fitting ending. Men had access to more land than women did, on average, although more men than women are completely landless (87 percent versus 61 percent). Table 6.7 shows that for men, in particular, a strong positive relationship exists between land access and trading profits. The association is uneven, but those with access to more land tended to make more profits in trade. They were also likely to have more start-up capital. For women, however, profits fell somewhat when access to land rose above eight acres, probably because women put in more work farming. The sum of this evidence shows strong class differentiation among men traders, but only weak differences among women traders, while virtually all the statistical differences between women and men are significant at the .00 level.[10]

Men and women traders' profits also differ within commodity groups as a logical consequence of differential access to capital and withdrawal of profits for family needs. Although there is a tendency for men to concentrate in more profitable commodities, such as used and new clothing and

Table 6.6. Average gross profits of traders, on good and bad days, by age and gender, 1987–1988 (in Kenyan shillings)

Age group	Good day		Bad day	
	Women	Men	Women	Men
15–19	153.6	274.0	90.0	74.5
20–29	140.4	363.8	45.4	106.9
30–39	151.8	254.8	46.6	64.8
40–49	120.0	346.5	40.4	113.4
50–59	114.8	57.8	28.0	11.9
60–69	97.8	116.3	24.7	50.8
70+	105.1	128.0	35.0	55.6
Average all ages	132.9	318.1	41.5	93.3

Table 6.7. Distribution of land access and trading profits by acreage and gender, 1987–88

Acreage	% with land access		Average profits (good day)	
	Women	Men	Women	Men
< than 1	33.1	19.1	109.80	150.00
1–3.9	46.6	56.1	107.42	342.64
4–7.9	11.7	14.6	208.58	286.17
8 +	8.6	9.8	142.09	395.00

housewares (as shown in table 6.8), the differences in profits are significant even within commodity groups. Table 6.8 ranks commodities by groups and profitability, while also showing the distribution of their sale by gender. Profits are average gross profits for a good day. Some commodities have undoubtedly fallen in level of profitability. The sale of fresh vegetables was probably more profitable, for example, before better transport brought more competition. Nici Nelson's study (1979:293) included some vegetable sellers whom she considered to be quite poor.[11] Thus, women's entrance in large numbers into vegetable selling may have coincided with a loss in profitability. Conversely, the used-clothing trade may have become more profitable than previously due to its illegality. It existed as far back as World War I but has now grown considerably. It is extremely profitable for the business owners, but the many young sellers are paid low daily wages by the owners, rather than commissions.

The most significant results in table 6.8, however, are the lower profits of women than men in all trades except the selling of meat, fish, and milk (where only two men gave profit information), and the lesser involvement of women in trades where profits are higher. The dried-staples trade, a mainstay for women, is the lowest by far in terms of profitability. For most traders, subsistence trade is the equivalent of subsistence farming. Many women selling dried staples have attitudes about profits that fit this profile. They calculate their profits based on how well they meet the basic needs of themselves and their families. Three women responded to the question "How do you calculate your profits?" as follows: "By buying the children clothes"; "I don't calculate the profits. What I count is the daily bread that I get. . . . If I can afford a packet of maize meal, this is my profit"; "That's what I spend. . . . I first count to ensure that the money used in buying is back, then the rest I can spend."[12] A woman in a rural market said about her bean trade in the 1960s and 1970s, "The best thing is to find a sympathetic wholesaler who will sell to you using a bigger calabash." When asked about the problem of eating her capital, she replied, "What can you do if you care? I used to go [to the market] for my consumption needs and nothing else."[13]

Most dried-staples sellers were poor women selling in open space that cost little, in accordance with their means, and that in Nairobi is illegal. Their concentration in such areas increases competition, to which some

Table 6.8. Profitability of trade in various commodities and distribution by gender, 1987–1988 (in Kenya shillings)

Commodity	Average daily profits (N=823)			% selling commodity (N=1000)		
	Women	Men	Total[a]	Women	Men	Total
Clothing, used	285.04	546.92	462.63	4.7	25.5	11.6
Agricultural supply	140.00	550.00	345.00	0.3	0.6	0.4
Clothing, new	262.94	286.51	276.30	9.9	20.2	13.3
Housewares/school supply	250.60	278.00	195.79	3.7	14.4	7.2
Prepared/canned food	94.43	229.50	166.45	3.3	7.4	4.6
Clothing, accessories	n.a.	162.66	162.66	0.3	4.3	1.6
Fresh vegetables	109.17	277.85	140.84	32.4	15.6	27.0
Meat/fish/milk	147.27	32.85	136.87	3.0	0.9	2.3
Fresh fruit	130.15	148.21	133.49	8.4	4.3	7.1
Dried staples	105.70	167.90	110.14	33.9	6.1	24.9

a. Listed in order of decreasing amounts of total profits.

reacted by group buying and setting prices. The poorest of the poor are the itinerant hawkers, but even the average staples traders are poor. As a consequence, they and many other traders generally have a low commitment to selling their commodity; most say they would rather sell anything more profitable, but they lack capital to do so. This is a precarious foundation for the trade that feeds Nairobi, made even more precarious by government persecution.

Traders' Coping Strategies

The coping strategies adopted by many traders derive from the very precariousness of their living. Such strategies are where social and economic changes meet, demonstrating how gender and class differences translate into people's lives.

The chief dilemma facing most traders is poverty. How did the traders' profits meet standard-of-living requirements in Nairobi in 1987–88? After subtracting the costs of doing business, net profits were approximately 12 percent of gross profits, according to information given by traders. On this basis, in June 1987, mean average daily earnings of women traders were 10.45 shillings (approximately U.S. 61¢) compared with 24.7 shillings (about U.S.$1.45) for men. Both figures were well below the minimum daily wages in Nairobi of 30.8 shillings (approximately U.S.$1.81).[14]

The 1987 *Statistical Abstract* for Kenya defined poor households as those with incomes of less than 700 shillings ($41.18) per month. Middle-income households were defined as those earning 700 to 2499 shillings (up to $147), and upper-income as 2500 shillings and up (more than $147).[15] Male traders were earning an average of 669.12 shillings (approximately $39.40) per month, compared with 229.12 shillings (about $13.50) for women, who less often had household income supplemented by other earnings.[16]

In a small sample of fifty-six female dried-staples traders drawn from the large sample, a quarter of the women had supplemental income beyond that from trading, averaging 193.65 shillings per month (or 6.45 shillings daily), not including such costs as rental maintenance or farming inputs.[17]

Most of that additional income came from selling crops or milk separately from the market trade. It was clearly not enough to make a significant difference in the standard of living for most women, except for three who received more than 700 shillings per month. Only one woman had income from wage work: casual agricultural labor that yielded 700 shillings per month on average.

Trade as a survival strategy for women is intimately affected by their substantial family obligations. The usual pattern was for older women to trade, leaving younger women (their daughters and daughters-in-law) to farm and care for young children and/or elderly husbands. When traders were asked why they began selling, more than a fourth of the women cited family needs as primary, compared with less than 7 percent of the men. Moreover, 13 percent of the women mentioned landlessness, widowhood, divorce, or insufficient earnings by the husband. Women also cited poverty about twice as often as men did (6 percent versus 3 percent). In general, women's reasons for trading pointed to economic necessity more than men's did (58 percent versus 50 percent of reasons mentioned). Men's reasons in this category were more often to support themselves rather than their families (16 percent versus 8 percent for women), or their failure to find wage employment (23 percent versus 7 percent for women). Among the positive factors attracting people to trade, profitability was most important for both men and women (25 percent for men; 20 percent for women), and men were more likely to be seeking economic independence (14 percent versus 7 percent for women).

It is in the different patterns of women's and men's involvement with trade, however, that the most crucial differences are evident. Although women averaged more years in business due to their greater age, men's businesses endured longer on the whole, showing both women's greater potential for bankruptcy and their tendency to begin later (N = 897 businesses). However, 43 percent of the businesses of the women trading in 1987–88 lasted five or more years, compared with only 29 percent of those of the men, and fewer women had businesses with durations of a year or less (15 percent of women compared with 21 percent of men). The biggest difference favoring men was in businesses enduring 1.0 to 4.9 years, which included 51 percent of men's and 41 percent of women's businesses.

These results reflect both women's lack of other opportunities and their greater age, as well as men's tendency to move in and out of trading according to their access to wage work, which provides some with other options. A few men even took up trading as a retirement occupation.

Women averaged fewer occupations over their lifetime than men did; among those aged fifty to sixty-nine, women averaged 2.9 occupations compared with 3.9 for men (N = 132). Women aged seventy and over averaged only two occupations: farming and trading. Intensive interviews with fifty-six women staples sellers yielded the information that there were erratic patterns of growth and shrinkage in quantities bought. Over time, half of their businesses grew and half shrank, with the length of time they had been in business making no difference to that pattern. Parker and Dondo's study (1991, 22, 27) of small enterprises in Kibera found the same pattern for women's businesses, but steady growth as a characteristic of men's businesses. Moreover, when women's businesses failed, they were more likely to become unemployed; men were more likely to start up again. McCormick (1988:223) also found that women owners of garment businesses had more family expenses than did men, as well as shorter-lived businesses.

The same patterns prevailed when traders listed reasons for quitting occupations. Both women and men named unprofitability as their chief reason, in identical proportions (39 percent for both); but for women, family reasons were next (19 percent versus 2 percent for men). Of the women citing family reasons, 3 percent said the husband's disapproval was their reason for quitting. More common were factors such as caring for a sick child, going bankrupt from eating the commodities, paying school fees, or moving. For men, reasons related to wage jobs were most important—being fired or having a wage-work opportunity open up, for instance. Such reasons applied to 29 percent of the men but to only 12 percent of the women.

Among other reasons for quitting, women named the following more often than did men: problems with harassment or licensing from authorities (3 percent versus 2 percent for men), problems with supply or spoilage (8 percent versus 6 percent for men), high competition or a poor selling location (4 percent versus 2 percent for men), and health problems (8 percent versus 6 percent for men). Men seemed more willing to quit a job for personal reasons such as disliking the boss or wanting self-employment (14 percent versus 9 percent for women). Overall, it was clear that family reasons loomed most important for women, while wage-related opportunities were more likely to affect men's choice of occupation.

One of the most serious factors diminishing women's profits, probably as important as lesser start-up capital, is the fewer hours they spend selling in the markets. The gender division of labor that assigns to them exclusive caretaking functions for household members is evident. Men less often tended to their own subsistence activities, which aided their profits. Many of the women in the large sample were divorced (14 percent), widowed (13 percent), or never married (19 percent), but most had children—an average of 4.1 per woman (compared with 2.2 for men). On average, women provided most of the support for 28 percent of their 5.5 dependents, compared with men providing most of the support for 15 percent of their 5 dependents. But women not only had fewer critical resources available to them to help with that support, they also had less time available to them to that end.

For instance, women traders in daily markets put in an average of 58.3 hours per week there, and in periodic markets, 38.2 hours. Men in the same markets worked on average 69.4 and 54.5 hours weekly, respectively. Those in periodic markets often circulate between three two-day markets six days per week, but they also spend significant amounts of time in farm labor, most of it unpaid. A few traders supplemented trade earnings with paid plantation labor. Even many urban traders put in significant hours in farm work; some Kamba women were in the habit of spending six weeks or so at home on their farms during planting and harvesting.

The average number of hours spent trading per week for men was 66.9 (or 6.3 days), versus 50.6 hours (5.1 days) for women. Some young men who were employees of older male traders picked up daily, weekly, or monthly jobs and were expected to put in longer regular hours in the markets. The high competition for these jobs left them little discretion in determining their work hours.

By contrast, women were overwhelmingly self-employed and found the flexibility that allows them to accommodate their family obligations to be one of the most desirable aspects of trade. Women's business hours were curtailed because they usually cooked breakfast and took children to school before going to the markets; they frequently took time off or left early to deal with children's illnesses or with schooling requirements. Because 46 percent of the women had no spouses (an additional 7 percent support elderly or disabled husbands), and because grown sons did not usually help with housework but lived elsewhere, more than half of the women did not even have the possibility of sharing domestic responsibilities with men.

In addition, a considerable proportion of married women and men (19 percent and 62 percent respectively) lived separately from their spouses in order to trade. Even without collecting specific data on performance of household chores (which were beyond the scope of this study), it is evident that sharing household and child-rearing responsibilities was uncommon. This impression is reinforced by the widespread societal ideology, which supports a segregated gender division of labor within households. Some women noted that a few husbands left in rural areas had shouldered some of the responsibility for work usually considered to be "women's," but when pressed, most admitted that their older daughters were doing it.

The labor value of daughters keeps some out of school, thus recapitulating the whole system of male privilege. "Domestic" obligations, then, have a daunting impact on women's economic productivity, while at the same time fueling the necessity for that productivity.

Conclusion

Women traders in the Nairobi area have fewer resources and a larger work and dependency load than men traders, on the whole. That workload often extends to farming and inevitably to "domestic" work, which in turn has distinct implications for the women's "public" functions in earning a living. Women also have less time to spend on recreation or organizational activities (Robertson 1996). Women more often than men are the sole support of a family. No single men reported supporting the children they had had with a lover, but many women did, even if that support meant that a woman sent money to her own mother on a farm, where she was caring for her grandchildren. A few young men also reported turning such children over to their mothers to support, in some cases at the wish of the children's mother.

Data such as these are not usually factored into analyses of the business performance of small entrepreneurs (Parker and Dondo 1991). Policy makers proceed oblivious to the social costs of persecuting traders in Kenya and elsewhere; programs designed to improve traders' businesses often carry requirements for entry that make women ineligible to participate. Child care is usually not provided; literacy requirements may be stringent; and the cost of the program may be prohibitive.

Steps taken by the Kenyan government to provide infrastructure for the manufacturing portion of the informal sector omit women by definition: the gender division of labor assigns to men the manufacture of metal goods and of shoes. The manufacturing industries with large female involvement—the garment and basket industries—are not privileged to the same extent. The dried-staples traders are often persecuted by police raids, extortion, and beatings (Robertson 1993). Therefore, women also have lesser access to the critical resource of government benefits.

Male privilege prevails in both the "public" and the "private" spheres, which are not separate for these women. If Nairobi is to be fed satisfactorily in an ever more demanding environment, women traders need reinforcement, not supermarkets or jailings that drive them out of business. They need child care at training centers and elsewhere, affordable and appropriate training and technology, and a malleable gender division of labor wherein the employed and the unemployed, regardless of gender, do the housework and care for the children in more than superficial ways.

Factoring housework and child-rearing costs into the gross domestic product would help with economic planning. At the very least, academics must factor such considerations into research plans and results, with the goal of producing positive change that will feed more people.

Notes

1. The Grameen Bank experiment, initially founded to provide loans to small-business persons, regardless of gender, eventually had to take measures to reduce male privilege in order to increase the viability of women's businesses.

2. To cite books only: Clark 1994; Robertson 1990; White 1987; Sudarkasa 1973; Kaba 1982; and Cordonnier 1987. For southern Africa, there is only Horn 1994. For a more detailed comparison of women's trade in Accra, Ghana, and Nairobi, Kenya, see Robertson 1995.

3. For purposes of comparison, Mitullah's sample of 425 Nairobi street hawkers in 1988–89 showed that 73 percent were landless, while those with land averaged 1.8 acres (Mitullah 1990:41). Rutten (1992:35) describes Kenya as belonging to the group of countries in Africa with the highest inequality in land distribution, with female farmers being particular victims.

4. MacKenzie (1990a) says that the cultural rationale that women have no property rights is a relatively recent one, but, aside from some women in the past being granted use rights by their fathers until they married, there seems to be no basis for this assertion. Women's ownership of their houses is acknowledged, but this is a weak position, since husbands regularly now sell land regardless of the houses on it. What seems to have lapsed is the courtesy of asking the women's permission to do so.

5. Republic of Kenya, UNICEF/Central Bureau of Statistics, *Situation Analysis of Children and Women in Kenya 1984*, sec. 1, 30.

6. Republic of Kenya, Central Bureau of Statistics, *Population Census of Kenya, 1979*, vol. 3, Urban Population, 24–25.

7. Republic of Kenya, UNICEF/Central Bureau of Statistics, *Situation Analysis of Children and Women in Kenya 1984*, sec. 3, 51–77.

8. Periodic rural markets include Wangige, Gitaru, Karuri and the open-air sections of Kiambu, Kawangware, Kangemi, and Limuru markets. Daily markets include Gikomba, Shauri, Moyo, Kariakor, Westlands, Toi, Gachui, Ngara and Ngara Bean, Nyamakima, and the stalls at Kiambu, Kawangware, and Kangemi.

9. These data answer the question posed by Parker and Dondo (1991:30) regarding why women's businesses at Kibera show lower survival rates than men's; had their survey research lasted longer than twenty-two days, they might have confirmed this finding.

10. A USAID study of Kutus Market (USAID *Newsletter*, October 1989), one of the fastest-growing markets in Kenya's Central Province, found similar gender differences: women had a fourth to a third of the start-up capital and half the sales that men did; they had less access to capital; and they had greater time constraints

due to domestic chores (presumably, agricultural labor was classified under domestic chores for women). Women traders also spent more on locally produced products and had a higher rate of return on their capital, indicating their willingness to put in long hours for little profit.

11. Livingstone (1981:6, 18–19) gave the following order of profitability for the informal sector, from highest to lowest: (1) auto repair, metalwork, food kiosks (average weekly income 500–600 shillings); (2) retailing, furniture making (300 shillings); (3) charcoal making, tailoring, shoe making, hairdressing (110–190 shillings); (4) shoe shining and repair, clothes repair (60–100 shillings). The omission of many women's trades was unfortunate.

12. Interview D. Gitaru, 6 July 1988; No. 118 Nyamakima, 7 January 1988; No. 123 Nyamakima, 18 December 1987.

13. Interview H. Karuri, 26 October 1988.

14. Republic of Kenya, Central Bureau of Statistics, *Statistical Abstract, 1987,* 257.

15. Republic of Kenya, Central Bureau of Statistics, *Statistical Abstract, 1987,* 260.

16. This calculation factors in the lower average number of days worked per month for women than for men analyzed below. It also assumes the lower profit margin associated with the dried-staples traders, who are most numerous in the sample and almost universally female. It therefore understates the earnings of men and women dealing in more profitable commodities. It does not subtract the cost of food purchased and consumed by men or women traders in the markets, nor that of edible commodities consumed by their family members. This phenomenon, mentioned more often by women, sometimes results in bankruptcy.

17. Mitullah (1990:19) found that the vast majority of Nairobi hawkers had no supplemental source of income outside hawking.

References Cited

Clark, Gracia. 1994. *Onions Are My Husband: Survival and Accumulation by West African Market Women.* Chicago: University of Chicago Press.

Cordonnier, Rita. 1987. *Femmes africaines et commerce: Les Revendeuses de tissue de la villa de Lome* (African women and trade: the fabric retailers of Lome). Paris: Editions l'Harmattan.

Cowen, Michael, and Kabiru Kinyanjui. 1977. Some Problems of Capital and Class in Kenya. University of Nairobi IDS Occasional Paper no. 26.

Davison, Jean, and the Women of Mutira. 1989. *Voices from Mutira.* Boulder, Colo.: Lynne Rienner Publishers.

Horn, Nancy. 1994. *Cultivating Customers: Market Women in Harare, Zimbabwe.* Boulder, Colo.: Lynne Rienner Publishers.

Kaba, Brahima D. 1982. *Profile of Liberian Women in Marketing.* Monrovia: USAID/University of Liberia.

Livingstone, Ian. 1981. *Rural Development, Employment, and Incomes in Kenya.* Addis Ababa: ILO.

MacKenzie, Fiona. 1990a. Gender and Land Rights in Murang'a District, Kenya. *Journal of Peasant Studies* 17 (4):609–43.

———. 1990b. "Without a Woman There is No Land": Marriage and Land Rights in Small-Holder Agriculture, Kenya. *Resources for Feminist Research* 19 (3–4):68–74.

McCormick, Dorothy. 1988. Small Manufacturing Enterprise in Nairobi: Golden Opportunity or Dead End? Ph.D. dissertation. Johns Hopkins University.

Mitullah, Winnie V. 1990. *Hawking as a Survival Strategy for the Urban Poor.* Report submitted to the Ford Foundation, Nairobi.

Nelson, Nici. 1979. How Women and Men Get By: The Sexual Division of Labour in the Informal Sector of a Nairobi Squatter Settlement. In *Casual Work and Poverty in Third World Cities,* edited by R. Bromley and C. Gerry. New York: J. Wiley and Sons.

Parker, Joan, and C. Aleke Dondo. 1991. Kenya: Kibera's Small-Enterprise Sector Baseline Survey Report. GEMINI Working Paper No. 17 (April).

Republic of Kenya. Central Bureau of Statistics. 1979. *Population Census of Kenya.* Vol. 3, *Urban Population.*

———. 1987. *Statistical Abstract.*

Republic of Kenya. UNICEF/Central Bureau of Statistics. 1984. *Situation Analysis of Children and Women in Kenya.*

Robertson, Claire C. 1986. Women's Education and Class Formation in Africa, 1950–1989. In *Women and Class in Africa,* edited by C. Robertson and I. Berger. New York: Holmes and Meier.

———. 1990. *Sharing the Same Bowl.* Ann Arbor: University of Michigan Press.

———. 1993. Traders and Urban Struggle: Ideology and the Creation of a Militant Female Underclass. *Journal of Women's History* 4 (3) (Winter):9–42.

———. 1995. Comparative Advantage: Women and Trade in Accra, Ghana, and Nairobi, Kenya. In *African Market Women and Economic Power,* edited by B. House-Midamba and F. Ekechi. Westport, Conn.: Greenwood Press.

———. 1996. Grassroots in Kenya. *Signs* 21 (2) (Spring):615–42.

———. 1997. *Trouble Showed the Way: Women, Men, and Trade in the Nairobi Area, 1890–1990.* Bloomington: Indiana University Press.

Rutten, M. M. 1992. *Selling Wealth to Buy Poverty.* Saarbrucken: Verlag Breitenbach.

Stamp, Patricia. 1991. Burying Otieno: The Politics of Gender and Ethnicity in Kenya. *Signs* 16 (4) (Summer):808–45.

Sudarkasa, Niara. 1973. *Where Women Work: A Study of Yoruba Women in the Marketplace and the Home.* Ann Arbor: University of Michigan Press.

U.S. Department of State. Agency for International Development. 1989. *Newsletter.* October.

White, E. Frances. 1987. *Sierra Leone's Settler Women Traders.* Ann Arbor: University of Michigan Press.

7. Overcoming Challenges: Women Micro-entrepreneurs in Harare, Zimbabwe

Nancy E. Horn

The entrepreneurial behavior exhibited by fresh produce market women in Harare, Zimbabwe, incorporates various aspects that allow women to overcome the many challenges they face in establishing and maintaining their enterprises. These include cultural traditions delineating the rural division of labor and economic responsibilities, the historical development of the southern African labor reserve economy, and the present-day economic difficulties brought about by the Economic Structural Adjustment Program (ESAP) and by drought. Most important of all is the essence of entrepreneurship that these women personify in daily business operations (Horn 1994a, b).

This chapter first analyzes the challenges faced by women in the historical development of their entrepreneurial niche and then considers specific challenges that women vendors must continue to overcome to maintain their businesses. Contemporary challenges include the sectoral location of women's enterprises in the informal economy, the failure of agricultural policy makers and practitioners to recognize the role of women in the distribution of horticultural commodities, the hardships created by the ESAP and by drought, and the tenets of women's successful entrepreneurship.

The Gendered Landscape: Transforming a Weakness into a Strength

The link connecting women to microenterprises in Zimbabwe is in the roles and responsibilities that women fulfill in their households and in their skills and abilities to manage complicated lives in which they must respond to multiple demands from their families, households, and businesses. Ownership and operation of a microenterprise situates women in a web of biologically, socially, politically, and economically based relationships that are both a product of their own making and a context that shapes their daily lives. The Shona-speaking women's adage—"work, nothing comes without it"—guides and shapes both women's ideology and their praxis in domestic and public spheres.

Meeting the responsibilities of their roles as mothers and household food provisioners, urban women in lower socioeconomic categories seek to employ their skills and abilities efficiently. That the choice of jobs and income-generating activities is limited is a problem of the broader macroeconomic environment, gender biased and selective in the emphasis it places on women's traditional roles over their need to earn an income (see Bourdillon 1993:31 for how men reinvent culture as they move from urban to rural areas). While employment opportunities have been and remain limited, women's innovativeness coupled with necessity have led many to establish microenterprises in the so-called informal sector of the economy.

Once in this domain, women must contend with a number of constraints. Not the least of these is found in the commodities they sell (Daniels 1994). The amount of profit that can be generated is limited to the number of customers, but what is not sold can be brought home to eat. Hence, while their incomes are just enough to replenish stocks, their urban families may be nutritionally better off because they have a constant source of fresh produce. Despite the overwhelming obstacles they face on a daily basis, women utilize their business acumen, their self-taught insights into management, their knowledge of the market and of their customers, and their understanding of their urban roles to overcome challenges to their ability to do good business. To establish and maintain microenterprises, however, women have had to overcome many challenges posed by patriarchal cultural beliefs about women and by the historical development of the labor reserve economy.

At the outset of the ten-year period (1985–95) when this research was undertaken, 3,426 mostly women vendors were found selling from market stalls, from roadside tables, or in shopping centers throughout the city of Harare.[1] From this number, 325 vendors were interviewed intensively. Approximately 74 percent of the sample population migrated to Harare from Zimbabwean rural areas, 14 percent came from surrounding countries, and 12 percent were born in Harare. Educationally, 19 percent had never attended school, 63 percent had achieved between grades one and seven, and 18 percent had some secondary education. Concerning marriage, 73 percent were married, 26 percent were either divorced or widowed and living single, and 1 percent had never been married. Vendors had an average of five children, with most still living at home. Of those born outside the city, 63 percent migrated after they married. Most of the vendors left their rural homelands prior to independence (70 percent), with 40 percent having been in Harare since 1940. In 1985, 36 percent had been selling from five to thirty-four years, while 55 percent had established their enterprises since independence in 1980. The remainder had established their businesses within the previous year. These data demonstrate the tenacity of many vendors and attest to their resilience in overcoming the many challenges discussed in this chapter.

The Rural Division of Labor and the Labor Reserve Economy

In the rural areas, a woman's domain over garden crops in her patrilocal domicile and her ability to harvest enough to feed her family are traditional indicators that her husband's ancestors have accepted her and will bless the family with fertility—both in the womb and in the garden (Lan 1985). Any surplus produced by the woman's *mawoko* (labor of the hands) can be disposed of in any way she deems functional to the welfare of her family (May 1983; Schmidt 1992). This includes bartering with other families, and, since the arrival of foreigners, selling or trading surpluses at periodic markets (see Bhila 1982 for a discussion of how the Portuguese trading fairs established a locus for provisioning Europeans). Food trading networks are made possible by women's production, and trading enhances family food security.

The labor reserve economy created by colonial encroachment beginning in the 1890s robbed rural households of their male inhabitants. Made to pay hut taxes in cash, male household heads sought means to create alternatives to leaving their homes in order to work in white-owned plantations, mines, and growing industries. Women figured prominently in one strategy: they grew greater surpluses and sold them for cash, thus providing the amounts that husbands and fathers needed to pay their taxes (Ranger 1985).

Staving off labor migration was short lived, however, and as the need for labor increased, so did regulations against Africans selling agricultural commodities. Consequently, more men had to migrate to earn cash to pay their taxes. In Harare, African men resided in barracks, and obtaining food was an issue. White shop owners did not stock traditional foods, and Africans were not permitted to own shops. Again women came to the rescue. Both colonial and traditional culture viewed women as dependent on their male counterparts. They were not seen as constituting a political threat, and the pass laws governing the movements of men were not as stringently enforced against women (Barnes 1987). With greater freedom of movement, women growing surpluses in the Harare environs came daily to sell fresh vegetables, fruits, and maize meal to the labor migrants. By so doing, they created a marketing niche that they developed further in the ensuing years.

When a permanent African labor force was needed, a demand was created for African family housing. This led to the development of African townships, referred to today as high-density suburbs. Another problem arose, however. Men's wages were never adequate for the maintenance of the family in either the rural or the urban areas. When women migrated with their husbands, women's ability to fulfill their cultural role of family food provider was severely challenged. Housing plots were too small to grow gardens, and cultivating open areas was prohibited by ordinance. Income-earning opportunities for women were limited by patriarchal cultural beliefs and practices, held by colonial and African males alike. Women faced the dilemma of how to provide food for their families without the means to do so. Many overcame this problem by building on their rural expertise in fruits and vegetables to expand the fresh produce marketing niche established by their foremothers: they began selling fresh fruits and vegetables in their neighborhoods.

At first they "ordered" from the women who came to Mbare hostels to sell their harvests. As needs grew, and as the wholesale market at Mbare grew, vendors purchased their daily stock from the wholesale *musika* (market) and returned to their neighborhood township markets to resell. By earning a bit of profit, and by obtaining larger quantities of foodstuffs at a cheaper price, many women were able to meet the needs of their culturally based food provisioning roles. Thus, while the labor reserve economy extracted labor directly from men, it extracted labor from women indirectly in order to meet the economic demands of the household.

The Challenge of the Informal Economy

In making the decision to become fresh produce vendors, women encountered other obstacles. Ordinances about business ownership discriminated against Africans, particularly women. Denied licenses to trade, women became vulnerable to police harassment.

Policy Context

The development of the urban informal economy occurred as a consequence of at least four variables: the city was seen as the domain of white people, with Africans only "temporary sojourners"; business licenses were not granted to Africans; women were not viewed as serious income earners; and colonials did not perceive the market they were creating by increasing the demand for permanent labor.

Because wages provided for Africans were not adequate, the incomes they earned were not sufficient to buy the types or quantities of commodities offered in the shops. With urban influx laws limiting the movement of Africans in white areas, Africans had to find daily provisions they could afford. To keep the city segregated, a parallel market was developed in African townships. The goods and services Africans could afford became the basis of trade in the informal economy.

After independence, the number of people who migrated to the city "exploded" to the current population level of 1.5 million, 96 percent of whom are of African origin (Government of Zimbabwe 1994a). Women, as well as men, came to the city looking for means to generate an income. Many found their way to the informal sector because of their gender and because of their lack of education. By 1985–86, 62 percent of the vendors had not found formal sector employment. Of the 38 percent who had, the employment they had found was as domestics, or else in clothing factories, nursery schools, hospitals, and hotels. The more educated had found work as teachers, receptionists, and shop girls.

Lack of Capital and Credit

Establishing a microenterprise requires initial capital. Until very recently, funds were not available for microenterprise development, generally because bank policies would not accommodate small loans. In the past few years, SEDCO (Small Enterprise Development Corporation), Opportunity International/ZAMBUKO Trust, and other nongovernmental organizations have established microlending opportunities for both production and trading enterprises.[2] Women in Harare, who had established enterprises selling fresh produce prior to these opportunities, accessed funding through their spouses, siblings, parents, and other kin. Once established, however, vendors' daily cash flow allowed them to join a revolving savings and credit society. By 1985–86, 40 percent of vendors belonged to a marketwide savings society, and 57 percent were members of a more selective, smaller group (Horn 1994a:96).[3] By 1994, more than half of the vendors had joined burial societies as a form of life insurance for their families.[4]

Regulations and Bylaws

Formal sector enterprise regulations remaining from colonialism, as well as labor laws enacted since independence, both serve as barriers to the establishment and maintenance of microenterprises.[5] Up until 1994, these laws could be enforced through periodic inspection or through the granting of licenses. Since the imposition of the ESAP, however, many of these laws have been relaxed and are not being enforced. This has given rise to the ad hoc establishment of enterprises on every street corner in downtown Harare and in residential areas of the low-density suburbs, a situation not tolerated before the ESAP.

The barriers that women have overcome are historically rooted in uninformed patriarchal colonial policies and in patriarchy practiced within traditional culture. While vendors have experienced a significant degree of success, the current challenges posed by the agricultural sector, by the ESAP, and by droughts are formidable.

The Challenge of the Agricultural Sector

Women's horticultural production is still not viewed as having any consequence in the food-security equation. This is because production, on an individual basis, is limited to the size of the garden allocated to a woman through traditional tenure. If aggregated, however, women's production and sales contribute significantly to the domestically consumed food supply. Nevertheless, women's agricultural roles have not received as much attention as they should. Since independence, AGRITEX, the agricultural extension service, has increased the number of female agents and has begun to address women's agricultural information needs. However, Mbare Musika market in Harare is the only outlet identified to market women's horticultural crops.

The challenges that vendors face in conducting business include those of throughput (that is, the quantity of products that must be assembled) and transportation; other problems lie in sourcing supplies and in the location and structure of the markets. Each difficulty serves to impede the progress of vendors and challenges their economic viability.

Disconnected Linkages to the Agricultural Sector

Although the majority of the stocks that vendors purchase wholesale emanate from commercial farms and are sold to informal sector wholesalers, there is no acknowledgment that white producers rely heavily upon urban African market women for the ultimate distribution of their crops. Hence, commercial producers do not realize the integral role that women play in crop distribution. Data collected in 1985–86 (when the population of Harare was approximately 800,000) on the throughput of both the formal and informal market in fresh produce indicates women's distributive capabilities in at least eight different crops (table 7.1).[6] Since the population of Harare has almost doubled in the ten years since these data were collected, and the number of fresh produce vendors has increased (but is as yet un-counted), the quantities distributed by vendors have increased exponen-tially. These data make a compelling argument for the acknowledgment of vendor-distribution capabilities.

However, almost all vendors have problems with transport from home to Mbare market and from Mbare to their vending sites. As the system currently operates, women vendors must deal with *makoronyera* (thugs in the market, who steal from both wholesalers and retailers) at Mbare, with bus drivers who refuse to load their wholesale purchases, with emergency taxi drivers who also refuse to load the baskets of fresh produce onto ve-hicle roofs, and with pushcart operators who fail to deliver vendor pur-chases to their market sites. If vendors were acknowledged for their horti-cultural crop distribution activities, it would be logical for vendors and producers to reach an agreement for delivery of wholesale purchases.[7]

Sourcing Wholesale Stocks

At the outset of this research, women's networks worked informally to disseminate information as to where to purchase commodities at the cheap-est price. Vendors also consulted the daily published wholesale fruit and vegetable prices provided to the *Herald* by the Independent Market (a for-mal sector wholesale agency). Vendors had a choice of where to purchase a

Table 7.1. Estimated volume of selected crops sold through formal and in-formal sector marketing channels in Harare, 1985–1986

Crop	Formal sector commodity tonnage	Informal sector tonnage (N = 325 vendors)
Avocado	31	20
Cabbage	253	87
Lemons	129	16
Onions	14,119	43
Oranges	3,717	50
Potatoes	83,175	138
Sweet potatoes	735	45
Tomatoes	1,484	210

Source: Field notes.

given commodity; they could go to either Mbare Musika, Mbare farmers' market, formal sector wholesalers, formal sector agencies, the Fruit and Vegetable Co-op, commercial farmers, or to market gardeners in the Harare environs.

For the past few years, however, vendors' choices have been limited to Mbare and local producers; formal sector wholesalers do not readily make their commodities available to vendors, since their numbers have skyrocketed with changes in the policy environment. Moreover, the publication of wholesale prices has ceased. Consequently, any commodity that a vendor sells is limited to whatever is offered at Mbare or at neighboring gardens and farms.

Market Sites and Market Architecture

When marketplaces were designed by the city council, it was believed that stalls similar to those originally constructed in farmers' markets during colonial times would meet vendors' needs. Consequently, it is possible to find stalls for a hundred vendors in one location. Selling from such stalls creates another set of challenges: women must find ways to attract customers; they must always have the freshest commodities; there is no "privacy in selling," in which a vendor might try to gain a comparative advantage over her neighbor vendors; and only a handful of markets have storage space in which to keep fruits and vegetables overnight (Nachudwa 1995:142–44).

The location of markets also poses a challenge. Many markets are situated where there are no pedestrian thoroughfares. Consequently, in order to develop a customer pool, vendors may pay rent for their stalls but sell at bus stations or shopping centers during times of peak pedestrian activity. Managers of supermarkets in suburban shopping centers have registered complaints about this practice, but the police have not been directed to halt it, because government does not perceive that the women pose any real threat to supermarket profits (Bloch 1995:6; Ncube 1995:15, 20).

The Economic Challenges of Structural Adjustment and Drought

Vendors have been specifically challenged since 1991, when Zimbabwe became a part of the World Bank and International Monetary Fund Structural Adjustment Program.[8] The program seeks to create a more liberalized economy, but the effects felt by vendors include increased wholesale prices, cost recovery fees imposed by the Harare City Council on the rental of vending sites, and increased transportation costs attributed to currency devaluation and inflation rates of between 24 percent and 30 percent.

Horticultural commodity prices were also affected by the droughts of 1991–92 and 1994–95. Producers with irrigation were unable to satisfy the demand for fruits and vegetables, thus increasing wholesale prices even more. Vendors could no longer buffer seasonal price fluctuations and passed their increased costs on to their customers. The combination of the ESAP and drought has created deleterious effects on the agricultural economy as a whole. The following points are particularly relevant when vendors' distribution activities are seriously considered.

Horticultural Crop Production and Export

Commercial and communal farmers ultimately depend on vendors for the distribution of a significant portion of the national fresh produce crop. Liberalization of foreign exchange regulations has led to at least a 20 percent increase in production for export over the past year.[9] However, it is not clear how the liberalization of foreign currency availability will affect the domestic food supply of fresh produce. There may be less for domestic consumption unless acreage planted expands significantly.[10]

Expanding horticultural crop production by communal farmers involves complex requirements. These include, among other things: (1) the production and availability of pest- and disease-resistant seeds; (2) an agricultural extension service that can reach communal farmers with information on horticultural crops and that can address women's expertise in this area (Moyo, Mutuma, and Magonya 1989; Moyo and Page 1992); (3) the development of reliable irrigation systems; (4) prices that will make production possible; (5) availability of credit for the production of horticultural crops; (6) accessible marketing infrastructure and alternative markets; and (7) a system that recognizes women's domain over horticultural production. Increasing smallholder horticultural production for domestic consumption and for export must become a priority policy issue if the country's supply of fresh produce is to be adequate.

Women cannot automatically expand production of their crops, because of several factors: demand for their labor in rain-fed grain crops and for household chores; lack of access to land, except through their spouses or sons; lack of credit, because of both their gender and the sociopolitical bias against their owning land; and lack of water with which to irrigate (see Chidzonga 1993:190–98 for a further analysis of constraints that women face in the agricultural sector).

But even if production is increased significantly, marketing opportunities will be another bottleneck. The marketing system is predicated on the premise that all horticultural production is sent to Harare for redistribution. Most recently, local markets have been developed in areas adjacent to irrigation and resettlement schemes in order to reduce transportation costs and waste (Mazhangara, Manzungu, and Brown 1994). Transportation, poor quality of produce, and oversupply are issues that both producers and traders confront. Hence, in order for women to respond to the increased demand for more produce, a key problem that will have to be addressed is the development of decentralized, nonmonopolistic marketing channels.

Unemployment and the Informal Sector

To maintain their businesses, vendors require both a flow of fresh produce commodities and a paying clientele. With unemployment rising due to retrenchment and the inability of the economy to provide jobs for increasing numbers of school graduates, fewer families can afford the increased prices of food. Also, with relatively few new hirings, more men and women have joined the informal sector. In 1994 bylaws and legislation were relaxed, resulting in a further "explosion" of trading enterprises throughout the city.

From 1991 to 1993, during the first few years of the ESAP, the number of microenterprises grew from 836,337 to 941,944, representing a growth rate of 6.1 percent (Daniels 1994:E-3). Employment in these microenterprises increased 14.4 percent, from 1,350,908 in 1991 to 1,546,938 in 1993 (Daniels 1994:10). In the urban areas, where approximately 25 percent of Zimbabwe's population resides, microenterprises grew at a rate of 3.6 percent, or from 238,141 in 1991 to 255,541 in 1993 (Daniels 1994:E-3). Trading in fruits and vegetables—once the domain of women—is now being taken over by men, primarily downtown rather than from stalls and table-vending sites in the high-density suburbs. Women vendors must thus face the challenge of competition in heretofore unheard-of proportions.

Wages, Inflation, and the Cost of Living

Vendors are also affected by double-digit inflation and several devaluations: "Real wages have declined by more than 40 percent in the past five years" (Worker). The sales tax on all goods and services was increased with the 1995–96 budget to 15 percent (Sunday Mail 1995a, 6).[11] The cost of clothing will increase as the result of a 45 percent import tax that will limit family options to purchase clothes.[12] For those who have electricity, increased rates will include a 5 percent tax. Most injurious to vendors is the increase in import duty on gasoline and diesel fuel that will have an impact on the rural-urban movement of many commodities. Daily commuter buses used by vendors between Mbare and the high-density suburbs have already increased their fares (*Herald* 1995e, 1).

Coupled with the ravages of drought and the national budget, the increases in housing and utilities have placed many urban families at extreme risk: monthly housing rents have increased 25 percent, while sewerage costs have gone up 14 percent, waste management 30 percent, water 25 percent, electricity rates 26 percent, and administration fees 25 percent. Annual hawkers' fees were increased to 50 Zimbabwean dollars as of January 1996 (Mahove 1995:3, 7). Mbare wholesale market rental fees were raised to 257 dollars per month, and producers will pay 5 dollars per day to sell at the farmers' market (the latter three will ultimately be passed along to retail produce vendors). Small kiosk owners will have to pay either 100 or 200 dollars annually for licenses.

The cost of foodstuffs increased twice during 1995. In March, the following increases were put into effect: maize meal 14 percent, bread 56 percent (to Z$3 per loaf), cooking oil 12 percent, beef 10 percent, and beer 40 percent. Food price increases in July–August 1995 are indicative of that year's drought: the price of bread jumped to Z$3.60 per loaf, or another 17 percent (reflecting a 22 percent increase in the cost of flour); the price of roller meal increased by 38 percent (*Herald* 1995f, 1). These increases follow on those of 1994, which yielded a 330 percent jump in the consumer price index since 1990, or 572 percent since 1989 (Horn 1994b:11).

Effects of the ESAP on Market Women

For far too long, women's economic activities have been seen as inconsequential to the national economy. The argument has been that their income-generating strategies are merely an extension of their domestic roles (Lue-Mbizvo 1991:8; Makoni 1995). Their participation countrywide in microenterprises in 1993, however, constituted 71 percent of the total. With fewer formal sector opportunities, women join the illicit branch of the informal economy and become prostitutes. Women who have chosen this economic path blame the ESAP and say that it is better to earn an income through prostitution than "to die from starvation" (*Weekly Sun*, 19–25 July 1995, 11).

Women's ability to provision their households presents yet another challenge. Since the ESAP was implemented over the period of two droughts, the accessibility of food at affordable prices has continuously spiraled downward. Forced to choose among housing, durable goods, and food, families choose food (Mahove 1995:3), but many have had to reduce their meals from three to two per day (Kanji and Jazdowska 1993).

The impact of the ESAP and the effects of drought on fruit and vegetable vendors is reflected in their declining incomes (Horn 1994b) and in the commodities they sell. In more affluent neighborhoods in the high-density suburbs, for instance, *tsunga* (a green, leafy vegetable) was sold by many vendors in 1985–86. The 1995 data indicate that the proportion of vendors selling this vegetable has declined, while the proportion selling *covo*—a cheaper green leafy vegetable—has increased.

In summary, the ESAP and droughts have given rise to increased prices, decreased wages, increased unemployment, and an increase in the number of informal sector operators. For the vendors, the ESAP and droughts have challenged both their ability to generate an income and their role as family food providers—these are the principal reasons they became vendors.

Ten Tenets of Women's Entrepreneurship

The activities and experiences of the female fresh produce vendors of Harare are more broadly applicable to microentrepreneurs elsewhere. The essence of their operations, distilled into "ten tenets of entrepreneurship," can serve as a guide to policy makers as they consider how best to meet the needs of women microentrepreneurs in the informal sector.

1. Entrepreneurship is a gendered activity. Women's responsibility for nurturing children is a prime motivator for women to establish micro enterprises (see Jiggins 1994 for similar arguments applied in other economic arenas). In an overwhelming majority of interviews, vendors indicated that their motivation to establish and maintain their businesseses was their children—the need to provide food and create future opportunities for them. Hence, for women, entrepreneurship is motivated by the responsibility for the family's survival.

2. Entrepreneurship requires risk taking. Women take the risk of diverting a portion of their meager resources into trading or production enterprises that may or may not generate a profit. Moreover, incomes are generated on a daily basis, thus enabling women to meet daily expenses, to restock their commodities, and to participate in daily revolving credit societies.

Women also learn how to spread their risk. As the market women saw their incomes dwindle over the period of economic reform, they consistently began to diversify their income-earning activities. Some started to crochet "on contract" for women vendors who traded in South Africa; others began to sell used clothing in flea markets. Diversification, however, is not oriented toward the growth of the vendor's enterprises; rather, it is for the increased cash flow needed to meet the upwardly spiraling cost of living (Grown and Sebstad 1989; Tinker 1987).

3. Entrepreneurship requires opportunity. Women create microenterprise opportunities themselves. They perceive a niche they can fill and then proceed to do so. Opportunity begins with an idea, then develops as information is gathered, and blossoms with the realization that the opportunity includes a market and access to resources and inputs, and that it has a cost advantage such as low overhead (Mead 1993:41). In the case of the fresh produce vendors, a culturally based indigenous knowledge system guided women in past decades to increase production and establish trading relationships. In more recent days, women have built upon the ideas of their foremothers and established competitive enterprises.

4. Entrepreneurship requires initial investment capital. Women do not have access to the formal credit and lending opportunities that men do, because they do not have collateral. Consequently they rely on spouses, kin, and moneylenders, as well as on their own savings, for their initial business investment. Amounts needed, however, are comparatively small. With the growing interest in microenterprise development, more funds are becoming available for enterprises, though the emphasis is on those involved in production rather than in trade.

5. Entrepreneurship requires market intelligence and reliable wholesalers. Market women, prior to the economic reform program, had to know where to buy stocks at the lowest price. Since the implementation of the ESAP, options have been limited. Most useful to vendors and producers alike would be a dual-benefit production-marketing partnership.

6. Entrepreneurship requires knowledge of potential clientele. Vendors know how to satisfy their customers' needs in terms of price and quality. For this reason, vendors do not lump their purchases and buy any number of boxes of tomatoes. Rather, they buy the particular size and quality of tomatoes that they know will satisfy their clientele. Vendors also go out of their way to purchase more "exotic" produce in demand, for example, cauliflower. If a customer knows the lengths to which a vendor will go to meet a demand, he or she is more likely to become a regular customer.

7. Entrepreneurship requires business acumen. Many women apprentice themselves to more experienced vendors who, more likely than not, are relatives. Other women have had experience as young girls helping their mothers after school. By learning how to manage wholesale purchases,

identify quality produce, arrange retail displays, attract customers, manage money, and the like, vendors develop their operations to meet their customers' needs.

8. Entrepreneurship requires operational space. Vendors have had to adapt their marketing techniques to fit their particular selling locales, from ad hoc tables under trees to proper marketing stalls. As the economy recovers from economic reform, women will again have to redefine their niches, as well as their legitimacy.

9. Entrepreneurship requires the ability to make a profit. The profit margins that vendors experience are limited by the amount that customers are willing to pay for food and by the amount that vendors must pay for wholesale stocks. The number of vendors competing for customers has increased significantly since the ESAP began, and women who have operated their businesses for many years have had to innovate in search of ways to maintain their customers.

10. Women's entrepreneurial activities entail freedom from domestic chores. To be successful in a business, time must be spent on cultivating customers, making wholesale purchases, and creating retail displays. This time is not available to vendors if they must tend to domestic responsibilities, including child care.

Conclusion

The challenges faced by entrepreneurs demand a response from policy makers, planners, growers, urban and rural councils, as well as from the vendors themselves. New patterns of organization and new policies to augment the economic viability of microenterprises must be established. Policy should promote an arena in which all members of the horticultural subsector benefit: smallholder and commercial producers, marketers and truckers, wholesalers and retailers, and market women. These policies must address the longevity of the informal sector by creating opportunities to finance the establishment or maintenance of microenterprises. The policies must also address women's ability to own property, especially their market sites, and they must address taxation. Consideration must be given to the question of what would be a fair way for government to benefit from individual entrepreneurship without burdening microentrepreneurs to the extent that they are forced out of business.

The historical bifurcation of the horticultural subsector along racial lines is reemerging in Zimbabwe as a result of policy. Liberalization of access to foreign exchange has produced a shift in production from the domestic to the export market. As more horticultural commodities leave the country, and as droughts continue to play havoc with water for smallholder irrigation, the quantities of fresh produce for domestic consumption are reduced.

To ensure the countrywide distribution of crops, it is appropriate for planners and producers to determine a more efficient system that will not be so costly to those who can least afford it. The first step must be the recognition of women's roles in distribution. Women are providing a cheap marketing service to both producers and wholesalers. While it might be argued that this is the way business is done, the situation is highly inefficient and favors one group over another, that is, wholesalers or producers over women retail vendors.

However, women who have little education or who have been unable to find alternative employment have few other options for earning an income. The marketing system is constructed "on the backs of women," yet recognition of their contribution and of their role in food distribution is minimal. Vendors constitute the end point in a production-marketing chain from which both they and commercial producers could benefit. The ultimate beneficiaries, however, would be the consumers, who would have an improved food supply, a less costly food basket, and families who are nutritionally satisfied.

Notes

Author's note: Funding for this research is from a number of sources: in 1985–86, from a Fulbright-Hays Dissertation Research Abroad award and a National Science Foundation grant; in 1993, partially from the U.S. Peace Corps; in 1994, from Cornell University; and in 1995, from the opportunity provided by the Fulbright-Hays Group Projects Abroad Program, which I led to Zimbabwe. All newspapers cited are published in Harare, Zimbabwe.

1. The analyses presented in this paragraph are those presented in Horn 1988 and 1994a.

2. SEDCO is currently undergoing privatization itself, because government cannot provide the capital to meet loan demand (*Business Herald* 1995b). The Indigenous Business Women's Organization has promoted the creation of a trust that will make loans available to women seeking to establish and maintain enterprises at all levels, on the order of the Grameen Bank of Bangladesh. The Zimbabwe Women's Finance Trust is an affiliate of Women's World Banking, and when the bank is fully functional, it is anticipated that 10 million Zimbabwean dollars will be available for loans (*Business Herald* 1995a; Jiri 1994:18).

3. These societies have flourished and have gained an international reputation to the extent that Namibian women came to Zimbabwe to learn how to manage these clubs (*Herald* 1995d, 5).

4. Upon the death of a vendor or a member of a vendor's family, each member of the society contributes three Zimbabwean dollars and fresh produce for the fu-

neral. Each participant in the society is guaranteed $3,000 as well as food to feed those who attend the funeral.

5. Legislation affecting this sector falls into these categories: zoning; operating hours; licensing; registration; labor regulations; title deeds; foreign exchange; and tax rates (Daniels 1994; Saito 1990). Enterprises that sell foodstuffs must also conform to Ministry of Health regulations, which are open to interpretation by inspectors (Saito 1990:35).

6. Linking informal sector retailers with producers is not a new concept. The Anglo-American corporation played a key role in organizing the Informal Sector Association of Zimbabwe by forming a venture capital company—Hawk Ventures—to assist small businesses with start-up capital. This multinational corporation sees the benefit of assisting microentrepreneurs with their production-oriented enterprises.

7. This throughput sold by vendors remains in Harare, while that sold through formal sector wholesalers is packaged and reshipped to supermarkets and greengrocers, the army, hospitals, schools restaurants, and other institutional buyers throughout the country. It is important to note that the throughput for vendors is reported only for the 325 who were intensively interviewed. If these numbers were multiplied to reflect the throughput of the entire population of vendors found in 1985 (3,426), quantities of fresh produce distributed by vendors would be sizable.

8. The goals of the ESAP were to reduce the government's deficit from 10 percent to 5 percent of the GDP by fiscal year 1994–95; making public enterprises more efficient; shifting from a centralized to a market-oriented foreign exchange allocation system through trade liberalization; liberalization of price controls and relaxation of labor controls; investment promotion and domestic deregulation; monetary policy and financial sector reform; and implementation of a SAP to assist the poor and vulnerable members of society (Brand, Mpedziswa, and Gumbo 1992; Government of Zimbabwe 1994b).

9. Export of horticultural crops by commercial farmers has increased steadily since independence, from 1.5 million Zimbabwean dollars in 1980 to 154 million dollars in 1994–95 (*Herald,* 25 June 1995, 1). This growth was facilitated by irrigation, largely on commercial farms, as producers sought to diversify production. Commercial farmers developed their own irrigation regimes with loans accessed through the Agricultural Finance Corporation and other sources, while communal farmers have been able to expand production on irrigated fields only through schemes developed and implemented by government (Rukuni and Makadho 1994:127).

10. Agricultural production statistics indicate an increase in acreage planted in selected horticultural crops (tomatoes, onions, potatoes, sweet potatoes, oranges, and bananas), owing to expanded irrigation facilities on communal, resettlement, and small-scale commercial farms. Commercial farmers also increased horticultural crop acreage in response to export incentives.

11. Informal sector operators do not include these additional charges in their

prices. In the unlikely event that taxes have been included in the calculation of the wholesale prices, the vendor prices unwittingly include taxes paid by either wholesalers or producers.

12. This tax was levied because of the disastrous effects of the importation of second-hand clothing on the local textile industry (*Sunday Mail* 1995a, 3; *Herald* 1995b, 9, 11).

References Cited

Barnes, Terri. 1987. African Female Labour and the Urban Economy of Colonial Zimbabwe, with Special Reference to Harare, 1920–1939. Master's thesis, Department of History, University of Zimbabwe.

Bhila, H. K. 1982. *Trade and Politics in a Shona Kingdom.* London: Longman.

Bloch, E. 1995. Several Sides to Street Vendor Problem. *Financial Gazette,* 20 July, 6.

Bourdillon, M. F. C. 1993. *Where Are the Ancestors? Changing Culture in Zimbabwe.* Harare: University of Zimbabwe.

Brand, V., R. Mpedziswa, and P. Gumbo. 1992. *Women Informal Sector Workers Under Structural Adjustment in Zimbabwe.* Harare: University of Zimbabwe, School of Social Work.

Business Herald. 1995a. Business Women Set to Establish Their Own Bank. 13 July, 2.

———. 1995b. SEDCO Awaits Cabinet Nod. 6 April, 1, 8.

Chidzonga, M. 1993. The Situation of Women in Agriculture in the Communal Areas of Zimbabwe. In *Food Policy and Agriculture in Southern Africa,* edited by R. Mkandawire and K. Matiosa. Harare: SAPES Books.

Daniels, Lisa. 1994. Changes in the Small-Scale Enterprise Sector from 1991 to 1993: Results of a Second Nationwide Survey in Zimbabwe. Washington, D.C.: GEMINI Project, Technical Report no. 71; Bethesda, Md.: Development Alternatives International.

Government of Zimbabwe. 1994a. *Census 1992: Provincial Profile: Harare.* Harare: Central Statistical Office.

———. 1994b. Estimates of Expenditure for the Year Ending June 30, 1995. Paper presented to the Parliament of Zimbabwe 1994. Harare: Government Printer.

Grown, C., and J. Sebstad. 1989. Introduction: Toward a Wider Perspective on Women's Employment. *World Development* 17 (7).

Herald. 1995a. Fund for Women's Bank Launched. 24 June.

———. 1995b. Help Urged for Textile Sector. 14 July.

———. 1995c. Horticultural Export Earnings Top $514m. 24 June.

———. 1995d. Namibian Women End Savings Groups Study. 24 June.

———. 1995e. Petroleum Fuel Prices Go Up. 1 August.

———. 1995f. Roller Meal, Flour Prices Up. 18 July.

———. 1995g. Workers Lose Jobs As Farmers Fail to Repay Loans. 2 August.

Horn, Nancy E. 1988. The Culture, Urban Context and Economics of Women's Fresh Produce Marketing in Harare, Zimbabwe. Ph.D. dissertation. Department of Anthropology, Michigan State University.

———. 1994a. *Cultivating Customers: Market Women in Harare, Zimbabwe*. Boulder, Colo.: Lynne Rienner Publishers.

———. 1994b. Horticultural Crop Production and Marketing Among Smallholders in Zimbabwe. Paper presented at the Workshop on Smallholder Horticulture in Zimbabwe, 31 August–2 September, Harare, Zimbabwe.

Jiggins, Janice. 1994. *Changing the Boundaries: Women Centered Perspectives on Population and the Environment*. Washington, D.C.: Island Press.

Jiri, M. 1994. Women and Access to Credit. *Zimbabwe Women's Resource Centre and Network. News Bulletin* 3 (1):18.

Kanji, N., and N. Jazdowska. 1993. Structural Adjustment and Women in Zimbabwe. *Review of African Political Economy* 56:11–26.

Lan, David. 1985. *Guns and Rain: Guerrillas and Spirit Mediums in Zimbabwe*. Harare: Zimbabwe Publishing House.

Lue-Mbizvo, C. 1991. *The Role of Women in Small-Scale Bread, Brick, and Beer Industries in Rural Zimbabwe*. Working Paper no. 30. Harare: Zero Publications.

Mahove, C. 1995. Food or Housing—Dzivarasekwa Residents in Quandary. *High Density Mirror*, August, 3.

Makoni, M. 1995. How Women Are Playing a Big Role in the Informal Sector. *Herald*, 9 April.

May, Joan. 1983. *Zimbabwean Women in Colonial and Customary Law*. Gweru, Zimbabwe: Mambo Press.

Mazhangara, E. P., E. Manzungu, and M. W. Brown. 1994. Characteristics of Four Rural Horticultural Markets in the Southeastern Lowveld of Zimbabwe. Paper presented at the Workshop on Smallholder Horticulture in Zimbabwe, 31 August–2 September, Harare, Zimbabwe.

Mead, Donald. 1993. Identification of Micro Business Opportunities. Report of Workshop 5 at the Zimbabwe National Chamber of Commerce and the Friedrich-Naumann Foundation Workshop on Development and Growth of Micro Business Activity in Zimbabwe, 3–4 March, Monomotapa Hotel, Zimbabwe.

Moyo, S., P. M. Mutuma, and S. S. Magonya. 1989. *An Evaluation of Agricultural Extension Services Support to Women Farmers in Zimbabwe, with Special Reference to Makonde District*. Consultancy Reports 12. Harare: Zimbabwe Institute of Development Studies.

Moyo, S., and H. Page. 1992. *A Review of the Class and Gender Basis of Agricultural Extension Service in Zimbabwe's Communal Areas*. Discussion Papers 16. Harare: Zimbabwe Institute of Development Studies.

Nachudwa, D. 1995. Women in Micro-Enterprises: The Case of Mbare, Zimbabwe. In *Gender Research on Urbanization, Planning, Housing, and Every Day Life, Phase 1*, edited by S. Sithole-Fundire, A. Zhou, A. Larsson, and A. Schlyter. Harare: Zimbabwe Women's Resource Centre and Network.

Ncube, J. 1995. State Dithering Delays Vendors' Street-Legal Status. *Horizon*, 15 July, 20.

Ranger, Terence. 1985. *Peasant Consciousness and Guerrilla War in Zimbabwe*. Harare: Zimbabwe Publishing House.

Rukuni, M., and J. Makadho. 1994. Irrigation Development. In *Zimbabwe's Agricultural Revolution*, edited by M. Rukuni and C. K. Eicher. Harare: University of Zimbabwe Publications.

Saito, Katherine. 1990. The Informal Sector in Zimbabwe: The Role of Women. Report No. 9006-ZIM. Washington, D.C.: World Bank.

Schmidt, Elizabeth. 1992. *Peasants, Traders, and Wives. Shona Women in the History of Zimbabwe, 1870–1939*. Portsmouth, N.H.: Heinemann.

The Sunday Mail. 1995a. Sales Tax Hikes Prices of Basic Commodities. 19 March.

———. 1995b. Customs Suspends Donation of Second Hand Clothes. 16 July.

Tinker, Irene. 1987. The Human Economy of Microentrepreneurs. Paper presented at the International Seminar on Women in Micro- and Small-Scale Enterprise Development, 26 October, Ottawa, Canada.

The Weekly Sun. 1995. Prostitution Is Now at Its Most Alarming Rate. 19–25 July.

The Worker. 1995. ZCTU Calls for Reasonable Wages. 26 July, 1.

8. Entrepreneurs and Family Well-Being: Agricultural and Trading Households in Cameroon

Judith Krieger

This chapter concentrates on choice of economic strategy and control of money as keys to understanding the relationship between women's income-generating activities, household food supplies, and child growth in a Cameroonian near-urban location. The household food stocks and child growth characteristics of women primarily engaged in commercial production of food and firewood are compared with those of entrepreneurs who deal primarily in foodstuffs and prepared food. A group of women whose husbands provide their primary income is compared with both. The research shows that the children of women entrepreneurs are significantly taller and heavier for their age than those of primary producers, and that there is a greater variety of food in their mothers' kitchens. These results have implications for development policy and programs.

For the women of a village on the outskirts of Bamenda, the capital of Cameroon's North West Province, the city means economic opportunity, a ready market for the firewood, crops, and foodstuffs they produce and a source of food and commodities for home use and trade. Most village women are subsistence farmers, responsible for their family food supply. They also earn their own money through sales of firewood, food crops, and foodstuffs. There is no question about subsistence food production: it is constructed as women's responsibility, as is the operation of the farms that produce family food.

But women have financial responsibilities as well, and they are expected to develop independent income sources. Production of food and firewood for the cash market is the primary income source for many women, while others engage primarily in business and trading. Although research shows that women's income is often linked to family welfare, neither of these routes to cash has received government, nongovernmental organization (NGO), or agency program support until recently.

Men's export crop production (for example, coffee) has been supported for years by development agencies such as the United States Agency for International Development (USAID) and the Swiss development agency Helvetas. Women's small-scale business enterprises have not received much attention at all in this rural-based area, being relegated to the category of "petty trading," although such enterprises can have a major effect on family welfare. Women's farms and small-scale enterprises are documented and discussed in the anthropological and historical literature of this area of Cameroon (Chilver 1992; Goheen 1991, 1996; Kaberry 1952; Krieger 1995; van den Berg 1992), but they have not received systematic attention from development agencies until recently.

Newer development and NGO strategies target women's small business, as well as women's agriculture, as areas of program development. It is timely to ask which emphasis best benefits women and their families—entrepreneurship or agriculture—and under what conditions.

The role of women in agriculture was a focus for research, and, to a lesser degree, for policy formation in the 1980s (DeWalt 1993; Frankenberger 1985). West African market women have received increasing attention in a developing literature on economic and social roles (Clark 1994; Dwyer and Bruce 1988; Robertson 1984, 1995). Child health studies have emphasized the links between women's work and breastfeeding, limited to studying infants and very young children (Leslie and Paolisso 1988). The present study assesses the growth of young children in the context of women's economic strategies and household food, using data collected in 1991 in a near-urban West African setting.[1]

It is by now commonplace to state that women's farms are the primary source of food for their own households and for the burgeoning cities in much of Africa. Cameroon is no exception to this pattern. The primary objectives of Cameroon's national food policy are food security (self-sufficiency) and low urban consumer cost (Guyer 1984, 1987). Responding to increasing demand from urban areas, many Cameroonian women have become commercial food producers, increasing their production and their income by working longer hours growing and selling food crops (Guyer 1984; Henn 1989). Other women, while continuing to farm for household provisioning, have become entrepreneurs, organizing and managing their own small businesses to earn money, often in sales and resales of raw and processed food (van den Berg 1992).

Food policy and development theorists assume that aggregate household income has a positive effect on family well-being and nutritional status. However, the relationship between income from commercial farming (the production of food or nonfood crops for sale), household food security, and child health in farming families is inconsistent. Variables such as choice of crop, control of production and income, allocation of household labor, land tenure, pricing policies, and the maintenance of subsistence production are identified as crucial in understanding the impact of agricultural commercialization on the nutritional status of rural people (DeWalt 1993). Each of these variables has a gender dimension in West Africa, where women earn their own incomes and feed their own children, and where households operate with separate purses for each marital partner.

Various studies demonstrate linkages between women's economic activities and the welfare of their children. Three of these are cited here to represent this larger literature. Tripp (1981) showed that women in northern Ghana who earned money through market trading were able to invest it to feed their children better than women who stayed at home, although market activities took place away from the household. Popkin and coworkers in the Philippines showed that women who worked as traders did not have time to gather and prepare leafy vegetable sauces (Popkin and Solon 1976). Their children were less well nourished in terms of vitamin A status than were the children of "nonworking" women. In India, Kumar (1978) found that women in Kerala who earned high incomes from seasonal agricultural labor raised children whose health and growth were poorer than those of children whose mothers earned less money. Kumar hypothesized that the women did not have the time or energy to prepare adequate food during the agricultural season.

These studies show that child well-being as measured by child growth is related both positively and negatively to women's occupation, income, and time use, and that the association with women's occupational choice must be seen in the context of very local social, cultural, and economic conditions.

Bamenda Grassfields women have a long history of commercial activity at the local level (Kaberry 1952). In 1991, village women increased their activity, responding to market signals from diverse urban populations, including a nearby urban center requiring a steady supply of locally preferred food staples; more remote cities requiring food crops at the wholesale level; and some segments of both transient and local populations in need of complete meals, ready-to-eat or nearly so, and more substantial than casual street foods such as roasted corn or fish. Food production in this context ranges from household subsistence (for all women) to that destined for international export, and from raw foodstuffs to processed and prepared foods.

Study Site

This study was carried out in 1991 in Bamendankwe, a village and chiefdom within the Bamenda Urban Area, North West Province, Cameroon.[2] The region is about four degrees north of the equator and more than 2,000 meters high. The terrain is hilly and mountainous, with a relatively cool climate and monsoonal-type rainfall of approximately 2,500 millimeters (90–120 inches) annually. The chiefdom has a population density of at least 250 inhabitants per square kilometer, residing on at least thirty-five square kilometers of land.[3]

Culture and social organization of the study area are similar to those of many other societies in West Africa. Politically organized as a chiefdom, the patrilineal and patrilocal village was first settled in 1901. Communal land is allocated through the *fon* (chief) to family heads, who then assign it to individual men, and, through them, to women, wives, and daughters. Polygynous compounds are organized matrifocally (see Uchendu 1965). That is, husbands have separate houses, while each wife has her own living quarters and kitchen and is expected to feed only her own children and other dependents. Additionally, because she is dependent on her sons for access to land after her husband's death, and on her daughters for care in old age, she must work to augment her husband's money for medical care and education that will lead to success for her children in a situation where co-wives may be competing for benefits for their own children.

Women farm, while men's major responsibilities include land clearing and preparation, building construction and maintenance, hunting, propagation and care of trees and tree crops, governance, craftwork—especially metal crafts—and trade. Men's incomes provide shelter, medical help, school fees, and some foodstuffs, especially meat. Under British colonial administration, the area was governed from Lagos as part of Nigeria and was used as a labor reserve for rubber and palm oil plantations on the Cameroon coast, without a great deal of interference. As a result, much of the traditional life and indigenous systems of government are still in place.

Family food security is the responsibility of women. Corn (maize), a European introduction replacing the indigenous millet, and cocoyams are the main subsistence crops and dietary staples, augmented by sauces and soups that are served alongside. Secondary staples include a variety of yams, plantains, bananas, and other seasonally available items. Soups and sauces are prepared in various ways, often with red palm oil as a base and a variety of spices and flavorings. Beef, chicken, goat, and other meats are thought of as festive rather than everyday dishes. Many kinds of fish and fish products—dried, smoked, frozen, or fresh—add variety and protein to the diet as ingredients of soups, sauces, and relishes, which may also include wild or gathered ingredients, such as squash seeds, groundnuts, and other nutritionally valuable components. Many of these are purchased, as they are not otherwise available in this high, inland area.

Research Methods

The participating compounds were randomly selected from qualified compounds in the core quarters of the village. All participating women were married, and thus had access to farmland through the husband's lineage. Each woman had at least two children, one of which—the target child— was between twenty-four and sixty months old.

This age was chosen to eliminate breast milk as a source of nutrients, as weaning is generally completed by twenty-four months. Recent research also suggests that nutrition during the period 24 to 60 months is critical to the development of cognitive ability (Calloway, Murphy, and Beaton 1988; Sigman and Neumann 1989).

In this study, there were 110 mother-child pairs and 95 husbands. Methods of data collection included participant observation, key informant and focus-group interviews, a questionnaire survey, and child anthropometry. Two commonly accepted indicators—household food diversity and child growth—were used to assess household food adequacy and child health.

Household food diversity indices are based on the idea that consuming a variety of foods is more likely than is a restricted diet to result in adequate amounts of the nutrients needed for normal human growth and body maintenance. This diversity can be assessed by enumerating unique food items (Hoddinott and Haddad 1991). These indices are developed in several ways, for example, from records of foods eaten, foods served, or foods available at the household level. The latter method has been employed here, enumerating the items available in each pantry with a list developed and standardized for the village (table 8.1).

Child growth was calculated using the child's age (as determined by a birth certificate or clinic registration card), weight, and height measurements. Growth indicators are expressed as Z scores, as is the commonly accepted practice. Weight for age (WAZ) is an indicator of current food intake and health, and a WAZ score of less than -2.0 is termed underweight. Height for age (HAZ) measures growth over time, long-term food intake, and health. An HAZ score of less than -2.0 is termed *stunting* and indicates

Table 8.1. Specific foods in household pantries by women's source of cash (in percentages)

	Producers[a] (N = 69)	Entrepreneurs (N = 25)	Collaborators (N = 12)	Total (N = 106)
Staple foods				
Cocoyam	74	92	83	79
Corn or cornmeal	33	56	33	39
Gari (cassava)	32	48	50	38
Irish potatoes[b]	59	68	58	52
Plantain	20	16	17	19
Rice	19	16	58	23
Sweet potatoes	36	44	25	37
Yams (all kinds)	4	4	8	5
Protein sources, animal				
Beef	43	44	25	42
Crayfish	25	40	58	32
Egg	12	8	0	9
Fish, dry or frozen	10	40	16	18
Kanda	38	32	16	34
Njanjimoto	25	32	33	27
Protein sources, vegetable				
Beans[b]	96	2	100	95
Cowpeas	4	8	17	7
Egusi	64	8	50	49
Groundnuts	19	64	58	34
Soyabeans	1	20	25	8
Vegetables				
Amba	52	32	50	47
Avocado pear	29	32	33	30
Banana	65	60	66	95
Cabbage	16	4	17	18
Jakato	12	0	16	9
Njama-Njama	39	40	25	38
Okra	12	24	25	16
Onion	46	60	66	52
Pumpkin	62	84	58	67
Tomato	16	36	42	24

a. The column numbers are to be interpreted thus: "Amba was found in 52% of all household pantries of women producers."
b. End use (i.e., for sale, home consumption or planting) was not specified, but item was stored in a secure pantry.

low food consumption over a long duration. Weight for height (WHZ) is a measure of current food intake. A WHZ of less than -2.0 is termed *wasting* and indicates low current food consumption or high current energy expenditure. The effects of gender on child-growth scores show no significant difference between boys and girls, and so the growth scores are aggregated.

The participating women were grouped according to the source of their major income, primary production, entrepreneurial and trading activities, and collaboration with husbands who provided income (table 8.2). Primary producers collected and sold firewood or farmed commercial food crops. Entrepreneurs consisted of traders, small-business operators, and vendors of processed food. The term *collaborative* is used in this study to describe the group of women whose main household income was supplied by the husband. All women were also subsistence farmers who grew staple household food.

Results

Out of the study sample, 51 of the 110 children (46 percent) were classified as stunted, with an HAZ score of -2.0 or less. This was greater than the expected ratio of about 28 percent (ROC 1978). As shown in table 8.2, the children of primary producers were significantly shorter and lighter in weight for their age than were the children in the other two groups. This could be the result of food unavailability and/or chronic health problems. The children of entrepreneurs were significantly heavier for their height

Table 8.2. Child health and household characteristics by women's first income type

Income type	N	Child health indicators				Socioeconomic status (Index = 100)	
		HAZ (height/ age)	WAZ (weight/ age)	WHZ (weight/ height)	Diet pantry items (diversity index)	Material status (MSL)	Social status (SSL)
Producers	70	-2.1[a]	-.9[a]	.5	17	93	88
Entrepreneurs	26	-1.5	-.3	.8[b]	19[c]	63	92
Collaborators	11	-1.2	-.3	.6	17	92	57

Note from text: stunting, HAZ < -2.0; underweight, WAZ <-2.0; wasting, WHZ<-2.0
a. Significantly different from collaborators at the .05 confidence level.
b. Significantly different from producers at the .05 confidence level.
c. Significantly different from producers and collaborators at the .05 confidence level.

than were the producers' children, which indicates a greater food intake and better health over an extended period, resulting in sustained growth.

The pantries of the entrepreneurial women showed a greater diversity of items than did the producers' pantries, reflecting comments made by many of these women, such as, "I sell and use some for my own children." They tended to bring home foods and snacks that could not be home produced. Diversity scores were calculated by summing the presence or absence of each food for each pantry. A difference of 2 in the aggregate group scores meant that on average, pantries of producers had fewer items, while traders' pantries had more, and that this tendency was not due to chance.

Two indicators—material status of life (MSL) and social status of life (SSL)—reflect material and social aspects of men's income use. These are based on frequency counts of material items in men's possession. The MSL indicator approximates socioeconomic status (SES) using a variety of material items: electric power, sewing machine, cupboard, vehicle (motorcycle, auto, or truck), upholstered chairs, radio, television. The SSL also enumerates men's ritual paraphernalia associated with village social life and status, a set of values referred to as "our tradition." It represents another set of men's consumption choices and therefore is another measure of SES. The regalia included flintlock rifles (Dane guns), Grassfield gowns, ceremonial spears, cutlasses, drinking horns, drums, and juju or dance ownership.

For both MSL and SSL, the frequency of each item in a compound was recorded and the percentage of compounds with the item were determined. For each item recorded in a compound, a weighted score was given by using the following formula: 100 percent minus the percentage of compounds having the item. For example, if 85.7 percent of the compounds had a radio, the weighted score given to a compound for *radio* would be 14.3 (100 minus 85.7). The weighted scores for each item found in a compound were then summed to get the total score for that compound. Compounds were classified according to producers, entrepreneurs, and collaborators. A mean total score was determined for each of these categories of compounds. For example, in table 8.2, the material status of life (MSL) score for producers' compounds is 93, and the social status of life (SSL) score is 88. The mean score for all of the compounds was 84.4.

Even though the differences shown in table 8.2 appear large, they are not statistically significant because there is a considerable amount of variation within the groups. Men's income use is, in general, not related to women's occupations. The indices (pantry item diversity, MSL, and SSL) are based on frequency counts of categorical data; thus the apparent large difference between numbers has no intrinsic meaning but reflects the wide variation and lack of central tendency in each group.

The child growth measures, on the other hand, are based on ratio level data that are standardized as Z scores and then compared to Z scores derived from data collected from an economically and ethnically representative sample of American children and analyzed by the National Center for Health Statistics, a global standard reference in child health. These scores are sensitive to small variations among populations, hence small differences in the measures between groups can be both statistically significant and socially important.

In these children, stunting is indicative of long-term chronic dietary restriction. Dietary restriction and chronic mild malnutrition in this preschool age group are linked to inadequately developed brain structures and to changes in behavior that impair the ability to learn and to take full advantage of educational experiences as an older child or adult (Brown and Pollitt 1996; Calloway, Murphy, and Beaton 1988; Sigman and Neumann 1989). These chronic deficits are indicated by suppressed longitudinal growth that occurs over a relatively long period of time.

Discussion

Commercial Farmers

Production of food crops for sale was the main income generating activity for fifty-two mothers. Of these, thirty-eight grew potatoes, the major women's commercial crop. Women used other staples, particularly cocoyams, to feed their families, since potatoes are considered, locally, to be very inferior food, and most are exported to markets in major cities and to other countries, such as Gabon. Women's comments about potatoes ranged from "They don't fill the belly" to "You can't work on them" to "They give the children diarrhea."

Twenty-four of the commercial potato cropping women were from compounds where the husbands worked coffee farms as their major income source. All of these women contributed labor on their husbands' coffee plantations. Many made more from their potato farms than did their husbands from coffee. These women's pantries had the lowest food diversity scores, and their children were more likely to exhibit longitudinal growth deficits, although the family income could be quite high.

One informant's story was typical. Ngenue started "seriously" to sell food crops in the late 1960s, even though coffee provided cash, and even though her husband paid education and health expenses and bought meat and oil. She needed an independent income for things of "her own," such as shoes and clothing, children's schoolbooks, kitchen equipment, and other items. At first she sold yams, but she discontinued this production when soil fertility declined and yams did not produce well. She started selling potatoes and *njama-njama* (*Solanum scabrum L.*, see FAO 1988), a leafy green vegetable used as the major sauce ingredient for several dishes. By the 1980s, when the urban market was well developed, she could clear 100,000 FCFA (about U.S.$350) each year on potatoes alone. To put this number in perspective, the household per capita income figure for all of Cameroon in 1985 was 393,000 FCFA (about U.S.$1,310).[4]

The potato harvest begins in late June and ends by October; women expect to have their potato money in hand by September. In a good year, a good farmer can make more than her husband. But her money is mainly spent on education and health, even though education is generally considered a father's responsibility. In the past, women did not expect to pay school fees. Since women are able to earn a lot of money selling potatoes, and since men's incomes have declined, many women find that their husbands refuse to pay school fees. As one compound head noted, "If she wants them to [go to] school, she must pay."[5]

Women identify land and labor as major constraints to expansion of their farming activities. As the area has urbanized, women farmers have been finding it harder to locate good farming land. They are understandably reluctant to intensify production or permanently improve their farm plots, because they do not have secure tenure; improvements would only benefit the owner. They farm intensively in their compound plots where tenure is secure, using fertilizers when they are available.

The second major constraint to increased production is labor. Women no longer depend on their children to help them in the farms, since the children are occupied with school during most of the year. They hire other women to work labor contracts, or they arrange to work on a reciprocal basis (usually with relatives). But there is a limit to any one woman's time and energy, especially as she ages. Thus, commercial farmers must come to grips with an important labor question: Will they pay contract labor and farm more plots at increasing distances from the villages, or will they farm fewer plots and use only "free" family labor?

Clearly these women are experienced, competent farmers. They grow food for their families and for commercial crops for a strong market. Why should their children show signs of undernutrition? There are a number of reasons. Potatoes, fresh corn, and beans are conceptualized as cash crops, not as family subsistence crops. They are used as family food when available during harvest (the family consumes whatever is not appropriate for sale), but the family food supply is conceptually based on cocoyams, cassava, plantains, and dried corn, which in this area is usually purchased. Women remark that although potatoes may be all right "for city people," they are not appropriate foods for working men or for women farmers. Cocoyams, cassava, and plantains are available year round, while potatoes, corn, and beans are seasonal, are harvested at one time, and suffer from severe storage problems. The separation of food and cash crops follows the pattern commonly seen in cash cropping areas: selling higher-value crops and retaining the lower value crops for family use (DeWalt 1993; Frankenberger 1985).

Entrepreneurs: Traders and Vendors

Food-related trading managed by village women varies widely in scale and by commodity. It ranges from buying a sack of rice or a tin of oil for repackaging and reselling to larger scale, long-distance operations in which women travel to other areas, buy larger quantities of nonlocal commodities, and return to sell or reship them. Some of these women manage a two-way trading circuit, and it is not uncommon for them to deal in multiple commodities.

Women like to trade because it brings a steady income that can be sustained throughout the year. It is less physically demanding than commercial farming, it is more social, and children can help in some of the selling. It does require investment. One informant, with five children between the ages of three and nineteen, outlined her business operation.

In May of 1991, she had a sack of ninety unripe avocados that she had purchased in Bamenda for 1,000 FCFA (U.S.$3), or 11 francs each (U.S.5¢). As the avocados ripened, she planned to have her daughter sell them in the village market for 20–25 francs each and double her money. Of course, not all would ripen and not all would sell, but she would make a small profit and feed what did not sell to her children. Meanwhile, she would buy rice, gari (a preparation of cassava), dried corn, cocoyam, and beans by the sackful in town or along the road for resale in the village; in this way she would subsidize her family's food.

Buyam-sellams, who circulate between country and city to buy and sell, have become essential participants in the urban and rural food supply since the government of Cameroon formally turned to the private sector for the provisioning of the cities (ROC 1986). Intercity trade in foodstuffs is often carried out by women. One informant regularly traveled to Wum, a smaller center in a different ecological region, to trade. She carried Irish potatoes purchased in Bamendankwe for sale, bringing back smoked "bush meat" and Ibo yams. Both of these commodities had ready buyers and commanded "a fine price" in Bamenda. She organized her system of production, using regular suppliers and customers in both locations along with her kin network. She did not let lack of transport stop her; in 1991,[6] she said her profits were so high because of the shortages of bush meat in the city. Having recognized the potential income, she said, she "couldn't afford to sit."

Once goods were found and purchased, they were transported by poorly maintained vehicles over often only marginally passable roads. Women told stories of loaded pickup trucks overturning on remote country roads, or of mechanical breakdowns that stranded them for days while their produce spoiled. Additionally, they worried about their families at home and about their own farms, both of which were often left in the hands of family members—sisters, mothers, or older children. Women sometimes borrowed money for these trading ventures only to lose it all in one accident, thus ending up in debt. More than one woman decided the risks were too great for the amount of gain involved, particularly with high-bulk, low-value, perishable produce such as cocoyams, cassava, or tomatoes. However, with skill, experience, good connections, and luck, fine profits could be made.

Prepared-food vending operations were used by many as supplementary-income sources, but 10 of the 105 women in the study used it as their primary income source. This trade is mostly in *achu*, the pounded cocoyam staple that is sold to restaurants or to regular customers.[7] Women generally prefer to use their own production, which requires no financial investment, and many prepare two batches for sale each month. The price for bundles varies according to cocoyam availability.

The women in this study expected to generate about 1,000 FCFA ($3.00) per batch of achu, and often they remarked that they used the money for their monthly rotating credit associations. Again, the key issues for them were not the size of the income but its steadiness, as well as the possibility of raising small amounts of money quickly. The Bamenda cattle market also provided opportunity for women residents of the quarter. They used the twice-weekly market as a resource, selling several kinds of prepared meals, snacks, and beverages. Several women depended on the mar-ket to generate money, and to do so relatively close to home. The profit gained from these kinds of prepared-food sales was usually small but steady, and it could be earned from the compound, with low initial investment and risk, and with equipment and skills that women possessed or could easily access.

Are such women as these entrepreneurs? Using a standard definition of the term as "someone who risks his or her money in a venture in hopes of making a profit," they are indeed (Spencer 1990:21). They follow a common pattern in assembling the factors of production—raising money, organizing management, making policy decisions, and reaping the gains or suffering the losses. Innovation, another key to entrepreneurship, is seen in the small details of operation. Variation in recipes, quick response to new opportunities, the shaping of products to fit niche markets, all provide rich examples of the flexibility, creativity, and innovation required of small-scale operations. There is a general pattern, an "indigenous business plan," with individual variations.

First, a woman should carefully study her situation and resources, keeping in mind that she will always need to have a farm for her family's staple food. Her resources include her own time and her own skill and experience and, possibly, the skill, experience, and connections of her kin. Money can be raised in a number of ways. She may get a loan from her husband, from her family or friends, or she may accumulate money in a savings society. Women rarely use banks, preferring to use the indigenous credit or savings associations that help to conceal the amount of their income, as they fear that their husbands may gain access to their bank accounts.

Women have clear ideas about the kinds of income they need (small or large, steady or periodic) and about the kinds of enterprises that generate income. Small-scale food sales are often a starting point, but many women have more elaborate schemes.

One woman identified three phases in her entrepreneurial plan. First, she needed one enterprise to provide a small but steady income, suitable for daily expenses. To this end, she hoped to buy an ice-cream maker, set it up downtown, and hire someone to sell the cones: "Small money, but steady, you can buy your food."

Next she would raise money quickly, through cattle sales. This would require more money but could generate large returns quickly. The risk would be higher but so would be the profits, earmarked for housing, clothing, children's school expenses, and to accumulate money for the third venture. This was to be a specialized import business, more secure and potentially more profitable than either of the first two. The woman wanted to be ready to take advantage of any turnaround in the economy.

Why should trading and marketing as economic choices foster improved child welfare in this setting? Analysis of pantry data showed that market and trading women generally had more purchased items on hand. These items included several kinds of fish and fish products, groundnuts, egusi seeds (squash seed), dried corn, flavoring cubes, and spices.

Some of these—especially fish, groundnuts, and egusi—are good protein and micronutrient sources. The presence of dried corn, flavoring cubes, and spices indicates the preparation of a wide variety of dishes that also use small amounts of purchased ingredients.

These women worked in what might be called a "food-enriched" environment, that is, they tended to bring their children snacks and treats and to use trading or food-preparation leftovers in family meals. All of this enhanced the children's diet and welfare.

Collaborative Households: Husband's Income, Wife's Farming

Husbands completely supported family expenses in 11 of the 105 compounds. Women of these compounds were able to concentrate their time and energy on subsistence food production and on child care. As a group, they farmed significantly fewer plots than did the women in the primary producer compounds, indicating that they were spending less time and labor on the farm plots. Their children were significantly heavier and taller than those from primary producer compounds.

Several of the husbands depended on steady incomes from government service or on wages from secure jobs and occupations. As one woman said, "I work the farm and get the cash from him." It is important to note that most of these women had some way of generating independent income for obligations to their natal families, even though their husbands provided the primary income. These households were vulnerable, as male income was dependent on jobs and professions that are always under pressure in conditions of continuing economic decline. As government and private agencies and corporations continue to cut back, jobs disappear and salaries decline. Thus, these households may suffer serious setbacks.

The pattern of male migration for work is well established in North West Province, used as a labor reserve by the British in the colonial period. Men often leave home in search of work; the women and children are usually left behind to work the farms and subsist as best they can, waiting for remittances from absent husbands and fathers. Women who are not accustomed to earning their own income and have not developed the social networks that make it possible may be at a severe disadvantage. Dependence on male income is a risky economic strategy for many families.

Women's Occupation and Family Welfare

There is striking unanimity in the use of money. The major expenditures for all categories of compounds, for both men and women (table 8.3) are health and education. These expenditure categories represent long-term investments in children and family, a concrete expression of cultural values that identify education and health as keys to a better life in the future. Many women, especially older women, mentioned that they valued health care as the most important consequence of economic development, and that "the women and the children don't die as they used to. There are doctors and medicines, and roads to get to them." Parents try to educate all children through the primary levels of school, and they support talented and "serious" youngsters to university level if they can. Women use their own income if those of the husband or father are not available.

Entrepreneurial women's families have several advantages. One is the small but steady income stream. Research shows that different kinds of income are spent in different ways (DeWalt 1993; Frankenberger 1985). "Lump" income tends to be spent for big-ticket items, while small, steady income is used for daily expenses. The income from potatoes can be a large

Table 8.3. Men's and women's expenditures by priority (in percentages)

Expenditure category	Priority ranking			
	First	Second	Third	Total
Men				
Health	45.7	38.1	12.6	95.4
Education	44.7	34.0	12.6	91.3
Food	4.3	16.5	38.9	59.7
Celebrations	3.2	5.2	15.8	24.2
Clothing	0.0	4.1	14.7	18.8
Problems	1.1	2.1	3.2	6.4
Personal	1.1	0.0	1.1	2.2
Women				
Health	40.2	30.2	11.8	82.2
Education	31.3	30.4	6.4	68.1
Food	12.5	16.1	29.1	57.7
Clothing	4.5	9.5	20.9	34.9
Celebrations	7.1	4.5	9.1	20.7
Problems	0.0	1.7	5.5	7.2
Personal	0.9	0.0	6.4	7.3

lump sum that is often used by women for big purchases such as clothing or donations to family celebrations. But a large amount of income, especially when it comes at a specific season, is obvious to husbands and relatives. Many husbands, knowing that women will receive large amounts of money at specific times, withhold school or health payments, forcing the women to make up the deficits in school fees and medical treatments (culturally constructed as a husband's and father's responsibility) out of their own purses. Income from small sales can be as steady as the women wish, and it is easier to conceal.

There are other benefits of small, food-related enterprises. Some of the commodities can be used for feeding families (for example, cooking oil), while others promote hygiene (soap) or lighting (kerosene). Small amounts of money are easier to conceal from husbands and other relatives, reducing household friction and increasing women's autonomy in spending decisions. Such amounts can be quietly invested in savings societies, some of which are set up to buy kitchen essentials (oil, salt, flavor cubes). And, as women often mentioned, leftovers are used to feed the family.

Recent studies of West African women document and analyze women's trade and entrepreneurship as economic choices of *urban* women (Clark 1994; Robertson 1984, 1995). These women are not all married, nor do they have their own farms. Thus the setting is profoundly different from that of the Cameroonian case presented here, where all women were married and had their own farms for family subsistence production. Additionally, child welfare data using measures of child growth, especially long-term measures such as attained height for age, were not collected for the urban groups. Thus these specific welfare measures cannot be associated with variation in urban women's economic choices.

The point to be emphasized is that available choices and associated results depend on very local factors, including women's access to and use of resources. Access to farmland and the maintenance of subsistence production, as previously mentioned, are critical in the production of family welfare for agricultural families, while it simply may not be possible for women in the urban milieu. It is quite possible that the maintenance of subsistence production explains at least part of the difference between this Cameroonian population in its near-urban area and the urban ones in Ghana studied by Robertson and Clark.

But there is another issue; that of managerial competence. Successful entrepreneurial women are equipped by selection and training (often begun in childhood) to compete in the commercial sphere. They make sound economic decisions, manage their money and time, and take advantage of commercial opportunities. The skills and competencies developed may well carry over into the noncommercial side of their lives, enhancing their ability to manage resources for their own and family benefit.

Trading and entrepreneurship, with much of the family food supply coming from the women's farms, is, in this near-urban setting, an economic choice that is associated with improved child welfare. For some, the economic explanation of increased income suffices. The background to economic success, however, is not so simplistic. There are complex social and cultural factors involved. Recent research (Clark 1994; Musisi 1995; VerEecke 1995) and ethnographic observations (Krieger 1991, 1995) suggest that recruitment, training, and mentoring of girls and women by established traders may promote the development of managerial skills that are also related to improved family welfare. Cultural and social factors such as the local definition of family social status (not necessarily socioeconomic status) and family connections, and their relationship to women's economic success, may also play major roles here and will merit further study.

Robertson (1984, 1995) finds that the urban trading women in Accra and in Kenya are being increasingly marginalized by the effects of international capitalism, and that trading for them is the last economic resort. Married women in Bamendankwe are marginalized also, and by the same kinds of economic and social factors that Robertson so persuasively details.

In Bamendankwe, however, firewood sales were the last resort for marginalized women. They had, at least for the moment, land to farm for subsistence, and although the household food supply may have been limited in variety, it could be produced with little to no cash outlay.

The issue of women's relationship to external economic forces is critical to the issue of family welfare and should not be neglected. Within the constraints of these conditions, however, it is obvious that some women succeed and some do not. Studies of variation and diversity will continue to illustrate ways in which success, at whatever scale, can be enhanced; such studies will also continue to provide models for future action.

Conclusion

The village women who supply a variety of foods to the city are also subsistence farmers, who depend to a great degree on their farms for household food. Their interactions with the urban markets are aimed at generating income that they themselves control. The types of income strategy and market interactions that they choose are associated with the household food supply and the health of their children.

The pantries of women who were primarily engaged in firewood or food crop production had significantly fewer kinds of foods than did the pantries of entrepreneurs, and the children of the former were more likely to be stunted and significantly lighter in weight. There was a positive association between women's trading and improved child welfare.

White (1985) persuasively argues that it makes good economic sense to investigate, acknowledge, and encourage entrepreneurship among women, rather than to subsume such activity under the general heading of housewife or petty trader, thus overlooking patterns such as those differentiated in this study. The results here indicate the need for policy analysis and recommendations to rely on more than the simplistic measure provided by total household income or even women's income.

Policies and programs must also be sufficiently flexible to respond meaningfully to variation in local social and cultural conditions and particular settings, noting profound differences between urban and rural milieus and the relationships between them. Female entrepreneurship, as well as agricultural production, must be considered a major avenue for improving well-being among children and families, and policy choices should encourage and support activity that allows women to determine the amount, timing, and control of their own incomes.

The processes of recruitment, training, and mentoring in the development of managerial skills are likely to be critical to both business success and family welfare. They should be further investigated, acknowledged, and encouraged when appropriate.

Notes

1. This research was supported by a Fulbright Institute for International Education Research Fellowship and by a Social Science Research Council/American Council for Learned Societies Program for Fellowships for Training and Dissertation Research in Africa.

2. The Bamenda Urban Area is a designated administrative unit with a set of specifically urban land-use regulations that allow subsistence and commercial farming in the outskirts.

3. Land area and density of inhabitants are from my own calculations.

4. The FCFA (the Central African franc) is pegged to the French franc at the rate of 100 FCFA/French franc. Amounts given in U.S. dollars are rough equivalents in predevaluation 1991 dollars.

5. This kind of conflict between husband and wife over children's educational expenses is not uncommon. S. Ardener, in a personal communication, 1995, terms it "gender blackmail" as it is in the *mother's* best interest to educate her children well.

6. In 1991, roads were closed and there was no public or private transport on weekdays due to political problems.

7. *Achu* is prepared from cocoyams and small green bananas, steamed and pounded into a paste in a wooden mortar. After preparation, the paste is wrapped in banana leaves in packages of 300–500 grams.

References Cited

Brown, J. Larry, and Ernesto Pollitt. 1996. Malnutrition, Poverty and Intellectual Development. *Scientific American*, February, 38–43.

Calloway, D. H., S. P. Murphy, and G. H. Beaton. 1988. *Food Intake and Human Function: A Cross Project Perspective*. Berkeley and Los Angeles: University of California.

Chilver, Elizabeth M. 1992. Women Cultivators, Cows and Cash Crops in Cameroon. In *Persons and Powers of Women in Diverse Cultures*, edited by Shirley Ardener. Oxford: Berg.

Clark, Gracia. 1994. *Onions Are My Husband: Survival and Accumulation by West African Market Women*. Chicago: University of Chicago Press.

DeWalt, Kathleen. 1993. Nutrition and the Commercialization of Agriculture: Ten Years Later. *Social Science and Medicine* 36 (11):1407–16.

Dwyer, Daisy, and Judith Bruce, eds. 1988. *A Home Divided: Women and Income in the Third World*. Stanford: Stanford University Press.

FAO (Food and Agriculture Organization of the United Nations). 1988. *Traditional Food Plants*. Food and Nutrition Paper no. 42. Rome: FAO.

Frankenberger, Timothy. 1985. *Adding a Food Consumption Perspective to Farming Systems Research*. Washington, D.C.: USAID Bureau for Science and Technology, Office of Nutrition.

Goheen, Miriam. 1991. The Ideology and Political Economy of Gender: Women and Land in Nso, Cameroon. In *Structural Adjustment and African Women Farmers*, edited by Christina R. Gladwin. Gainesville: University Press of Florida.

———. 1996. *Men Own the Fields, Women Own the Crops: Gender and Power in the Cameroon Grassfields*. Madison: University of Wisconsin Press.

Guyer, Jane. 1984. *Family and Farm in Southern Cameroon*. African Research Studies no. 15. Boston: African Studies Center, Boston University.

———. 1987. Feeding Yaounde. In *Feeding African Cities*, edited by Jane Guyer. Bloomington: Indiana University Press.

Henn, Jeanne. 1989. Food Policy, Food Production, and the Family Farm in Cameroon. In *Proceedings of a Conference on the Political Economy of Cameroon: Historical Perspectives*. Research Report no. 35, June 1988. Leiden: African Studies Center.

Hoddinott, John, and Louis Haddad. 1991. Household Expenditures, Child Anthropometric Status, and the Intrahousehold Division of Income: Evidence from the Côte d'Ivoire. IFPRI (mimeo).

Kaberry, Phyllis. 1952. *Women of the Grassfields*. London: Her Majesty's Stationery Office.

Krieger, Judith. 1991. Field notes.

———. 1994. Women, Men, and Household Food in Cameroon. Ph.D. dissertation. University of Kentucky.

———. 1995. Field notes.

Kumar, Shuba. 1978. The Role of the Household Economy in Child Nutrition at Low Incomes: A Case Study in Kerala. Cornell University Occasional Paper no. 95.

Leslie, Joanne, and Michael Paolisso, eds. 1988. *Women, Work, and Child Welfare in the Third World.* Boulder, Colo.: Westview Press.

Musisi, Nakanyike B. 1995. Baganda Women's Night Market Activities. In *African Market Women and Economic Power,* edited by B. House-Midamba and F. Ekechi. Westport, Conn.: Greenwood Press.

Popkin, Barry M., and Florentino S. Solon. 1976. Income, Time, the Working Mother, and Child Nutrition. *Journal of Tropical Pediatrics and Environmental Child Health* 22:156–66.

Robertson, Claire. 1984. *Sharing the Same Bowl: A Socioeconomic History of Women and Class in Accra, Ghana.* Bloomington: Indiana University Press.

———. 1995. Comparative Advantage: Women in Trade in Accra, Ghana, and Nairobi, Kenya. In *African Market Women and Economic Power,* edited by B. House-Midamba and F. Ekechi. Westport, Conn.: Greenwood Press.

ROC (Republic of Cameroon). 1978. *National Nutrition Survey.* Yaounde: Government of Cameroon.

———. 1986. *Sixth Five-Year Economic, Social, and Cultural Development Plan.* Yaounde: Government of Cameroon.

Sigman, M., and C. Neumann. 1989. Cognitive Abilities of Kenyan Children in Relation to Nutrition, Family Characteristics, and Education. *Child Development* 60 (6) (December):1463–74.

Spencer, Milton H. 1990. *Contemporary Macroeconomics.* New York: Worth.

Tripp, Robert. 1981. Farmers and Traders: Some Economic Determinants of Nutritional Status in Northern Ghana. *Journal of Tropical Pediatrics and Environmental Child Health* 27:15–22.

Uchendu, Victor. 1965. *The Igbo of Southeast Nigeria.* New York: Holt, Rinehart and Winston.

van den Berg, Adri. 1992. *Women in Bamenda: Survival Strategies and Access to Land.* Research Report no. 50. Leiden: African Studies Center.

VerEecke, Catherine. 1995. Muslim Women Traders of Northern Nigeria: Perspectives from the City of Yola. In *African Market Women and Economic Power,* edited by B. House-Midamba and F. Ekechi. Westport, Conn.: Greenwood Press.

White, Sylvia. 1985. African Women as Small-Scale Entrepreneurs: Their Impact on Employment Creation. In *Women As Food Producers in Developing Countries,* edited by J. Monson and M. Kalb. Berkeley and Los Angeles: University of California Press.

PART III

Entrepreneurial Management Styles
and Characteristics

◇◇◇◇◇◇◇◇◇◇◇◇◇

9. A Historical Perspective on African Entrepreneurship: Lessons from the Duala Experience in Cameroon

Yvette Monga

The poor performance and gloomy forecast of the economies of most sub-Saharan African countries have raised concern over how they can be successfully integrated into the international economy. These concerns have been underlined by studies that point to the so-called lack of an indigenous foundation of business skills. Other studies have used culture to explain Africa's economic problems. Such studies have juxtaposed an "ethos of munificence" (or *politique du ventre*), to an "ethos of retention" (or *tirelire vitale*) (Bayart 1989; Bayart, Mbembe, and Toulabor 1992; Warnier 1993; Warnier and Miaffo 1993). The second attribute is praised as representing the Weberian ideal of hard work and asceticism said to be characteristic of an authentic spirit of entrepreneurship, while the first is depicted, in contrast, as a reprehensible pattern of consumption leading to the evaporation of surpluses. These authors conclude that the consumption of resources and nonaccumulation of surpluses are the major impediments to the development of African entrepreneurship.

Yet, as other researchers have found in the study of African precapitalistic societies, a number of strong examples of progressive economic behavior are embedded in particular features of indigenous social organizations (Austen 1987; Ayittey 1991; Cooper et al. 1993; Duignan and Gann 1975). This chapter presents the Duala,[1] a small Bantu-speaking group located in coastal Cameroon, who emerged in colonial Cameroon as a powerful economic force. Their entrepreneurial strategy was based on a twofold social network: a lower network, composed of dependents whose loyalty was secured by a patron-client relationship, and an upper network, whose members were linked by marriage alliances. These social networks enabled Duala entrepreneurs to take full advantage of German economic policies in Cameroon after 1884, as well as to circumvent French administrative obstacles to their commercial success. This study reveals how Duala entrepreneurs manipulated their system of social relations to enter the cocoa industry. It also presents an analysis of their strategies for revenue investment and adjustment to change. The conclusion provides theoretical and practical insights that may be applicable to African entrepreneurs in general.

Duala Cocoa Planters during the German Administration, 1884–1914

Precolonial Duala society was made up of four major segments claiming to share a common ancestor: the Bell and the Bonaberi, belonging to the Bonandoo clan (*bona* means "people of"); and the Akwa and the Deïdo of the Bonakuo clan. Duala rulers emerged during the precolonial period as "big men" able to control the slave and ivory trade. During the second half of the nineteenth century, the slave trade was replaced by trade in palm oil. Palm oil, unlike slaves, could be collected and traded by anyone. Consequently, any ordinary Duala could use this to obtain foreign goods such as guns and gunpowder, scarlet uniforms, top hats, and so on. As a result, the authority of earlier Duala merchant princes was challenged and the consequent social instability prompted them to seek outside intervention.

When Germany finally established a protectorate over Cameroon in 1884, the ambition of the Hamburg traders behind that move was to strengthen their commercial positions in the coastal Cameroon region and eventually to gain access to the networks that supplied tropical products from the interior. But from the beginning, some German traders and businessmen were also eager to create large plantation estates in the country (Jaeck 1960).

In 1895, Governor Jesco von Puttkamer announced his policy of strong support for the creation of German plantations in Cameroon, especially to produce cocoa. Cocoa was considered a highly sophisticated crop to be grown only by Europeans, so the local population was not perceived as a source of potential competition. At that time, Africans—ironically, the Duala, whom Europeans had known earlier as commercial brokers and middlemen—were depicted as idle people unable to perform any productive work.[2] The only role allowed for Africans in the cocoa plantations was that of menial laborers (Etoga 1971; Michel 1970). But, as the German authorities would later discover, the Duala brokers and middlemen had an agenda of their own that they pursued vigorously.

After 1889, the colonialists launched military expeditions to open up the interior to direct European trade (Austen 1983; Dominik 1908; von Morgen 1982). This resulted in the Duala brokers being eventually evicted from their role as exclusive middlemen. From then on, they faced competition from both European agents and local petty merchants; palm oil trade became less profitable and lost its attraction, especially for the most influential and successful brokers. The latter had invested large resources in that activity, and the only way left to survive economically was to reinvest in a new lucrative venture.

Cocoa growing provided such an opportunity to these formerly rich Duala middlemen. They entered this booming industry not as the laborers as prescribed by their colonial masters, but as entrepreneurs, owners of large cocoa plantations, and, later, as investors in many other moneymaking ventures.

To secure both the land and labor necessary for their new business, these Duala cocoa entrepreneurs used their social networks. Two categories of networks can be distinguished: the lower network and the upper network. The lower social network was composed of dependents, or "juniors." They were the poor segments of the Douala society, including both the freeborn Duala (*wonja*) and the slaves (*bakum*). The seniors formed the segments of the Duala society that controlled the economic riches, regardless of their origin. They were the local elite of "big men" observed in other precapitalist societies.

At the upper level of social relationships, the coastal Duala entrepreneurs built profitable trade alliances with the neighboring groups in the interior. These alliances were consolidated through closed societies, the *losango*, as well as through tactically important marriages with inland women (Austen 1983; Gouellain 1975). Using these social foundations, each of the four Duala patrilineal segments carved out valuable and sometimes exclusive commercial zones for protected trade with allies and clients. After the formal abolition of the local slave trade in 1840 (Brutsch 1955), Duala merchants obtained from their allies and clients additional lands on which to settle their slaves (Gouellain 1975:33).

Slave villages appeared in this way and were devoted to producing food crops for the coastal Duala masters and serving as relay stations in the long-distance trade. When the palm oil trade ceased to be lucrative in the mid-1890s, Duala middlemen transformed their slave villages into plantation villages for cocoa growing. The existence of precolonial links later smoothed land transactions between Duala entrepreneurs and the landowners, favoring the expansion of Duala cocoa plantations along the inland river valleys where their trade zones had once been located.

An extensive survey of Duala cocoa plots in 1913 showed that the location of cocoa plantations matched that of the former precolonial trade zones, illustrating the Duala alliances with inland groups.[3] The Deïdo plantations, for example, were located along the Dibombe river in the Abo region from where one of their forefathers had originated, and where they traded during the precolonial period. The Bell and the Bonaberi owned their plantations in the Moungo valley for the same reasons and became the most important Duala cocoa planters. They were the most successful brokers during the precolonial period, and the last traders to lose control of their trade zones under colonialism (Austen 1983).

While the upper social network of allies and clients enabled an easy access to lands, the lower social network of dependents comprised the labor force of the Duala entrepreneurs. During the period of precolonial trade, the dependents of the Duala entrepreneurs were either domestic slaves living on the coast and assisting their masters in the long-distance trade, or they were settled in inland slave villages to produce food crops and palm oil. The dependents provided the labor force for the cocoa industry in the form of servile workers until 1908.

During the precolonial period, Duala middlemen had chosen talented juniors as right-hand men, and afterward, they were entrusted with goods to trade in the interior. During the colonial period, Duala entrepreneurs employed the former juniors as overseers' agents in their works in the plantations, as managers in their stores, and as cocoa salespersons during the campaign seasons.[4]

Duala entrepreneurs also provided other support for their dependents: they paid for bride wealth, granted plots of land upon which to grow food, paid school fees for children, gave financial assistance when needed, offered hospitality when dependents traveled to the coast, provided for medical care, and so on.[5] Dependents could eventually grow to the position of seniors. The most telling example in that respect is that of the successful entrepreneur David Mandesi Bell, who started as a dependent of King Bell. There developed a patron-client relationship between the Duala entrepreneurs and their dependents, with mutual rights and obligations on both sides.

However, in the early 1900s, this labor system was affected by two imperial decrees. In 1907, a decree prohibited the payment to laborers in kind, and in 1908 another decree generalized the mandatory payment of a head tax for any male adult able to perform work.[6] The head tax regulation provided that employers could pay the tax on behalf of their employees. Consequently, Duala cocoa planters began buying tax tokens for their workers and eventually added a moderate wage.

Taxation thus indirectly introduced capitalist labor relationships into

Duala cocoa plantations. But Duala entrepreneurs somehow managed to encapsulate it within the framework of their own system of production by reinventing it as a relationship couched in terms of the former patron-client alliance. For instance, laborers were recruited through personal contacts with the village chiefs; they lived in the plantations and farmed a plot of land for their own. Duala planters still sometimes paid bride wealth on their behalf. Many laborers married local women or even Duala women, and their offspring were considered Dualamen.

In general, Duala entrepreneurs based their economic strategy on exploiting their social networks to succeed in the cocoa industry. The first inland plantations were created in 1894, or perhaps earlier.[7] From 1894 to 1907, Duala agricultural endeavors grew in scope. But knowledge of these inland cocoa plantations was hidden from most of the German officials, though it is difficult to tell whether the Duala did this on purpose.[8] Only after 1907 were they officially "discovered," on the occasion of a land conflict between Duala planters and a German tobacco company. German public opinion was then still being affected by the Herero and Nama wars in southwest Africa and by the Maji Maji rebellion in East Africa, and officials were aware of the political risk in a policy that supported large capitalistic plantations against efforts by the local African people (Clarence-Smith 1993). As a result, in 1907 German officials directed colony economic policy toward the promotion of peasant cocoa growers, following the example of the British colony of the Gold Coast.

The goal of the Volkskultur policy, as this German directive was called, was to foster the emergence of a peasantry that was allocated one hectare of cocoa plantation per family, and that employed domestic labor. In practice, however, German officials did nothing to impede the development of large cocoa plantations such as those developed earlier by the Duala, based on extra-family labor. The Duala entrepreneurs took advantage of the new colonial policy to expand their plantations further. Duala plantations extended toward the Tiko plain, and again their social upper network served their economic goals. Indeed, Teckla Njanjo Douala Manga Bell, daughter of the paramount chief Rudolph Douala Manga Bell, married the Bakossi chief Ntoko Epee. And it was not surprising that the Bell people, including members of the ruling family, benefited most from the expansion of cocoa cultivation in the Tiko plain, located in the Bakossi region.

Because of the Volkskultur policy of 1907, many Duala with economic backgrounds other than those of brokers entered the now-booming cocoa industry. They were civil servants, teachers, or clerics, like Modi Din and Kuoh Issedou, two Protestant ministers who opened cocoa plantations, to the great disapproval of their colleagues (Derrick 1989: 184; Van Slageren 1972:188). These newcomers owned smaller plantations, but they still were large by Volkskultur standards. They operated their plantations parallel to their first profession, employing extra-family labor. By the end of the German administration in Cameroon, rich Duala cocoa pioneers had started to invest their cocoa revenues in new ventures. The diversification of Duala entrepreneurs' activities went on further during the French Mandate period.

Strategy of Investment and Reaction to Change during the French Mandate, 1914–1930s

After being defeated during the First World War, Germany lost its colonies, and Cameroon became a joint British and French Mandate Territory. The most important Duala plantations were located in the French zones, and they soon suffered from French policy. Indeed, French officials suspected the Duala entrepreneurs of having German sympathies; they also resented Duala promptness in sending petitions to international institutions, as well as their demands to be treated on equal footing with Europeans on the grounds that their forefathers had signed the annexation treaty that had placed the country under German rule. The French disliked the Duala ambition to be the country's most influential population group. It was, then, not surprising that the new cocoa policy was directed to favor the emergence of a new peasant bourgeoisie in the south and the center regions of the country to counteract the Duala influence (Guyer 1980, 1981).

To adjust to this hostile environment, Duala entrepreneurs invested their revenues and energy in new additional ventures. During the 1920s and 1930s, they added coffee, rubber, and bananas to cocoa plantations, but the planters invested foremost in the real estate businesses. The will of the paramount chief Rudolph Douala Manga Bell indicated in 1914 that he had rented at least four houses and several urban lands.

So did many other Duala entrepreneurs (Derrick 1979, 1989). In 1929 alone, twenty-six new planning permissions were granted in the city of Douala. The boom in the housing industry went along with the success of the timber and sawmills businesses. Between 1923 and 1926, David Mandesi Bell acquired at least three tracts of forest land for cutting timber in the Moungo region (Derrick 1979:192, 200). Some entrepreneurs operated import and export businesses, others traded goods on their plantations, and all sent their children to Europe to complete their education.

To cover these expenditures, Duala entrepreneurs had two main sources of income, different in both their amount and their regularity: cocoa plantations and real estate properties. David Mandesi Bell signed several sale contracts with European companies for the delivery of cocoa: a contract of 62,500 French francs (FF) in 1919, 98,250 FF in 1930, and 6,000 FF in 1935. Considering the moderate labor and transportation costs, it can be presumed that his net profit was equally substantial.

The statement of revenues and expenses of such a prominent businessman as Rudolph Douala Manga Bell shows that cocoa sales provided more substantial revenues than did house rentals. In 1919, cocoa incomes amounted to 14,252 FF, whereas the houses yielded only 6,004 FF. Cocoa labor and transport to coast cost 1,742 FF, meaning that the planter was left with the still considerable return of 12,510 FF.

However, while cocoa revenues were earned only during the cocoa sale/trading seasons, real estate properties provided regular, albeit moderate, incomes. This pattern of cash flow enabled the entrepreneurs to plan their expenses in two separate ways. The first category of expenses encompassed the costs of keeping up the plantations (payment of laborers' salaries; dowries to provide some workers' with wives), constructing new houses, and maintaining existing rental properties. These expenses could be referred to as purely economic, since they were devoted to creating wealth and renewing resources. Because these expenditures arose sporadically and required substantial investments, income from cocoa plantations usually covered them.

The second category of expenditures included payment of living allowances; house repairs; receptions and hospitality; and customary expenses such as gifts, family members' dowries, and financial aid to members of the dependents' networks (Derrick 1979:445). These expenses could be qualified as social, because, unlike those in the first category, they were absorbed into so-called unproductive sectors. They were quite frequent, some occurring on a monthly basis and paid for by income from house rentals.

Monthly reimbursements of bank debts and payment of school fees were covered by both plantations and real estate incomes. But Duala entrepreneurs also spent substantial sums of money on luxury goods: motorcycles, imported furniture, and clothes from Paris. The family budget of a rich Duala businessman in the 1920s listed a total of 1,760 FF for clothing, nearly half his budget of 3,977 francs (Derrick 1979:216, 445).[9] Yet, the significance of the social expenses and of Duala consumption habits should be reviewed in the context of their economic strategy.

At first glance, there were two main categories in the Duala entrepreneur's budget: the "productive" investments of cocoa revenues, and the daily "unproductive" expenses of moderate real estate earnings. But regarding the importance of social networks in the Duala entrepreneurial strategy, these so-called unproductive expenditures counted for nothing less than long-term investment, since they were employed to create, maintain, or renew the very human resources that enabled the production of wealth. Besides, the economic aspect of display and consumption of luxury goods should also be stressed. Duala entrepreneurs showed off their riches as a self-advertisement directed to both the lower and the upper social networks: they indicated that one was a successful senior or businessman, worth working for or being allied to.

The role of these networks was still crucial during the French Mandate period. The lower networks of dependents continued to provide a cheap labor force to run Duala entrepreneurs' different businesses, while the matrimonial alliances built at the upper level provided entrepreneurs with the social resources to strengthen their economic positions and adapt their entrepreneurial attitude to the political context of the French administration. Thus in 1929, David Mandesi Bell, Franz Mudute Bell, and Erdmann Njo Eteki, three successful planters, wanted to set up a commercial company to sell cocoa directly to Europe and obtain more profit for their products.[10] Njo Eteki married Mudute Bell's sister Yonde; his daughter Irma Makongue married Mandesi Bell's son Sam (Derrick 1979:382).

The Duala also put their energy into sociopolitical agitations aimed at reversing an administrative decision regarding expropriation of their lucrative urban lands. This project dated back to the German period, and the Duala opposed its being continued by the French. Duala entrepreneurs collected money and sent a representative to Paris in 1929 to argue their case (Derrick 1979:280; Moume-Etia 1991:43). They expected support from the Senegalese-born French deputy Blaise Diagne and his friends. Diagne was related to the Duala elite through the marriage of David Mandesi Bell's daughter Maria with a Senegalese railways technician, Mamadou Yande Diop. However, there is no clear indication as to whether the Duala received the expected support from Blaise Diagne (Derrick 1979).

Because of their status in the upper social network, Duala entrepreneurs and their descendants continued to play a major role in Cameroon's sociopolitical life well into the second half of this century. In the late 1950s, Duala matrimonial links with the Bakossi chief Ntoko Epee brought them some support for Cameroonian reunification in some anglophone regions (Moume-Etia 1991:93). Sam and Jean Mandesi Bell and Gaston Kingue Jong, all sons of cocoa planters, were among those who pioneered the syndicalist movements and newspapers in Cameroon in the 1930s and 1940s.

The descendants of Duala entrepreneurs occupied the first liberal professions in Cameroon as lawyers, physicians, and journalists. They also participated in intellectual debates at the continental level. David Mandesi Diop, grandson of David Mandesi Bell, became a well-known poet; he animated the Afrocentric *Mouvement de la Négritude* and in the late 1940s, with Alioune Diop, his sister Christiane's husband, he launched the review *Présence Africaine*, which still exists in Paris (Kala-Lobë 1983).

Conclusion

Duala entrepreneurs were able during the German and French colonial administrations to retain a leading position in Cameroon due to their use of social relations and their entrepreneurial networks. The effectiveness of social networks was somewhat eroded by the introduction of wage labor. In addition, the adaptation to capitalistic labor relationships had its share of difficulties. The most critical was the late payment of the tax tokens and laborers' salaries.

Social networks and human resources were the key factors of Duala entrepreneurial strategy. In that respect, social expenses should not be condemned as a mere waste of surpluses resulting from an antieconomic attitude ingrained in a presumably African—in this case, Duala—culture.[11] There is, in fact, no "social rational" separate from a "purely economic rational" in African systems of production; both interact and inform each other (Mbembe 1992; Labazee 1992). This study has put forward the rationale behind social expenses and highlighted how the social element was integrated within the framework of economic actions.

Contrary to assumptions made in many mainstream analyses, it takes more than capital savings and hard work to succeed in entrepreneurial ventures. The case of Duala entrepreneurs emphasizes the importance of both the entrepreneurial strategy and social networks. However, this study does not use the cultural generalizations of postmodernist thought to claim an "African" pattern of entrepreneurship. Considered closely, there is indeed only a difference of degree between the Duala social networks during the colonial period and more current market networks that determined the success in Latin America of immigrant Jews, Lebanese, Arabs, Italians, and Germans (Hirschman 1970; Gillis et al. 1990), as well as that of Chinese communities in many other parts of the world, and that of Indians, Lebanese, and Chinese in postcolonial Africa.

In that regard, this study is an invitation not to couch the weaknesses of current African entrepreneurs exclusively in terms of lack of capital, nor to blame cultural barriers. More significant is the existence of valuable partnerships, as well as the connection and access to market networks and information. These are some of the factors that can empower and strengthen African entrepreneurs more effectively than just more finance capital.

Beyond the obvious existence of a local spirit and model of entrepreneurship already observed elsewhere in precolonial and colonial Africa, this study helps to test the validity of some of the most widely accepted theoretical frameworks presented by both economists and socioeconomists. The information recorded from the experiences of the Duala entrepreneurs of Cameroon challenges the universal applicability of both the Braudelian prerequisites of capitalism and the Weberian view of entrepreneurial spirit as the only way to entrepreneurial success.

Notes

1. *Duala* refers to the people, *Douala* to family names and to the name of the city.

2. Lederbogen, W. "Der Charakter der Duala und ihre Erziehung zur Arbeit," *Kamerun in Reichstag*: 1902, 450–52, 486–87; 1903, 5.

3. For details, see Archives Nationales de Yaoundé. German materials 4/926, agronomist Frommhold's report, 26 October 1913, 62.

4. Mandesi Bell's family archives; several business letters. Buea Archives No Ta 1933/1, Kunz Kwa Mutome to British Resident, 28 April 1933.

5. David Mandesi Bell's will, Mandesi Bell's family archives (MBFA); Rudolph Douala Manga Bell's will, 7 August 1914, Douala Bell's family archives.

6. *Die Deutsche Kolonial-Geseztgebung*, vols. 11 and 12. Berlin: S. Mittler und Sohn, 1908, 1909.

7. The first attempt was made on the coast in 1890, and the experiment failed. A sale contract between D. Mandesi Bell and a landowner stated that the latter had already planted some cocoa trees in the land sale (MBFA, sale contract, 25 April 1894).

8. Von Brauchitsch, who served as chief of the region in Douala, might have known of the existence of Duala cocoa plantations, but probably not of their scale. Many Duala informants recall his name as someone who supported their economic development (Reichskolonialamt, for the Archives of German Colonial Office, 4301, Report from German Consulate, Lugano, 26 March 1929).

9. Pastor Russillon, who lived in Douala at that time, condemned the pattern of consumption among wealthy Duala, which he saw as harmful to a productive economic activity and contrary to the Christian virtue of moderation.

10. Archives of Aix-en-Provence, Agence FOM, C 1003 D 3518, Report to Commissioner of Republic in Cameroon. 2 August 1929.

11. Warnier (1993) uses a simplistic framework to conceptualize and divide the Cameroonian people into two main cultural groups: the Grassfield and the Muslim Fulani entrepreneurs with an "ethos of retention," whom he refers to as *"tirelire vitale"*; the others, including the Duala and the Beti people, with an "ethos of munificence," also referred to as *"politique du ventre"* (Bayart 1989).

References Cited

Austen, Ralph. 1983. The Metamorphoses of Middlemen: The Duala, Europeans, and the Cameroon Hinterland. *International Journal of African Historical Studies* 16 (1):1–24.

———. 1987. *African Economic History.* London: James Currey and Heinemann.

Ayittey, George. 1991. *Indigenous African Institutions.* New York: Transnational Publishers.

Bayart, Jean-François. 1989. *L'Etat en Afrique: La Politique du ventre.* Paris: Fayard.

Bayart, Jean-François, Achille Mbembe, and Cormi Toulabor. 1992. *La Politique par le bas en Afrique noire.* Paris: Karthala.

Brutsch, Jean-René. 1955. Les Traités camerounais. *Etudes Camerounaises* 47–48:9–42.

Clarence-Smith, William-Gervase. 1993. Plantation Versus Smallholder Production of Cocoa: The Legacy of the German Period in Cameroon. In *Itinéraires d'accumulation au Cameroun,* edited by P. Konings and P. Geshiere. Paris: ACS-Karthala.

Cooper, Frederick, et al. 1993. *Confronting Historical Paradigms.* Madison: University of Wisconsin Press.

Derrick, Jonathan. 1979. Duala under the French Mandate, 1916 to 1936. Ph.D. dissertation, School of Oriental and African Studies, London.

———. 1989. Elitisme colonial au Cameroun: Le Cas des Douala dans les années trente. In *Histoire du Cameroun,* edited by M. Z. Njeuma. Paris: L'Harmattan.

Dominik, Hans von. 1908. *Von Atlantik zum Tschadsee.* Berlin: S. Mittler und Sohn.

Duignan, Peter, and L. H. Gann. 1975. The Economics of Colonialism. In *Colonialism in Africa, 1870–1960.* Stanford: Hoover Institution.

Etoga, Eily Florent. 1971. *Sur les chemins du développement.* Yaounde: CEPER.

Gillis, Malcom, et al. 1990. *Economie du développement.* Brussels: DeBoeck.

Gouellain, René. 1975. *Douala: Ville et histoire.* Paris: Institut d'Ethnologie, Musée de l'Homme.

Guyer, Jane. 1980. Head Tax, Social Structure, and Rural Incomes in Cameroon, 1922–1937. *Cahiers d'Etudes Africaines* 20 (77):305–29.

———. 1981. The Depression and the Administration in South-Central Cameroun. *African Economic History* 10:67–77.

Hirschman, Albert. 1970. *A Bias for Hope.* New Haven: Yale University Press.

Jaeck, Hans-Peter. 1960. Die deutsche Annexion. In *Kamerun unter deutscher Kolonialherrschaft,* edited by H. Stoecker. Berlin: Rütten und Loening.

Kala-Lobë, Iyiwe. 1983. "Ensemble" avec mon frère. In *David Diop. Témoignages-etudes.* Paris: Présence Africaine.

Kennedy, Paul. 1988. *African Capitalism.* Cambridge: Cambridge University Press.

Labazee, Pascal. 1992. Les Patrons de commerce Ouest-Africains: Hommes d'affaires ou spéculateurs? (mimeo).

Mbembe, Achille. 1992. Pouvoir, violence, et accumulation. In *Le Politique par le bas en Afrique noire,* edited by Bayart, Mbembe, and Toulabor, q.v.

Michel, Marc. 1970. Les plantations allemandes du Mont Cameroun. *Revue Française d'Histoire d'Outre-Mer* 57 (207):182–213.

Morgen, Curt von. 1982. *A travers le Cameroun, du sud au nord*. Paris: Serge Fleury.

Moume-Etia, Léopold. 1991. *Cameroun: Les Années ardentes*. Paris: Jalivres.

Van Slageren, Jaap. 1972. *Les Origines de l'Eglise Evangélique du Cameroun*. Leiden: E. J. Brill.

Warnier, Jean-Pierre. 1993. *L'Esprit d'entreprise au Cameroun*. Paris: Karthala.

Warnier, Jean-Pierre, and Dieudonné Miaffo. 1993. *Accumulation et ethos de la notabilité chez les Bamileke*. Paris: African Studies Center–Karthala.

10. Managers and Their Entrepreneurs: Power and Authority in Indigenous Private Manufacturing Firms in Nigeria

Chikwendu Christian Ukaegbu

Until about a decade ago, most Nigerian business people concentrated their investments in trade rather than in manufacturing. The bulk of indigenous investment went into wholesale and retail commerce, export and import activities, and transport. Some of these trading businesses became prosperous, and their owners achieved considerable wealth and prominence in their respective communities. Although trading ventures are still widespread, some wealthy Nigerian entrepreneurs have begun to invest in medium and large manufacturing and processing ventures. They are part of a small "industrializing elite." A fundamental question is whether this growing class of indigenous industrialists is capable of creating a sustainable industrial base for Nigeria.

Entrepreneurs play many roles in the process of industrialization. They innovate, open new markets, and bear risks; they find new combinations of materials, processes, and products. They create employment, commercialize new inventions, and invest in new opportunities (Marsden 1990; Kilby 1971; Schumpeter 1961). Obeng (1988) states that in order for entrepreneurs to fulfill these roles, they must possess certain qualities of leadership. These qualities include imagination, foresight, motivation, and drive. Further, Obeng specifies, the entrepreneur-manager should be proficient in such skills as decision making, organizing, delegating, and communicating.

Although studies of economic change in Africa have shed considerable light on certain characteristics and dynamics of the indigenous bourgeoisie (Lubeck 1987; Hopkins 1988; Riddel 1990; Forrest 1993; Brautigam 1994; Himbara 1994), not much is known about organizational processes in the growing numbers of medium- and large-scale private manufacturing ventures. These organizational processes include power relations between owner-entrepreneurs and their managers, as well as the effect of those relations on the operation and success of the enterprise. This chapter is primarily concerned with identifying and evaluating the organizational skills of owner-entrepreneurs; it addresses this issue by analyzing how managers perceive them.

Examination of the managerial perceptions of entrepreneurs is important for several reasons. It helps highlight organizational factors that may handicap or facilitate the goal of enterprise survival. It allows informed suggestions to be made about the effective management of the enterprises. Socialization theory holds that society, or the group, is a mirror through which the individual evaluates acceptability or nonacceptability of his or her values and actions. Similarly, this chapter suggests that by using managers as mirrors of the owner-entrepreneur's behavior, entrepreneurs can be prompted to change detrimental behavior or encouraged to retain profitable patterns of action.

Methodology

Data for this study were obtained from medium- and large-scale indigenous private manufacturing enterprises in four states of eastern Nigeria: Abia, Anambara, Enugu, and Imo. I collected observational, survey, and interview data during six months of intensive fieldwork in 1991. The primary objective of the study was to explore the extent to which entrepreneurial and managerial roles in indigenous private manufacturing firms facilitate or handicap the chances of survival and success of the firms. The results presented in this chapter are based primarily on data collected from managers and owner-entrepreneurs in firms founded and owned by private Nigerian businessmen and employing more than fifty workers. (Owners may be individuals, families, or partners.)

A total of twenty functioning manufacturing firms participated in the study. Firms were selected from a variety of industries: pharmaceutical, paper, shoe, automobile parts, machine tools, beverage, plastics, paints, chemicals, and grain processing. A total of 114 questionnaires were distributed to managers; 78 were returned, and 73 were usable.

As a highly literate group, the managers completed their questionnaires themselves; additionally, in-depth interviews were conducted with a sample of thirty of them. Questions were asked about working conditions and about the responsibility factors of work, managerial practice, structure of ownership and control, attitudes of entrepreneurs, organizational commitment, present and future problems of the enterprises, and the managers' suggestions as to how such problems could be solved.

By contrast, the owner-entrepreneurs were generally reluctant to complete their questionnaires, for several reasons. They had less time because they were constantly busy and itinerant, in search of production inputs and business networks. In addition, some could not write and so could not fill out the questionnaires themselves. Those who attempted to cooperate were selective of the items to which they responded. Personal interviews with them proved more useful, but only eleven entrepreneurs were interviewed. Consequently, the data on entrepreneurs are not as extensive as those on managers.

The Theoretical Context

An organization is a collection of people working together in a division of labor to achieve a common purpose (Schermerhorn, Hunt, and Osborn 1982). The collectivity may be a social club, a voluntary association, a religious body, a government agency, or a profit-making business enterprise. In formal business organizations, participants are normatively arranged in a hierarchy, each with specific roles and responsibilities. Dahrendorf (1959) and Kerr (1964) contend that in a postcapitalist industrial society, ownership of the means of production is widely dispersed among numerous stockholders, while effective control is exercised by professional managers and executives. High-level managers may own significant amounts of shares in their corporations. Their controlling power does not derive from this partial ownership, but from occupancy of positions of authority within the enterprise (Dahrendorf 1959).

By contrast, in countries in early stages of industrialization, family ownership of the means of production is more common (Kerr 1964). Enterprise control tends to be determined primarily by ownership, rather than by expert or managerial knowledge. This can contribute to a struggle for power between the owner and the manager, a struggle for control of the enterprise's operations.

According to Weber (1978), power is the probability that one actor within a social relationship will be in a position to carry out his or her will despite resistance. Authority is the probability that a command with a specific content will be obeyed by a given group of persons. The important difference between power and authority, Dahrendorf (1959) suggests, is that whereas power is tied to the personality of the individual, authority is always associated with social positions and roles.

Following Dahrendorf, therefore, it is hypothesized that as owners of production resources, entrepreneurs of indigenous private enterprises command power rather than authority. As employers upon whom the livelihood of the managers depends, entrepreneurs can wield coercive power and issue rewards to elicit managerial compliance with their entrepreneurial strategies even if these are not in the best interest of the enterprise (French and Raven 1959).

Although they worked in enterprises owned by sole entrepreneurs, most of the managers in this study had received training that had prepared them for work in corporations with depersonalized ownership structures and modes of administration. In that regard, managers would expect the expert knowledge that they had acquired through university education to be put to the best use possible. They would also expect the bureaucratic elements of the division of labor and delegation of authority to apply. Put somewhat differently, managers would expect the principles of equality of authority and responsibility to guide their daily work activities. By this principle, Fayol (1949) prescribes that once a responsibility is assigned to a subordinate, commensurate authority must be allocated for effective consummation of the assignment.

Ideally, bureaucratic control is achieved through directives coming from the top of the pyramid (Burack 1975). Empirical assessments of bureaucracies have, however, shown that overconcentration of controlling power at the top is a constant source of alienation among incumbents below. The implicit assumption is that the subordinate is lazy, short-sighted, selfish, and liable to make mistakes; has poor judgment; and may even be dishonest (Haire 1962). This perception of human behavior is incompatible with the skill, expertise, confidence, and sense of autonomy that professional education instills in managers. Hence, it is likely for them to have negative perceptions of entrepreneurs if the latter are seen to concentrate much organizational power in themselves.

In organizations, power and authority find expression in the ability of incumbents to exercise the freedom to make decisions relevant to or commensurate with the positions they occupy. In that regard, managers will be enthusiastic to use their knowledge and abilities to allocate resources, design work processes, motivate workers, and contribute to redirection of the organization if the latter is perceived to be moving toward an unprofitable path. When managers cannot exercise initiative, managerial commitment to the organization may wane.

Organizational commitment is the degree to which an employee identifies with the goals of the organization and is willing to exert effort to help it succeed (Kalleberg and Berg 1987). Mueller, Wallace, and Price (1992) define it as the degree of an employee's affective, or emotional, attachment to the organization. This emotional attachment that influences the employee to stay or leave depends on his or her assessment of the profitability of continuing the current employment against that of working elsewhere (Halaby and Weaklien 1989). In some cases, the decision to stay may be more a function of the lack of preferred alternatives than a reaction to the attractions of the present job.

Some questions to be asked are: How do managers perceive their entrepreneurs? How much are the former involved in decision making, and is that involvement related to power structure in the enterprise? What are the implications of the perceived entrepreneurial behavior for the future of the investment?

Medium- and Large-Scale Indigenous Private Manufacturing Firms: Structure and Characteristics

As stated earlier, the interest of local businessmen in medium- and large-scale manufacturing started to increase about a decade ago, particularly in eastern Nigeria. About 80 percent of the firms used in this study started operations in the 1980s, primarily between 1980 and 1988.

Also, 60 percent of the firms were sole proprietorships and 25 percent were partnerships ranging from two to eleven persons. The remaining 15 percent had previously been sole proprietorships and had become public a short while before this study. Founders of sole proprietorships and partnerships often included wives, children, and other relatives as part of the ownership. In that regard, 85 percent of the firms (that is, seventeen of the twenty) were family owned. Where a firm or a group of firms was owned by an individual, the owner was usually known as chairman or managing director. In the case of partnerships, one of the owners was appointed chairman and the co-owners were called directors.

Of the founders, 76 percent had little formal education, having started as traders and contractors, while 24 percent were university graduates and former employees of the civil service and multinational corporations. Those entrepreneurs who were illiterate tended to depend on their managers to read business letters and other information to them in order to make organizational decisions. However, being illiterate had not prevented them from becoming effective entrepreneurs. They had been able to assemble these large production facilities because of hard work, creativity, risk taking, and ability to perceive and pursue new economic opportunities.

Analysts of early European industrialization have shown that lack of formal education was no handicap to entrepreneurial success among pioneers (Bendix 1974). The Nigerian entrepreneurs interviewed had few years of formal schooling, but they were high in entrepreneur-specific human capital, as shown in their prior self-employment experience in other forms of private enterprise.

In some of the firms, the owners did not physically participate in administration. Instead they preferred to pay greater attention to their trading business, while a relative was appointed deputy managing director to oversee the daily affairs of the factory. In some cases, the deputy managing directors did not have their offices at the factory site. Rather, they occasionally visited the factory from their own trading post or from the trading headquarters of the founder. At times, this surrogate owner had little or no knowledge of production management. It was this kind of a situation that prompted a general manager of a brewery to say: "This company is being run by remote control; managers or executives are here as figure heads."

Most of the firms under consideration were owned by individuals, and a few by partners or families. The monetary value of each ran into millions of naira. Each had a significant amount of land space, perhaps in anticipation of future expansions. They employed or had the capacity to employ more than fifty workers, and 87 percent of the firms employed more than one hundred workers. Most of the employees who occupied managerial and high-level technical positions were university graduates or had other forms of tertiary education. Founders emphasized academic specialization in the recruitment of managers.

The data in table 10.1 show that a majority of the managers (78 percent) had higher education. It was found that most of the managers with low education had previously worked for the entrepreneurs in other businesses prior to the founding of the manufacturing firms. Others were individuals who had acquired considerable technical experience from working in other firms and had been recruited to provide some technical leadership in the new firm.

Because these production organizations demanded scientific and technical knowledge, science and engineering graduates made up the majority (51 percent) of the managerial cadre (table 10.1). Also, a knowledge of business theory, as well as practical management experience, were felt to be necessary, and 40 percent had these qualifications. A significant percentage of the managers had degrees in various areas of business studies (accounting, finance, marketing, personnel management, and public relations). In addition, other data showed that 33 percent of the managers had master's degrees in business administration.

In the course of the interviews, two main forms of managerial recruit-

Table 10.1. Education specializations of managers (frequency and percent)

	N	%
Educational attainment		
Low (primary and secondary)	12	16
Intermediate (ordinary diploma)	4	6
High (higher diploma, bachelors, masters)	57	78
Total	73	100
Areas of specialization		
Arts and social sciences	5	9
Business studies	23	40
Science and engineering	29	51
Total	57	100

ment were identified: the "sympathetic" and the "conventional." Sympathetic recruitment refers to entrepreneurs hiring managers in order to help them become gainfully employed. The managers who were hired had usually been managers before but were now unemployed as a result of retirement, dismissal, or because their company had gone out of business. In response to a question about how he had recruited his managers, one entrepreneur stated: "I employed [my general manager] to help him. He had a problem where he was before. But he is intelligent and experienced."

Asked the same question, another entrepreneur said, "Some of my managers have worked in other places before. They might have been sacked because of small things. When I see such people, I try to help them because I can tolerate them."

When asked how they had lost their previous positions, some managers said that they had had "problems" with their previous employers, but none stated the nature of the problems. In many cases, managers who had been recruited because of sympathetic considerations were kinsmen of entrepreneurs, or their friends, or former business or political associates, or persons recommended by other close associates.

Conventional recruitment, by contrast, refers to managerial selection based primarily on objective criteria related to the requirements of the position. Managers in this study were recruited in both ways.

The average annual salary of the managers was 11,310 naira (the same as a senior lecturer's starting salary before the revised salary scale for academics went into effect in 1992). Most of the companies provided housing and company cars for their managers, or provided housing and automobile expense allowances. Some of the companies had health clinics, while others contracted with external physicians through retainer fees. Pensions and gratuities were not common, and there tended to be no clear lines for promotion into higher positions. Opportunities for additional training were rare. However, some entrepreneurs sent relatives hired as managers for additional training, either overseas or within Nigeria, with the intention of preparing the trained relatives for higher positions in the firm.

Managers' Perceptions of Entrepreneurial Behavior: Aspects of Working Conditions, Power, and Control

Managers generally recognized and appreciated the entrepreneurial abilities of their employers. Most managers regarded their entrepreneurs as energetic, creative, and courageous individuals who deserved respect for establishing a major manufacturing enterprise. During the interviews, the managers also exhibited characteristics of high intelligence, insight, and vision. They were analytical, articulate, and had good communication skills. In their critical evaluations of their organizations, they emphasized issues that exposed the weaknesses of their enterprises not as a result of prejudice, but as problems requiring sound and durable solutions. Managers who were not relatives of entrepreneurs tended to be more critical and analytical of enterprise problems than were relatives. Relatives tended to be more protective of entrepreneurial weaknesses and often evaded the interviewer's questions about problems in their organizations.

Drawing from his experience as a senior manager in a large family business, Tuyo (1990:53) is quite critical of such lack of objectivity by relatives: "Regrettably, the average family business director is unqualified to hold his position. Not only does he lack an understanding of the company and its industry, his kinship ties to the founder preclude the effective discharge of his evaluative role as a director. Several family business directors are collaborators rather than directors. They exist merely to rubber-stamp the dictates of the owner who, of course, is always the Chairman or Managing Director."

Much of the managers' criticisms against entrepreneurs centered around an owner's hold on the real power and authority within a company. In a few cases where general managers were given a free hand to provide leadership in the management of the enterprise, they exhibited entrepreneurism. For example, they demonstrated the ability to recognize and analyze problems, implement solutions, and take advantage of opportunities for constructive change. Most of the managers felt that owners were too dominant. This caused them to feel uncertain of their positions of authority within the organization.

The responses in table 10.2 show that a majority of the managers (87 percent) saw their work as challenging. Much of the challenge, especially among those in technical divisions, derived from long hours of work (including working late and on public holidays), production deadline pressures, and the requirement for making technical decisions on the job. Most said they were actively involved in the daily and overall operations of their companies and felt that their ideas were respected, with many of their suggestions implemented (79 percent and 86 percent, respectively). But the extent of some of the managers' involvement in decision making appeared to be somewhat limited; 44 percent agreed with the statement made by one of them on the questionnaire that "the owner makes all the decisions in the company."

In most cases, the owner and founder was the sole signatory to company accounts. For example, one brewery suspended production for a week because the owner was on a business trip overseas and was not available to release funds for the procurement of raw materials. The production manager of the company, a highly experienced brewer who had been attracted from a leading multinational corporation, expressed extreme dissatisfaction. "He never lets go," he said. "He will pick up the best crop of managers but [he] never allows them to use their brains, particularly where

Table 10.2. Managerial perceptions of selected work characteristics

	Agree		Disagree	
	N	%	N	%
Responsibility factors				
My tasks are challenging	61	87	9	13
Owner makes all decisions	29	44	37	56
As a manager I don't know what goes on in the company	14	21	53	79
I can't put my ideas into use in my present job	9	14	53	86
Extrinsic factors				
I am satisfied with my salary	26	38	42	62
Promotions are fast here	12	32	45	68
Commitment factors				
As soon as I get a job elsewhere I will leave this place	21	33	42	67
My future is in this company and I will work hard for the company	56	82	13	18
I want to work in another company	19	31	43	69

money is concerned. So for three or four days there will be no brewing operations, and none can start up until he comes back from abroad."

Of the twenty functioning firms in the study, in only five of them did managers say that significant power had been delegated to them or to other supervisors in the company. Two of these firms were owned by highly educated entrepreneurs who had previously been employees of multinational corporations; one was owned by an uneducated entrepreneur who had an executive director with a doctorate degree in business administration. The fourth firm was headed by a general manager who was a younger brother of the absentee owner; thus, the general manager's freedom and authority could have been dependent on the familial relationship. The fifth company was owned by two illiterate partners who had concentrated on their trading activities and left the factory in the hands of several managers, one of whom was a relative of one of the partners.

Table 10.2 also shows that a high proportion of the managers were dissatisfied with the extrinsic rewards of work. Apart from unhappiness with their salaries, many cited dissatisfaction with dead-end jobs that had no clear lines of promotion. However, a large majority of the managers (82 percent) said they were committed to staying with their companies. This high level of commitment was probably due to the tight labor market in Nigeria, making it difficult for people to secure alternative employment.

Commitment to staying with an organization may also be due to the relationship between the employee and the owner. This is a function of sympathetic recruitment. Managers hired through sympathetic recruitment tend to remain at the organization even when they are dissatisfied, in order to show their appreciation to the entrepreneurs for their help when the manager was seeking employment. Kinship relationships between an entrepreneur and a manager also influence the latter to remain with the enterprise despite dissatisfaction with the job.

Apart from the monopoly of power and unwillingness to delegate authority, managers complained about other behaviors of owners. Most entrepreneurs were averse to the formation of workers' unions, but many managers saw unions as avenues to opening up or improving employer-employee communication. Managers who discouraged unions often did so to go along with the wishes of the entrepreneur.

Some managers were also exasperated by the entrepreneurs' habits of conspicuous consumption, which they referred to as "high living." This included taking ceremonial titles such as chief, expending large sums of money on festivals and ceremonies, and making large social or political financial donations. One personnel manager emphatically resented the behavioral pattern of entrepreneurs, saying: "Sometimes the owner uses funds to acquire prestigious property for millions of naira but he is unable to provide 40,000 naira for paying monthly salaries. The chief engineer needed 3,000 naira to buy parts to repair a broken machine. It took him two weeks to get it. But within the same period, a political aspirant got 100,000 naira as a donation, yet at the end of the same month workers had to wait for six days before they were paid."

Because of the spontaneity with which owners, and sometimes members of their families, withdrew and used company funds, the accounting departments at these companies were rendered inefficient and, in some cases, irrelevant. Entrepreneurs were also said to promote interpersonal conflict among the employees by acting on gossip. In one interview, an entrepreneur endorsed gossip as a means through which both workers and owners may achieve their objectives.

In the questionnaire, respondents were asked (1) as a manager, what in your opinion are the problems faced by this company now? and (2) what future problems or concerns do you anticipate within the enterprise?

Table 10.3 shows that most of the managers believed that the current problems of their firms were due to inadequate operational resources. Perhaps protecting themselves, few cited poor management as being a major problem. The problem of resources as specified by managers included insufficient equipment and spare parts, financial problems caused by excessive borrowing and high interest rates, inadequate supply of raw materials, unreliable supply of utilities, and import difficulties attributed to high duties and scarcity of foreign exchange. Those (27 percent) who listed managerial problems referred to broader problems such as too much concentration of control by the owner, unmotivating working conditions, misuse of company funds, poor marketing of company products, and unclear policies toward management by the owner.

The managers were asked what changes or problems they anticipated in the future. They noted that there would eventually come a time when the owner would no longer be able to direct the affairs of the enterprise because of old age or death. About 40 percent of the managers expected their companies to develop management problems in the future, compared with the 27 percent who listed this as a current problem (table 10.3).

The managers mentioned specific problems that they foresaw could arise in the future, including conflicts among the managers or within the family, inefficiency and waste due to low staff loyalty, and a real possibility that the enterprise itself would cease to exist.

Six nonfunctioning firms were also included in this study. In three of

Table 10.3. Managers' perceptions of present and future problems of their enterprises (in percentages)

	Present problems		Future problems	
	N	%	N	%
None	0	0	17	35
Inadequate work resources	33	73	12	25
Poor management	12	27	19	40
Total	45	100	48	100

them, the founders had died and the operations had been shut down by court order as a result of disputes among the owner's children over ownership and assets; often the children were products of polygynous marriages. This situation in itself warrants further study to determine its effect on succession and on the long-term sustainability of enterprises in Africa. The other three of the six nonfunctioning firms had closed down because of lack of trust and cooperation among partners.

These findings are paradoxical and ironic. On the one hand, credit must be given to the owners-founders for putting together the resources to establish and maintain major manufacturing enterprises for as long as some of them had done so. On the other hand, the future of enterprises such as these is uncertain, due to the lack of a plan for the leadership of the business after the owner is no longer able to exert control.

Table 10.4 lists managers' suggestions of ways to improve a company's possibility of survival. One way was to sell company shares to the public, thus allowing the enterprise to acquire a larger amount of operating capital, and, just as important, facilitating the "deconcentration" of power and delegation of authority. The latter result is likely in enterprises that "go public," because management has to be accountable to its shareholders in making decisions, particularly in the disbursement of revenues.

Whether or not selling stock in companies is a realistic alternative is questionable under current economic conditions in Nigeria. However, deconcentration of power and delegation of authority by appropriate means would allow more important operational decisions within an enterprise to be made by qualified professionals.

Conclusion

Kerr (1964) observes that in intermediate stages of industrialization, managers as hired subordinates of proprietary capitalists or of family patriarchs may feel indignant at taking orders from persons they deem to be

Table 10.4. Managers' suggestions for enterprise durability

	N	%
Sell shares to public	15	22
Decentralize and delegate authority	20	30
Provide more work resources	24	36
Improve working conditions	8	12
Total	67	100

technically incompetent. Managers seem to feel that owners sometimes use their control of an enterprise to the point of autocracy. One explanation is that most owners start business as traders, making use of the services of a small number of illiterate and personal servants who only take orders and run errands. Upon the establishment of complex production firms that employ many people with diverse skills, experience, and needs, most entrepreneurs are unable to recognize that a new approach to business management is required. Therefore, the autocratic paternalistic behavior exhibited in small-scale trade remains dominant. This is supported by Nafziger (1988), who states that conservatism about delegation of authority and paternalism in employer-employee relationships are two of the setbacks of family entrepreneurship in developing countries.

Another explanation relates to trust. Most entrepreneurs explicitly expressed reluctance to give a free hand to their managers because of what they described as subordinates' insatiability, which had the potential of leading the latter to divert organizational resources for personal use. According to a co-owner of a machine tools factory, "Running a corporation within the African environment is complex because you have many factors to deal with. Poverty is glaring. The worker needs shelter. If he can lie, embezzle, or gossip to get that, he will do so." This is consistent with Kilby (1988), who observes that African entrepreneurs often complain that raw material wastage, pilferage, and embezzlement by employees contribute to the rising costs of production.

Entrepreneurs also tend to feel that a democratic or participatory administration will expose their managers and workers to the sources of their business success. This orientation finds practical expression in entrepreneurial secrecy. Forrest (1993) refers to the same phenomenon as a culture of secrecy that effectively blocks delegation, rules out partnership, and undermines chances for succession. Entrepreneurial secrecy is not the same as the conventionally known industrial secrecy, in which enterprises protect their research results or new production processes to maintain an edge over competing firms. Rather, it refers to the tendency and practice of owners to keep to themselves the strategic knowledge on which their firms' operations are based.

Entrepreneurial secrecy has several elements. The owner-founders are the only persons who know the amount and sources of the company's financial and physical resources. They are the sole allocators of strategic organizational resources, especially money. They retain exclusive knowledge of and interaction with crucial business networks (both within and outside the country), such as those concerned with borrowing and lending, foreign exchange, and supply of essential capital equipment.

Entrepreneurial secrecy gives the enterprise an appearance of viability as long as the owner remains in control. But it portends enormous costs upon the exit of the founder. When the founder dies, for instance, business associates of the enterprise may be lost, sources of operational resources may not be known, and steady supply of production input may cease to exist. The result is managerial confusion and, perhaps, the death also of the enterprise. This scenario approximates "corporeuthanasia," a term used to describe the owner's act of willfully killing off the business he loves by failing to provide during his lifetime for a viable organization with clear continuity (Tuyo 1990:53). Excess control by entrepreneurs coupled with their imperviousness to change are very high on the list of causes of corporeuthanasia in Nigeria (Tuyo 1990).

The question is what is to be done. Some managers suggest that their enterprises sell shares to the public to diversify ownership. Expectedly, a wider ownership structure may diffuse power, reduce the burden of administration on the owner-founder, attract more funds, professionalize management, and introduce a greater degree of administrative rationality. However, there are certain preconditions before a company can go public. The company's books should show that the probability of sustained profitability is high. The feasibility of continued acquisition of inputs and sustained operations should also be favorable. And potential stockholders should develop confidence in the marketability of the products. Just as important, the enterprise should have a systematic accounting procedure. Many of the indigenous private firms under consideration do not yet possess these qualities. Hence these preconditions constitute constraints to their being listed on the stock market.

However, for most managers, entrepreneurial willingness is even more problematic than the official constraints. This skepticism derives from the jealous affection with which entrepreneurs guard and manage their enterprises. The owner of a chemical plant reacted to a question about going public thus: "You would not like somebody to squander what you have taken so many years to build." In the same vein, the owner of a large shoe factory said, "If we go public, a lot of ideas and intrigues will come that will ruin the company. Going public will destroy our ideas."

Not only may many entrepreneurs find it difficult to relinquish power and control, they are not likely to subject themselves to the financial discipline required of public liability companies. Hence the suggestion that enterprises sell shares to the public at this stage of their development is not likely to be a viable option. It is therefore an option that should be left to time and the forces of change. Owners of family businesses should make deliberate efforts to direct the education of some of their children in areas that equip them to acquire relevant managerial and technical competence for effective participation in the management of the enterprises. Where an owner has no children, capable members of the extended family should be incorporated. This prescription is based on the assumption that the goals of the enterprise will usually coincide with the aspirations of family members. It is an endorsement of patrimonial management in which ownership, major policy-making positions, and a significant proportion of other top jobs in the establishment are held by members of the extended family. According to Kerr (1964), if members of the family are competent, well educated, and diligent, patrimonial management (which recorded success in Japan and Germany) can be quite dynamic, and family enterprise can be an effective agent of industrialization.

However, it may happen that neither the children of the founders nor the members of their extended family are interested in, or capable of, playing the role required of them for effective patrimonial management. Therefore, in addition to encouraging active involvement of members of the family, the owner-founders should involve their managers in decision making, as well as exposing them to the strategic knowledge on which the enterprise operations are based. A combination of patrimonial and professional management is useful because where one system fails, the other acts as a buffer by which the enterprise can be sustained.

Deconcentration of entrepreneurial power and control cannot take place without some conscious intervention. Specifically, owner-founders require focused education about the demands and complexities of formal organization within informal ownership structures. The substance of such an education should include the importance of deconcentration, the benefits of cultivating financial discipline, and ways of building trusting relationships with their subordinates. Entrepreneurs should be made to understand that their skepticism about deconcentration and delegation can be allayed by their effective supervision of managers. They should also be helped to realize that expansions in business are facilitated by transformations in managerial practice initiated by founders and their managers (Chandler 1962, 1992).

Entrepreneurial education should enable owner-founders to internalize the benefits of providing good working conditions for employees. In this regard, in addition to other job rewards, the issue of post-employment security (gratuity and pension) should be stressed, because where it is present, it can constitute a source of employee attachment to the enterprise. But where post-employment security is absent, managers normally seek such security elsewhere. The natural result is employee turnover and its attendant costs to the enterprise.

But solutions to the problem of post-employment security should not be left to the education and discretion of entrepreneurs alone. The profit motive may prevent them from according it the attention it deserves. Government should, therefore, enact and monitor legislation making it mandatory for firms to build such security into the conditions of service. In this regard, every firm in the class under consideration should be made to submit properly documented conditions of service to the Ministries of Industries and Labor.

Apart from reinforcement of the importance of administrative rationality, the content of education for professional managers and the founders' families should stress honesty, trust, diligence, and commitment to the success of the enterprise. If this conscious intervention (through education) enables both owners and managers to recognize their mutual interests as organizational participants, an organizational culture based on convergence of interests could emerge for the long-term benefit of the enterprises and of industrial development.

Author's note: A version of this paper also appears in the *Scandinavian Journal of Development Alternatives* 16 (1) (March 1997).

References Cited

Bendix, Reinhard. 1974. *Work and Authority in Industry.* Berkeley and Los Angeles: University of California Press.

Brautigam, Deborah. 1994. African Industrialization in Comparative Perspective: The Question of Scale. In *African Capitalists in African Development,* edited by B. J. Berman and C. Leys. Boulder, Colo.: Lynne Rienner Publishers.

Burack, Elmer. 1975. *Organizational Analysis: Theory and Applications.* Hinsdale, Ill.: Dryden Press.

Chandler, Alfred D. 1962. *Strategy and Structure: Chapters in the History of the American Enterprise.* Cambridge: MIT Press.

———. 1992. Organizational Capabilities and the Economic History of the Industrial Enterprise. *Journal of Economic Perspectives* 6 (3):79–100.

Dahrendorf, Ralf. 1959. *Class and Class Conflict in Industrial Society.* Stanford: Stanford University Press.

Fayol, Henri. 1949. *General and Industrial Management.* London: Pitman Publishing Company.

Forrest, Tom. 1993. *The Advance of African Capital: The Growth of Nigerian Private Enterprise.* Charlottesville: University Press of Virginia.

French, John R., and Bertram Raven. 1959. The Social Bases of Power. In *Studies in Social Power,* edited by D. P. Cartwright. Ann Arbor: University of Michigan Press.

Haire, Mason. 1962. The Concept of Power and the Concept of Man. In *Social Science Approaches to Business Behavior,* edited by G. B. Strother. Homewood, Ill.: Dorsey Press.

Halaby, Charles N., and D. Weaklien. 1989. Worker Control and Attachment to the Firm. *American Journal of Sociology* 95 (3) (November):549–91.

Himbara, David. 1994. *Kenyan Capitalists, the State, and Development.* Boulder, Colo.: Lynne Rienner Publishers.

Hopkins, Anthony G. 1988. African Entrepreneurship: The Relevance of History to Development Economics. *Africa* 26 (2):8–28.

Kalleberg, Anne, and Ivar Berg. 1987. *Work and Industry: Structures, Markets, and Process.* New York: Plenum Press.

Kerr, Clark. 1964. *Industrialism and Industrial Man.* New York: Oxford University Press.

Kilby, Peter. 1971. *Entrepreneurship and Economic Development.* New York: Free Press.

———. 1988. Breaking the Entrepreneurial Bottleneck in Late Developing Countries: Is There a Role for Government? *Journal of Development Planning* 18:221–50.

Lubeck, Paul M. 1987. The African Bourgeoisie: Debates, Methods, and Units of Analysis. In *The African Bourgeoisie: Capitalist Development in Nigeria, Kenya, and the Ivory Coast,* edited by P. M. Lubeck. Boulder, Colo.: Lynne Rienner Publishers.

Marsden, Keith. 1990. *African Entrepreneurs: Pioneers of Development.* Washington, D.C.: World Bank.

Mueller, Charles, Jean Wallace, and James Price. 1992. Employee Commitment: Resolving Some Issues. *Work and Occupations* 19 (3):211–36.

Nafziger, E. Wayne. 1988. Society and Entrepreneurship. *Journal of Development Planning* 18:172–52.

Obeng, Ahwireng F. 1988. Entrepreneurial Revolution for the African Third World: The Case of Ghana. *Canadian Journal of Development Studies* 9 (1):19–34.

Riddel, Roger C. 1990. A Forgotten Dimension? The Manufacturing Sector in African Development. *Development Policy Review* 8 (1):5–23.

Schermerhorn, John, James Hunt, and Richard Osborn. 1982. *Managing Organizational Behavior.* New York: John Wiley and Sons.

198 | Chikwendu Christian Ukaegbu

Schumpeter, Joseph. 1961. *The Theory of Economic Development.* New York: Oxford University Press.

Tuyo, Kunle. 1990. Corporate Death of Family Businesses. *Crown Prince,* March, 53–54.

Weber, Max. 1978. *Economy and Society,* vol. 1, edited by G. Roth and C. Wittich. Berkeley and Los Angeles: University of California Press.

11. Entrepreneurial Characteristics and Business Success in Artisan Enterprises in Ghana

Barbara E. McDade

The focus of economic development in Africa has shifted from favoring the public sector and government to promoting the private sector and individual entrepreneurs. Within the private sector, the largest proportion of businesses are small-scale indigenous enterprises. These enterprises create employment, provide services, and produce goods for the majority of people in Africa. Usually owned and operated by a single individual, a few partners, or a family, small-scale enterprises gain their vitality from the ongoing actions of these individual entrepreneurs.

Certain attributes of business owners have been identified with business success (Elkan 1988; Nafziger 1977; Kilby 1971; McClelland 1961). These include education, innovation, work experience, and ethnicity. This chapter looks at the relationship between selected characteristics of entrepreneurs involved in traditional artisan enterprises in Ghana and the success of their enterprises.[1]

The artisans in this study were cane and rattan weavers in both rural and urban environments. In recent years, there has been a revival of crafts industries in the economic sector in Africa, because of both a growing middle class with disposable income and the loosening of trade restrictions (Biggs et al. 1994). Some studies have shown the contribution that a sizable rural crafts sector can make to the economies of developing countries (Tambunan 1994; Cable and Weston 1986; Rogerson 1986). World Bank and national census data taken from nineteen countries in Africa, Asia, and Latin America show that in thirteen of these countries, at least 20 percent of the rural work force is now engaged primarily in artisan and crafts activities. The urbanization of developing countries has also expanded the scope and type of artisan activities. New industries have appeared in the cities to produce modern product lines such as aluminum tools and implements, ceramic cookware, and decorative items. These newer crafts activities coexist with traditional ones, such as basket weaving and blacksmithing (Ofori-Amoah 1988). Craft production supplies utility goods such as tools, storage containers, and cooking utensils for the farm and household, as well as decorative and ceremonial artifacts. In addition, there is an international market for handicrafts exports.

In this study, business success was measured by the amount of revenues generated from sales of the crafts products. Other factors, such as length of time in business, can also be used to indicate whether a business is successful or viable. However, the urban enterprises had been in operation for an average of only three years, so longevity was not an appropriate measure in this study. And since many of the rural enterprises had no definite starting date (most of the rural artisans had begun weaving in their youth), longevity for these enterprises was not a good measure of business viability.

The data for this study were collected through personal survey interviews and observations of artisans in both rural and urban locations. The rural sample consists of forty-nine artisans from the rural village of Enyiresi, randomly selected from a population of 400 adult artisans aged eighteen and over. The urban group consists of all of the twenty cane- and rattan-weaving enterprises that could be found in the capital city of Accra. Enyiresi is the first area in Ghana where cane and rattan weaving emerged as a major occupational craft; it is known countrywide for the quality of its cane and rattan products (Asamoah 1980). Until recently, artisans who produced traditional crafts items worked primarily in rural areas, hence the small number of urban enterprises found.

The Artisan Entrepreneur

In Ghana, cane and rattan weaving is traditionally a male occupation, but women are entering this profession. Still, when the initial survey was done in 1988, there were only ten women weavers among the approximately 400 occupational weavers in Enyiresi. Of the two rural women interviewed, only one said that weaving was her main occupation. The woman in the urban group was an apprentice.

In the initial study in 1988, the average rural artisan was a married man of thirty-one years of age with a middle-school education, who had practiced weaving as an income-producing venture for seventeen years. Although born in the village of Enyiresi, where he had informally learned his craft, the artisan also had migrated to work elsewhere. In Accra, the average urban artisan's profile was similar: he was married, thirty years old, with a middle-school education. He had learned his craft as an apprentice to a master weaver or as a student in school. He had owned and operated an enterprise in Accra for about three years. Although the average age of the businesses surveyed was only three years, most of the urban artisans had been weaving for most of their adult lives. Table 11.1 summarizes the demographic characteristics of both the rural and the urban artisans.

The artisans had a higher level of education than do most Ghanaians, only one-fourth of whom have a middle school (or junior secondary school) education, compared with nearly two-thirds of the artisans. This higher level of education is consistent with the findings in other studies of entrepreneurs in Africa (for example, Kallon 1990). For most Ghanaians who reach the middle school level, formal education ends there because sec-

Table 11.1. Demographic characteristics of artisan entrepreneurs

Characteristic	Rural artisan (N = 49)	Urban artisan (N = 20)
Age		
<20 years	3	0
20s	19	9
30s	15	9
40s	10	2
50s–60s	2	0
Sex		
Male	47	19
Female	2	1
Marital status		
Married	32	14
Not married	17	6
Highest level of formal education		
None	4	1
Primary school	9	0
Middle school	32	13
Secondary	1	3
Postsecondary	3	3
Weaver training		
Parents/elders	19	4
Self-taught	17	3
Apprenticeship	9	10
School	4	3

Source: Author.

ondary schools are few and are expensive to attend; admissions are limited, and students who attend these secondary schools usually are required to live on campus.

Earlier studies of small-scale artisan enterprises in Africa have shown that a primary reason they remain small is that as soon as apprentices learn the minimum skills of the craft, they leave to start their own operation (Steel and Webster 1991; Garlick 1971). Garlick concludes that the reason for this is that most Africans do not want to work for others. This results in the continuous setting up of many micro and small enterprises that compete with each other instead of consolidating so that they may have a chance to grow into medium- to large-scale enterprises.

However, in this study, most of the Accra artisan entrepreneurs had previously worked as apprentices or paid employees in other weaving enterprises. The terms of their employment ranged from two to four years before they left to start their own businesses. In Enyiresi, two-thirds of the artisans had worked in other weaving enterprises elsewhere at some point in their careers. Thus, there seemed to be an inclination among some of the artisans to work as employees in an established enterprise for a while before starting their own business.

Determinants of Business Success among Cane and Rattan Entrepreneurs

The indicator in this study used to measure business success was amount of weekly sales revenues. Business revenue is the gross amount of sales and is not the same as artisan income. Other possible indicators for business success include profits, labor productivity, increase in assets over time, and age of the business. However, these were not used for this study, after reviewing previous studies such as that by Beveridge and Oberschall, who state that "profits are often volatile and difficult to establish accurately" (1979:208). Kennedy (1980) observes that few small African firms keep records detailing labor productivity or asset changes.

Since half of the urban enterprises in Accra in this study were less than one year old (average longevity was three years), longevity was not considered an appropriate measure. The age of the rural enterprises was ambiguous, since the artisans could not provide a definite date, in most cases, when the artisan activity had become a separate business entity.

The weekly revenue figure for the weaving enterprises, considered to be a reasonably accurate estimate, was obtained from observing production and from recording sales transactions during field research, as well as from the artisan's own records, when available.

Characteristics Associated with Business Success

This study identifies individual characteristics and behaviors of the artisan entrepreneurs that are related to success (making and sustaining sales revenues) of their businesses. The theoretical basis for this approach is found in the works of Weber, Schumpeter, and McClelland. Weber (1930) argues that the Calvinist doctrine espoused by Christian capitalists in sixteenth-century Europe encouraged a propensity to save and invest, to seek accountability in business transactions, and to see material wealth as a sign of salvation. As noted in chapter 1 of this volume, Schumpeter ([1934] 1961) believes that individuals who take risks by instituting changes or innovations are most likely to become successful entrepreneurs. By contrast, McClelland (1961) believes that entrepreneurship is related to socially induced goals for personal achievement, while Beveridge and Oberschall (1979) caution that the emphasis on individual characteristics might underestimate the complexity of societal factors and conditions that contribute to successful business enterprises. Since the focus of this study is on the individual artisan entrepreneur, the variables chosen were primarily those that involved individual characteristics, rather than economic indicators of the Ghanaian economy.

Some of the personal and business characteristics analyzed in this study were derived from previous studies of business success (Chuta and Liedholm 1985; Kennedy 1980; Beveridge and Oberschall 1979). They were divided into two descriptive categories: personal characteristics (acquired and attributive) and business characteristics. The acquired personal characteristics were education, weaver training, apprenticeship experience, previous employment experience, and migration activity. The only attributive personal characteristic considered was age.

Ethnicity, an attributive characteristic, has been used elsewhere in studies of entrepreneurial qualities (Nafziger 1977; Hagen 1962; Weber 1930). However, almost all of the residents of Enyiresi are from one large Ghanaian ethnic group, the Akan. For urban artisans, business characteristics included (1) whether the weaving operation was full time or part time; (2) number of artisans; (3) number of paid employees; (4) whether the owner planned to remain in the weaving business; (5) whether he or she had ever received a loan to start or operate the business; (6) whether the rural artisans sold to wholesale traders other than those living in Enyiresi; (7) what investments the owner would make if he or she had more money for such activity; (8) whether the enterprise had made innovations or changes in its products; and (9) a composite innovation variable that indicated actual and potential use of innovations. Ethnicity was not queried.

Of the above characteristics, innovation was of particular interest because of its relationship to entrepreneurial activity and success. Even the propensity to innovate is an important indicator for estimating economic growth potential in developing countries (Kilby 1971). However, people engaged in traditional enterprises in Africa are usually not thought of as innovative (Marsden 1990). Consequently, this survey evaluates whether these "traditional" artisans innovated, as well as if they had a propensity to do so.

Two variables were used to measure innovation. The product-change variable identified if the artisan had changed his or her products by introducing different styles, types of products, or materials. The composite variable measured the artisan's propensity to innovate now or in the future by identifying current or planned strategies to enhance the business and sales. The composite variable was composed from answers to questions about the source of the artisan's creative ideas for products, the use of various marketing methods, experience in or interest in export trade, and capability and responsiveness for increasing production. All of the characteristics (variables) from the quantitative analyses are listed in table 11.2.

Table 11.2. All characteristics of artisans used in statistical analyses of rural and urban enterprises

	Rural	Urban
Weekly revenue (in cedis)	x	x
Age of artisan in years	x	x
Formal educational level attained	x	x
Weaving learned in formal school	x	x
Weaving learned as an apprentice	x	x
Plan to remain in weaving	x	x
Received start-up or operating loan	x	x
Investment in weaving	x	x
Product change	x	x
Composite innovation variable	x	x
Full-time or part-time weaver	x	n.a.
Migrated to rural Ghana	x	n.a.
Migrated to urban Ghana	x	n.a.
Migrated outside Ghana	x	n.a.
Uses outside traders	x	n.a.
Number of paid employees	n.a.	x
Number of apprentices	n.a.	x
Experience as weaver employee	n.a.	x

Note: x means this variable was used in the analysis for the rural or urban artisan; n.a. means the variable was "not applicable" to this group.

Analysis of Characteristics Associated with Business Success

A correlation analysis of the hypothesized characteristics associated with business success is carried out to measure the strength of their association. Correlation analysis measures relationships between two variables (for example, between weekly revenue and formal education). However, it can underestimate the strength of relationships among several variables (for example, weekly revenue, formal education, migration, and number of employees).

Multiple regression analysis is used to address this deficiency. The value of multiple regression is in its ability to measure the combined influence of several independent variables interacting together. In the statistical model designed for the multiple regression analyses, weekly revenue is the dependent variable that varies among the observed enterprises due to the influence or impact of the independent variables, the previously described personal and business characteristics.

The correlations for the independent variables with weekly revenue, the business success variable, are listed in table 11.3. The correlation coefficients for rural and urban entrepreneurs are given in the same table in order to compare strength (or magnitude) of correlation (or association) for characteristics that are common to both rural and urban entrepreneurs. In table 11.3, the correlation coefficients marked with asterisks indicate the variable that has a statistically significant level (of one-on-one association) with weekly revenue.

Correlation for Personal Characteristics

For the Enyiresi rural artisans, none of the personal characteristics showed statistically significant levels of correlation with weekly revenue (business success). However, for the Accra artisans, two of the four personal characteristics showed a statistically significant correlation with business success. Both of them were related to how the artisan had learned weaving—either in a formal school setting or as a workshop apprentice. Weekly revenue had a positive correlation (0.54) with having learned to weave in a formal school setting, and it is statistically significant at the .01 level.[2]

There was also a strong correlation (-0.45) between weekly revenue and having learned to weave in an apprenticeship. This correlation is statistically significant at the .05 level. The sign is negative, but this may not necessarily imply an inverse relationship.[3] Half of the urban artisans reported they had learned the skill as apprentices, an important and common method of skills transfer in Africa.

Correlation for Business Characteristics

For the rural entrepreneurs, three business characteristics show statistically significant correlation with weekly revenue. They are whether the artisan received a start-up or operating loan (0.28), whether the artisan used traders outside of the village to market products (0.30), and the composite innovation variable (0.45). For the urban entrepreneurs, the only variable showing a significant level of correlation with weekly revenue is the number of apprentices employed. The product innovation variable, however, is second to number of apprentices in strength of association (0.29), although it is not statistically significant.

Table 11.3. Correlation analysis of business success with entrepreneurial characteristics

	Rural	Urban
Attributive personal characteristic		
Age	-0.02	0.09
Acquired personal characteristic		
Formal education	0.09	-0.03
Learned weaving in school	-0.23	0.54*
Learned as apprentice	0.21	-0.45**
Experience as weaver employee	n.a.	-0.12
Full-time weaver	0.21	n.a.
Rural to rural migration	-0.21	n.a.
Rural to urban migration	0.21	n.a.
Foreign migration	0.26	n.a.
Acquired business characteristic		
Number of paid employees	n.a	0.23
Number of apprentices	n.a.	0.55*
Plans to remain in weaving	0.15	0.15
Received business loan	0.28**	0.24
Uses outside traders	0.30**	n.a.
Investment in weaving	0.22	0.16
Innovation		
Product change	0.22	0.29
Composite	0.45*	0.23

Note: Significant at *.01 and **.05 confidence levels; n.a.=variable not applicable to this group of either urban or rural artisans.

The Multiple Regression Model

Rural Entrepreneurs

Multiple regression is used in the second phase of the analysis to develop a model to explain business success for these enterprises. Table 11.4 shows the best model for the rural artisans that is generated in the stepwise multiple regression process. This model has the highest R-square and F values, .48 and 8, respectively. The variables that appear in this model are migration (foreign and internal), composite innovation, use of outside traders, and learning weaving formally in school. In stepwise multiple regression, the computer enters the variables into the analysis one by one, until the highest R-square value possible is achieved. The interpretation of the R-square value in this model is that 48 percent of the variations in weekly revenue among the rural enterprises can be explained by the influence of the five independent variables that were entered.[4]

Urban Entrepreneurs

Table 11.5 shows the results of the multiple regression analysis for the urban artisans. The values of R-square and F are .83 and 12.3. This indicates that 83 percent of the variations in weekly revenue can be accounted for by the five variables selected. For the urban artisan, business success is associated with whether (1) the enterprise has apprentices and paid employees, (2) the artisan learned the weaving skill in a formal educational setting or school, and (3) the artisan has experience working as a weaver in another enterprise before establishing his or her own business.

Table 11.4. Multiple regression analysis of business success for rural artisans

Dependent variable = weekly revenue	
Independent variable	Relative effect on weekly revenue
Foreign migration	0.43
Innovation composite	0.37
Uses outside traders	0.33
Rural to urban migration	0.28
Learned weaving in school	-0.22

R-square = 0.48   F = 8   N = 49
Significant at .01 confidence level.

Discussion of the Characteristics that Contribute to Business Success

Rural Enterprises

Three of the variables generated in the multiple regression model fall under the category of acquired personal characteristics: whether the artisan learned weaving in a formal school setting, rural-to-urban migration, and migration outside Ghana. The other two variables selected in the multiple regression procedure are business characteristics that involve decision making: the use of outside traders and the creation of innovations in the operation of the enterprises. The value for one, weaving in school, has a negative sign that seems to indicate that it has an inverse relationship with business success. Almost none of the Enyiresi artisans learned weaving in school. They learned from parents, elders, or were self-taught.

A possible explanation for the negative sign may be that a rural artisan who has to learn weaving in school may have started later, has less experience, or is not adept enough to pick up the skills by observation. This would have an adverse effect on his or her ability to produce quality products in sufficient quantities and, therefore, would negatively affect weekly revenues. Alternatively, it may be a kind of mathematical glitch (see note 3).

Thus, it may be stated that for the rural Enyiresi artisan, business success is associated with innovation, the initiative to migrate to other places, and use of several marketing avenues (for example, other traders). The weekly revenue of the artisans spans a wide range of values. However, for the rural entrepreneurs, nearly half of this revenue variation is accounted for by the influence of the variables mentioned.

Foreign migration shows the strongest contribution toward success of all of the variables in the rural model. Several of the artisans had previ-

Table 11.5. Multiple regression analysis of business success for urban artisans

Dependent variable = weekly revenue	
Independent variable	Relative effect on weekly revenue
Learned weaving in school	0.83
Prior experience as weaver employee	0.71
Number of apprentices	0.59
Number of paid employees	0.46
Age	0.25

R-square = 0.83   F = 12.3   N = 20
Significant at .01 confidence level.

ously traveled to Nigeria, Côte d'Ivoire, or other neighboring countries and gained experience as self-employed artisans or as paid workers at larger weaving enterprises. It is likely that from these experiences, they acquired knowledge to improve production and organizational skills in their own enterprises. Internal migration to cities within Ghana, the urban migration variable, is also included in the model. The reason for its impact on revenue is probably similar to that of foreign migration, although its influence is not as strong.

The outside traders variable indicates whether the village artisans use more than one method of marketing for their products. In Enyiresi, women traders within this village are the primary sellers of artisans' products. However, by using additional traders from outside the village, the artisans increase the range of their market area and the number of potential customers. This apparently results in the sale of more products and in higher revenues.

Innovation is significantly and positively related to business success among the rural artisans. With the second largest standardized estimate of the variables (0.37) in the model, it is highly associated with business success. Artisans who incorporate innovations in their operations appear to earn more revenues. An artisan who introduces a new product or style that is attractive to customers enjoys the advantage of a brief monopoly, until the change is adopted by other artisans.

The artisans' responses indicated that innovation and change were not infrequent occurrences among small-scale business persons, including artisans who practiced a traditional craft. The survey responses show that thirty-nine (80 percent) of the rural artisans had introduced changes and/or had indicated a propensity to change. In Accra, sixteen of the twenty (also 80 percent) artisans stated that they had introduced changes in product types and styles, as well as in their production operations, within the previous three years. Table 11.6 lists the various kinds of changes that the artisans had introduced.

Urban Enterprises

The attributive personal characteristic of age is entered during the stepwise multiple regression process, although it has a lower standardized parameter estimate than do the other variables. The probable reason it is selected is that the two oldest urban artisans had the highest weekly revenues. These entrepreneurs had been in business in Accra for many years and had the advantage of reputation and experience, loyal clientele, and business contacts.

Table 11.6. Weaving industry product and process changes reported by artisans

Product changes
  New styles, and "names"
  Plywood inserts
  New kinds of products (e.g., clothes hampers, TV stands, and VCR shelves)
  Use of colored paints as decoration
Production changes
  Splitting cane (for lighter weight products)
  Using helpers to peel and split cane (elements of assembly line division of labor)
  Using nails and hammers in fabrication process
  Using propane torch to kill insects, bend thick cane
  Using varnish finish as preservative, insecticide
  Women entering this male-dominated craft
Supply changes
  Contacting with cane supplier for village
  Renting truck for cane delivery
Marketing changes
  Using several traders or wholesale buyers to sell products
  Traveling to regional bazaars and organized crafts fairs
  Participating in or interest in foreign export
  Attending international trade show
  Locating urban shops near major roads or consumer base

Age does not show up at all in the model for the rural entrepreneurs. In the more informal rural setting, age does not seem to be significant either, as a limitation on physical activity or as an advantage in contacts or business experience. Among the urban artisans, however, age may be associated with other factors, such as experience, customer loyalty, proven credit worthiness, or more business contacts, that contribute to the success of a business. These do create an advantage in the more competitive urban business environment.

The other factors that show statistical significance and that appear in the urban model include prior work experience in weaving before starting an enterprise, number of paid employees, and number of apprentices. Most (over 70 percent) of the urban enterprises used either paid workers or unpaid apprentices in their production operations.

The coordination of the production effort among several employees is primarily a feature of the urban enterprise. For many of these enterprises, the production process involves some division of labor. Apprentices and less experienced workers do basic tasks, such as cleaning and peeling the cane and preparing other materials. The complex and more creative work is then completed by the skilled artisans.

Neither of the innovation variables (product change or composite) appears in the urban model. This seems contradictory, since previous statements have associated innovation with business success. However, it appears to be a nuance of the statistical model and quantification technique.

The reason that the innovation variable does not come out in the multiple regression procedure is that there was no variation among the artisans for this characteristic. All of the urban artisans incorporated innovative practices and continually changed their products.

Although innovation does not appear in the multiple regression model, in the correlation analysis, product innovation is second only to number of apprentices in strength of association with weekly revenue. In the preceding section it is shown that innovation is significant in the model for rural artisans where greater variation in use of innovations exists. Since revenues among the urban artisans are higher than those of rural artisans, it is reasonable to say that innovation is a contributing factor in the higher revenues for the urban artisans as a group. (However, other factors that differentiate rural from urban enterprises exert more influence on revenues of enterprises in these two locales.)

The urban artisans were involved in various types of innovative activity, such as introducing new types of products, creating new designs and features for standard products, reorganizing the production process to incorporate division of labor according to skill levels of the workers, indicating an interest in the export market, already participating in marketing their products for export, and securing wholesale orders from large firms or government ministries (see table 11.6). Therefore, with respect to the use of innovation among the urban artisans, this variable does not stand out in the model.

The two factors that are differentially distributed among the urban artisans and that show a statistical significance in business revenue (that is, success) are prior experience in another business and the number of workers that the enterprise has.

The Economic Viability of Small-Scale Artisan Enterprises

Programs to promote small-scale indigenous businesses sometimes are less effective, because these enterprises are believed to generate little more than subsistence income for the artisans. However, the average monthly income of the artisans in this study exceeded that of wage earners in the Ghanaian economy, though there was wide revenue variation among the enterprises.

Table 11.7 shows that the average monthly income for employees in the nine economic sectors in Ghana ranged in 1991–92 from a low of 7,800 cedis (about U.S.$51) in the agriculture sector to a high of 19,500 cedis ($127) in the mining sector. The overall average for the nine sectors listed is 11,200 cedis ($73). By comparison, the average monthly income for the Enyiresi rural artisans was 23,800 cedis ($118); for the urban artisans, the average was 84,000 cedis ($416). This shows that small-scale entrepreneurs can establish and operate lucrative enterprises and achieve satisfactory income levels

Conclusion

The hypothesis that certain characteristics that contribute to business success can be identified is supported by both qualitative and quantitative analyses of the data. The quantitative results also indicate the relative strength of the association of certain characteristics with business success.

The characteristics that contribute to success are classified in this chapter as business-related characteristics that involve conscious decision mak-

Table 11.7. Average monthly earnings in Ghana by economic sector[a] compared with average for rural and urban weavers in survey[b]

Sector	Cedis	U.S.$
Agriculture	7800	51
Commerce	9200	60
Services	10,300	67
Finance	10,800	70
Construction	11,100	72
Electricity, utilities	11,300	73
Transportation	12,500	81
Manufacturing	14,000	90
Mining	19,500	127
Average	11,200	73
Rural artisans	23,800	118
Urban artisans	84,000	416

a. *Source:* EIU Country Profile, Ghana, 1991–92.
b. *Source:* Author.

ing and management. Certain other characteristics are classified as acquired personal characteristics. These acquired characteristics suggest that entrepreneurs have attempted to improve or advance themselves. They include the decision to migrate. The primary reason people migrate is for economic opportunity (de Souza 1990). In the continuing debate over whether entrepreneurship results from psychological and cultural characteristics (Hagen 1962; McClelland 1961) or from responses to economic opportunity (Elkan 1988; Kilby 1971), the results of this analysis seem to support the latter argument. Small-scale artisans working in a traditional crafts industry in Africa make rational business decisions and incorporate innovative approaches in their enterprises that contribute to the success of their enterprises.

This analysis identifies factors that may be most important to sustaining a successful and viable business in a developing economy such as that of Ghana. International-development institutions now actively promote the private firm as the most effective and efficient generator of economic growth. For the past two decades, small-scale industries and indigenous businesses in developing countries have been given ideological support. By studying these firms through the behavior of the individual entrepreneur-owner, private and public policy makers are provided with corroborative information that supports measures that can be taken to promote small-scale (even so-called traditional) enterprises and enhance business success. Finally, the entrepreneurs themselves can benefit from studies such as this to evaluate their behavior and decision making in the management of their operations.

In studies of developing countries, especially in Africa, the failure of industrial and commercial ventures has received widespread attention. While lessons can be learned from the experiences of failure, perhaps even more effective lessons can be learned from the glimpses of successful enterprises operating under the same conditions. Whether or not these successes are related to behavioral characteristics of the entrepreneurs, to the manner in which the entrepreneurs operate the enterprises, or to proactive decisions taken, if the successes have common components, they can be recommended and encouraged in other business endeavors. Thus the successes can be replicated over and over again.

Notes

1. Ghana has a population of 18 million people. According to a United Nations survey, its 1990 per capita income of $400 places Ghana in the middle range of developing countries. Its gross domestic product in 1990 was $9 billion. Its GDP

growth rate since the institution of economic reforms in 1983 averages 5 percent a year.

2. In statistical analysis, the levels of confidence or significance refer to the probability that the strength of the association (the correlation coefficient) would be as reported, if there is no relationship between the variables. A statistically significant level of .01 (or .05) means that there is only a 1 in 100 (or 5 in 100) chance that these correlation coefficients would be generated, if there is no relationship between the two variables.

3. The correlation coefficient for weekly revenue and apprenticeship training for the urban artisan has a negative sign. This does not necessarily mean an inverse relationship between the two, because the apprenticeship variable is quantified as a nominal variable. In this analysis, the experience of apprenticeship training for the artisan-entrepreneur is indicted nominally by a 1 (yes) or a 0 (no).

In a correlation in which there is a nominal or ordinal (rank) variable, the sign (plus or minus) of the correlation coefficient may not matter (Beveridge and Oberschall 1979). In this case, the coefficient number means that there is a statistically important association between these two variables; it does not necessarily mean that the relationship is inverse.

4. The F value of 8 suggests that this model is a reasonably good one. The F value indicates whether the research hypothesis tested in the model can be supported. Generally, an F value of 4 or greater (given the number of observations and variables) suggests that the research hypothesis can be supported and that the relationships are less likely to be a statistically significant but realistically improbable coincidence.

References Cited

Asamoah, Leonard. 1980. Rural Industry: Assessment of the Impact of the Basket-Weaving Industry on Income Level at Enyiresi. Honor's bachelor's thesis, University of Ghana, Legon.

Beveridge, Andrew, and Anthony Oberschall. 1979. *African Businessmen and Development in Zambia.* Princeton, N.J.: Princeton University Press.

Biggs, Tyler, Gail R. Moody, Jan-Hendrik van Leeuwen, and E. Diane White. 1994. Africa Can Compete! Discussion Paper no. 242. Washington, D.C.: World Bank.

Cable, V., and A. Weston. 1986. *Commerce of Culture: Experience of Indian Handicrafts.* New Delhi: Lancer International.

Chuta, Enyinna, and Carl Liedholm. 1985. *Employment and Growth in Small-Scale Industry.* New York: St. Martin's Press.

de Souza, Anthony. 1990. *Geography of the World Economy.* Cincinnati: Merrill Publishing Commune.

Diomande, Mamadou. 1990. Business Creation with Minimal Resources: Some Lessons from the African Experience. *Journal of Business Venturing* 5:191–200.

Economist Intelligence Unit. 1991. *Ghana. Country Profile, 1991–1992.* London: Business International Limit.

Elkan, Walter. 1988. Entrepreneurs and Entrepreneurship in Africa. *Finance and Development* 25:20, 41–42.

Garlick, Peter. 1971. *African Traders and Economic Development in Ghana*. Oxford: Clarendon Press.

Hagen, Everett. 1962. *On the Theory of Social Change: How Economic Growth Begins*. Homewood, Ill.: Dorsey Press.

Kallon, Kelfala. 1990. *The Economics of Sierra Leonean Entrepreneurship*. Lanham, Md.: University Press of America.

Kennedy, Paul. 1980. *Ghanaian Businessmen*. London: Weltforum Verlag.

———. 1988. *African Capitalism: The Struggle for Ascendancy*. Cambridge, Mass.: Cambridge University Press.

Kent, Calvin, Donald Sexton, and Karl Vesper. 1982. *Encyclopedia of Entrepreneurship*. Englewood Cliffs, N.J.: Prentice-Hall.

Kilby, Peter. 1971. *Entrepreneurship and Economic Development*. New York: Free Press.

Marsden, Keith. 1990. African Entrepreneurs: Pioneers of Development. International Finance Corporation Discussion Paper 19. Washington, D.C.: World Bank.

McClelland, David. 1961. *The Achieving Society*. Princeton, N.J.: Van Nostrand.

Nafziger, E. Wayne. 1977. *African Capitalism: A Case Study in Nigerian Entrepreneurship*. Stanford: Hoover Institution.

Ofori-Amoah, Ben. 1988. Improving Existing Indigenous Technologies as a Strategy for the Appropriate Technology Concept in Ghana. *Industry and Development* 23:57–79.

Rogerson, C. M. 1986. Reviving Old Technology: Rural Handicraft Production in Southern Africa. *Geoforum* 17:173–85.

Schumpeter, Joseph. [1934] 1961. *The Theory of Economic Development*. New York: Oxford University Press.

Steel, William, and Leila Webster. 1991. *Small Enterprises under Adjustment in Ghana*. World Bank Technical Paper 138. Washington, D.C.: World Bank.

Tambunan, Tulus. 1994. Rural Small-Scale Industries in a Developing Region: Sign of Poverty or Progress? *Entrepreneurship and Regional Development* 6:1–13.

Weber, Max. 1930. *The Protestant Ethic and the Spirit of Capitalism*. New York: Scribner.

PART IV

Public Policy and Private Initiative in Entrepreneurial Development

12. Policy Lessons from the Kenyan Experience in Promoting African Entrepreneurship in Commerce and Industry

David Himbara

Fostering an African entrepreneurial class in Kenya became a national priority not only after independence in 1963, as is widely believed, but, in fact, beginning in the 1940s. Before 1963, the existing microentrepreneurship was seen as the base from which small-scale and informal operations would be enhanced to graduate into the formal economy. The postindependence program abandoned this course, however, opting for what has come to be called capitalism from above. The new policy sought to hoist Kenyan Africans directly into mainstream commerce and industry (Government of Kenya 1964). However, the principal beneficiaries were overwhelmingly drawn from upper echelons of reigning political classes and higher levels of the civil service.

The argument here is that the exclusion of microentrepreneurship was a serious policy error, and that attempts at instituting capitalism from above were flawed in many ways. The shortcomings in regard to capitalism from above included the preoccupation with such concerns as provision of loans, offices, and business sites, while more decisive factors were accorded less attention. These factors included acquisition of business skills, technical know-how, collective organizational competence, and the important question of establishing relationships with existing mainstream commerce and industry. As is argued here, it seems that some hard lessons were learned, as indicated by the 1986–89 policy reversals that not only questioned the prudence of capitalism from above, but reinserted the small-scale and informal sectors in the overall policy regime.

Pre-1963 Policies of Fostering African Entrepreneurship

Both academic and Kenyan official literature after independence converged on the myth that the colonial state had hindered African entrepreneurship in order to stifle competition with preferred settler estates in Kenya. Such a legacy, according to Kenyanist literature, was bound to affect outcomes of subsequent periods adversely. Marris and Somerset, for example, argued that the poor quality of African businesses was a direct result of a colonial administration that was "indifferent or restrictive, directing openings for trade towards the immigrant communities" (1971:228). The isolation of African businessmen, they concluded, "can be seen as a consequence of policies which ignored the opportunity to train and finance them" (ibid.).

Brett emphasized that the failure of Africans to move upward into business did not "stem in any way from any of the attributes supposedly associated with the traditional values" (1973:294). On the contrary, he said, it was the full power of the colonial state that eliminated African middlemen (and small-scale Asians) "who were competing only too effectively on the market where opportunities existed. Their failure stemmed directly from the limits imposed on the free operations of the market system by the State" (ibid.). Swainson added her support to these views, invoking "the extensive restrictions placed in the way of indigenous capitalism during the colonial period" (1987:140).

If the above mistaken views had been merely academic, it is possible that limited or no harm would have resulted. However, the postcolonial officialdom reflected a similar propensity, leading to dubious policy reversals and gullible anticipations of instantaneous ascension of a vibrant class of Kenyan African entrepreneurs. It could be officially declared in 1964 that economic opportunities that existed in Kenya were not available to Africans. That being the case, the government was obliged to "promote vigorously increased African participation in every sphere of the nation's economy" (Government of Kenya 1964:41). Statements such as "we must have a sort of monopoly so as to get our people into business" were widespread. It was asserted that, after all, colonial policy had protected "their [European] big businessmen" (Balala 1964:2723).

The reality of the colonial period was not that simple, especially during the early 1940s, when tailor-made policies aimed at facilitating African entrepreneurship began to take form. The initial phase was signaled by the establishment of the Rural Industries Committee, set up essentially in response to the increase in the African population, overcrowding in "native reserves," unemployment, and an increase in rural-urban migration. To this set of issues must be added the unexpected and sharp surge in formal African business establishments, a novelty that called for policy. In explaining the rationale for setting up the Rural Industries Committee, it was stated that the government attached considerable importance to the early development of rural industries in the native areas of the Colony. Hence there was a need to appoint "a suitably qualified officer to devote his whole time to the important task of ascertaining what progress can be made and of ensuring that such steps as are possible are taken" (Roughton 1944). This led to the appointment of J. S. Stirton, whose 1945 report became the cornerstone of the official thinking on African entrepreneurship up to independence.

Before examining the policy package that evolved in the subsequent period, it is necessary to outline briefly the African entrepreneurship that existed earlier, and how it influenced policy options. The 1940s witnessed extraordinarily large numbers of businesses being established by Africans, not only in small and informal sectors, but also in more complex business forms of limited liability and in public companies based on shareholding. The principal source of capital for these businesses was pooled funds by returning African ex-soldiers from World War II. As was then officially noted, there was steady pressure from a large number of Africans for facilities to engage in trade in Kenya, particularly in the Central Province, as well as around Machakos region. In regard to limited liability and shareholding firms, a report by the Registrar of Companies indicated that the first companies incorporated by Africans were registered at the end of 1945. It was further stated that 1945, 1946, and 1947 were boom years, and to a lesser extent 1948; but there was a very great falling off in 1949 that continued through 1950 (Registrar of Companies 1950).

In terms of the amounts of capital involved in these African ventures, it was revealed that by 1949, seventeen African "public companies" with a nominal capital of nearly 4.3 million Kenyan shillings were incorporated, while fifty-three African "private companies" with a nominal capital of 2.7 million shillings had been established (Registrar General 1949).

Most of the enterprises, however, tended to disintegrate as soon as they formed, leading officials to call for curbing their activities, as they often resulted in significant losses on the part of their members. The Registrar of Companies warned that African managers and promoters of companies were "defrauding shareholders of the funds of companies that they are running," and that since their African shareholders had no knowledge of the provisions of the law, some "tightening up of the legislation on this score appears to be necessary" (Registrar General 1949). This call was repeated several times, with the registrar stating in 1950 that there was no single African company "whose affairs I can honestly describe as satisfactory" (Registrar of Companies 1950). It was further officially stated that African capital "without the ability to use it properly can achieve no improvement—it can merely lead to disaster on a grander scale" (Penwill

1950). The seriousness of the problem was illustrated by the fact that it reached the upper levels of the state, with the Executive Council concluding in 1950 that the formation of companies by Africans was causing considerable hardship among African subscribers. The council advised that the matter should be investigated.

It is, therefore, not surprising that the Stirton report of 1945 that was issued in the midst of the rise and fall of African enterprises advocated a "bottom-up" approach to facilitating African entrepreneurship, rejecting "anything requiring large capital and the importation of expensive machinery," which was not within the Africans' "means just yet." On the contrary, it was essential "to commence at rock-bottom and to look to the future" for the emergence of an industrious African entrepreneur.

In the short term, however, microentrepreneurs should be encouraged to engage in such spheres as production of building materials, construction, and crafts including blacksmithing, shoe making, tailoring, soap making, and furniture making. While these were "not regarded as fully fledged industries," it was upon them that formal industry would be built to "cater for African markets, and ultimately absorb large numbers of persons in employment not directly concerned with land." In Stirton's view, it was wise to concentrate on and encourage such activity as was already established, instead of engaging "in frantic efforts to introduce something that is likely to fade out with the first signs of failing enthusiasm" (Stirton 1945).

The propositions of the Stirton report were reiterated in 1950, when the previous schemes of rural industries were reassessed and broadened. The same thinking was yet again evident four years later, in the introduction of what became the most ambitious project of creating an African entrepreneurial class during Kenya's colonial period: the Assistance to African Industrialists, Artisans, and Businessmen Scheme. Funded by the United States government through the International Cooperation Administration (ICA), with matching funds from the Kenyan government, the pilot phase of the scheme became operational in 1953 in Nyanza Province; it was introduced to the rest of the country in 1954 (Ministry of Commerce and Industry 1954).

By 1959, in addition to Nyanza Province (Elgon, Kisumu, and Kericho), the project was well established in Central Province (Kiambu, Nyeri, Embu, and Meru), Southern Province (Machakos, Kitui, Kajiado, and Narok), Rift Valley (Nandi, Elgeyo Marakwet, and Eldoret), and the Coast Province (Kwale, Kilifi, Teita, and Mombasa). As in the original Stirton report on rural industries, the bottom-up philosophy of the scheme called for directing aid and technical assistance to any African applicant in trade, business, or industry who indicated "through his own efforts" that he had "the necessary ability to operate his business with a reasonable measure of success" (Ministry of Commerce and Industry 1954).

It must be pointed out as well that since the Stirton initial report, business education had been considered a crucial component in fostering African entrepreneurship, particularly since it was widely believed that African business persons lacked elementary business knowledge, a tendency reflected in the events of the 1940s. By the time of the ICA scheme, provision of basic education for African entrepreneurs had become almost as important as granting them loans.

The Jeanes Schools at Kabete (Central Province) and Maseno (Nyanza Province) were commissioned to provide tailor-made educational packages that included such elementary aspects as arithmetical calculations involving money, weights and measures, simple accounting (for example, daily sales and stock books, cash and trading accounts), business methods (credit, transport, and wholesaling facilities), purchasing, costing, and banking. Acquisition of skills in these areas, or, more specifically, having "suitable qualification granted by a recognized technical school," in effect became part of the requirement for successful loan application on the part of African entrepreneurs (Ministry of Commerce and Industry 1954).

It was in this arena that the state successfully mobilized mainstream industry to help facilitate African capitalism. Besides involving prominent business executives in guest lectures, visits to their factories and commercial establishments were incorporated into the educational scheme in an attempt to provide potential African business persons with "role models." On the participation of local business communities in this program, the Commerce and Industry's officials could state within two years that "we are extremely indebted to these gentlemen who give so freely and willingly of their time" (Ministry of Commerce and Industry 1956).

Finally, toward the end of the colonial period, the state (specifically, the Ministry of Commerce and Industry, together with the district administration and registrar of societies) sought to increase the organizational capacity of African entrepreneurs by assisting them to initiate their own chambers of commerce. The pilot scheme in this project was the Kiambu African Chamber of Commerce, established in 1959. It is worthwhile to note that the inaugural secretary of the Kiambu chamber was Njenga Karume, probably the most accomplished Kenyan African industrialist and businessman to date (Simmance 1959).

In their assessments of the progress during the 1950s, it appears that government officials were not optimistic regarding short-term prospects of African entrepreneurs, but were more hopeful for the future. Bureaucrats at Commerce and Industry could write in the late 1950s that they found that the African tended "to be an individualist who resents any form of organization in his commercial activities, and this tendency will have to be overcome before there can be a really profitable partnership with him in such activities." The officials, however, were not dismissive of long-term prospects, particularly in regard to the Kikuyu community. It was suggested that the Kikuyu were most "likely to realize the advantages . . . more quickly than others" (Maddison 1956).

In the case of the ambitious scheme of the African Industrialists, Artisans, and Businessmen, it was acknowledged in 1959 that "we seem to be faced with too many traders and a marked reluctance to repay loans." It is worthwhile to emphasize, however, that government officials still believed that long-term educational and technical support for African businessmen would eventually lead to desired outcomes. Hence the call for further governmental concerted efforts "to adjust the attitude of mind which is clearly holding up the implementation of the scheme" (Maddison 1959).

Policy Reversals after Independence and Outcomes

The above pre-independence history, if known, was ignored by the post-1963 policy makers who assumed that the previous state had actively hindered the development of African entrepreneurship. Thus the immediate task became the removal of assumed past impediments to enable black entrepreneurship to take its place in the formal economy. Eliminated almost entirely from policy consideration was microentrepreneurship.

Accounts of programs and implementing institutions that were established during the 1960s and early 1970s to foster capitalism "from above" abound (Leys 1975; Himbara 1994). Suffice it to note that leading among these were the Industrial and Commercial Development Corporation (ICDC) and the Industrial Development Bank (IDB); these two parastatal bodies were to provide commercial or industrial know-how, as well as funds to Africans to enable them to purchase existing firms, acquire shares in them, or found new ones. Those with a more specific mandate included the Kenya National Trading Corporation (KNTC), which sought to specialize in promoting African traders, a task supplemented by the Joint Loan Boards (JLBs). The National Construction Corporation (NCC) sought to support African contractors in the building and construction industry.

That the beneficiaries of these programs came directly from ruling circles and upper levels of Kenyan civil service has been established in previous accounts (Himbara 1994). The early crop of groomed entrepreneurs was almost synonymous with who's who in the Kenyatta family and in Kenyatta's closer political circles, particularly those affiliated with the quasi business-ethnic-cultural group known as the Gikuyu, Embu, Meru Association (GEMA) (Kaplinsky 1982:193–221).

As for the civil servants, it is a well-known fact that the 1971 presidentially appointed Ndegwa Commission openly advocated their participation in business. According to the commission, "there ought in theory to be no objection to the ownership of property or involvement in business by members of the public services to a point where their wealth is augmented perhaps substantially by such activities" (Republic of Kenya 1971:13–14). Almost ten years later, another presidential commission of inquiry decried the "misuse of official positions and official information in furtherance of civil servants' personal interests. There are officers who live beyond their means and who cannot honorably account for the wealth they have amassed" (Republic of Kenya 1980:37–38).

Yet it does not appear that the "amassed" wealth on the part of the political class and senior civil servants necessarily translated into productive entrepreneurial activity. It became apparent, in fact, that creating capitalism from above, in Kenya's particular conditions, could not lead to the desired effect. Some Kenyan leaders soon realized that preoccupation with such issues as loan portfolios, business premises, and the like, was not enough. Equally important was the need to create means of training the emerging African businessmen in basic organization, markets, and the acquisition of know-how.

In light of difficulties facing many newly created African companies throughout the 1960s, some leaders pointed out that giving loans in itself was not sufficient. What was called for was "drastic steps to enable our people to understand business methods as opposed to just getting loans, putting up a shop or an industry. Business is a profession and needs some learning. . . . For our people to be able to engage in big enterprises requires that they be advised by highly trained people, how to plan and understand the intricacies of modern business. . . . I think it is important that the present established companies already in Kenya should . . . lend a hand and take a few of our people who are interested in business and give them some form of training to enable them to understand the complexities of running a big business" (Wariithi 1964:2717).

Similarly, it was advised that instead of expelling or harassing Indian or other "foreign" business persons (see below), the Kenyan government "should keep them here, so that the African small traders can be taught, be given directions as to how to handle their business and keep their cash books properly" (Oduya 1963:2725). As the 1960s drew to a close, the Ministry of Commerce and Industry revealed the wisdom of statements such as these. There was no point in anyone "pretending otherwise," said its minister, for the available African managerial cadre had not "really performed to the satisfaction either of their shareholders or anyone in the Government" (Kibaki and Republic of Kenya 1969:3199). The 1970s and early 1980s confirmed this reality, as Kenya witnessed spectacular African business failures recalling the 1940s.

Two related additional failings of the post-1963 program need to be noted, namely the organizational arena beyond individual business and the realm of state mediation of various levels of enterprise. In contrast to attempts to instill in "the African" organizational business sense by introducing African chambers of commerce in 1950s, the integrated Kenya National Chamber of Commerce and Industry (KNCCI) cannot be credited with such a role from the early 1960s onward. There was little effort by way of organizational empowerment. By the 1980s, the chamber had become almost synonymous with political intrigue, mismanagement, and corruption. Far from becoming a learning arena, as well as an effective business lobby for its membership, the KNCCI became an embarrassment, as was consistently reported (*Daily Nation*, 25 April 1983; *Sunday Times*, 7 September 1986; *Industrial Review*, September 1989). The image that the chamber presented was "not of business people in a unity of purpose but of people driven by hunger for power. These are politicians in business garb" (*Sunday Nation*, 28 June 1987).

As for state mediation, in contrast to earlier official initiatives to involve mainstream commerce and industry in facilitating African capitalism, the post-1963 posture was closer to a go-it-alone stance on the part of the government. The case of the Trade Licensing Act of 1967 demonstrated this policy shift. The act empowered trade licensing officers to determine who, among non-Kenyan Africans, could give up his or her trading concern through a "quit notice" to create space for incoming Kenyan African business persons. The act also designated zones and commodities that non-citizens could not trade (Republic of Kenya 1972:5). The act was subsequently amended via Legal Notice No. 229, 1974, to sanction similar African takeovers of manufacturing firms. As the chief executive of the Kenyan Association of Manufacturers (KAM) remarked, this amendment meant that any firm "might be given a quit notice by a Trade Licensing Officer under the new Amendment at any time," a development that ultimately implied "a threat to their investments" (Wanjui 1975).

This view was soon proved right, when some manufacturing firms (especially those owned by local Indians) were actually earmarked for takeover by Kenyan Africans. These included the Flora Garment Factory (valued at 400,000 shillings in 1975, with eighty employees); Capital Knitwear (2 million shillings, one hundred employees); Pactco Industries (4 million shillings, fifty employees); and Karania Packers (4 million shillings, sixty employees), all of which were issued with quit notices in 1975. The state realized, however, that it could not successfully authorize the takeover of these firms, as this clashed with its broader developmental strategy based on private initiatives. Put differently, the state could not pursue a capitalist path while forcing the very vehicle of the strategy to behave according to official dictates.

That was precisely the argument successfully used by the KAM to defeat the amendment. The association argued that the takeover of companies by the government contradicted its official pronouncements inviting both foreign and local investors to participate in local manufacturing industries (Tyrrell 1975).

But the most remarkable thing about the post-1963 policy package was how Kenyan policy framers failed to modify it in light of glaring shortcomings that became apparent almost immediately. This did not occur until two decades later, during the 1980s, when it was provisionally acknowledged that post-1960s policies had been misguided. The turning point was in 1986, when it was granted that a major blunder—namely, the omission of the small-scale and informal sector—had adversely affected the entire policy package on African entrepreneurship.

It was now argued that although the informal sector suffered from a negative public image, it possessed many positive characteristics and had a vital role to play. Among the reasons for this reversal was the fact that the activities associated with the sector "require very little capital to create jobs, rely primarily on family savings, often provide their own skill training at no cost to the Government, and are a prime training ground for future African entrepreneurs. . . . They fulfill key functions in support of agriculture and other local production by marketing inputs such as fertilizer, making and selling small tools, maintaining vehicles and equipment, marketing produce, and providing local inhabitants with a wide range of inexpensive basic consumer goods and services for everyday life. Small local firms can be especially efficient at producing bulky or heavy items such as building materials, especially bricks and tiles, and furniture, thus saving on transport costs" (Republic of Kenya 1986:54–55).

The 1986 policy reversal toward a bottom-up strategy resembled the Stirton report issued forty years earlier. There were other similarities as well. In calling for the promotion of rural industries, Stirton had understood entrepreneurship to be a solution to a multifaceted problem of high population growth leading to high unemployment. He had seen entrepreneurship as having the potential to arrest rural migration into urban centers and to promote general wealth and development.

The 1986–89 official call for encouraging the informal sector in rural areas was thus a repeat of the 1945 Stirton agenda. As was editorialized in 1989, the introduction of the rural informal sector had many built-in benefits, including promoting self-employment, addressing the escalating unemployment problem, and containing rural migration, as urban centers were becoming increasingly unable to cope with the influx (*Standard*, 13 December 1989).

It should perhaps be noted as well that the International Labour Organization (ILO) had advocated a scheme similar to that of the Stirton report as far back as 1972. In the view of the ILO, the Kenyan government should have been promoting, instead of harassing, the informal sector. This sector seemed capable of "offering virtually a full range of basic skills needed to provide goods and services for a large though often poor section of the population" (ILO 1972:5).

The 1986 tentative admission of policy lapse turned into a full-fledged official admission of outright failure in 1989. Regarding the ICDC schemes, even where they initially had assisted in transferring businesses from "non-indigenous to indigenous businessmen, [they] reverted to the former through the back door" (Republic of Kenya 1989:161). The KNTC fared equally badly; contrary to its mission of facilitating African capitalists in commerce and trade, its "monopolistic status led to inefficiencies and unprofitable operations," while it failed "to compete effectively with older and well established non-Kenyan businesses" (159). The JLBs faced such problems as poor management, false accounting, and the issue of fictitious loans, in addition to massive defaults by its clients (159–60). Almost the entire parastatal sector, including principal parastatals such as the ICDC, had since the late 1970s been found to be badly flawed, with various commissions of inquiry advocating their privatization or outright liquidation (Republic of Kenya 1979; Republic of Kenya 1982). The case of the National Construction Company was indicative of the scale of the problem at hand. It had survived only long enough to found one construction company, the International Construction Company, which had ceased to operate in 1978.

It was not all gloom, however, for success stories were recorded during the 1980s and early 1990s, particularly in microentrepreneurship. Through their in-house supplier development programs and retention of quality and design controls, large- and medium-size Kenya-based firms pursued a strategy of cutting costs by experimenting with subcontracting to smaller and informal operations. For their part, the latter hoped to gain skills, credit, and ready-made markets, as well as any benefits from the association with mainstream economy. The subsectors involved included textile, automobile, and construction industries. In the automobile industry, small-scale or informal operators manufactured such items as car seats and upholstery, while in textiles they undertook such tasks as stitching and attaching buttons. Leading firms such as Kenya Breweries, East Africa Industries, and British American Tobacco trained their distributors, more or less guaranteeing their niche in the market for mutual interests of effective distribution of their products.

The most advanced system of subcontracting was by far in the building and construction industry. Prompted by the need to enhance such developments, leading Kenya-based firms established the Kenya Management Assistance Program in 1986. Its mission was to free their top and middle-level executives for one day per month to counsel clients registered with the program (Morara 1990). It appears that the state had little or no choice but to follow the advice of Kenyan mainstream business and leading multilateral funding agencies. These groups successfully persuaded the government that the private sector constituted the best avenue of promoting African entrepreneurship in Kenya (KAM 1990).

Lessons from Kenyan Policies on African Entrepreneurship

There are several important lessons to be drawn from the Kenyan experience at attempts to facilitate African entrepreneurship. The first has to do with the role of the state in this task. In the period 1944–63, the state appears to have recognized its limits and actively sought in several ways to involve the private sector in developing entrepreneurship. Business executives participated in the Jeanes educational programs, and so-called role-model programs enabled African entrepreneurs to visit factories and exchange views.

The post-1963 program was suspicious of mainstream firms, subjecting some to threats of forced takeovers. This period can, in fact, be described to a large extent as a go-it-alone stance on the part of the state. Yet the state and its parastatal sector was in no position to deliver, as it suffered the same shortcomings in technical skills and financial resources as did the African entrepreneurs it had hoped to assist. The go-it-alone stance appeared to give way to tentative recognition of the need to cooperate with the private sector. This awareness came about as a result of both the poor outcomes of official strategies and the notable success in the area least subjected to state action: microentrepreneurship associated with in-house supplier programs of larger firms.

The second lesson concerns the most elementary prerequisites in nurturing a productive entrepreneurial class. The Kenyan case shows that despite its paternalist and patronizing tone, the 1944–63 program appreciated the complexity of this exercise. Hence the call for a fuller range of support mechanisms that at the very least included education, finance, and organizational initiates. The 1945 Stirton program pioneered these principles. Subsequent modifications and amendments to this wisdom throughout the late 1940s and the 1950s contributed to attempts at developing a fairly complex and integrated African business class.

However, in the postindependence period, this approach was abandoned. Related to this shortcoming was the absence of an effective chamber of commerce to assist the state in spreading business ideas and organizational imperatives in the African business community. The post-1963 chamber, as shown above, was almost irrelevant in regard to these issues. Without an effective and supportive parastatal sector, with the state having essentially alienated big business, and without a productive association of their own, how were African entrepreneurs to gain organizational experience?

The third lesson revolves around the social forces from which entrepreneurial material can spring. As has been argued in another context, "much ink has been spilt in attempts to identify the sources from whence came the entrepreneurs." These attempts have met with limited success, as evidence remains flimsy and incomplete. In fact, "they came from every social source and every area" (Wilson 1972:388).

In the Kenyan situation, the framers of the 1944–63 program identified the small-scale and informal sectors as the terrain from where a substantial pool of entrepreneurs could emerge on the basis of their already proven exposure to business. With technical, financial, and organization support, such forces could first of all fill a gap in local African markets, eventually graduating into the formal economy. The post-1963 program opted instead to assist Africans to vault directly into the large-scale commerce and industry. In light of inappropriate state support and poor outcomes, however, a policy reversal in mid-1986 returned to the pre-1963 view. This development signals a positive change on the part of Kenyan policy makers.

In conclusion, it cannot and should not be inferred from the above discussion that it is impossible to develop a capitalist class "from above" successfully, as was attempted in postindependence Kenya. Perhaps with a more effective state, a better parastatal sector, consistent support mechanisms, and better-informed policies, such an objective could have been attained. History shows that some countries have succeeded with this approach very well (Amsden 1989).

The point here is to demonstrate that in Kenya, the state lacked the capacity to implement appropriate policy because implementing governmental institutions were weak and inconsistent. With such profound flaws, the prospects for creating capitalists from above were unlikely. The ill-advised policies assumed a false dichotomy between the formal and informal economic sectors that resulted in neglect of microentrepreneurship. In fact, integrated economic systems comprise a range of businesses, from small to large. Indeed, in African countries, as well as in other countries, the small-scale sector accounts for a large measure of progress in economic development (Shiek 1992).

References Cited

Amsden, Alice. 1989. *Asia's Next Giant: South Korea and Late Industrialization.* New York: Oxford University Press.

Balala, M. P. 1964. *The National Assembly, House of Representatives Official Report.* Vol. 3 (pt. 2). Nairobi: Government Printer.

Brett, Edward. 1973. *Colonialism and Underdevelopment in East Africa.* New York: NOK Publishers.

Government of Kenya. 1964. *Development Plan, 1964–1970.* Nairobi: Government Printer.

Himbara, David. 1994. *Kenyan Capitalists, the State, and Development.* Boulder, Colo.: Lynne Rienner Publishers.

ILO (International Labour Organization). 1972. *Employment, Incomes, and Equality.* Geneva: ILO.

Kaplinsky, R. 1982. Capitalist Accumulation in the Periphery: Kenya. In *Industry and Accumulation in Africa,* edited by M. Fransman. London: Heinemann.

Kenya Association of Manufactuters (KAM). 1990. Annual Report.

Kibaki, Mwai, and Republic of Kenya. 1969. *The National Assembly Official Report.* Vol. 17 (pt. 2). Nairobi: Government Printer.

Leys, Colin. 1975. *Underdevelopment in Kenya.* Berkeley and Los Angeles: University of California Press.

Maddison, V. A. 1956. Scheme of Assistance to African Industrialists, Artisans, and Businessmen. Ministry of Commerce and Industry, 11 September. MCI/6/782, Kenya National Archives (KNA).

———. 1959. Ministry of Commerce and Industry, 29 June. MCI/6/1275, KNA.

Marris, Peter, and Anthony Somerset. 1971. *African Businessmen.* London: Routledge and Kegan Paul.

Ministry of Commerce and Industry. 1954. Circular No. 7/55 30: Extending the

Scheme of Loans to African Traders and Industrialists to Other Parts of Kenya. November. In MCI/3/144, KNA.

———. 1956. Loan Instructions to Town Clerks and Joint Boards. 12 July. MCI/3/144, KNA.

Morara, A. N. 1990. Linking Industry for Faster Development. Paper presented at the Seminar on Industrial Subcontracting, 4–9 March, Nyeri.

Oduya, M. P. 1964. *House of Representatives Official Report*. Nairobi: Government Printer.

Penwill, D. J. (district officer, Nyeri District). 1950. Cited in The African in Business: Memorandum for Meeting of Provincial Commissioners. Ministry of Commerce and Industry, February. MCI/6/782, KNA.

Registrar of Companies. 1950. African Companies. Ministry of Commerce and Industry, 12 October. MCI/6/789, KNA.

Republic of Kenya. 1971. *Ndegwa Commission*. Nairobi: Government Printer.

———. 1972. *Laws of Kenya*, Trade Licensing Act. Nairobi: Government Printer.

———. 1979. *Review of Statutory Boards*. Nairobi: Government Printer.

———. 1980. *Report of the Civil Service Review* (or the *Waruhiu Report*). Nairobi: Government Printer.

———. 1982. *Report and Recommendations of the Working Party on Government Expenditures*. Nairobi: Government Printer.

———. 1986. *Sessional Paper No. 1 of 1986 on Economic Management for Renewed Growth*. Nairobi: Government Printer.

———. 1989. *Development Plan, 1989–1993*. Nairobi: Government Printer.

Roughton, J. F. G. 1944. Acting Chief Secretary, the Secretariat, to Provincial Commissioners. Ministry of Commerce and Industry, 2 December. MCI/6/1833, KNA.

Shiek, G. S. 1992. *"Boss" Island: The Subcontracting Network and Micro-Entrepreneurship in Taiwan's Development*. New York: Peter Lang.

Simmance, A. J. F. 1959. Application for Kiambu African Chamber of Commerce, from the Registrar of Societies. Ministry of Commerce and Industry, 22 April. MCI/6/750, KNA.

Stirton Report. 1945. Ministry of Commerce and Industry. MCI/6/1833, KNA.

Swainson, Nicola. 1987. Indigenous Capitalism in Postcolonial Kenya. In *The African Bourgeoisie*, edited by P. Lubeck. Boulder, Colo.: Lynne Rienner Publishers.

Tyrrell, T. W. 1975. T. W. Tyrell, Executive Officer, KAM, to Dr. J. G. Kiano, Minister for Commerce and Industry, 30 May. KAM files.

Wanjui, J. B. 1975. J. B. Wanjui, Chairman, KAM, to Hon. Dr. J. G. Kiano, Minister for Commerce and Industry, 25 February. KAM files.

Wariithi, M. P. 1963. In Parliamentary Debates, Government of Kenya, *House of Representatives Official Report*. Vol. 2. Nairobi: Government Printer.

Wilson, Charles. 1972. The Entrepreneur in the Industrial Revolution in Britain. In *Europe and Industrial Revolution*, edited by S. Lieberman. Cambridge, Mass.: Schenkman Publishing.

13. Institutional Constraints on Entrepreneurship in Kenya's Popular Music Industry

Robert A. Blewett and Michael Farley

African popular music provides an excellent illustration of African entrepreneurial dynamism in an industry dependent upon creativity and continual innovation. As the international marketplace of East Africa, Nairobi seemed destined to become an economic and creative force in Africa's emerging popular music industry. The establishment of Kenya's independence in 1963 marks a period in which Nairobi became a major center for the creation, production, and distribution of an identifiably Kenyan popular music. This music was well on its way to reaching audiences throughout Africa, but Kenya's contribution to African popular music has all but disappeared in the last twenty years.

This chapter explores the reasons behind the collapse of Kenya's popular music industry. It is simplistic to assume that Kenyan music fell victim to changes in taste—that it was simply a short-lived musical fad in Africa. Neither was this collapse due to a lack of indigenous entrepreneurial ability. As other chapters in this volume can attest, there is no shortage of African entrepreneurial talent. However, successful entrepreneurship does not occur in an institutional vacuum. This study argues that Kenyan popular music ceased to innovate and develop due to the unintended consequences of certain policies implemented after independence.

Although these policies were intended to foster development of African industries and markets, they imposed institutional constraints on entrepreneurs that disrupted the indigenous music industry's growth and development. Africanization policies disrupted marketing and distribution networks, effectively reducing the regional and international market for Kenyan recordings. Import, visa, and foreign exchange restrictions also reduced flows of peoples, ideas, music, and technologies from the rest of the African popular music industry. These flows, and the resultant interactions, supply the necessary conditions for a dynamic and innovative popular music scene. With effective international demand for its products reduced, and with the supply of resources essential for continued innovation also reduced, it was inevitable that Nairobi ceased to be a major force in the African pop music scene.

Materials for this case study were obtained from extended interviews with current and past participants in the Kenyan music industry, as well as with other informants familiar with conditions in the industry. The extensive literature descriptive of the Kenyan and other African popular music scenes (both past and present) was also accessed, but there is no previous literature providing analytic work concerning the economics or institutions of the African popular music industry. This case study proceeds by first examining the socioeconomic conditions that influence and give growth to popular musics, followed by a description of the structure of the Nairobi music industry. Next, evidence is offered to demonstrate that Nairobi was a major center for African pop music in the 1960s, and that it is now a pop music backwater. Africanization of the industry is then analyzed, in order to explain how it adversely affected entrepreneurs in the industry. Finally, other contributing factors related to Kenya's relative isolation from the rest of the pop music world are considered, using the successfully entrepreneurial Zairian music industry as a contrast.

The Development of Popular Music

The importance of popular music—or any other aspect of culture, for that matter—cannot be measured in terms of business activity or contributions to the gross domestic product. Popular music not only fulfills individual needs, it also affects groups within society. However, there is no clear consensus as to the meaning of the designation *popular music*. In general it may be said that the term delineates one of three ways of thinking about the function of music in society. (The other two might be referred to as art music and traditional music.) In this study, popular music has the following attributes:

- The music is a product of "a relatively highly developed division of labor and a clear distinction between producers and consumers" (Manuel 1988:2).
- The music product is "created largely by professionals, sold in a mass market and reproduced through the mass media" (Manuel 1988:2).
- The music is "primarily urban in provenience and audience orientation" (Nettl 1972: 218).

· The music is financially successful according to the degree to which it sells across ethnic and economic boundaries (Small 1984).
· The production and marketing of this product is intensely affected by, and responsive to, changes and developments in technology (Manuel 1988:3–4).
· The popularity of any particular product or style of product is relatively short lived (Small 1984).

Certain economic and social conditions are conducive to the rise of a popular music industry. The fundamental catalyst seems to be rapid urbanization. Peter Manuel states: "Rapid urbanization often brings together members of distinct ethnic, racial, linguistic, and/or tribal origins. Such groups may find themselves interacting with, and living alongside one another, and confronting shared socio-economic challenges" (1988:17).

Jacobs (1969) has described the interaction that results from the spatial concentration of large groups of diverse peoples as a phenomenon that often generates and facilitates innovation by entrepreneurs. As an industry that is driven by adaptation and change, innovation is crucial to the success of a popular music. The popular music that results from interaction between ethnic groups is not only an incredibly viable product, it may also act as an important agent of socialization. "For many, the changes wrought by urbanization and modernization are accompanied by considerable alienation, exploitation, and impoverishment. As such the creation of a new social identity assumes a crucial rather than incidental role in survival and adaptation to the new environment. To those immersed in the struggle, popular music may serve as a powerful and meaningful symbol of identity, functioning as an avenue of expression and mediation of conflict" (Manuel 1988:16).

The music that facilitates the development of this new identity must tread a narrow path. "For the city dwellers of the developing world, neither traditional 'folk' forms nor imported Western styles may fully express social identity. Rather, new musics are generated which syncretize and reinterpret old and new elements [of identity] in a distinctive metaphorical expression" (Manuel 1988:17).

In Africa, this newly created, syncretic expression must be "at once authentic and modern, indigenous but not isolated or provincial, African, but not ethnically exclusive" (Coplan 1982:125). In Africa, and throughout the world, the most successful music must be an interethnic form of expression in order to fulfill this needed function. Popular music is the result of a process in which musical ideas are shared between ethnic groups and blended. As mass media become available, these ideas are shared and blended at a much faster rate. Roberts (1972:240) cites the introduction of the radio and phonograph as central to the development of popular music in Africa.

Popular music, then, is an outgrowth of and an influence upon the interaction of diverse ethnic groups within an urban area. The growth of a popular music industry is stimulated by a number of concomitants of urbanization. These conditions create a demand for popular music and also lead to its supply:

· Immigrants to urban areas arrive in response to employment opportunities. Those who find employment have more discretionary income, leisure time, and a desire for entertainment. Thus a demand for popular music exists.
· Urban areas are typically the hubs for distribution and retail networks. As such, they tend to attract entrepreneurs who are willing to take risks and willing to finance the technology necessary to produce the music.
· Urban areas are typically the site of major broadcast facilities. With access to mass media, ideas are shared and blended between ethnic and economic groups at a much faster rate.

Nairobi as a Popular Music Center

By the time Kenyans established independence in 1963, Nairobi possessed all the prerequisites for being a center for popular music. Migration from rural areas caused a rapid increase in population with an increasing ethnic diversity. The mass media of radio and phonographs were available during this period as well. As the commercial center of East Africa, Nairobi had the business climate and distribution networks necessary to market African popular music locally and internationally.[1]

It might be expected that there would be little interaction among races, given the long history of stratification along racial lines under colonialism. However, despite ethnic and racial distrust and the acrimony that accompanied the independence movement, the overall political mood after independence was optimistic. Kenyan leaders and musicians asserted the importance of learning to live together in a new Kenyan state. John Storm Roberts described the subject matter of Kenyan popular music: "The stressing of the positive point, the uniting of once mutually distrustful tribes, is typical. . . . The man who sings 'Sisi wote ndio wananchi, si Waafrika, Wazungu na Wahindi, tufurahi ya Uhuru kwetu wa Kenya—Let all we inhabitants, Africans, Europeans and Asians, rejoice in our Kenyan independence' expresses the universal attitude of these songs to immigrant groups taken as a whole" (1968:40).

Under the influence of these conditions and attitudes, Nairobi became an ideal site for the development of a popular music industry. An examination of the institutions that existed at that time provides an excellent illustration of the kind of exchange among ethnic groups that creates a viable popular music product.

One of the legacies of the colonial system was that a license was required to conduct almost every type of business in the city. In marketing a music, individual aspects of the enterprise—recording, production, distribution, retailing, and broadcasting—required separate licenses. Each of these activities tended to be dominated by different ethnic groups in Kenya. As a result of ongoing efforts to cultivate an African market, Europeans tended to hold licenses for record pressing, while Europeans and Asians held the licenses for recording. Since the early 1920s, Asian traders had maintained a highly successful system for the distribution and retail of music that they imported from India (Stapleton and May 1990:261). Thus Asians held licenses for distribution and retailing. By the time independence had been established, African Kenyans had assumed control of Nairobi's KBC (Kenya Broadcast Corporation, the major broadcast facility for most of East Africa). Therefore, Africans held the "license" for broadcasting. The only aspect of the enterprise that did not require a license was probably the most interesting in the light of the earlier description of innovation resulting from interaction among ethnic groups: the creation of the music itself.

During the 1950s, a distinctly Kenyan music was being created in the western portion of Kenya, where there was a need for a music that would serve the needs of two ethnic groups, the Luo and the Luyia. Though both groups had individual and vital musical traditions, there was a market for contemporary music that could serve the needs of the growing, multiethnic populations in cities such as Kisumu and Nairobi. The musicians in western Kenya were also under the influence of recordings of guitar music that served the interethnic mining camps in eastern Zaire (then the Belgian Congo). By the late 1950s, they had forged a uniquely Kenyan blend of Congolese guitar music with music based on Luo and Luyia traditions. Sung in Kiswahili, the trade language of the area, this music appealed across ethnic boundaries.

All of these activities came together in a trading center within Nairobi known as River Road. Originally a lower-income Asian district on the edge of the Asian bazaar, River Road became an ethnically mixed area where

238 I Robert A. Blewett and Michael Farley

Africans tended to shop and sell goods (Hake 1977). By independence, River Road had become the center for the production and distribution of popular music.[2] Studios in the River Road area would record on reel-to-reel tapes. (By contemporary standards, the recording process was a somewhat primitive undertaking, with one or two microphones and a technician who would merely turn on and off the tape recorder.) The artist or producer would then take the tape to a distributor. The distributor would evaluate the marketability of the recording, heavily relying on the advice of African friends and employees. If the recording was deemed marketable, arrangement would be made to have the records pressed at East Africa Records (a subsidiary of the multinational Polygram and the only pressing plant in East Africa). The finished product would be marketed in local, Asian-run retail shops and promoted to contacts within the radio station. Particularly promising products would be distributed across eastern and southern Africa. Kenyan records were sometimes distributed and retailed as far away as Monrovia in West Africa and even Europe.

What Went Wrong?

Nairobi possessed the necessary conditions and characteristics to be a popular music center. The fact that it actually was a major center of African pop in the mid-1960s is widely accepted, although there are no supporting sales figures available. (A vibrant, ever-changing recording industry does not readily lend itself to monitoring by government statisticians.) Fortunately, these three indicators confirm that a thriving popular music industry existed in Nairobi: the migration to Nairobi by many artists from surrounding areas; the pan-African and international success of Kenya-based artists; and the number of record labels and distributors that existed in Nairobi.

Nairobi became the center of the infant East African music business by the end of the late 1950s. Several top guitarists from Katanga in eastern Zaire moved to Nairobi during this time. They provided the inspiration for the first generation of Kenyan guitarists such as Fundi Kande, Fadhili Williams, David Amunga, and Daudi Kabaka. These artists were also drawn to Nairobi in the 1950s. Radio broadcasts from Nairobi in the 1960s promoted the careers of the next generation of Kenyan stars, including George Mukabi, John Mwab, and Isaya Mwin (Ewens 1992: 159–65). Also in the 1960s, stars from the Ugandan music scene came to Nairobi to record, as did artists from Zaire trying to escape the domination in their homeland of the superstar Franco. Interviews with local musicians also confirmed that during this time, musicians and would-be artists from all over East Africa were being drawn to Nairobi.

The music products of Nairobi were not for local consumption only. As noted above, the more promising Kenyan recordings were distributed throughout Africa. There were also some international hits of Kenyan music (for example, "Malaika"). There was a large number of record labels and record releases in Nairobi. The number of local labels had risen to more than forty as early as 1957 (Harrev 1991:109). By 1964, a number of labels had emerged as top contenders for the Kenyan market: Equator Sound, Associated Sound, Mzuri, New Jambo, and Nissenhut Studio. Numerous small labels also proliferated throughout the city. Releases on Nairobi-based labels were substantial. In 1962, 420 releases were listed in a catalog from Capital Music Stores, while a 1964 catalog from Associated Sound showed 160 releases. Approximately 1,000 records were issued around the same period by the Jambo series; Nairobi was indeed a center for African pop music (119).

However, Kenyan popular music stagnated by the late 1970s. The developing "Nairobi Sound" lost its commercial appeal, and an identifiable Kenyan music product or style had failed to surface (Stapleton and May 1990:272). There are many indications that Nairobi today certainly cannot be considered a center for African popular music. The recording studios consist of equipment that is ten years out of date and often in disrepair. Informants state that there are no artists who can make a living from recordings alone.[3] The kiosks of Nairobi are filled with cassettes of pirated foreign music and some local ethnic music (but none that sell internationally). The producer for the most popular group in Kenya, Them Mushrooms, said there is no export market or international distribution of their recordings, with the possible exception of the occasional sale to a tourist or the odd ethnomusicologist passing through Kenya. There is no comparison between the Nairobi music scene of the 1960s and that of the 1990s.[4]

It is simplistic to hold that the collapse of the Kenyan music industry was merely the result of changing musical fashion. Kenya had been a center for too long for this to be true.[5] In other parts of Africa, notably Zaire, music continued to innovate and change. The question is, Why did Kenyan music fail to continue to innovate? What conditions allowed entrepreneurs in Zaire to continue as the dominant source of African popular music while Nairobi became a pop music backwater?

Africanization

The Nairobi Sound fell victim not to changing fashion but, unintentionally, to policies imposed after independence. Africanization policies inadvertently disrupted the institutional arrangements that had evolved within business networks that were essential for successful entrepreneurship (Himbara 1994). This, in turn, disrupted the production and distribution of music for international markets. Incentives arose to produce ethnic music that had limited appeal, diverting resources away from interethnic pop music in Kenya.

Described earlier was how the production and distribution of popular music were run out of the Asian *dukas* (shops) in Nairobi's River Road area. At independence in 1963, the residents of Kenya chose between Kenyan and British citizenship. Many Europeans and Asians declined Kenyan citizenship. Given their standing as middleman traders—unpopular minorities in a land where many Africans viewed them as foreigners, if not economic parasites—many risk-adverse Asians felt more secure remaining British subjects with British passports. This is a particularly understandable decision given the treatment later of Asians who owned commercial enterprises in other parts of Africa, particularly Uganda and Tanzania.

Many African countries in the postindependence era enacted laws, regulations, and other policies to bring about the indigenization of manufacturing and trade. Kenya was no exception. The Trade Licensing Act of 1967 excluded noncitizens from owning certain types of businesses. Thus, many of the Asian noncitizens had to sell their dukas, some at distress-sale prices. It was during the late 1960s and early 1970s that the River Road area became primarily African as the low-income Asians were displaced.

A large proportion of the subsidized loans from the government-sponsored Industrial and Commercial Development Corporation went to African Kenyans to buy out the businesses of noncitizen Asians during this period (Kennedy 1988:64). The vast majority of these Africans were Kikuyu.

Constituting some 20 percent of Kenya's total population, the Kikuyu predominate in Nairobi and the surrounding Central Province. The Kikuyu are also Kenya's commercial, educational, and political elite among Africans in the postindependence era. They now control the record shops formerly run by Asians in the River Road area, along with their other commercial endeavors. Never before had there been a significant Kikuyu presence in the music industry.[6]

A serious problem with the Kikuyu takeover of the music industry was the inability of the Kikuyu entrepreneurs to replicate the business networks of the Asian community. Without these networks, international marketing became problematic. These networks had not only provided the distribution and marketing of the products, they had also served as a source of credit and insurance to firms. To understand the problems Kikuyu businessmen faced, a brief explanation of the role of transactions costs is required.

All but the simplest contracts have transactions costs. These costs are associated with the screening, monitoring, and enforcement problems. Time and effort must go into screening potential customers and suppliers, so as to ascertain the risk of default. Contracts must be monitored to ensure that the parties to them take actions that minimize the likelihood of default. Enforcement in the event of default, or as a credible threat to potential default, also has associated costs. If these costs are high, they can prevent otherwise mutually beneficial trades from taking place. In some cases, these costs can preclude the existence of markets for certain types of credit and insurance (Hoff and Stiglitz 1990).

The risk associated with uncertain cash flows and other shocks to businesses lead to a demand for credit and insurance. The absence of credit-reporting bureaus, the relatively high costs of enforcement by the legal system, and the lack of other means for coping with transactions costs imply that markets for these business services are likely to be missing or not highly developed in Africa. If markets for credit and insurance are missing or incomplete, business enterprises lack long-run sustainability. To overcome this problem, many contracts have credit and risk-sharing (that is, insurance) arrangements tied to the exchange of goods or services. This bundling of contracts allows for other institutions to be used to minimize the costs of contracts (Boot, Greenbaum, and Thakor 1993; Zame 1993).

Repeated dealings or trades can make it easier for parties in a transaction to obtain information about each other, thereby reducing screening costs. Monitoring of behavior is also made easier as the parties continue to deal. Personalized relationships are established that develop trust (Gambetta 1988). This trust can be viewed as collateral in the event of contractual default. Trust must be built up over time, invested in like a capital good, by repeated trades or deals that do not involve implicit credit or insurance. This "social" capital good, once acquired, provides access to credit and insurance services (Coleman 1988). Continued dealings allow for the maintenance of this capital asset, while default would cause the asset to be lost. Thus, trust is very much like physical collateral in regard to its ability to be used as a mechanism of enforcement.

Reputation may serve as an enforcement mechanism that, unlike trust, does not require personalized business relationships (Greif 1989, 1993). Like trust, reputation can be viewed as a social capital good that can be used as collateral in business contracts (also see Fafchamps, this volume). Loss of reputation, however, will impose a higher cost on a defaulter because the information concerning reliability will spread to many potential business contacts. For reputation to be an effective mechanism, there must be methods of sharing information among groups of traders. For this reason, business networks are often established among ethnic minorities, or along geographical, religious, or social class lines. There needs to be some basis for repeated contact in order to share information, news, or gossip about others in the group. This screening of people by group affiliation can even lead to the monopolization of a group over particular business activities (Fafchamps 1994).

The Asian communities of Kenya had—and still have—such networks. However, in the River Road area, Africanization of the studios and retail establishments by Kikuyu entrepreneurs led to the disruption of the contractual networks established in the music industry. The Africans did not have the contacts, trading history, or reputation mechanisms with the Asian community (or among themselves) to replicate the credit and insurance arrangements available to their Asian predecessors (Fafchamps et al. 1994). The Kikuyu may have been able to purchase the physical capital, but they still lacked the social capital necessary to sustaining a viable and dynamic popular music industry.

Artists suffered as well from the Africanization of the music business. Informants from many ethnic groups (including Kikuyu) confirm that, lacking enforcement mechanisms, many Luo and Luyia musicians found that their contracts for payment often became "loans" used for working capital to Kikuyu business owners. One musician described dealing with Kikuyu shop owners during that period: "When you produce music, you need a distributor. You need a retailer. They will come and buy from you. They're not paying cash. They are getting them [the records] on credit. Hopefully, they pay you by the end of the month. . . . Now the music, the supply [of records] you give to them to sell and then go for your check at the end of the month, that is the money they use to record their own [ethnic music]. If you went up for your payment, they tell you, 'I spent all the money. You try next time.' Take them to the lawyer, he'll go up there and say, 'Yes, I'm owing this man twenty thousand bob [shillings], but I'll pay him five hundred shillings per month.' The [record pressing] factory is charging you cash."

Such opportunistic behavior is not unexpected if the mechanisms to encourage the keeping of contracts are not in place. Without this social capital, Africans were at a disadvantage—not in that the pressing plants demanded cash from African entrepreneurs, but in that, as suggested by other evidence, non-African firms did not face such a requirement (Wallis and Malm, 1984). This disadvantage persists to the present. A study by Fafchamps et al. (1994) indicates that African-Kenyan businesses are less likely to purchase on trade credit than are Asian-Kenyan firms.

The inability of African entrepreneurs to market their goods internationally, or even nationally, without access to credit and distribution networks resulted in a move into the production of Kikuyu ethnic music. Luo and Luyia urban residents may have had the musical skills, but they did not have the economic resources of the Kikuyu. The effective demand in the local market was Kikuyu. Or, as an informant said concerning Kikuyu businessmen, "What a Luyia cannot buy from them, the Kikuyu *can* buy. They have all the money they want."

But there is a major problem with marketing Kikuyu music. As noted earlier, a popular music is successful according to the degree to which it crosses traditional ethnic boundaries. Although there is a local ethnic market for Kikuyu music, it did not appeal across ethnic boundaries. There are three reasons for this. First, only one ethnic group understands Kikuyu, whereas Kiswahili and Lingala (the language used in Zairian popular music) are trade languages that are shared among many ethnic groups. A second related problem with Kikuyu music is that it tends to be more text-oriented. There is more storytelling, with allusive messages or allegories that tend to be lost on members of other ethnic groups (even without being obscured by language). Allusive messages and allegories are also common in Kiswahili and Lingala music. However, they tend to be allegories that transcend ethnic boundaries.

A third problem has to do with the sound of Kikuyu, relative to the trade languages Kiswahili or Lingala. In the process of transcending ethnic boundaries, a language becomes simpler, in regard to both the number of words available for use and the number of messages that may be conveyed using combinations of these words. As a result, the prosody (that is, the rise and fall) of the voice becomes more important in imparting a message. The prosody of these trade languages is therefore more pronounced. Kiswahili and Lingala are mellifluous languages with a slow delivery rate and graceful, arching curves that are easily discernible. In comparison, Kikuyu is known for its rapid-fire delivery and lack of notable prosody. Kikuyu music, therefore, lacks the grace and sinuosity of Kiswahili and Lingala music. Or, as a devotee of Nairobi's discotheques put it, "Kikuyu music is not seductive. It is not good for dancing."

Selling Kikuyu music across ethnic boundaries, let alone across national boundaries, was therefore problematic. The Kikuyu music was different. The difference was not only due to the different language, but also to a difference in style and sound. This is seen (with a considerable amount of ethnic bias) in a musician's comments about the Kikuyu takeover of the industry and the product they put out:

> Now, when Africans took over the shops . . . the shops were distributed unfortunately on ethnic considerations. And unfortunately those who took over the shops were not musically-oriented people. They loved the music, but they were not musically oriented people. . . . But when shops, the most important part of our industry, fell into the hands of these people . . . they just developed an interest in recording out [Kikuyu ethnic music]. They're just . . . storytellers. . . .
>
> And now what you hear . . . is not actually Kenyan music. It is ethnic music. Now you find, because they are not guitarists, what they do, they compose a melody, a song. And they bring a Luyia or a Luo to play. Now a guitarist who likes to be shown how he is going to play. A composer must be able to arrange how a song is going to be. They don't do that. They just say, "You just play the way my melody goes." . . . Now, when you listen to the song, a listener gets bored. And the singing is poor.

The Kikuyu community represented a much larger local market, so the Kikuyu owners of record shops saw the profitability of selling their own ethnic music. However, unlike the Asians, these entrepreneurs were for all practical purposes cut off from the larger international markets.[7] Without the business networks to provide credit and risk sharing, the African businesses could not profitably produce records with broader appeal. The result was that the institutional changes wrought by Africanization led to a diversion of resources in the Kenyan music industry. The diversion to a local ethnic market meant that resources were not being devoted to the creation of innovative music with a broader pan-African appeal. The stagnation of Kenyan popular music was the inevitable result.

Other Contributing Factors

Africanization and the resultant breakdown of distribution networks essential for entrepreneurship reduced the effective demand for Kenyan popular music. This is only a partial explanation for the marginalization of Kenya's music industry. While demand conditions did play an important role, there were also supply-side conditions necessary for a sustainable and innovative music industry. These conditions brought about by import, visa, and foreign exchange restrictions in Kenya, suppressed vital interactions among peoples, ideas, musics, and technologies. Kenya was effectively isolated from the rest of the African popular music industry.

The music industry in Zaire, with its freer flows of musical resources from the outside world, stands in stark contrast to its Kenyan counterpart. Examining conditions in Zaire provides a useful contrast to help understand why the music produced by Zairian entrepreneurs became so successful, while Kenyan music stagnated. Kinshasa is now the undisputed center of popular music in Africa. There is a long history of a popular music culture in Central Africa. In the 1920s, Cuban rumba music was introduced there. It had a strong influence on the popular music that developed in Brazzaville and Zaire, an influence felt to this day.

The government in Zaire was more supportive of popular music. Zairian government officials became aware, after independence, of the political influence of popular musicians. They were anxious to utilize that influence. "By the end of the 1960s, the two top Zairian singers were acting as unofficial government spokesmen, explaining its actions and singing in praise of President Mobutu. In return, they received official sponsorship, along with instruments and equipment" (Stapleton and May 1990:150). On the other hand, the Kenyan government not only had "no officially determined cultural policy" (Bender 1991:126), it also subjected the importation of instruments and equipment to high tariffs and foreign exchange controls.

But a far more important advantage that Zairian musicians had over Kenyan musicians stems from their connections to Parisian facilities and institutions. These connections enhanced and encouraged continued progress and innovation in Zairian pop. The ease of travel between France and Central Africa, combined with an easily convertible currency, the CFA franc, has resulted in the two-way transfer of resources and technology between the two regions. For example, the entry of recordings and equipment into Zaire is relatively easy, given the linkages between France and Brazzaville and between the latter and Zaire (MacGaffey 1991; MacGaffey and Bazenguissa 1994).

Paris is also a center for the production of African pop. In many regards, it should come as no surprise that a European city has become a center for African music. Many of the requisite conditions for becoming such a center, as discussed previously concerning Nairobi, are present in Paris. With its multiethnic concentration of African populations, the French capital has become the center of African culture in Europe. Many African artists congregate there, and this enhances the diffusion of innovations in musical styles and techniques. Paris is the conduit for interactions not only among Zairian artists but among musicians from many different countries and regions of Africa.

Mass media outlets, another factor supporting popular music, are also available in Paris. There is a significant number of broadcast facilities that devote extensive programming to African popular music. These include Radio France International (which broadcasts to Africa), Radio Gilda, Radio Nova, and Radio Monte Carlo (Bergman 1991:130). This creates a larger and more profitable market for Zairian popular music.

Recording and distribution is also easier in Paris. The connections between Zairian or Congolese musicians and Parisian studios and production facilities are well documented (Bender 1985; Bergman 1985; Graham 1988). It is not unusual for Zairian or Congolese artists to record in Paris, where the latest technology is available and where artists feel they have more control over their product. Contractual obligations are more likely to be kept and are more easily monitored in Paris. The distribution of recordings to the international market—not only in Africa but in Europe as well—can be facilitated from Paris. While Kenyan musicians lost their Asian networks, Zairian networks were not disrupted, and the Central Africans still had their Paris connections.

Zairian entrepreneurs were able to access and exploit the institutional resources of a foreign land so as to support their domestic music industry. This is somewhat ironic, given the stereotype of exploitive economic linkages between Europe and Africa. This irony is not lost on artists from the Third World. In the words of African musician Ismail Toure, "We're here [in Paris] because of the business system, cosmopolitanism, structure, technology . . . it's a question of having the equipment, too, and sometimes we say, laughing, that we came to colonize them" (Bergman 1985:130).

In comparison, Kenyan artists had little contact with the London music industry and far less with Paris. There is a London-based African pop music scene that is mostly populated with Nigerian and South African artists (Stapleton and May 1990:297–302). Difficulties in obtaining visas, protectionist tariffs on instruments and equipment,[8] as well as exchange controls and the nonconvertiblity of the Kenyan shilling, all removed opportunities for Nairobi's musicians to innovate and develop in contact with the larger world of popular music. The essential conditions necessary for successful innovation and entrepreneurship were missing.

It was not always this way in Kenya. In the heady days just before independence, there was free movement of peoples and musics in East Africa. Entrepreneurs and artists from Tanganyika, Zanzibar, Uganda, and the Swahili Coast were able to interact freely in an economic region without trade barriers and with a common shilling (Ewens 1992). It may not be mere coincidence that it was in the early 1960s that the Nairobi music scene was at the height of fervency and creativity.

In an industry in which it is crucial to remain on the cutting edge of technology and production techniques, Kenyan musicians were cut off from the rest of the world. The musical product of Kenya became stylistically dated. By the late 1970s, it was also obvious that the technical quality of the recordings failed to keep up with that of international competitors (Stapleton and May 1990). The Kenyan popular music industry's lack of international competitiveness was inevitable, given the institutional constraints.

Conclusion

Kenya was once a vibrant and dynamic center of the African popular music industry. However, this is no longer the case. The industry became stagnant in the 1970s as the unintended consequence of institutional changes brought about by policies intended to lead to economic development. Foremost among these policies was the effort toward Africanization of Kenyan businesses. Entrepreneurs require social capital or social infrastructure to enforce contracts, provide credit, and ensure risk-sharing arrangements among firms. Institutions that provided this social infrastructure were present in the Asian business community that controlled the distribution of Kenyan popular music. African business people may have taken over these Asian enterprises in the late 1960s and early 1970s, but the enterprises did not have the necessary social capital. As a result, Kikuyu entrepreneurs were effectively cut off from the international market and were induced to produce for a local ethnic market. This diversion of resources slowly strangled the dynamism out of the Kenyan popular music scene.

Other policies that restricted contact and interaction with the outside world were even more important in dooming Nairobi to be a pop music backwater. Import, visa, and foreign exchange restrictions severely reduced the flows of peoples, ideas, musics and technologies from the rest of the African popular music world. These policies were disastrous for entrepreneurs in an innovative and dynamic music industry. Contrasted with the Zairian music industry, with its extensive linkages with Paris, and via Paris with the rest of francophone Africa, it is clear that Kenya's industry, isolated, failed to provide the institutional capacity for entrepreneurs to remain competitive in the ever changing pop music scene.

It is tempting to apply the lessons learned from this case study of entrepreneurs in the Kenyan popular music industry to entrepreneurs in other industries in Kenya or other parts of Africa. However, a careful analysis of the particular institutional context of each case should be undertaken before making any broader generalizations. What is known is that institutions matter. Entrepreneurship does not take place in an institutional vacuum. In the case of African popular music, institutions that allow for greater interaction among peoples and musics also give rise to the necessary conditions for a dynamic and innovative industry that can remain internationally competitive.

Notes

1. The nightclub scene can provide a source of income to musicians, as well as a venue to develop music and musical styles. But unlike other major and minor centers of African pop music, Nairobi lacked a sizable live performance market. Given its population, the city had relatively small African patronage in its clubs. While these establishments could provide jobs to supplement the incomes of musicians, they were unlikely to serve as incubators for cutting-edge African pop. However, lack of a vibrant African nightclub scene did not prevent Nairobi from being a center of African pop. In contrast, the more vibrant African night life of Kampala did not enable the Ugandan capital ever to become more than a very minor center of popular music.

2. Popular music tends to develop in lower-income residential and commercial districts where ethnic groups intermingle and conduct business (for example, Storyville in New Orleans, Tin Pan Alley in New York City, the *favela* known as Manguira in Rio de Janeiro, and the Malonge district of Kinshasa, Zaire). River Road was such an area.

3. There are two artists who do come close to being able to earn a living from recordings alone: Daniel Owino Misiani, a Luo who records popular music, and Joseph Kamaru, a Kikuyu who now records gospel music. Both have been able to cross over and appeal to other ethnic groups.

4. The nature of the music industry in the two periods is not comparable either. Cassette tapes and inexpensive cassette players have completely changed the recording industry. Worldwide, vinyl record sales peaked in 1978, with 1988 sales being only 42 percent of peak levels (Hung and Morencos 1990).

5. Some places can have short periods of success due to a music fad, for example, Liverpool and Manchester in the mid-1960s, starting with the success of the Beatles and the "Merseyside Sound." However, it was only a few years before London again became the center of British pop. Nairobi was a center of African pop for over fifteen years, going through several "generations" of pop music before its demise.

6. The Luo and Luyia, whose ancestral homes are in the western portion of the country, were the innovative and creative forces in the industry. There are strong feelings among members of these communities that Kikuyu dominance was the result of political favoritism based on ethnic considerations. However, these ethnic

groups were never well represented among the commercial interests in their own homelands, let alone in Nairobi.

7. Multinationals CBS Records and EMI did enter the Kenyan market in the 1970s. While the primary reason for this was to produce and import for the domestic market, there was also the hope of finding African music suitable for export. These large recording companies tend to be on the lagging edge of musical innovation in any country or area of the world. Seeming to have a particularly unsuitable organizational structure for innovation, these corporations tend to rely on more entrepreneurial, independent companies to discover new talent and to create new musical trends. In the late 1950s and 1960s in Kenya, Asian entrepreneurs searched the rural roads to find talented musicians. Without such local entrepreneurial efforts, the multinationals failed to exploit Kenyan musical resources. Both corporations left Kenya by the late 1970s after substantial losses.

8. Restrictions on the importation of the computer hardware and software that facilitate the production of popular music became a particularly important limitation in the Kenyan music industry by the 1980s.

References Cited

Bender, Wolfgang. 1991. *Sweet Mother: Modern African Music.* Chicago: University of Chicago Press.

Bergman, Billy. 1985. *Goodtime Kings: Emerging African Pop.* New York: Quill.

Boot, Arnold, Stuart Greenbaum, and Anjan Thakor. 1993. Reputation and Discretion in Financial Contracting. *American Economic Review* 83 (December):1165–83.

Coleman, James. 1988. Social Capital in the Creation of Human Capital. *American Journal of Sociology* 94 (supplement):S95–S120.

Coplan, David. 1982. The Urbanization of African Music: Some Theoretical Observations. *Popular Music* 2:113–29.

Ewens, Graeme. 1992. *Africa O-Ye! A Celebration of African Music.* New York: Da Capo.

Fafchamps, Marcel. 1994. The Enforcement of Commercial Contracts in Ghana. Paper presented at the annual meeting of the African Studies Association, November, Toronto.

Fafchamps, Marcel, Tyler Biggs, Jonathan Conning, and Pradeep Srivastava. 1994. Enterprise Finance in Kenya. Regional Program on Enterprise Development, Africa Region. Washington, D.C.: World Bank (draft).

Gambetta, Diego. 1988. *Trust: Making and Breaking Cooperative Relations.* New York: Basil Blackwell.

Graham, Ronnie. 1988. *The Da Capo Guide to Contemporary African Music.* London: Da Capo.

Greif, Avner. 1989. Reputation and Coalitions in Medieval Trade: Evidence on the Maghribi Traders. *Journal of Economic History* 49 (December):857–82.

———. 1993. Contract Enforceability and Economic Institutions in Early Trade: The Maghribi Traders' Coalition. *American Economic Review* 83 (June):525–48.

Hake, Andrew. 1977. *African Metropolis: Africa's Self-Help City.* New York: St. Martin's Press.

Harrev, Flemming. 1991. Jambo Records and the Promotion of Popular Music in East Africa: The Story of Otto Larsen and East African Records, Ltd., 1952–1963. In *Perspectives on African Music,* 2d ed., edited by Wolfgang Bender, 102–19. Bayreuth, Germany: Bayreuth University.

Himbara, David. 1994. The Failed Africanization of Commerce and Industry in Kenya. *World Development* 22 (March):469–82.

Hoff, Karla, and Joseph Stiglitz. 1990. Introduction. Imperfect Information and Rural Credit Markets—Puzzles and Policy Perspectives. *World Bank Economic Review* 4 (3):235–50.

Hung, Michele, and Esteban Morencos. 1990. *World Record Sales, 1969–1990: A Statistical History of the World Recording Industry.* London: The International Federation of the Phonographic Industry.

Jacobs, Jane. 1969. *The Economy of Cities.* New York: Random House.

Kennedy, Paul. 1988. *African Capitalism: The Struggle for Ascendancy.* New York: Cambridge University Press.

MacGaffey, Janet. 1991. *The Real Economy of Zaire: The Contribution of Smuggling and Other Unofficial Activities to National Wealth.* Philadelphia: University of Pennsylvania Press.

MacGaffey, Janet, and Rémy Bazenguissa. 1994. The End of the Rainbow: Three Case Studies of Women Traders from Central Africa. Paper presented at the annual meeting of the African Studies Association, November, Toronto.

Manuel, Peter. 1988. *Popular Music of the Non-Western World: An Introductory Survey.* New York: Oxford University Press.

Nettl, Bruno. 1972. Persian Popular Music in 1969. *Ethnomusicology* 16 (2):218.

Small, Christopher. 1984. *Music of the Common Tongue: A Celebration of Afro-American Music.* New York: Riverrun Press.

Roberts, John Storm. 1968. Kenya's Pop Music. *Transition* 4 (19):40–43.

———. 1972. *Black Music of Two Worlds.* Tivoli, N.Y.: Original Music.

———. 1983. *Before Benga, vol. 2: The Nairobi Sound.* Compact disc, OMCD 022. Tivoli, N.Y.: Original Music.

Stapleton, Chris, and Chris May. 1990. *African Rock: The Pop Music of a Continent.* New York: Dutton.

Wallis, Roger, and Krister Malm. 1984. *Big Sounds from Small People: The Music Industry in Small Countries.* London: Constable and Company.

Zame, William. 1993. Efficiency and the Role of Default When Security Markets Are Incomplete. *American Economic Review* 83 (December):1142–64.

14. Trade Credit in Zimbabwe

Marcel Fafchamps

Firms need funds or financing to operate. Entrepreneurs with insufficient funds cannot invest in new equipment and machinery, they find it difficult to reach out for new markets and products, they cannot cope with temporary cash-flow problems, and they are slowed down in their desire to innovate and expand. Access to external finance is particularly critical for poor entrepreneurs who, on their own, may never gather funds proportional to their ambitions. Understanding how African firms access external finance is essential to assessing entrepreneurship in Africa, as well as its effect on the prospects for future growth on the continent.

Studies of enterprise finance in Africa and elsewhere typically focus on bank credit; more particularly, on bank loans. However, banks are not the primary source of external finance for most African firms. Rather, trade credit—that is, credit offered by suppliers—dominates the picture. Trade credit is particularly important to small and medium firms (Staley and Morse 1965). Unlike bank loans and overdraft facilities, trade credit is not guaranteed by formal collateral or mortgageable assets. The often heard argument that credit constraints are due to lack of collateral is clearly inapplicable to trade credit transactions. Yet microenterprises appear to encounter about as many difficulties in accessing supplier credit as they do in receiving bank credit. There are, therefore, other obstacles to credit than lack of collateral. Understanding how suppliers select trade credit recipients should thus throw some light on how credit markets operate and provide a more accurate picture of how enterprise finance in Africa really works.

This chapter examines evidence on the use of trade credit among Zimbabwean manufacturing firms. (A conceptual framework for the detailed descriptive analysis presented here can be found in my recent studies [Fafchamps 1996a, 1996b, 1996c].) After reviewing the relative importance of different sources of enterprise finance and illustrating the role of trade credit, access to trade credit and determinants of trade credit terms are studied in detail. The enforcement of trade credit contracts is discussed next. Evidence on screening and monitoring procedures is presented, together with a discussion of contract compliance and flexibility practices. The respective roles of reputation, trust, and socialization are examined in detail (for example, Raub and Weesie 1990; Kandori 1992; Greif 1993). The conclusion focuses on the obstacles that small enterprises and African-owned firms must surmount to escape the vicious circle created by their weak financial base, their resulting unreliability as debtors, and their inability to access credit and thereby expand. Possible remedies are suggested at the end.

The data in this study were derived from two sources: a panel survey of Zimbabwean manufacturing firms and a series of case studies by the Regional Program for Enterprise Development (RPED) of the World Bank. The panel-survey data consisted of 200 industrial enterprises located in Harare, representing four subsectors of manufacturing: food processing, textile and garments, woodworking and furniture, and metalworking.

Two basic criteria were used in drawing the panel sample: each firm had at least five employees, and each was in charge of making its own investment decisions. The first criterion excluded most microenterprises and informal sector firms; the second excluded certain company divisions and subsidiaries of mother companies.

Among the 114 RPED firms located in Harare, 40 firms were randomly selected for a follow-up study on enterprise finance. An additional 28 firms were selected as possible replacements. Of the initial 40 firms, 16 declined to be interviewed and 15 replacements were interviewed in their stead, resulting in a sample of 39 manufacturing firms interviewed in August 1994. Most of the initially selected Asian firms and half of the African firms declined the interview.[1] Large firms were less likely to decline than firms of small and medium size. A smaller proportion of firms in the metal and food-processing sectors agreed to be interviewed.

As a result, the final case study sample tends to overrepresent large firms, firms owned or managed by whites, and firms in textile and garments manufacturing. African and Asian entrepreneurs, smaller enterprises, and firms in the wood sector tend to be underrepresented compared with the panel sample. Table 14.1 shows categories of the firms in the study classified by ethnicity, size, and sector of activity.

In addition to manufacturing firms, eighteen trading firms representing a cross section of suppliers and clients of manufacturers were interviewed. They all operated in the same four sectors of economic activity as

Table 14.1. Description of firms by ethnicity of owner, size, and production sector (in percentages)

	Panel sample (manufacturing) (N = 201)	Case study sample (manufacturing) (N = 39)	Case study sample (nonmanufacturing) (N = 18)
Ethnicity[a]			
African	33	23	22
European	46	64	56
Asian	13	5	6
Other	8	8	17
Size[b]			
Micro	20	15	6
Small	3	28	22
Medium	23	21	17
Large	24	36	56
Sector			
Food	24	23	33
Textile	13	44	17
Wood	44	13	22
Metal	18	21	11
Mixed	n.a.	n.a.	16

Source: RPED panel data, 1993, and case study sample, 1994.
a. Ethnicity of the owner or manager is not known for 7 of the originally selected 40 firms. The percentages shown refer to those firms for which ethnicity could be determined.
b. Micro, 1–10 employees; small, 11–100 employees; medium, 101–250 employees; large, 251+ employees.

did the manufacturing firms—food processing, textile and garments, wood products, and metal products. Some were active in several of them at the same time. Of the trading firms, eleven were primarily in the retail business; the others were involved in wholesale. In the absence of a readily available census of enterprises involved in trade, trading firms could not be randomly chosen and the selection approach was essentially ad hoc. Therefore, the sample may not be representative of the population of trading firms in Harare.

An effort was made to select firms of various sizes and ethnic origin. Partly due to a bias in those that declined to be interviewed and partly as a result of the domination of chains of retail outlets over the retail sector in Harare, the sample of 18 trading firms includes mostly large firms and only one microenterprise. The proportion of black traders interviewed was small—a consequence of the inability to secure interviews with micro-enterprises in the trading sector. Only five of the 57 surveyed firms (manu-facturing and nonmanufacturing) were owned or headed by women, a proportion substantially lower than that of female owners in the panel survey (19 percent).

Among the firms interviewed, most of those owned or managed by Africans turned out to be microenterprises or small firms (11–100 employees). There was only one medium-size firm (101–250 employees) headed by an African, and four large African-managed firms. Some of these were parastatals. To gain a better perspective on the problems faced by black entrepreneurs, interviews were conducted with an additional half-dozen black entrepreneurs heading medium to large private firms. These firms were not, obviously, randomly selected and were not included in the quantitative results presented in this report. However, they added to the interpretation of the survey data.

The Relative Importance of Different Sources of Finance

Manufacturing firms in Zimbabwe get funds from a variety of sources. This variety is reflected in their outstanding balances in table 14.2. On average, supplier credit is the most important source of funds, accounting for a quarter to a third of all outstanding balances in all firm size categories. Supplier credit is a form of short-term finance, but, because it is typically renewed with each order, it can last indefinitely.

Loans from nonbank financial institutions (that is, finance houses, building companies, pension funds, and government credit programs) come next. Unlike supplier credit, these loans benefit mostly large firms. Moreover, nonbank loans are unevenly distributed within each firm size category: their large share in average outstanding balances is due to a small number of large loans.

Bank overdrafts come next by order of importance. Because overdraft facilities are typically renewed annually, they contribute to firms' long-term financing in the same way that supplier credit does. Together with trade credit, they are de facto the longest-lasting form of finance manufacturing to which firms have access.

Overdrafts represent a large proportion of the funds received by microenterprises because they receive little credit from elsewhere, except from suppliers. This is confirmed by the fact that only a small percentage of microenterprises have an overdraft facility. Bank loans, like loans from nonbank financial institutions, are more important for larger firms, although for the largest firms, they are superseded by nonbank finance. Borrowing from informal sources such as friends and relatives, money lenders, groups,

Table 14.2. Outstanding balances by size of firm

	Micro (N=40)	Small (N=64)	Medium (N=45)	Large (N=44)	All (N=200)
Inflows of funds (in Z$000)					
Gross outstanding	11	406	2,799	2,5771	6,812
Category of outstanding					
Overdrafts	64%	17%	30%	21%	23%
Bank loans	0%	12%	20%	14%	14%
Nonbank loans	0%	9%	11%	30%	28%
Informal borrowing	9%	34%	8%	4%	5%
Owed to suppliers	27%	26%	30%	30%	30%
Owed to clients	0%	1%	0%	0%	0%
Outflows of funds (in Z$000)					
Gross outstanding	-9	-372	-2,054	-13,613	-3,682
Category of outstanding					
Informal lending	11%	1%	2%	6%	5%
Due from suppliers	0%	0%	2%	1%	1%
Due from clients	89%	99%	96%	94%	94%
Net balances (in Z$000)					
Net outstanding	2	33	744	12,157	3,129
Net trade credit	-5	-258	-1,180	-5011	-1,461
Net informal credit	0	134	202	358	168

Source: RPED panel data, 1993. A few firms could not be classified by size due to missing data; they are nevertheless included in the panel average. Positive number represents inflow of funds; negative number represents outflow of funds.

and competitors is not important for large firms, but it is occasionally important for smaller firms.

Most informal credit recorded in the panel survey consist of short-term loans of equipment and materials. These loans, repaid in kind, survive from the Unilateral Declaration of Independence period, during which shortages of raw materials and spare parts were severe, and manufacturers learned to share whatever they could find. With trade liberalization, the practice is likely to disappear. Unlike in Ghana (Cuevas et al. 1993; Fafchamps 1996a) and in Kenya (Fafchamps et al. 1994), advances from clients are a negligible source of funds for Zimbabwean manufacturers, even for microenterprises. This may, however, be an artifact of the sampling frame that ignores the smallest firms in which this form of credit may be important.

On the lending side, customer credit dominates the picture. Advances to suppliers were rare. Informal loans went mostly to employees. Some loans of equipment and materials by surveyed firms were also recorded. Net outstanding balances were positive for all firm categories: firms were net recipients of credit. The net contribution of informal lending was positive but small, a reflection of the extent of borrowing and lending among firms: on average, many of these transactions cancel out. On the other hand, manufacturing firms in all size categories were, on average, net providers of trade credit. A more detailed analysis reveals that 135 of the 200 panel firms were net granters of trade credit; 36 were net recipients; and 16 had a zero position due to their nonparticipation in trade credit transactions.

The fact that trade credit represents a net drain on manufacturing firms' financial resources is hardly surprising. The credit that firms receive from their suppliers covers only raw materials, but the credit that they give to their clients must cover the value of their finished products. The difference between the two is value added. The more thoroughly raw materials are transformed in the manufacturing process, the larger the value added, and the larger the need for other sources of finance to fill the gap between supplier and customer credit.

These results are confirmed by the proportion of firms using various sources of finance. It appears that the overwhelming majority of small, medium, and large firms received and gave trade credit. Most of them also had an overdraft facility. In contrast, large firms were much more likely to receive a bank loan. To the extent that frequency of use was an indicator of ease of access, microenterprises appeared to have no easier access to supplier credit than they had to bank overdrafts. In fact, microenterprises were twice as likely to give credit to their customers as they were to receive credit from their suppliers. The following section attempts to provide an explanation for this.

Access to Trade Credit and Determinants of Credit Terms

An examination of the survey responses shows that larger firms and non-black firms were more likely to receive trade credit. There seemed to be discrimination against black firms, independent of firm size. This result is similar to that obtained for Kenya by Fafchamps et al. (1994). Bade and Chifamba (1994) conducted an in-depth analysis of the same data. They concluded that firms were more likely to get credit from their suppliers when: they purchased regularly and in bulk; the trade discount was large; their end-of-year stock was high relative to sales; they were more profitable; and they had an overdraft facility. They found that firms were less likely to receive supplier credit when the supplier's share of that input was large and when the firm was black- or foreign-owned.

Firms' need for credit did not seem to be the sole determinant of trade credit, since those firms with an overdraft facility were more likely to receive trade credit. Bade and Chifamba (1994) suggested that suppliers were more willing to extend credit for large purchases (meaning large trade discounts and bulk purchases) and to regular clients (those who made regular purchases). Monopolists were less likely to grant credit than were competitive suppliers. Credit enforcement considerations seemed to play a role because firms with an overdraft facility and higher profits found it easier to get trade credit.

The survey responses showed that larger firms and non-black firms were more likely to give credit to their clients. The effect of race was less marked than in the case of supplier credit, however. Firms in the food sector were less likely to give credit to their customers, presumably because goods are perishable and turnover rapid. In their detailed analysis of the same data, Bade and Chifamba (1994) showed that firms were also more likely to grant credit when: they negotiated prices with buyers; spent less on advertising; sold to wholesalers and retailers; and received credit from their own suppliers. These results suggest that the inability to grant trade credit is another obstacle that small firms must overcome to compete successfully with large firms.

Many of these results were confirmed by the case study. As in the panel data, most of the purchases and sales made by manufacturing firms were on credit. On average, purchases on credit accounted for 81 percent of all purchases (table 14.3). Again, there were sharp differences across ethnic groups and firm sizes. White entrepreneurs in the case study sample pur-

Table 14.3. Percentages of total purchases and sales made on credit by ethnicity of ownership and size of firm

	All Firms	African	White	Other	Micro	Small	Medium	Large
				Credit purchases				
N=	52	10	34	8	4	15	10	23
	81%	57%	91%	79%	29%	81%	97%	90%
				Credit sales				
N=	55	13	33	9	7	15	10	23
	64%	41%	73%	53%	19%	65%	86%	61%

Source: Case study sample, 1994.

chased virtually all their inputs on credit; black entrepreneurs in the sample, on the other hand, only bought a little more than half on credit.

The pattern of supplier credit use was similar to that of overdraft facility: usage was high in all firm size categories except for microenterprises. It appears, therefore, that suppliers are not significantly better than banks in their ability to reach microenterprises. This result somewhat contradicts expectations from the theory: since suppliers gather information on their clients as a byproduct of the sale, it would be expected for them to use that information to screen trade credit applicants more effectively than banks do—and thus to grant credit to clients who have no access to banks. If this finding is confirmed by other studies, it implies that there is little hope of channeling more credit to microenterprises by granting more credit to their suppliers.

Similar patterns emerged with regard to credit sales, with African firms and microenterprises less likely to sell on credit than were other firms. Large enterprises sold a smaller fraction of their output on credit than did medium-size firms. Survey results indicated that large firms both purchased and sold more on credit than did small firms. African and other non-white firms purchased less on credit than did white firms, and African firms sold less on credit. Manufacturers bought less and sold more on credit than did retailers and wholesalers. That retailers sold less on credit is not surprising, since the bulk of their clients were anonymous consumers. Food-processing firms sold less on credit than did firms in other sectors. This is probably because perishable items with a short shelf space receive shorter credit terms (Schwartz and Whitcomb 1979).

The firms in the case study were asked why they bought on credit. The most common response, cited by firms of all sizes and ethnic groups, was that credit improves a firm's ability to manage its cash flow. White firms, however, were more likely to cite other reasons as well. Some, for instance, said that buying on credit was more convenient than cash from an accounting standpoint, and that it was safer than using cash for transactions because of concerns about theft. Some respondents also said they bought on credit because the supplier did not offer a cash discount, or because the implicit cost of trade credit was cheaper than alternative sources of finance. Only large firms stated that credit was automatically offered, suggesting that reputation and market power facilitated the provision of trade credit.

Firms were also asked why, if at all, they used cash for purchases. The most common reason cited was that the supplier did not offer credit. African firms were more likely to cite the supplier's unwillingness to grant credit as the only reason for buying with cash. Other firms often volunteered other reasons as well. Some said they preferred to take the cash discount; others said that cash purchases were for small, occasional purchases not worth the hassle of applying to the supplier for a line of credit. A handful of firms, all microenterprises or small firms, stated that they do not like to incur debt and preferred to pay cash.

Self-rationing is consistent with the models of demand for credit developed by Zeldes (1989), Carroll (1992), and Zame (1993); these firms probably shied away from credit because they feared that a cash-flow shock could reduce their ability to pay, lead to default, and have disastrous consequences on their personal assets. Consistent with this interpretation, most of the self-rationed firms kept precautionary savings to deal with emergencies, but only one indicated that it had other sources of income upon which it could draw in a crisis.

Asked why they sold on credit, most firms answered that it was an important dimension of their ability to compete. Some of their customers did not like to pay cash, they said, and their competitors offered credit. Additionally, they could sell more by providing credit. Several firms, none of them microenterprises, cited accounting convenience as another reason for selling on credit. One firm explained that it was using factoring, and thus could sell on credit and get cash right away from the factor. From the point of view of the firms, therefore, sales promotion was the most important reason for providing credit to customers (Schwartz and Whitcomb 1979).

Firms were asked why, if at all, they sold on a cash basis. Enforcement considerations dominated respondents' answers. In most cases, the firm demanded cash because it believed it could otherwise not be paid at all. A client's failure to repay in the past was often cited as a reason for requiring a cash payment. Rationing of credit thus took place whenever firms did not believe they could trust their clients to pay them. Other reasons for selling for cash were similar to those cited for paying with cash: small, infrequent sales were mostly on a cash basis; some buyers preferred to pay with cash; and, in some cases, the firm was unable to provide credit to its customers.

There were no strong differences across firm sizes and ethnicity for cash transactions. Microenterprises were more likely to have customers who preferred to pay cash, a possible reflection of self-rationing on the part of buyers. Possibly, buyers also preferred to pay cash simply for convenience reasons. Indeed, microenterprises sold mostly to final consumers, who perhaps chose to pay on the spot to avoid coming back to pay and having to keep track of debt obligations. Evidence of rationing of trade credit was pervasive for the reasons cited above.

Trade Credit Duration

Credit terms appeared to be relatively standardized and did not differ substantially from those observed in developed economies (Dun and Bradstreet 1970; Dun's Analytical Services 1993). Table 14.4 shows 41 percent of all firms reported that they paid suppliers in full thirty days after delivery; 13 percent paid after forty-five days; and only 11 percent paid after sixty days. The average delay was forty-five days, which is very similar to the average delay between delivery and payment observed in the four sectors of inquiry in the United States (Fafchamps, Pender, and Robinson 1995).

The delay results from the combination of two elements: the time elapsed between delivery and statement, and the time between statement and payment. In Zimbabwe, suppliers normally use monthly statements. Three-fourths of the case study firms stated that they were given thirty days from the date of statement to pay their supplier. Fewer of the small firms received credit for more than thirty days. Thus, not only were larger firms more likely to qualify for supplier credit, they also received longer-term credit (table 14.4). Discussions with respondents suggested that this was due to the better reputations or relationships that these firms maintained with their suppliers, thereby reducing suppliers' fears about eventually getting paid. Credit duration can also be affected by market power, because monopsonistic (single-buyer) firms, which tend to be larger, often are able to dictate credit terms to their suppliers.

Panel firms were also asked about supplying credit to their customers. The survey distinguished five categories of clients: local private end users, local public end user, local private retailers and wholesalers, local public retailers and wholesalers, and foreign clients. Credit terms were similar to those given by suppliers (table 14.5). In more than a third of the cases, firms reported that clients paid their accounts in full thirty days after delivery. Large firms allowed their private trading customers longer to pay, on average, than other clients. Small firms gave long credit terms because they were more likely to deal directly with private end users, who took longer to pay.

The Offering of Cash Discounts

Explicit interest charges were rare: only ten such instances were recorded in the panel survey. In supplier credit transactions half of the panel firms reported that they could have obtained a cash discount for early payment (table 14.6). A little less than half of the panel firms also offered cash discounts to some of their clients.

Survey results showed that textile firms were much more likely than other firms to be offered a cash discount, and that metal sector firms were less likely to be offered one. Non-white firms were more likely to be offered a cash discount, possibly because they were perceived to be more risky and thus enticements were offered for them to pay early. On the giv-

Table 14.4. Number of days elapsed between delivery and payment to supplier by ethnicity of ownership and size of firm

	All firms	African	White	Other	Micro	Small	Medium	Large
N =	167	19	81	38	13	56	49	46
Delay between delivery and payment								
1–15 days	13%	11%	10%	18%	15%	7%	18%	13%
16–30 days	41%	42%	40%	39%	62%	43%	31%	41%
31–45 days	23%	16%	28%	16%	15%	25%	27%	22%
46–60 days	13%	11%	11%	21%	8%	18%	12%	7%
Over 60 days	11%	21%	11%	5%	0%	7%	12%	17%
Average delay (in days)	45	50	42	38	30	40	42	60

Source: RPED panel data, 1993.

Table 14.5. Number of days elapsed between delivery and payment by clients

	All firms	African	White	Other	Micro	Small	Medium	Large
N =	164	35	71	31	20	50	43	47
1–15 days	11%	26%	4%	16%	30%	16%	2%	4%
16–30 days	38%	37%	37%	35%	30%	42%	49%	26%
31–45 days	21%	9%	23%	29%	10%	14%	30%	23%
46–60 days	15%	14%	23%	10%	15%	14%	9%	23%
Over 60 days	15%	14%	14%	10%	15%	14%	9%	23%
Average delay (in days)	50	41	57	40	46	54	41	58
Average delay with private retailer or wholesaler (in days)	40	37	43	39	30	36	43	44

Source: RPED panel data, 1993.

Table 14.6. Percentage of firms receiving and giving cash discounts

	All firms	African	White	Other	Micro	Small	Medium	Large
N =	146	14	73	35	8	51	46	39
Percentage of firms receiving cash discounts from suppliers								
	47	64	41	54	38	45	57	36
Percentage of firms giving cash discounts to clients								
	42	21	51	53	18	42	58	52

Source: RPED case study sample, 1994.

ing side, African firms were significantly less likely to offer a cash discount. Most firms reported that credit terms varied across suppliers and customers. Some respondents indicated that they indeed used cash discounts to entice early payment by problematic customers. Others, in contrast, said that when they needed cash, they gave a big discount to their cash-rich customers to raise fresh money. These findings suggest that trade credit terms are not set unilaterally by the selling firm, but are subject to negotiation. This is consistent with Bade and Chifamba (1994), who found that firms that negotiate prices with their customers are more likely to provide trade credit.

The discount rate reported in the panel survey was 6 percent on average; the median was 3.3 percent. Similarly, case study firms reported that discounts for early payment averaged between 3 percent and 6 percent. One reason that many firms continue to use trade credit is that the implicit interest rate is lower than alternative sources of credit. Consider the average case in which the supplier must, in principle, be paid within thirty days of the date of statement. In practice, as the panel survey has shown, this means that the client has on average forty-five days to pay, from the date of delivery. In addition, penalties are typically charged only if payment has not been received by the next monthly statement. Thus, on average, a client has thirty days more to pay (fifteen days before, fifteen days after) than the explicit payment term written on the statement.

On this basis, the annualized interest rates that correspond to cash discounts of, say, 3 percent and 6 percent are 18 percent and 36 percent respectively (table 14.7). By comparison, lending rates of commercial banks at the time of the survey ranged between 29.5 percent and 47.5 percent per year (Reserve Bank of Zimbabwe 1993). The normal interest rate charged on overdrafts was around 30 percent to 35 percent per annum.

For many firms, then, trade credit is an attractive source of finance.[2] A cash discount of 6 percent or more is also equivalent to that of a money-market financial investment, but without the transaction costs. A large buyer

Table 14.7. Cash discounts expressed as annualized interest rate

Discount given by supplier								
N =	All firms 24	African 5	White 12	Other 7	Micro 0	Small 6	Medium 5	Large 13
minimum rate	18%	21%	17%	20%	n.a.	20%	18%	18%
maximum rate	36%	54%	25%	44%	n.a.	48%	24%	36%

Discount given to clients								
N =	All firms 19	African 2	White 14	Other 3	Micro 0	Small 6	Medium 5	Large 8
minimum rate	22%	26%	19%	31%	n.a.	25%	14%	24%
maximum rate	27%	26%	26%	31%	n.a.	25%	14%	37%

Source: RPED case study sample, 1994. Implicit annual interest rates were calculated on the basis of minimum and maximum reported cash discounts for respondents who gave a point estimate for the credit term, and by adding 30 days to the credit term (see text for details).

with ample excess cash may thus choose to take a 6 percent cash discount. Not everyone has access to the money market, however. The highest return that small investors can obtain is 18–20 percent on a savings account. The 18 percent annual return implied by a 3 percent cash discount is thus sufficient to attract payment from buyers with excess liquidities but no access to the money market. To summarize, there is evidence that market forces are at work in determining the level of cash discounts.

Survey results suggested that non-white firms were offered lower cash discounts, perhaps because they were too poor to have access to the money market. Therefore they received a lower yield on excess liquidities and were easier to lure into paying early. On the giving side, older firms tended to give lower cash discounts, possibly because they had reached maturity and were less concerned about their cash flow. Asian firms tended to give larger cash discounts. Firm size had no noticeable effect on the size of cash discounts.

Data on cash discounts also offered some information on the extent to which firms were affected by credit constraints. For example, six case study firms had to decline cash discounts equivalent to an annual interest rate of 60 percent or more. Credit at such high interest rates is uncommon in Zimbabwe. Presumably, firms that failed to take advantage of such good dis-counts had severe cash-flow constraints. If this was true, it would have made sense for suppliers to offer high cash discounts in an effort to entice prompt payment.

On the giving side, there were six firms in the case study sample that offered very high cash discounts; one of them also reported being offered very high cash discounts from suppliers. These firms composed a highly diverse bunch: two were large white-owned firms, two were small firms (one white and one of mixed ethnic ownership), and two were micro-en-terprises (one white-owned and one African-owned). Five of these firms had overdraft facilities, but four had borrowed up to their overdraft ceil-ing in the previous twelve months. Liquidity constraints may thus have been the reason that five of these six firms were willing to grant high cash discounts. The sixth did not appear to be financially constrained, but it had until recently been headed by an older woman who was averse to debt and may have sought to minimize collection costs in this way.

There were ten firms that had attempted to increase their overdraft facil-ity but had been unable to obtain as much credit as they desired, suggesting that the overdraft ceiling was binding for them. Only two of the high-dis-count-rate firms were among them. Taken together, there was reasonable evidence that at least thirteen of the fifty-seven case study firms faced bind-ing credit constraint and that, for five of them, the constraint had led to very high discount rates. One characteristic that some of these firms, but not all, had in common was that they were high-growth firms; their rapid expan-sion had made them overextended financially. As a result, they were in a cash crunch that, hopefully, would resolve itself in time.

These cases raise the issue of access to finance for rapidly growing firms, firms that attempt to seize expansion opportunities before they have been preempted by others. These firms constitute a category that would be ex-pected to emerge following a drastic realignment of relative prices, such as the one induced by structural adjustment. The effect of credit constraints on such firms may thus impede the pace of structural adjustment in Zim-babwe.

Procedures for Enforcing Trade Credit Contracts

Screening, Monitoring, and Collateral

Unlike credit from financial institutions, trade credit does not rely on for-mal collateral. Panel firms indicated that formal guarantees were required by suppliers in less than half the credit transactions recorded. The guarantee offered was, in two-thirds of the cases, simply a signed invoice. Similarly, panel respondents required formal guarantees from their clients in only a third of the cases, mostly in the form of signed invoices.

The attribution of trade credit clearly relies on a different mix of enforcement mechanisms than those of bank loans and overdrafts, and this is reflected in the screening process. The most common procedure to solicit credit is to fill out a credit application form and provide trade and bank references. In many cases, the firm's relationship with the supplier or its reputation in the business are important. Reputation is used more by large firms; having a prior relationship with the supplier is more important for micro and small firms. A few microenterprises or small-scale African-headed firms had been recommended directly to a supplier by a third party. This in itself suggests that reliance on the formal credit reference system was insufficient to dispel the supplier's doubts. A few large firms used their market power to dictate their own credit terms to their suppliers.

When dealing with their own customers, sample firms operated largely in the same way. Only one respondent claimed that over the years he had developed the ability to judge people and thus relied on his own judgment a great deal. Most others required clients to fill out a credit application form and to provide references. Many indicated that they took on customers on a trial basis to allow them to demonstrate their reliability. Many firms collected information about their clients directly; they inspected a client's business premises or home and asked friends and others about reliability. They also relied on previous acquaintance, on the reputation of the client, and on any other knowledge of the client that they had acquired over time. Several larger firms even required loan applicants to pass an independent screening by Dun and Bradstreet, by a credit insurance company, or by their factor. When suppliers were not satisfied, they could request the credit applicant to provide a deposit, a bank guarantee, or a personal guarantee to secure their line of credit.

Survey results revealed that African firms were both less likely to be formally screened and less likely to obtain credit from the first purchase. This seems to imply that some screening was done purely on the basis of the ethnicity of the applicant. Larger firms were significantly more likely to receive credit from the first purchase, suggesting the importance of reputation as a screening device. As providers of trade credit, large firms were more likely to use formal screening mechanisms, such as credit application forms and bank and trade references. Discussions with respondents suggested that there may have been economies of scale in establishing such formalized systems. Several respondents also pointed out that a formal credit application process minimized the risk of collusion between employees and clients. Firms in the textile sector were less likely to require formal screening of their clients. This may have been because the competition in this sector was fierce, and suppliers avoided being too suspicious and antagonizing clients. African firms were significantly less likely to provide credit to first-time customers. Many plausible explanations for this result can be ruled out by regression analysis. It is not because these firms were smaller or newer and thus more vulnerable to risk; it is not because African firms did not use formal screening mechanisms. The most likely explanation is that it was a reflection of the liquidity constraints that African firms faced.

This interpretation is reinforced by the fact that subsidiaries, which as a group are less credit constrained, are more likely to give credit on the first purchase. Alternatively, it may be that African firms sell mostly to other Africans, who, as a group, are poorer and therefore more risky debtors than are non-blacks, while subsidiaries sell mostly to other well-established firms, some of which are within their own group. Thus African firms must, in addition to having less access to credit, show extra caution in dealing with their own customers.

Contract Compliance and Flexibility

As Table 14.8 indicates, firms experienced problems with contract compliance in Zimbabwe similar to those in Ghana and Kenya, where similar questions were asked (Fafchamps 1996a; Fafchamps et al. 1994). Most panel firms experienced problems of late and nonpayment by customers. Large firms were more likely to run into such problems and face a larger number of problematic cases than were small firms, a possible reflection of the larger number of clients that the large firms had. Cases of late payment were much more frequent than cases of nonpayment.

Most firms' initial response when faced with a payment problem is to seek an amiable resolution through direct negotiation. Should these negotiations fail, firms hire a lawyer and threaten to go to court. Private arbitration is rare. Few firms ever threaten clients by calling upon the police. The majority of late payment disputes are settled and business is resumed. Nonpayment results in severing the commercial relationship.

Over 40 percent of the case study firms reported that their customers normally paid late, and nearly all firms had customers who had paid late at least once. Microenterprises were less likely to have customers pay late

Table 14.8. Frequency of contractual problems

	Micro	Small	Medium	Large	All firms
Percentage of firms last year					
Faced late payment by client	63%	72%	91%	93%	80%
Faced non-payment by client	48%	56%	80%	77%	64%
Number of occurrences of					
Late payment	24	18	98	101	61
Non-payment	4	6	6	19	9

Source: RPED panel data, 1993. The distinction between late payment and non-payment is based on the subjective perceptions of panel respondents. Non-payment typically corresponds to situations with little or no hope of collecting full payment.

and to charge interest penalties; when customers delayed payment to microenterprises, they also were less likely to pay more than thirty days late.

The reason for these findings undoubtedly is that microenterprises are typically so liquidity-constrained that they cannot afford to have their customers pay late. Whenever they give credit, which tends to be less frequently, it is for a shorter duration, and delays are also short. Interviews with respondents indicated that microentrepreneurs took the time necessary to harass their clients until they got their money. They could not survive otherwise. Firms owned by Africans and other non-white ethnic groups also appeared less likely to have customers pay late or delay for a long time.

Most firms view repayment delays of less than one month as part of doing business. It is understood that customers sometimes face temporary cash-flow problems that prevent them from paying on time. Such delays are no cause for major concern, especially if the customer has a good track record. After thirty days, firms get more annoyed and begin taking action. Many firms nevertheless indicate that what action they take depends upon their relationship with the customer and upon the extent of communication between the two.

Firms repeatedly stated that if customers came forward saying they were facing a short-term problem and then demonstrated a good-faith effort to pay, no action was taken beyond, perhaps, the imposition of interest penalties. If the suppliers felt that the customer was not behaving responsibly, however, or if the customer was not valued, the supplier could stop deliveries and, in extreme cases, take the client to court.

Firms typically have a hierarchy or sequence of responses when a client

268 | Marcel Fafchamps

fails to pay, beginning with contacting the debtor to find out what the problem is, then using repeated requests, perhaps coupled with threats to stop supplying the customer, then stopping supplies, then sending the customer a final notice, and finally turning the matter over to an attorney. There is some variation among firms, as large, monopolistic firms are quicker to stop deliveries, while others appear at a loss to prevent payment delays on the part of large or single buyers (monopsonists), including government agencies.

Conversations with respondents indicated that flexibility appeared to have diminished in recent years, as inflation and tighter monetary conditions had led to much higher nominal interest rates, increasing incentives to pay late and making default more likely. Firms were more anxious to receive payment on time and more willing to impose penalties for late payment. In many cases, they even had reduced the repayment period or stopped providing trade credit altogether.

Reputation, Trust, and Socialization

Trust and reputation play a central role in the way creditors screen debtors and in the way contractual difficulties are handled. As table 14.9 shows, nearly 90 percent of the sample firms indicated that they were familiar with their suppliers at least as business acquaintances, and many said that the relationship had social dimensions as well. Several respondents commented on the importance of a good relationship with suppliers, not just to have access to trade credit or flexibility in repayment, but also to help ensure that supplies were available, reliable, and of good quality.

Fewer microenterprises and African firms reported being acquainted with their suppliers, a feature consistent with the previous finding that suppliers are more likely to stop deliveries to such firms. Microenterprises and African firms were also less likely to be acquainted with their custom-

Table 14.9. Social relationships with suppliers and clients

	All firms	African	White	Other	Micro	Small	Med.-large	
N =	56	13	34	9	7	15	10	24
Percentage of firms claiming to have social relationships with								
suppliers	89	77	86	100	71	93	89	92
clients	73	62	77	78	57	67	70	83

Source: Case study sample, 1994. Other firms have either no personal interaction or minimal business contacts.

ers, and, in general, sample firms were less acquainted with their customers than with their suppliers. This is because firms generally have more customers than they do suppliers, but it also reflects the fact that for many years Zimbabwe was a supply-constrained economy in which the availability of raw materials and spare parts was problematic.

Reputation plays an important role in enforcing trade credit contracts. Most firms believe that defaulting on a particular supplier could result in losing credit from all suppliers. This perception is more common among larger firms. An implication of this is that larger firms have more "social capital" at stake, and so their reputation can be used as an enforcement mechanism. Most firms also indicated that delinquent customers could lose the ability to obtain credit from other suppliers. Microenterprises constituted an exception: only one such firm indicated that it could face a reputational penalty. This is important, because it may explain why microenterprises fail to get trade credit in the first place. Microenterprises also appear unable to impose a reputational sanction onto their own customers.

There are two most common means by which reputational penalties are imposed: the information published in the *Dun and Bradstreet Gazette*, and informal networks of suppliers who share information. Most firms nevertheless indicate their reluctance to spread "bad press" about a problematic client as long as there is a chance they may get paid. Reputational penalties are thus strongest in case of clear-cut default. The importance of formal credit ratings via Dun and Bradstreet suggests a degree of sophistication in the circulation of credit reference information not found in Ghana or Kenya, where firms rely exclusively on informal information networks, if on anything at all (Fafchamps 1996a; Fafchamps et al. 1994).

Taken together, these results support the importance of both reputation and personal relationships in commercial transactions, particularly in trade credit. Reputation is important in Zimbabwe because of the existence of several interconnected networks of credit reference information, at the center of which lies Dun and Bradstreet. The existence of these networks is what enables firms to rely on formal screening procedures and to grant credit to many first-time buyers. Thus, the system frees firms from exclusive reliance on personal relationships and past experiences, but it does not benefit all firms in the same way. Large firms with a well-established reputation are the major beneficiaries of the system. Many smaller firms eventually benefit from the system, once they have established a track record. But the reputation system represents a formidable hurdle for new firms. It generally fails to benefit microenterprises, because they often do not meet an essential prerequisite: registration with the Registrar of Companies. Registration is costly, as it requires the establishment of formal accounts and the payment of various fees.

Firms without a publicly visible track record must fall back on more rudimentary practices for establishing trade credit relationships of the kind that were documented in Ghana and Kenya, namely, personal recommendation and trust building. Those that do not pass formal screening often are given another chance to prove themselves over a trial period. They may be able to gain support from a third party who will vouch for them or even, in some rare cases, guarantee the payment of their debts. At every step of the screening mechanism, suppliers must assess the information in light of what they know of the general population of potential trade credit recipients. Because blacks as a group are poorer and black firms tend to be younger and less experienced, statistical discrimination probably affects how suppliers perceive them, particularly, but not necessarily, if it is reinforced by prejudice.

Conclusion

Zimbabwean firms typically finance their activities from a variety of sources. Trade credit is an important source of short-term liquidity for most firms, and terms are comparable to those in industrialized economies. Suppliers modulate credit terms by the type of borrower. Large firms tend to get credit for longer periods at lower interest rates; they are also more likely to be offered cash discounts. These findings may reflect market power and differences in credit costs due to the existence of fixed transaction costs. Variations in cash discounts and repayment periods reflect differences in suppliers' own conditions and differences among their customers.

The firms use a combination of formal screening, statistical discrimination, reputation, and acquaintance before granting trade credit. Most suppliers use sophisticated screening procedures and rely on the reputation of the credit applicant if it is easily assessed. Unknown clients may be provided credit only after a trial period. Large firms are more likely to obtain trade credit thanks to reputation and market-power effects.

The evidence again suggests that statistical discrimination may be used when assessing credit recipients. African firms are less likely to be formally screened, indicating that suppliers find it more difficult to collect and gauge information on African firms than on other firms. African firms themselves are also less likely to provide trade credit, a possible reflection of liquidity constraints and their own inability to identify trustworthy clients.

Reputation and relationships are important means of determining access to trade credit, as well as of enforcing repayment. The ability to use reputational penalties is fairly sophisticated in Zimbabwe, and the use of credit ratings by Dun and Bradstreet and other organizations is fairly common. Reputation effects are most important for large firms. Relationships are more important for small and medium firms. Microenterprises typically have neither. African entrepreneurs are less likely to know their bankers or their suppliers personally. Due to this lack of connections with the white- and Asian-dominated business community, African firms appear at a disadvantage in accessing credit beyond the difficulties inherent to their young age and small size.

There is ample evidence that certain Zimbabwean manufacturing firms are rationed in their access to credit. Evidence suggests that African firms are less likely to obtain trade credit than are other firms, controlling for factors such as firm size, age, and sector of activity. These findings suggest that differences based purely on ethnicity exist in Zimbabwe's trade credit market because of two factors. First, African firms as a group may be subject to statistical discrimination: they are perceived as being less reliable in repaying loans, possibly because they receive less credit and find it harder to smooth cash-flow shocks (Fafchamps, Pender, and Robinson 1995: chap. 6). Second, African firms are generally less well connected and have few acquaintances in banking and business. Socialization with potential sources of finance is low, and personal relationships are rare. Black entrepreneurs are thus disadvantaged by their lack of business contacts and by the difficulty of distinguishing themselves from the mass of financially insecure and short-lived African-owned businesses in Zimbabwe. A vicious circle is created between weak financial base, unreliability as a debtor, and inability to access credit.

Although it is hazardous to draw general policy recommendations from a limited sample, the analysis presented here suggests many ways to break this vicious circle. Credit delivery programs to microenterprises should focus on teaching loan recipients the rules of the business game and on helping promising entrepreneurs to graduate into the pool of medium-size firms. Encouraging financial discipline among small borrowers from targeted credit programs and circulating information about their repayment performance should provide the best of them with the track record required to gain access to overdraft facilities and supplier credit.

More opportunities for business contacts between black and white entrepreneurs should also be created. For instance, a selective program of internships in established firms could be set up to expose promising black entrepreneurs and college graduates to the business world. Alternatively, programs could be designed to encourage established firms to experiment with black subcontractors, for example by providing contract insurance at subsidized rates or by helping to screen potential subcontractors.

Author's note: I benefited from comments from and discussions with Tyler Biggs, Pradeep Srivastava, John Pender, Elizabeth Robinson, Jonathan Conning, and participants in various seminars, conferences, and symposia. The research upon which this chapter is based was financed by the World Bank.

Notes

1. In this chapter, Zimbabweans of African, European, and Asian origin are referred to as Africans (or blacks), whites, and Asians, respectively. The Asian population in Zimbabwe includes people from the Middle East (Arabs, Syro-Lebanese) and South Asia (Indians, Pakistanis).

2. Additional support for this interpretation is provided by the fact that 15 percent of the firms gave as a reason for using trade credit that it was cheaper than alternative sources of credit.

References Cited

Bade, Jan, and Ronald Chifamba. 1994. Transaction Costs and the Institutional Environment. In *The Manufacturing Sector in Zimbabwe: Dynamics and Constraints.* Regional Program for Enterprise Development (RPED) Country Study Series, Free University of Amsterdam. Washington, D.C.: University of Zimbabwe and World Bank.

Carroll, Christopher D. 1992. The Buffer-Stock Theory of Saving: Some Macroeconomic Evidence. *Brookings Papers on Economic Activity* 2:61–156.

Cuevas, Carlos, Rebecca Hanson, Marcel Fafchamps, Peter Moll, and Pradeep Srivastava. 1993. Case Studies of Enterprise Finance in Ghana. March. Washington, D.C.: World Bank and RPED (draft).

Dun and Bradstreet. 1970. *Handbook of Credit and Collection.* New York: Dun and Bradstreet.

Duns Analytical Services. 1993. Industry Norms and Key Business Ratios: Desk-Top Edition, 1992–1993. New York: Dun and Bradstreet Information Services.

Fafchamps, Marcel. 1996a. The Enforcement of Commercial Contracts in Ghana. *World Development* 24 (3):427–48.

———. 1996b. Market Emergence, Trust, and Reputation. Stanford: Stanford University, Department of Economics (mimeo).

———. 1996c. Ethnicity and Markets: Supplier Credit in African Manufacturing. Stanford: Stanford University, Department of Economics (mimeo).

Fafchamps, Marcel, Tyler Biggs, Jonathan Conning, and Pradeep Srivastava. 1994. *Enterprise Finance in Kenya.* Regional Program on Enterprise Development. Washington, D.C.: World Bank, Africa Region.

Fafchamps, Marcel, John Pender, and Elizabeth Robinson. 1995. *Enterprise Finance in Zimbabwe*. Regional Program for Enterprise Development. Washington, D.C.: World Bank, Africa Region.

Greif, Avner. 1993. Contract Enforceability and Economic Institutions in Early Trade: The Maghribi Traders' Coalition. *American Economic Review* 83 (3).

Kandori, Michihiro Kandori. 1992. Social Norms and Community Enforcement. *Review of Economic Studies* 59 (1):63–80.

Raub, Werner, and Jeroen Weesie. 1990. Reputation and Efficiency in Social Interactions: An Example of Network Effects. *American Journal of Sociology* 96 (3):626–54.

Reserve Bank of Zimbabwe. 1993. *Quarterly Economic and Statistical Review* 14 (3).

RPED. 1993. *First Report on the Zimbabwe Survey*. Free University of Amsterdam. Amsterdam: University of Zimbabwe and World Bank.

———. 1994. *The Manufacturing Sector in Zimbabwe: Dynamics and Constraints*. RPED Country Study Series, Free University of Amsterdam. Washington, D.C.: University of Zimbabwe and World Bank.

Schwartz, Robert A., and David K. Whitcomb. 1979. The Trade Credit Decision. In *Handbook of Financial Economics*, edited by J. Bicksler. New York: North-Holland.

Staley, Eugene, and Richard Morse. 1965. *Modern Small Industry for Developing Countries*. New York: McGraw-Hill.

Williamson, Oliver. 1985. *The Economic Institutions of Capitalism*. New York: Free Press.

Zame, William. 1993. Efficiency and the Role of Default When Security Markets Are Incomplete. *American Economic Review* 83 (5):1142–64.

Zeldes, Stephen. 1989. Optimal Consumption with Stochastic Income: Deviations from Certainty Equivalence. *Quarterly Journal of Economics* 104 (2):275–98.

PART V

Structural Adjustment and African Entrepreneurs

15. Negotiating Identities during Adjustment Programs: Women Microentrepreneurs in Urban Zimbabwe

Mary Johnson Osirim

Like their counterparts throughout much of sub-Saharan Africa, women who work as microentrepreneurs in urban Zimbabwe have faced increased hardships during the past eight years under the country's Economic Structural Adjustment Program (ESAP). Their difficulties include declining profits and increased competition, higher costs for business inputs, and escalating expenditures for family maintenance. Despite these problems, however, the women remain committed to their enterprises and continue to function as microentrepreneurs; they try to enhance their revenues, minimize their risks, and invest in the future of their businesses. Coupled with these activities, they continue to contribute to community and national development, namely through their investment in human capital.

This chapter seeks to examine the problems under adjustment faced by women who establish microenterprises in market trade, crocheting, sewing, and hairdressing in Harare and Bulawayo. A microentrepreneur is defined here as a person who began and owns a business employing no more than five persons.[1] Based on interviews with more than 100 women in these fields, this chapter presents a profile of these microentrepreneurs and explores the state's adjustment program and the role of governmental and nongovernmental organizations (NGOs) in providing support for women's businesses. Further, policy recommendations are offered to improve the status of women in these enterprises. To understand how these women define themselves and their decisions to become microentrepreneurs, this investigation begins with an analysis of the structural factors in the historical and contemporary periods that have restricted women's options in the Zimbabwean labor market. How have these women "negotiated their identities" in periods of social transformation?

Why Women Enter Microentrepreneurship: The Costs of Being Poor, Black, and Female

Small-scale agricultural production and microentrepreneurship are the two major areas of income earning for women in Zimbabwe (Saito 1990; Horn 1994). Women predominate in these spheres, precisely because of the structural blockage they experience in the society as a whole, and in the formal sector in particular, based on the legacy of colonialism, continued patriarchy, and gender-role socialization (Clark 1988; Meena 1991; Schoepf 1992; Osirim 1994). The current economic crisis and attempts to ameliorate it through the adoption of the ESAP further circumscribe the roles of poor and low-income women to farming and participation in the so-called informal economy. How can the historical underpinnings of the current crisis and the limitations that these women face in the labor market be understood?

In precolonial Zimbabwe, women and men were primarily involved in agricultural production. Among the Shona-speaking people, who constitute over 75 percent of the Zimbabwean population today, a gender-based division of labor existed where land for cultivation was allocated to married men by village headmen (Holleman 1951; Horn 1994). Married men in turn would allocate land for garden plots to their wives, and these plots would be used to feed the family, with any surplus to be used for trade. Men were responsible for clearing the land, felling trees, and soil preparation, while women were engaged in planting, weeding, and harvesting the crops. Thus, in the precolonial period, although a gender-based division of labor existed, both women and men had responsibilities for the overall maintenance of their households (May 1983; Horn 1994).

Settler colonialism in Zimbabwe enacted a severe toll on black Africans, especially on black women, and exacerbated the division of labor based on gender. The white colonial government established a system of Tribal Trust Lands for blacks and reserved the most fertile lands for white cultivation. Major restrictions were placed on the social and geographical mobility of blacks, to control the supply of labor and to ensure the hegemonic position of whites, who were far outnumbered by black Africans (Horn 1994; Osirim 1994). The state imposed taxes on blacks payable in cash, thus creating a need for black males to leave subsistence agriculture in the Tribal Trust Lands to pay these taxes (Horn 1994). Black males were drawn to the towns and cities to work in the mines and the factories, while black women remained in the reserves as subsistence farmers.

Even those few black women who eventually migrated to the cities and towns were clearly restricted in their activities to illegal beer brewing and trading, particularly in the indigenous foodstuffs that were not provided by the white commercial establishments (Seidman 1984). Throughout this period, many black men were provided with just enough formal education to enable them to fulfill their responsibilities in the labor market, while the majority of black women lacked opportunities for formal education in the Tribal Trust Lands (Seidman 1984; Osirim 1994).

During colonialism, black women were minors, subject to the control of their husbands, fathers, and other male relatives (Made and Whande 1989). Over a period of ninety years, then, their status had shifted from that of producers and reproducers in the precolonial period to that of reproducers and dependent minors under British colonialism (Osirim 1992). While both black men and black women suffered the injustices of colonialism, black men generally left this period with higher levels of educational attainment, majority legal status, and greater experience in the cash economy than their female counterparts.

Unlike previous colonial regimes, the postindependence government was committed to promoting equality between women and men in the society, particularly since both sexes had participated in the liberation struggle (Seidman 1984; Batezat and Mwalo 1989; Stoneman and Cliffe 1989; Osirim 1994). State efforts to improve the status of women were visible in many areas, from the creation of the Ministry of Community and Cooperative Development and Women's Affairs in 1981 and the subsequent change in women's legal status to the extension to women of educational opportunities, job training, and other social services. However, poor black women were not the major beneficiaries of these changes. They often lacked the access to resources and formal-sector networks where information about such programs was made available, and therefore, they continued to experience restricted social mobility.[2] Thus, poor women's low levels of educational attainment and restricted access to formal sector employment remain a legacy of British colonialism that has not adequately been rectified by the postindependence state.

Poor women with low levels of educational attainment can either participate in subsistence agriculture, work as agricultural laborers or domestics, or begin microenterprises. The decision to become self-employed carries with it a series of positive and negative factors; the entrepreneurs in this study maintained that the positive outweighed the negative. In addition to the constraints that they experienced in the educational sphere and the labor market, self-employed women were generally restricted in those avenues of trade and production that were open to them. They were concentrated in the trade of food and household goods, domestic service, food processing and/or preparation, beer brewing, prostitution, hairdressing, sewing, knitting and crocheting, pottery making, and other handicrafts (Moyo et al. 1984; Muchena 1986; Saito 1990; Osirim 1992).

Men were more likely to be involved in more lucrative areas with greater growth potential, including auto and electrical repair, metalworking, carpentry, shoe repair, tailoring, construction, upholstery work, and stone carving (Moyo et al. 1984). Not only were women channeled into the more traditional areas of microentrepreneurship through the messages and education that they received from their relatives and the school system, but contemporary training programs for the most part are still reinforcing these divisions. In several training programs sponsored by the city councils of Harare and Bulawayo in conjunction with foreign donors, few women received training in the nontraditional, male activities listed above (Osirim 1992, 1994).

Women who engage in the production and sale of foodstuffs also face a greater daily toll on their health and overall well-being than what is generally experienced by their male counterparts. Many of these women have to purchase food on a daily basis, since traders often lack refrigeration for their goods. Such purchases require the use of public transportation, which means increasing costs and long waiting periods. Most men's enterprises do not require daily purchases.

Poor and low-income women microentrepreneurs seldom receive loans for their businesses from commercial banks or from governmental or nongovernmental associations supposedly created to meet their needs. The major beneficiaries of such loans (after men) have been women from middle- and upper-middle-class backgrounds who have generally received higher education, are connected directly or indirectly (through their husbands) to formal sector networks in the state and in banking, have larger, more profitable enterprises, or can meet the collateral requirements posed by commercial banks. Most low-income women microentrepreneurs do not possess these characteristics and are often unaware of what opportunities exist to assist them.

The decision to enter microentrepreneurship does offer some advantages to poor and low-income women. First, as stated above, it is one of the very few avenues through which women can support themselves and their families. This situation has become even more essential as unemployment has escalated under adjustment and women find themselves increasingly heading households. In southern Africa, 25 percent to 40 percent of all households are headed by women (Made and Whande 1989). Second, microentrepreneurship enables women to fulfill their domestic responsibilities more easily. They have more flexibility in their work schedules (more than do most formal sector employees) and can combine their business tasks with child care. Older children often assist their mothers in such tasks as carrying items to the market or knitting, crocheting, and sewing segments of a garment at home. Through this process, women transmit skills to their daughters, even among those who attend school.

Recent changes in the Zimbabwean state and economy, however, present low-income microentrepreneurs with new challenges. Declining prices for primary product exports, destabilization in the region caused by South Africa in the 1980s, and several droughts in the 1980s meant that the government could not sustain the growth in employment and the expansion of social services it had embarked upon in the immediate postindependence period (Osirim 1994). To rectify the economic crisis, the Zimbabwean state enacted an ESAP in 1990 at the behest of the World Bank and the International Monetary Fund. This can be viewed as part of the larger process of the expansion of the global economy in which international lenders and Western governments have encouraged the adoption of "free-market" policies and the "shrinking of the state" (DAWN 1995).

Such adjustment programs are problematic for women microentrepreneurs for several reasons. Many men lose formal sector employment under adjustment, and this has a twofold effect on self-employed women. Women are expected to increase their contributions to the support of their families and households, and women experience greater competition from men and from other women who may enter the informal economy for the first time. Not only do women have to assume added responsibilities in sustaining the family, but the expenses associated with these responsibilities have increased because of the removal of subsidies from basic social services. Further, unstable economic conditions have also led to an escalation of violence against women in the household.[3]

The state encourages retrenched male workers to begin small and micro-enterprises as a means of earning a livelihood. As previously argued, men are generally advantaged over women, especially poor women, in their access to loans and other resources, thereby compounding the problems for women. Men also enter into competition with women in the sale of food, either through obtaining stalls in the market or through establishing produce stores, over which they enjoy a near complete monopoly. Thus, women are again disadvantaged at the same time as they are forced to shoulder more of the burdens to maintain their families.

The Economic Structural Adjustment Program: What Costs for the Poor?

Before exploring the specific impact of the ESAP on the business activities of women microentrepreneurs in Zimbabwe, it is worth noting the hardships that this program has wrought for poor and low-income families, especially for women and children. To improve the economy, Robert Mugabe launched an ESAP in 1990. There was little prior consultation with the major branches of government, nor with nongovernmental organizations working on the poor and/or women's issues. It was claimed that this was a "home-grown" program; however, it contained the features common to prior adjustment programs in southern nations: trade liberalization, reductions in government expenditures, and devaluation (Training Aids Development Group 1991; Moyo 1992).

The most adverse effect of the ESAP on Zimbabwe can be seen in the growing ranks of the very poor in that nation. As a result of such programs, it has been estimated that 60 percent to 70 percent of the population in southern Africa has become very poor. In 1991, one year after adjustment, of the 10.3 million residents of Zimbabwe, 6.6 million were estimated to be living in absolute poverty (Kamidza 1994; Osirim 1995). More than 40,000 state employees lost their jobs under this plan.

State investments in social services as a percentage of the federal budget noticeably declined in the first two years after adjustment. The percentages of the total budget allocated to health, transportation, and housing declined by over 20 percent, 40 percent, and 25 percent respectively in the first three years of the restructuring plan. All Zimbabweans now have to pay fees at hospitals and clinics to receive health services, unless they are among the few patients to receive a letter from the Social Welfare Department attesting to their poverty. One of the most devastating results of this plan has been the reductions in the numbers of women and children who seek health services (Kamidza 1994; Osirim 1995). The costs of adjustment have also resulted in shortages of necessary drugs and a further "brain drain" of health professionals seeking employment abroad (Nyambuya 1994).

The state's commitment to providing equal access to education has also been jeopardized under the ESAP. School fees have now been reintroduced, which are added to the expenses for uniforms, books, and transportation.

These costs have forced parents to make choices regarding which children to send to school; as a result, young women are again finding themselves shortchanged in these decisions.

The rise in poverty has perhaps become most apparent through the periodic shortages of foodstuffs and the increasing number of street children, idle and homeless, found in downtown Harare and Bulawayo.[4] Children have become much more aggressive in their begging for money and food from those walking along the downtown streets. Homelessness has become a more visible problem, with large numbers of people nightly lining Bulawayo's streets leading to the railway station.

To counter some of the economic burdens that the poor faced under the ESAP, the state established a Social Dimensions Fund. The U.S.$4 million allocated to this fund were not enough to meet the escalating demands for such support (Gibbon 1992). In addition, as has been the case with many governmental agencies and NGO programs, those who were most in need of the fund's resources lacked knowledge of its existence—for example, women microentrepreneurs. Furthermore, an interview with a Zimbabwe African National Union–Patriotic Front (ZANU-PF) official in 1994 revealed that both retrenched civil servants and those who had retained their positions were most often assisted by the fund.

Not only have poor women disproportionately borne the burdens of the ESAP, but poor and low-income women microentrepreneurs have frequently been bypassed by the state's efforts to assist women generally and women in business in particular. Middle- and upper-middle-class women have been the major beneficiaries.

Efforts to Enhance the Position of Women Microentrepreneurs: The State and NGOs

One of the earliest efforts of the state to advance the position of women and to assist women microentrepreneurs specifically was the creation in 1981 of the Ministry of Community and Cooperative Development and Women's Affairs. This agency was charged with helping women to gain economic independence by promoting their training in nontraditional skills and by developing the technology that would decrease women's work loads (Ministry of Community and Cooperative Development and Women's Affairs 1981; Osirim 1994). In addition, this ministry worked to ensure the provision of health care, day care, and community centers to meet the needs of employed mothers.

The government further tried to advance the position of self-employed women through the creation of loan funds. Zimbank provides small loans of up to 6,000 Zimbabwean dollars (about U.S.$750 in 1994) to women entrepreneurs with no collateral requirements. The bank also cooperates with the Small Enterprises Development Corporation to provide training for women in business. Women who began cooperatives could also receive up to 50,000 Zimbabwean dollars in loans from the Community Development Fund as part of the redesigned Ministry of Cooperative Development (the ministry was downsized after the ESAP, and Women's Affairs became a department in ZANU-PF).

Although these loan schemes exist, knowledge about and use of them remained very limited among the respondents in this study. In the first series of fifty-five interviews conducted in 1991, only 24 percent of those sampled had ever received loans from any source. This situation had worsened considerably by 1994, when only 6 percent of the fifty women interviewed had ever received a loan for their businesses. Low levels of educational attainment and the failures of these agencies to advertise their programs among poor and low-income microentrepreneurs help to explain the low knowledge base among this population.

Other government efforts to assist women microentrepreneurs have been insufficient. The city councils of Harare and Bulawayo have provided market stalls for fruit and vegetable vendors and ground sites for crocheters on which to make and sell their wares. However, many produce traders at sites such as Manwele market in Bulawayo and all of the crocheters studied in both cities lacked adequate protective covering from the elements. Many women sold their foodstuffs immediately adjacent to the market, since there was no more room available under the shed. They traded in dilapidated, makeshift stalls, and crocheters sat on the bare ground to do their work. Both groups of women are unlikely to see any major improvement in their worksites in the near future, since the government claims to be strapped for resources under the ESAP.

Local governments have also encouraged the formation of cooperatives and begun training programs for women in textiles and bead making. Other state programs have been started in the nontraditional areas of auto repair, carpentry, and welding. In the latter case, no respondents in this study (mostly mature women with families to support) could avail themselves of such training, since it was only available for recent school leavers, primarily of high-school age. Further, while such efforts to provide training in nontraditional skills are admirable, the results thus far have been minimal. Young women constituted less than 10 percent of the students in each of these courses.

While NGOs for women in business also exist, most have not targeted the needs of microentrepreneurs. Zimbabwe's Women in Business is one such organization that was started in 1988, but it has mainly served the needs of elite women. In addition to providing loan support, it has been committed to working with the state to enable women to obtain needed inputs for their enterprises. Through funding in the early 1990s from the Canadian International Development Agency and the Adenauer Foundation in Germany, another loan facility was established with $1.5 million Canadian. Women who have obtained loans have been mainly middle- and upper-middle-class entrepreneurs who have established businesses and are members of the organization. No efforts have been made to publicize the loan fund, and not one woman in the study had received a loan from this group.

Perhaps the one optimistic note on the loan front for women microentrepreneurs is the Zimbabwe Women's Finance Trust, an affiliate of Women's World Banking. This group has focused on the needs of poor women and began with an emphasis on training, not credit. Those who wish to obtain a loan need to have saved at least 10 percent of the amount they plan to borrow and must present a business plan. An evaluation of the business is then conducted by the loan committee; the evaluation includes representation from local entrepreneurs. Thus far, 153 loans have been granted averaging 3,000 Zimbabwean dollars (about U.S.$375), with a maximum repayment period of twelve months. The loan repayment rate has averaged 88 percent. Only one of the fifty women interviewed in 1994 had been granted a loan from this group.

While this chapter presents a brief overview of some of the many programs that exist in Zimbabwe to assist women microentrepreneurs, my research strongly suggests that poor and low-income women are rarely the recipients of such assistance. Who are these microentrepreneurs who lack access to such programs? What problems do they face under the ESAP?

Methodology of the Study

To discover who these women are who begin microenterprises in urban Zimbabwe, and to identify the problems they experience under the ESAP, fieldwork was conducted in Harare and Bulawayo in 1991 and 1994. The first study included fifty-five respondents, while the second included fifty. Only a few of the women from the 1991 study were located to be re-interviewed in 1994. The microentrepreneurs were intensively interviewed over several hours about their personal backgrounds, their roles and responsibilities in their households and families, and the operation of their businesses. I and several research assistants also spent time observing activities in the markets, shops, and street sites where these enterprises were located. The leaders of governmental and nongovernmental organizations that provided support to women in business were also interviewed.

The interviews of produce vendors were concentrated in two markets—Mbare market in Harare and Manwele market in Bulawayo. Both are located in high-density suburbs, the areas historically occupied by black residents and removed from the more affluent suburbs and downtown areas. These areas are still predominantly black and poor. Mbare Musika is a large building with over 1,000 vendors; Manwele market is small, with about twenty vendors trading under the shed and twenty working outside in makeshift quarters. Crocheters were interviewed at a number of sites, usually in shopping centers in the low-density suburbs (historically white areas). These areas included Newlands and Kamfinsa shopping areas in Highlands, Harare as well as Ascot shopping center and the tourist market at the City Hall in Bulawayo. Seamstresses and hairdressers were generally more scattered throughout the downtown buildings in both cities.

What types of goods and services do these microenterprises provide? Traders in this sample were engaged in fruit and vegetable vending of European and indigenous crops. Crocheters made and sold adult and children's sweaters, women's tops, bedspreads, tablecloths, and doilies. Seamstresses made and sold women's and some men's clothing. Hairdressers created all the latest styles using braids or chemical straightening.

Rather than examining all of the major issues addressed in these interviews, this discussion focuses on a demographic profile of the total sample and then explores by sector some of the major problems that the women face under adjustment.

Profiles of Microentrepreneurs in Harare and Bulawayo

The majority of participants in the 1991 and 1994 samples were Shona-speaking. The Shona constitute over 75 percent of the population of Zimbabwe, while the Ndebele make up about 16 percent (Kurian 1987). One-third of the respondents in the former study and about 20 percent of the latter were either Ndebele-speaking or members of ethnic groups from South Africa, Malawi, or Zambia. The mean age of the participants was about forty-one years in 1991 and forty in 1994. Only 7 of the 105 women interviewed in both periods had no formal education. The majority of businesswomen in each period had completed primary school (62 percent of the sample in 1991 compared with 61 percent in 1994). Women with the lowest levels of education in the sample were most often market traders and crocheters—occupations they could enter with few barriers (that is, occupations not requiring technical training and licenses in order to operate, such as hairdressing) and that they could perform using the skills they had learned from their mothers and female relatives. Although several women had begun secondary school, only 10 of the 105 women had completed their lower-level secondary education. Many microentrepreneurs reported that they could not complete their schooling because there was not enough money, or because their fathers were unemployed or had died. Traditional patriarchy and gender-role socialization patterns gave preference to men over women in the broader society and in the educational system in particular. When these realities were coupled with scarce resources, fathers would most often educate sons rather than daughters, or at least enable sons to complete more years of school.

In addition, young women had to complete many daily domestic tasks before and after school and had a very difficult time passing a sufficient number of O-level exams to enable them to attend upper-secondary school even if their parents could afford it. Finally, early pregnancies prohibited many young women from completing their education, since they were forced to leave school once they became pregnant. Therefore, as previously argued, these women microentrepreneurs faced many structural barriers that precluded them from completing postprimary education and severely limited their access to formal sector positions.

Although the majority of women in the study were married, 38 percent of those interviewed were currently the heads of households, mostly as a result of divorce. Some women were separated from their husbands, while others were widowed. The highest rates of divorce were noted among market traders, seamstresses, and hairdressers. Household headship led women either to seek income-earning activities if they were not already in the labor market, or to remain employed if they already had a job. Crocheters had a higher marriage rate than the other categories of microentrepreneurs studied, due to the selection of Newlands shopping center in Harare as the major site where crocheters were interviewed. This shopping center, which is the largest venue for crocheters in the city, is immediately adjacent to the major federal prison. Many of the crocheters at Newlands were the wives of men who worked as guards or police officers in the prison.

However, the fact that women in this study had an average of four children and that many of them were single parents tells only part of the story. Even in those households where husbands were present, women reported that they had additional financial responsibilities under the ESAP.

While men are responsible for the household expenses in traditional Shona- and Ndebele-speaking families, women are increasingly meeting full or partial costs of food and clothing, as well as many of the educational and health-related expenses for their children. Many men have lost their positions under the ESAP. For others, the removal of price controls has meant that food allowances they formerly provided for their wives are absolutely insufficient to meet the costs of even basic foodstuffs, such as cornmeal for porridge (*sadza*), vegetables, bread, and rice. There are often substantial price increases on these and other goods on a weekly basis; this not only makes it difficult to afford essential items, it also poses continuous anxiety for women as to whether they can feed their families. As one Mbare market trader noted: "There are particular problems for women in this society. Because the women will carry all of the problems of having enough money to look after the children, they have to worry about earning a good living. These are women's problems. You can barely sleep during the night; you're thinking what will I have to give the children tomorrow. How will I have enough money to feed them for tomorrow?"

Businesswomen in this study were adamant in their need to earn money to educate their children. After reinvesting profits to purchase needed inputs, their next major expense and most significant concern was in meeting these costs for education. In addition to using profits to meet these expenses, women also remarked that their participation in rotating credit schemes, known as "rounds" in Zimbabwe, were a critical source of revenue for educational expenses. For some women who belonged to these savings plans, the lump-sum payments they received in January were essential to meet deadlines for tuition payments and book purchases for the new year.

The women also had substantial responsibilities for extended family members who were not living with them. Most of these obligations involved monthly cash payments to parents and in-laws. In addition, many women assisted with the costs of educating their siblings and occasionally provided informal apprenticeships and employment for their sisters and other female relatives in their businesses, particularly in sewing and hairdressing.

What responsibilities for others were involved in the operation of their firms? Microenterprises, which had a mean age of nine years and a median age of eight years, provided regular and informal opportunities for income earning. The mean and median number of workers hired by hairdressers and seamstresses in this study was three, with many of the firms employing one worker who was a relative. In some instances, crocheters provided opportunities for subcontracting. In the making of bedspreads, for example, a woman sometimes hired other workers to make several segments of the product that were later stitched together to complete the bedspread. Although neither vendors nor crocheters in this study provided regular employment for others in these cities, they did provide some opportunities to hone new skills and earn some capital.

The Economic Structural Adjustment Program: Problems for Microentrepreneurs

Businesswomen in this study voiced problems with the ESAP both in the first year after the program had been inaugurated and four years later. But the difficulties had become more severe by 1994. The major problems were: increased competition and a reduction in the profitability of enterprises; a decline in customer base; escalating costs and difficulties in acquiring inputs; increased transportation expenses; and inadequate sites in which to work. These issues are discussed for each type of business, in the respondents' own words.

While over 50 percent of the women interviewed in 1991 reported that profits had declined in the first year after adjustment, 83 percent of those sampled in 1994 made this claim. Several factors were associated with the loss of profits, but the one most adamantly expressed by women in each category was increased competition. Crocheters explained that there were far too many women selling the same goods. One woman who was interviewed in 1991 and again in 1994 remarked, "Many women are crocheting. I think there are more now than in 1991. Therefore, customers can go to other crocheters, for example, at Ascot shopping center. . . . Too many people are crocheting to sell the same goods, such as doilies. . . . I am selling less than I did in 1991 because there are no customers now."

When questioned about sales, another crocheter commented: "I think we are getting less money because there are more vendors here [Newlands shopping center]. There are too many, about sixty-five. We were much fewer before."

Competition was perhaps an even greater problem for traders. "There are too many traders selling the same goods, so there are not so many customers," said one trader at Manwele market. "This is bad, because people are selling in the streets without having any check from the health department. The health department comes here to Manwele to check the foods."

"The unlicensed vendors are a problem," said another trader, at Mbare. "They don't have to pay any license fee or rent, and they divert possible customers from coming in here to buy from us."

A walk along the downtown streets in 1994, as compared with 1991, showed many women hawking goods along the streets in order to have direct contact with many more potential customers than traders had who remained in the markets. Women maintained that these street hawkers, frequently younger and more able-bodied than some of the businesswomen in this study, had taken away many of their customers and posed severe threats to the profitability of their enterprises. But many of these street vendors were also victims of the ESAP and of the structural barriers earlier discussed, and they had no choice but to engage in such work.

Visits to Mbare and Manwele markets, especially in 1994, showed that not only were there many vendors selling the same products, there were many men selling in the markets as well. Conversations with some of these male sellers revealed that they had recently lost their jobs, and, in the case of some younger men, were unable to find work in the formal sector, even with successful results on their O-level exams and sometimes on their A-levels as well. But in comparison with women traders, these men generally had better prospects for obtaining loans to start produce stores and other activities. Such shops posed additional competition for women vendors.

Seamstresses and hairdressers also noted increasing competition four years after the establishment of the ESAP. One of their more recent fears, in addition to their concern with the ESAP per se, was the effect on the Zimbabwean textile industry of the transition to majority rule in South Africa. As one seamstress remarked: "There is a lot of competition from large establishments that can afford to charge lower prices for garments. This means that those who place orders for resale will flock to South Africa to buy there at lower prices."

Connected to the issue of increased competition was the loss of customers experienced by women in each sector. In general, microentrepreneurs noted that the rise in unemployment and in prices for essential foodstuffs and vital social services meant that women had less money to spend on most items, especially any that could be considered luxuries. The microentrepreneurs described these problems as follows:

- Cost of living is high. People are buying less luxury foods like fruits, and would rather buy the type of food that feeds a family.
- Economic-reform programs are affecting the business because fewer people are coming to the market. It [ESAP] has not worked yet—we have not noticed changes yet in the economy or socially. People have been told that employment would be created and inflation would decrease. This has not happened yet.
- With a luxury business like hairdressing, no one can make them-

selves attractive while the stomach growls with hunger. ESAP has destroyed so many families. Some of my relatives are out of work and people have lost property due to the inability to pay the increasing rates.

Perhaps the one sector in which some (not all) of the micro-entrepreneurs did not experience a loss of customers, but spoke about the potential for expanding markets, was crocheting for the South African market since the coming of majority rule. Although many Zimbabweans had been engaged in cross-border trade with South Africa even under apartheid, crocheters now noted that many South Africans were visiting their roadside sites to purchase inexpensive sweaters and other crocheted and knitted goods to bring back to South Africa for sales or gifts. They also noted that some Zimbabwean women entrepreneurs were purchasing these goods to sell in South Africa.

The adjustment package, with its accompanying devaluation, has also meant increasing prices for licenses, rental fees, and inputs for production. Microentrepreneurs in every sector complained of major rent increases for market stalls (both in and outside of the official markets), for roadside plots used by crocheters, and for buildings used by hairdressers and seamstresses. Many crocheters commented that the rising costs of wool and cotton were also making their businesses less profitable, and that fewer crocheted goods now contained any dyed cotton, more expensive than beige yarn. "I used to buy a packet of wool for twelve [Zimbabwean] dollars," said one woman, "now it is seventy to eighty."

Hairdressers and seamstresses in particular experienced other problems in obtaining needed inputs, due to shortages of capital, high import duties, and restrictions on importing certain goods. As one microentrepreneur noted in 1991: "You can't get a license to order imported hair creams, because these are considered luxury items." Said another: "You can't import these products from abroad unless you have foreign currency or pay customs duty if someone sends it to you."

Many similar concerns were reiterated by dressmakers in 1994. Said one: "A problem I am facing is that I cannot get parts for my machines when they break down. I have more than six machines that are not working and I can't find parts." Another complained: "For me to get goods with [the South African] rand, the import duty is very high. There is 35–40 percent tax on goods."

Zimbabwe certainly should reduce its import bill under the current economic conditions; since some necessary inputs are not produced locally, however, it is difficult otherwise to maintain many microenterprises. Women are again disadvantaged in trying to obtain import licenses, not only because they generally have less access to capital than do men, but also because they lack the formal sector connections that facilitate the acquisition of such documents.

Transportation poses additional problems for microentrepreneurs in Zimbabwe, especially for market traders. During the first few years of the ESAP, many traders began lining up for buses at four o'clock in the morning, since with the shortage of spare parts in the country, few buses were available. Although this problem has been rectified somewhat by the legalization of many of the "emergency taxis" (that is, old Peugeot 404 station wagons), vendors face an additional problem because of the higher costs of such public transportation under the ESAP. Of all of the microentrepreneurs' problems studied, this one was most trying for traders, because they had to take several different buses and taxis to bring their produce to the market. The rising costs of such transportation coupled with the many hours spent waiting for buses also amounted to additional physical and emotional health risks for these women (see Horn, this volume).

Although inadequate sites for their operations was a problem prior to the adoption of the ESAP, the likelihood of this problem being solved in the near future is clearly related to the adjustment program. Many market traders and all of the crocheters interviewed were working in very poor facilities. Therefore, many vendors' products were frequently damaged by rain and excessive heat. Further, market traders in both locations lacked refrigeration and lost revenues on perishable goods. Crocheters faced similar problems at their roadside locations. Many women commented that working outdoors in the winter entailed health risks. They also lost valuable workdays in the rainy season, because they had no sheds or buildings in which to work.

While both traders and crocheters have been promised new facilities by the city councils, they face little possibility of gaining these anytime in the short term because of the costs of adjustment. But despite the problems that these businesswomen experience as a result of the ESAP, they continue to function as microentrepreneurs. They attempt to minimize their risks and continue to invest profits in their firms and in their communities. They have aspirations for the future that include expanding their current operations and beginning new and related activities, such as opening retail dress shops and mini marts, and starting factories to manufacture hair products.

Several entrepreneurs recognized that their problems were related to the ESAP and were angered by the burdens that adjustment had forced them to bear. One seamstress expressed the concerns of many that not all Zimbabweans have shared equally in this misery: "I see the government as being responsible for ESAP. They have cheated us. Ministers live rent free with healthy allowances, and they backdated a 64 percent pay hike by seven months. They live well and the rest of us suffer."

Policy Recommendations and Conclusion

This chapter has explored the historical and contemporary costs that women microentrepreneurs have faced in Zimbabwe based on their gender, class, and race. It has considered as well the current dilemmas they encounter as a result of the state's adjustment program. Based on intensive interviews with more than one hundred women working as market traders, crocheters, seamstresses, and hairdressers, this study has focused on the major problems these women have experienced under the ESAP: declining profits, increased competition, the loss of customers, increased costs and difficulties in acquiring needed raw materials, inadequate sites in which to work, and the rising costs of transportation and other vital services. To ameliorate the effects of the ESAP and improve the working conditions for these microentrepreneurs, several changes are required at the micro and macro levels.

First, city governments need to provide adequate facilities in which traders and crocheters can work. New comprehensive urban markets with refrigeration and child-care facilities could house the women who are currently working in and outside of the established markets, as well as the crocheters who are now working on bare ground. In light of the economic difficulties that the state also faces, such markets could be built as self-help projects, with the government providing the materials and the entrepreneurs and their families providing the labor.

Second, there is a need to improve the urban transportation system, especially for market traders. Their critical role in the food-distribution chain needs to be recognized by the state. Without these women, many urban residents would not have food (see also Horn, this volume). Therefore, the state needs to make some effort to lower the costs of transportation for them.

Third, with respect to training, the national and local governments should not only expand technical training courses, they should also alter their orientation regarding who receives such instruction. Educational opportunities for training and retraining need to exist for women across the age spectrum. In particular, classes in nontraditional fields such as welding and metalworking should be made more widely available to women. Active media campaigns to encourage women to enter nontraditional fields should be undertaken.[5]

Fourth, the family, the school system, and the larger society need to redress the process of gender-based socialization and gender-based inequalities that restrict women's social mobility. At the very least, the colonial system of secondary education, based on O-level examinations that can only be retaken if the student is enrolled in school (and pays the requisite school fees), requires a serious review: it discriminates against poor and low-income families. In general, the present system of education, with its inherent class and gender biases, limits the development of human capital, particularly among women. In turn, this retards national development.

Fifth, Zimbabwe needs to identify new markets for its goods. As the second most industrialized country in sub-Saharan Africa, it is now expert at making many products. Through the expansion of trade networks, additional revenues could be realized. For example, rather than dwelling on the fears that majority rule in South Africa could mean the end of Zimbabwe's textile industry, Zimbabwe should explore the possibilities for new outlets for it products, outlets beyond the African continent. Such actions would not only enhance the national economy, they would strengthen social and economic relations in the region.

Finally, greater attention needs to be paid to indigenous and regional development goals. When Zimbabwe adopted an ESAP, the emphasis rested on meeting the requirements of the multilateral lenders. Little attention was given to including Zimbabweans in designing the program, nor was much consideration given to the consequences of such an agenda. With the emergence of a stronger national economy and the removal of structural inequality based on gender, women microentrepreneurs in Zimbabwe would be likely to see a major improvement in the quality of their lives and in their contributions to national development. Such changes would certainly improve the life chances and further empower some of Zimbabwe's most deserving citizens.

Notes

1. In an effort to move beyond the pejorative connotations often associated with the term *informal sector* (which has brought to mind such qualifiers as *marginal* and *inefficient*), women and development researchers have increasingly used the term *microenterprises* to refer to small income-producing activities which are usuallly owned by women. The World Bank and the U.S. Agency for International Development (USAID) define the term *microenterprise* as encompassing activities based on

indigenous resources: "Microenterprises employ five persons or less, are located in home-based or makeshift quarters, and use family members and/or apprentices. They produce for local markets, use simple technology and locally produced inputs" (Otero 1987; Osirim 1994). While this definition bears some similarity to my own, my study used the number of employees in a business as the major criterion for selection.

2. Poor black women continue to experience structural blockage in access to education. They are barred from formal sector jobs if they fail to achieve the requisite number of O-level passes on their secondary-school examinations, but retaking the test requires students' enrollment in secondary school and payment of additional school and examination fees that are out of reach for poor families.

3. Peggy Antrobus and others have suggested that there is an association between the adoption of Structural Adjustment Programs and increasing violence against women (Conference on Gender, Justice, and Development, Amherst, Mass., 1993).

4. Due to the removal of price controls and the drought of 1992, Zimbabweans had to line up for maize meal under the protection of riot police. Consumers also experienced shortages of water, sugar, cooking oil, margarine, matches, and electricity (Moyo 1992; Osirim 1994).

5. Local and national governments, as well as NGOs, need to provide information and access to support services for women's microenterprises. In addition to advertising campaigns, this study encourages the use of urban outreach workers who could provide information about such programs to women where they work—in the markets, on the roadsides, in downtown office buildings. To reduce expenditures for an outreach program, upper-secondary-school and university students could be encouraged to assume these roles as internship or community-service projects in conjunction with their course work.

References Cited

Batezat, Elinor, and Margaret Mwalo. 1989. *Women in Zimbabwe.* Harare: Southern Africa Political Economy Series Trust.

Clark, Gracia, ed. 1988. *Traders Versus the State.* Boulder, Colo.: Westview Press.

DAWN (Development Alternatives with Women for a New Era). 1995. *Markers on the Way: The DAWN Debates on Alternative Development.* Platform for the Fourth World Conference on Women in Beijing. St. Michael, Barbados: Development Alternatives with Women for a New Era.

Gibbon, Peter. 1992. The World Bank and African Poverty, 1973–1991. *Journal of Modern African Studies* 30 (2): 193–220.

Holleman, John Frederick. 1951. Some "Shona" Tribes of Southern Rhodesia. In *Seven Tribes of Central Africa,* edited by Elizabeth Colson and Max Gluckman. Manchester: Manchester University Press.

Horn, Nancy. 1994. *Cultivating Customers: Market Women in Harare, Zimbabwe.* Boulder, Colo.: Lynne Rienner Publishers.

Kadenge, Phineas, Herbert Ndoro, and Benson Zwizwai. 1992. Zimbabwe's Structural Adjustment Programme: The First-Year Experience. In *Structural Adjustment Programmes in SADC*, edited by Allast M. Mwanza. Harare: Southern Africa Political Economy Series Trust.

Kamidza, Richard. 1994. Structural Adjustment without a Human Face. *Southern Africa: Political and Economic Monthly* 7 (6).

Kurian, George. 1987. *The Encyclopedia of the Third World*. New York: Facts on File.

Made, Patricia, and Myorovai Whande. 1989. Women in Southern Africa: A Note on the Zimbabwe Success Story. *Issues: A Journal of Opinion* 17 (2).

May, Joan. 1983. *Zimbabwean Women in Colonial and Customary Law*. Gweru, Zimbabwe: Mambo Press.

Meena, Ruth. 1991. Conceptual Issues of Gender in Southern Africa. *Southern Africa* 4 (10).

Ministry of Community and Cooperative Development and Women's Affairs. 1981. *Policy Statement*. Harare: Zimbabwe Ministry of Community and Cooperative Development and Women's Affairs.

Moyo, Jonathan. 1992. State Policies and Social Domination in Zimbabwe. *Journal of Modern African Studies* 30 (2).

Moyo, Nelson P., R. J. Davies, Guy C. Z. Mhone, and Logan Pakkiri. 1984. *The Informal Sector in Zimbabwe: Its Potential for Employment Generation*. Harare: Ministry of Labor, Manpower Planning, and Social Welfare.

Muchena, Olivia. 1986. *Women's Employment Patterns, Discrimination, and Promotion of Equality in Africa: The Case of Zimbabwe*. Addis Ababa: ILO.

Nyambuya, Muchaneta N. 1994. The Social Impact of Cost Recovery Measures in Zimbabwe. *Southern Africa: Political and Economic Monthly* 7 (6).

Osirim, Mary J. 1992. The Status of Women in the Third World: The Informal Sector and Development in Africa and the Caribbean. *Social Development Issues* 14 (2/3).

———. 1994. Women, Work, and Public Policy: Structural Adjustment and the Informal Sector in Zimbabwe. In *Population Growth and Environmental Degradation in Southern Africa*, edited by Ezekiel Kalipeni. Boulder, Colo.: Lynne Rienner Publishers.

———. 1995. Trading in the Midst of Uncertainty: Market Women, Adjustment, and the Prospects for Development in Zimbabwe. *African Rural and Urban Studies* 2 (1).

Otero, Maria. 1987. *Gender Issues in Small-Scale Enterprises*. Washington, D.C.: USAID.

Saito, Katrine, 1990. *The Role of Women in the Informal Sector in Zimbabwe*. Washington, D.C.: World Bank.

Schoepf, Brooke. 1992. Gender Relations and Development: Political Economy and Culture. In *Twenty-First Century Africa: Towards a New Vision of Self-Sustainable Development*, edited by Ann Seidman and Frederick Anang. Trenton, N.J.: Africa World Press.

Seidman, Gay. 1984. Women in Zimbabwe: Post-Independence Struggles. *Feminist Studies* 10 (3).

Stoneman, Colin, and Lionel Cliffe. 1989. *Zimbabwe: Politics, Economics, and Society.* London: Pinter Publishers.

Training Aids Development Group. 1991. Structural Adjustment: Changing the Face of Zimbabwe. *Read On* 3 (May–June).

16. The Role of Entrepreneurship in Improving Policy Credibility in South Africa

Willem Naudé

South Africa is moving away from state-led, import-substitution industrialization toward trade liberalization as a development strategy. Liberalization is generally driven by the need to achieve export-led growth and attract foreign investment. Evidence favors a positive relationship between liberalization and economic growth (Balassa 1984; Darrat 1987; Greenaway and Sapsford 1993).

Successful liberalization requires that entrepreneurs reallocate resources such as labor and capital from previously protected, nontradable goods production to investment in the production of tradable goods (Rodrik 1989:1). Recent theoretical contributions (for example, Persson 1988; Rodrik 1989) imply that unemployment might increase during liberalization, not only due to friction in the process of reallocation of resources (Cooper 1991), but also because investors and entrepreneurs may doubt the credibility of the liberalization.[1] Such policy incredibility tends to result in investors' and entrepreneurs' adopting a wait-and-see attitude until they are certain which sector (either tradable or nontradable) will eventually be the most profitable (Dixit 1989; Rodrik 1989:3). Thus liberalization may not necessarily alleviate unemployment and stimulate export-led growth. Moreover, the consequences of a failed liberalization might be more damaging than no liberalization program at all (Rodrik 1989:3).[2]

This chapter contributes to the understanding of the ways of improving the credibility of trade-liberalization efforts in South Africa. The underlying hypotheses are (1) that trade liberalization and policy reform are more likely to fail in an African country than elsewhere, due to a lack of entrepreneurial ability, and (2) that this microeconomic deficiency will result in macroeconomic policies losing credibility. It is suggested that the facilitation of entrepreneurial ability might improve the credibility of macroeconomic policies.

The focus is on South Africa because, as elsewhere in Africa after independence, the newly elected South African government has inherited a situation where entrepreneurial skills among blacks are less developed due to a deliberate policy under apartheid of preventing the emergence of a strong class of black entrepreneurs (Coetzee and Naudé 1996).[3] The South African government can choose to expand the state sector and state involvement in the economy by taking over entrepreneurial responsibilities (the choice that has been made elsewhere in Africa), or it can choose to minimize the role of the state to that of facilitator for private sector entrepreneurs.

This chapter first reviews the literature on the causes and consequences of policy incredibility. It also evaluates South Africa's policies against these. It then argues that the level of policy incredibility is inherently higher in Africa (including South Africa) due to dampers on entrepreneurial ability to exploit the opportunities and manage the risk created by policy reform. Finally, ways of enhancing entrepreneurship are outlined.

Policy Credibility in South Africa

Policy Reform

On the macroeconomic policy level, the foremost constraint on economic growth in South Africa is the balance-of-payments constraint (the trade gap). While the South African economy needs to grow by at least 4 percent to 6 percent per annum to make inroads into poverty, an economic growth rate of between 2 percent to 3 percent will result in a balance-of-payments deficit. This is due to the dependency of the South African economy on imported capital and intermediate inputs in the production process. In South Africa, this dependency was fostered by decades of inward-oriented growth and development strategies.

Changes in the international community and in the thinking on economic policies and government led to political and economic reform in South Africa. Most economic-reform measures, such as policies to encourage export growth and foreign direct investment, aim at creating a more stable business environment and easing the constraint imposed by the trade gap. The measures undertaken will result in a more open and outwardly oriented economy. Examples of the most important recent measures taken by South Africa in this regard include the scrapping of the dual-exchange rate system, the lifting of exchange control measures on nonresidents, the signing of the Uruguay Round of the General Agreement on Tariffs and Trade (GATT), and the enshrining of the operational independence of the Central Bank in the Interim Constitution.

Investment Response

The incentives offered by South Africa to potential foreign investors are similar to those currently being offered by countries in East Africa. In fact, peace and increasing political stability in southern Africa are paralleled in East Africa, for instance the ending of the war in Ethiopia, the solving of the Eritrean question, the consolidation of political stability in Uganda, and the adoption of World Bank Structural Adjustment Programs. However, East Africa received less than U.S.$20 million in foreign direct investment in 1991 and 1992, and some disinvestment occurred. The result of this in Kenya was that the stock of foreign direct investment dropped from U.S.$670 million in 1980 to just below $400 million in 1990 (UNCTAD 1994).

In South Africa, notwithstanding the measures adopted and the positive political changes, there seems to be a hesitancy among foreign investors. During 1993, there was a net capital outflow of around 15 billion rands (U.S.$5 billion). Indications are that foreign direct investment in South Africa since the April 1994 elections amounts to approximately U.S.$700 million. Most current bond issues and syndicated borrowing on international capitals remain short term. Foreign financiers seem to be unwilling to lend money to South Africa beyond the next general election.

In fact, existing foreign loans are referred to by some investors as "Mandela put options," indicating the underlying perception that the current favorable policies might be reversed when President Nelson Mandela leaves office. Jenkins and Naudé (1995) suggest that this might be an indication that South Africa's macroeconomic policies and trade reform are not perceived to be credible. Likewise, the poor response of potential foreign direct investors elsewhere in southern and eastern Africa to recent changes and incentives might suggest that foreign investors do not perceive the macroeconomic policies and trade reform measures to be credible.

The difficulty in making a definitive judgment on whether policy incredibility is the cause of the dismal investment response is that the credibility of policies is not directly observable (King 1995:3). Collier (1994a, 1994b) and Collier, Greenaway, and Gunning (1993) have pointed out that the necessary conditions for policies to be credible are that they should be compatible and dynamically consistent.[4]

Compatible Policies

A compatible set of policies is a configuration of trade, monetary, fiscal, exchange rate, and aid policies that result in external balance. There are many instances of incompatible policy configurations during liberalizations in Africa. For example, in the wake of balance-of-payments problems (due to overvalued exchange rates and unsustainable foreign borrowing), particularly in the early 1980s following the oil price shock and the debt crisis, many developing countries devalued their exchange rates in order to obtain expenditure switching and expenditure reduction effects. However, due to an inability to maintain fiscal discipline, the real exchange rates soon appreciated, eroding any advantages the devaluations might have conferred on the countries.

Thus, a major problem during trade liberalization is a lack of fiscal discipline. What can be said about the compatibility of South Africa's economic policy set? Data show that balance-of-payments surpluses during most of the 1980s have been achieved at the cost of domestic fixed investment expenditure and economic growth. The external constraints that forced the previous government into this specific configuration of policies (sanctions) fell away following the elections in 1994. Consequently, South Africa's balance-of-payments position turned from positive to negative. Given that foreign exchange reserves are rather low (about equal to six weeks of imports) and that a growing South African economy has always in the past demanded greater imports, especially of intermediate and capital goods, the current compatibility of policy measures is balanced on a knife edge.

A growing economy would demand more credit, especially in the export sector, where lags between outlays and receiving of payments are longer than they are in other businesses. Given the high level of current government debt (approaching 55 percent of the gross domestic product), unless careful fiscal control is maintained, export-oriented activities risk being crowded out by government borrowing.

It should also be noted that a large part of government expenditure and investment is on nontradable goods. These include goods that cannot be imported or exported due to their nature, whether they be services (for example, haircuts or tourist attractions), construction (such as road building), or even some goods that are restricted by governments for domestic commerce only (for example, beverages like beer in some African countries). Therefore, if a large part of government investment is in such goods, this will inevitably shift the internal terms of trade in favor of nontradable production by increasing its profitability. Although it is not yet the case, the government faces the risk that its fiscal policy will become incompatible with the needed export drive.

Dynamic Inconsistency

The essence of dynamic inconsistency is that any government economic policy would not be credible if the maintenance of that policy were against the government's own interest. An example of dynamic inconsistency is the taxation in many African countries of exports of primary commodities such as coffee (Collier and Gunning 1994:3). As a consequence, export production in those commodities dwindled. To rectify this situation, many governments lowered or eliminated the taxes on the exports in question. This is an optimal policy, since *ex ante* the government does not lose significant revenue, due to the collapse in export production. However, once farmers react to the incentive and produce more of the good, the temptation arises for the government to reimpose the tax.

A trade liberalization program can be perceived as dynamically inconsistent if the country's trade policy is endogenous and/or the government's intentions or motivation for the trade liberalization are misunderstood. Trade policy will be endogenous if it is a predictable response to some economic situation. For example, if the government is known to operate a trade policy in which, if the balance of payments deteriorates, it imposes import quotas and raises tariffs (and conversely in case of a balance-of-payments surplus, it lowers tariffs and eliminates quotas), private agents will be able to deduce that a trade liberalization will be reversed if external imbalances start occurring (Collier, Greenaway, and Gunning 1993:24).

An example is the 1978 Kenyan coffee boom (Reinikka 1994). The Kenyan government embarked on trade liberalization in the light of balance-of-payments surpluses. Exports and investment in export production failed to materialize; agents expected the trade liberalization to be reversed (since the coffee boom was clearly temporary) and started hoarding of imports. This reduced their fixed investments.

A government's intentions can be misunderstood by economic agents if the trade liberalization is accompanied by significant inflows of foreign aid (Rodrik 1989). Thus, many African governments might have no serious intention of permanently liberalizing and may be going along with donor conditionality for the sake of aid.

The question for South Africa is whether its current trade liberalization is a genuine policy-rule change or just an endogenous response to the change in external circumstances affecting the country. Related to this is the possibility that the government is only engaging in trade liberalization to attract foreign aid and loans over the short run in an attempt to be able to deliver quickly to the electorate before the election in 1999. It may be perceived that trade liberalization is an attempt by the new government to make the most of the current goodwill that exists toward South Africa in the world.

In other words, the impetus for the trade liberalization is external. It might be that for a resumption of loans and access to world financial markets to occur, South Africa is required to commit itself to trade liberalization measures, just as it needed to obtain a favorable rating from investment-rating agencies such as Moody's and Standard and Poor.

The implication is that the drive for trade liberalization should be seen to come from within South Africa. Trade unions and business forums should be solidly behind the trade reform. In this regard, entrepreneurs have an important role to play. It will be argued below that due to dampers on entrepreneurial development in South Africa, entrepreneurs may consider lobbying for protection to be vital to their survival. Potential foreign and domestic investors might perceive this possibility and thus refrain from investing in South Africa.

From the above discussion, the conclusion is that judged by the criteria of compatibility and dynamic consistency, South Africa's macroeconomic policies and trade reform may seem to be credible. But given the lack of sufficient investment response discussed, some other factor will have to be identified to account for the apparent high level of policy incredibility that foreign investors seem to attach to policies in South Africa.

The Role of Entrepreneurship

Ultimately, it is entrepreneurs who are responsible for the reallocation of resources toward the production of tradables. As an explanation for Africa's (and South Africa's) dismal record with respect to foreign direct investment and exports, policy incompatibility and dynamic inconsistency of policies do not, by themselves, seem to be enough. The nature of the causes of policy incompatibility and dynamic inconsistency is such that all countries' policies will be subject to some kind of incredibility. Rodrik points out that "at a fundamental level, no reform can be entirely credible because unforeseen circumstances and re-evaluation are always likely, requiring eventually some changes at the margin" (1989:4).

Many developing countries have been able, notwithstanding some marginal policy incompatibility and dynamic inconsistency, to attract significant inflows of foreign direct investment. Africa is the exception, which suggests that potential foreign investors view policy incredibility in Africa as much more serious than elsewhere. Why might this be the case ?

The similarity in many cases of the macroeconomic constraints and external shocks faced by Africa and other developing regions suggests that the answer might rather lie on a microeconomic level. In this regard, Collier has pointed to the fact that "what was peculiar about Africa upon independence was the negligible participation of Africans in large scale economic organizations, most particularly private firms, except as workers" (1994a:2).

Further, after independence, the public sector was biased toward indigenous Africans. This further diverted the already small stock of indigenous entrepreneurs from entering the private sector. Instead, corruption and rent seeking within the public sector became the principal means to power and wealth for potential ambitious entrepreneurs (Collier 1994a:3). The shortage of private entrepreneurs in Africa was exacerbated by the leading role that was assigned to parastatals (Lall 1991:267). Moreover, the state-centered approach to development suited many African leaders' desire to avoid the establishment of an indigenous business class that might serve as an opposition power base (Steel and Wangwe 1991:286). Although South Africa differs in many respects from the rest of Africa, similar considerations applied under apartheid.

Consequently, the private sector in South Africa is today largely characterized by small informal, unregulated, and unrecorded activities. In many cases, these only fulfill a survival function.[5] Local entrepreneurs lack the technical, managerial, accounting, marketing, and sales skills required for successful entrepreneurship in the global village (Kaunda and Miti 1995:375). Many entrepreneurs lack the ability to recognize that the nature of international competition is changing, and that exports need to be differentiated, of high quality, and tailor-made to the needs of the consumer (Ismail 1995).

Not only is the lack of such entrepreneurial ability a serious micro-economic constraint in South Africa, the lack of skills and education among workers is a serious constraint factor for the existing black entrepreneurs. In addition, entrepreneurs who do not have the necessary skills to manage the risks accompanying South Africa's changing circumstances may not be hiring labor (Collier 1994c:5), thus accounting for persistent unemployment.

Moreover, strategies by South Africa to increase manufactured exports may not be viewed as credible because the export of manufactures requires abundant skills that are lacking (Ismail 1995). The greater abundance of skills in the developed world and in other developing countries, such as East Asia and Latin America, generally explains Africa's inability to export manufactured goods (Wood 1994). In the case of Mauritius, arguably Africa's only export-led growth success, it was the country's combination of an abundant supply of inexpensive labor and high skill levels that was important in explaining its success (Rogerson 1993:191). Lall (1991:265) also identifies Mauritius's "strong indigenous entrepreneurial class" as one of the factors that differentiate it from the rest of Africa.

Table 16.1 shows that education levels in South Africa are not that different from those of the other developing countries listed. However, the adult literacy rate at 46 percent is considerably lower in South Africa than it is in the four other countries—South Korea, Malaysia, Brazil, and Mexico. This is a result of the differential access to educational opportunities for a large segment of the South African population under apartheid. Adults in the labor force are, therefore, deficient in skills that are needed in high-quality manufactured exports such as machinery and transport equipment. In South Africa, these types of exports account for only 3 percent of total exports, while in countries such as South Korea they make up 38 percent, and in Malaysia, 27 percent (Ismail 1995:40).

The importance of higher education levels, specifically in secondary education, to explain East Asia's superior export record relative to that of Africa has recently been emphasized by Nehru, Swanson, and Dubey (1995). Table 16.2 shows that, compared with all other developing regions, Africa has the lowest level of education. The gaps are particularly large in secondary and tertiary education. This presents a difficult challenge for Africa to catch up and compete with these other regions, especially East Asia, because the absolute magnitude and growth of the education level in East Asia is high (291).

The problem of lower levels of education has a double impact on the entrepreneur. He or she is constrained by limited knowledge of the effective use of business and policy strategies. In addition, lower levels of education in the general population mean that the pool of potential employees will have limited skills and training. Thus, economic strategies and trade orientation that incline toward export promotion (especially of manufactures) might be viewed with additional skepticism in South Africa, because entrepreneurs do not yet have the capacity to make these strategies work,

Table 16.1. Profile of education levels in South Africa and selected developing countries, 1990 (% of population)

	South Africa	South Korea	Malaysia	Brazil	Mexico
No education	28.6	13.3	26.7	27.4	27.5
Some primary	11.0	0.9	16.2	43.1	24.1
Complete primary	18.8	27.4	21.0	9.6	22.4
Some secondary	26.0	21.7	20.1	9.9	11.7
Complete secondary	13.9	27.5	14.1	5.7	4.2
Degree(s)	1.6	4.8	1.3	2.4	5.6
Adult literacy	46.0	94.7	74.0	78.5	84.7

Source: Ismail 1995.

Table 16.2. Level of education by region in 1989 (in average years per capita)

Region	Primary	Secondary	Tertiary	Total
East Asia	4.38	0.72	0.03	5.13
South Asia	2.39	0.88	0.12	3.39
Latin America	4.65	0.56	0.31	5.52
Africa	2.33	0.19	0.02	2.54
Industrialized countries	6.53	2.60	0.88	10.00
World average	4.38	1.17	0.29	5.85

Source: Nehru et al. 1995.

even though South Africa might have a marginally better-skilled labor force than those of many other African countries.

An implication is that South African entrepreneurs are likely to consider lobbying for some form of trade protection (or export promotion) to be vital for their survival. A recent survey of South African entrepreneurs found that 71 percent of entrepreneurs felt that current changes in South Africa's macroenvironment imply some risk for their enterprises (Coetzee and Visagie 1995:42–44).

Furthermore, most of South Africa's successful export-oriented firms are large conglomerates that are shedding employment opportunities in their desire to become internationally competitive. Because the Reconstruction and Development Program and the recent Presidential Committee on economic growth envisage job-creating economic growth in South Africa, such exports will not create an interest group with a stake in trade liberalization. In fact, political pressures for a different type of growth strategy will mount if export orientation does not create employment opportunities.

Generally in Africa, and also among black entrepreneurs in South Africa, employment creation is dominated by informal businesses and microenterprises (Oyejide 1991; Mapetla 1995; Coetzee and Naudé 1996), which should naturally be at the forefront of export-led growth. Although a number of studies have found a positive relationship between firm size and export capability (Patibandla 1995), for example in Taiwan, 70 percent of the work force is employed by small enterprises employing less than ten people (Mapetla 1995:33).[6] However, for South Africa to follow Taiwan's example in this, a similar level and growth of entrepreneurial quality would have to exist.

Enhancing Entrepreneurship

A number of studies confirm the positive impact of education on economic growth, but most focus on the quantity of education. However, evidence is accumulating that it is the quality rather than the quantity of education that is of importance. For instance, Oyejide (1991:279) points out that weakness of entrepreneurs in Africa is due to the fact that most have emerged from the ranks of craftsmen, and that it has been found that these skills are not easily transferable to diversified activities or larger types of enterprises. In a study of urban manufacturing workers in Kenya and Tanzania, Knight and Sabot (1990) found that the level of wages paid was related to the type of skills the workers possessed.

The indications are that in South Africa, the emphasis in coming years will have to be on the quality rather than the quantity of education and of education expenditure. For instance, the share of education expenditure in the central government budget increased from 13 percent in 1975 to 20 percent in 1990, and government spending on black education increased by 866 percent between 1970 and 1993. The efficiency of increasing government expenditure on schooling can be questioned, if the type of skills taught at school are not taken into account. For example, social rates of return to investment in the schooling of blacks were calculated by Hosking (1991, 1992), Archer and Moll (1992), Donaldson and Roux (1990), and Pillay (1991). Their estimates range from 5 percent to 18 percent, further suggesting that private returns to investment in schooling are higher than the social rates of return.

Clearly, the implication that the government should tax schooling or decrease expenditures thereon is contrary to any intuitive understanding of the South African situation. These results should be seen against the possibility that when more computational skills are taught to blacks, these returns on education will increase, because computational skills are better rewarded in the South African labor market (Moll 1995:13).

To raise the quality of education in South Africa, a reorientation in the emphasis placed on computational versus other skills might therefore be required. It would seem that South Africans especially lack computational and technological skills. Evidence for this was recently obtained from a new data set on South African households.[7] From an analysis of this data set, Moll found that the African primary-school system was a poor producer of computational ability and that "there appears to be a severe failing in the instructional process. The primary schools are not achieving what they set out to achieve" (Moll 1995:13).

Computational skills are needed by entrepreneurs for the sound financial management of their businesses, to adopt new technology, and to equip workers with the needed tools to manufacture high-quality, value-rich exports. Without adequate skills in financial management and other organization techniques, the size and complexity of the firms they can operate are limited. This represents an insurmountable obstacle to sustained and effective export growth.

The government in South Africa should not only improve the quality of education, it should also create incentives for the private sector to play a greater role in the provision of education and training. For example, on average in developed countries, about 4 percent of the annual wages bill is invested in education and training of a company's employees, while in South Africa, this figure is less than 1 percent (Hutton-Wilson 1995:45). It is even less in other southern African countries. As long as South African enterprises remain protected and relatively isolated, little incentive will exist for them to engage in training and education.

The opening up of the South African economy will thus have significant positive externalities. These constitute a case for government intervention. If the government can ensure that South Africans benefit from these positive externalities through the receipt of education from the private sector, a large interest group will be created that will favor trade liberalization. How this can be most effectively achieved in South Africa remains for future research to establish.

Conclusion

It was argued in this chapter that trade liberalization in South Africa needs to be accompanied by other steps to increase the skills of entrepreneurs. This is to allow them to respond to the incentives and opportunities created by liberalization and to manage the risks involved in an outward orientation. It was pointed out that, in general, Africa's relative lack of foreign direct investment, in comparison with such investment in countries in East Asia, might be explained by the lack of skills and training among its indigenous entrepreneurs.

In South Africa's case, it was emphasized that it is the quality of education that is inadequate, especially with regard to computational skills. The new Government of National Unity should take active steps to improve the computational skills of its population and to encourage the private sector to play a much greater role in providing education and training than it currently does.

Notes

1. In the context of economic policy, credibility refers to whether the policy makers' announced intentions are believable (King 1995:2).

2. Collier (1994b:21) and Collier and Gunning (1994) describe the negative consequences of limited credibility of trade reform, including speculation, hoarding of imports, and delayed investment.

3. Elsewhere in southern Africa, the emergence of local entrepreneurs was inhibited during colonial times by an absence of urban centers, economic activity, infrastructure, and colonial policies (Kaunda and Miti 1995:368).

4. Collier performed this exercise for Zimbabwe and concluded that "the government does not currently face a serious problem, but that it could improve the presentation of its reform program to enhance investor confidence"(1994b:31). Recently, however, the Zimbabwean government failed to meet the fiscal objectives it agreed to with the International Monetary Fund, leading to that organization's freezing its assistance.

5. Few of Africa's myriad informal and microenterprises develop into modern, medium-size firms (Oyejide 1991:281).

6. Large firms are expected to fare better than small firms in exports because of the economics of scale in production, research and development expenditure, and risk-taking abilities.

7. About 8,800 households were interviewed by the Southern African Labor and Development Unit and the Human Resources Division of the Southern African Department of the World Bank.

References Cited

Archer, Sean, and Peter Moll. 1992. Education and Economic Growth. In *Economic Growth in South Africa: Selected Policy Issues*, edited by I. Abedian and B. Standish. Cape Town: Oxford University Press.

Balassa, Bela. 1984. Adjustment to External Shocks in Developing Countries. World Bank Staff Working Paper No. 472. Washington, D.C.: World Bank.

Coetzee, Jos E., and Jan C. Visagie. 1995. SME Challenges in Reconstructing South Africa. *South African Journal of Entrepreneurship and Small Business* (May):37–50.

Coetzee, Rian, and Willem Naudé. 1996. The Historical External Constraints on the Structure of Black Urban Business in South Africa. In *Essays in Economic and Business History*, edited by H. Childs. Columbus, Ohio: Ohio State University.

Collier, Paul. 1994a. The Domain of African Government. Oxford: Centre for the Study of African Economies, University of Oxford (mimeo).

———. 1994b. Macroeconomic Aspects of Zimbabwean Trade Liberalisation. Oxford: Centre for the Study of African Economies, University of Oxford (mimeo).

———. 1994c. African Labour Markets. Oxford: Centre for the Study of African Economies, University of Oxford (mimeo).

Collier, Paul, David Greenaway, and Jan Willem Gunning. 1993. A Methodology for the Study of Trade Liberalisation. Paper presented at the AERC's [African Economic Research Consortium's] Launch Workshop on Regional Integration and Trade Liberalisation, 1–3 December, Nairobi.

Collier, Paul, and Jan Willem Gunning. 1994. Portfolio Responses to Trade Policy Incredibility. Paper presented at the Annual Conference of the Royal Economic Society, 28 March, Exeter.

Cooper, R. N. 1991. Economic Stabilization in Developing Countries. International Center for Economic Growth, Occasional Paper no. 14.

Darrat, A. 1987. Are Exports an Engine of Growth? *Applied Economics* 19 (2):277–83.

Dixit, Avinash. 1989. Intersectoral Capital Reallocation under Price Uncertainty. *Journal of International Economics* 26 (1):309–25.

Donaldson, Andrew, and André Roux. 1990. Education, Employment, and the Incomes of Black South Africans in 1985. Conference on Literary and Basic Adult Education in South Africa. Pretoria: Human Science Research Council.

Greenaway, David, and David Sapsford. 1993. Exports, Growth, and Liberalisation: An Evaluation. *Journal of Policy Modeling* 15 (1).

Hosking, Stephen. 1991. Social Rates of Return to Investment in Black Education. *Journal for Studies in Economics and Econometrics* 15 (3):43–55.

———. 1992. On Social Rates of Return to Investment in Education. *South African Journal of Economics* 60 (2):221–32.

———. 1995. A Critique of the Efficiency Case for Increasing Government Expenditure on Schooling in Post-Apartheid South Africa. *Journal for Studies in Economics and Econometrics* 19 (2):77–89.

Hutton-Wilson, David. 1995. Managerial, Technical, and Professional Skills: A Strength or Impediment to Growth and Foreign Investment in South Africa. Paper presented at the Europe–South Africa 1995 Business and Finance Forum, 27 June, Le Petit Palais, Montreux.

Ismail, Faizel. 1995. Education and the Ability to Export Manufactures: The Relevance to South Africa of the Wood Model. *Development Southern Africa* 12 (1):35–44.

Jenkins, Carolyn, and Willem Naudé. 1995. Reciprocity in South African-European Trade Relations. Paper presented at the Biennial Conference of the Economic Society of South Africa, 7 September, Rand Afrikaans University, Johannesburg.

Kaunda, M., and K. Miti. 1995. Promotion of Private Enterprise and Citizen Entrepreneurship in Botswana. *Development Southern Africa* 12 (3):367–78.

King, Mervin. 1995. Credibility and Monetary Policy: Theory and Evidence. *Scottish Journal of Political Economy* 42 (1):1–19.

Knight, John, and Richard Sabot. 1990. *Education, Productivity, and Inequality: The East African Natural Experiment.* Oxford: Oxford University Press.

Lall, Sanjaya. 1991. Human Resources, Technology, and Industrial Development in Sub-Saharan Africa. In *Economic Reform in Sub-Saharan Africa,* edited by Ajay Chhibber and Stanley Fischer. Washington, D.C.: World Bank.

Mapetla, N. 1995. Small Business Development in South Africa. Paper presented at the Europe–South Africa 1995 Business and Finance Forum, 27 June, Le Petit Palais, Montreux.

Moll, Peter. 1995. Human Capital, Cognitive Skill, and Schooling in South Africa. Paper presented at the Lunchtime Seminar, May, Centre for the Study of African Economies, University of Oxford.

Nehru, Vikram, E. Swanson, and A. Dubey. 1995. A New Database on Human Capital Stock in Developing and Industrial Countries: Sources, Methodology, and Results. *Journal of Development Economics* 46 (3):379–401.

Oyejide, T. A. 1991. Entrepreneurship and Growth in Sub-Saharan Africa: Evidence and Policy Implications. In *Economic Reform in Sub-Saharan Africa,* edited by Ajay Chhibber and Stanley Fischer. Washington, D.C.: World Bank.

Patibandla, M. 1995. Firm Size and Export Behaviour: An Indian Case Study. *Journal of Development Studies* 31 (6):868–82.

Persson, Torssten. 1988. Credibility of Macroeconomic Policy: An Introduction and a Broad Survey. *European Economic Review* 32:519–32.

Pillay, Punday. 1991. Education, Employment, and Earnings: A Study of the South African Manufacturing Sector. Ph.D. dissertation, University of Cape Town.

Reinikka, Riva. 1994. The Welfare Cost of Speculation During Kenyan Trade Reform. Centre for the Study of African Economies Working Paper no. 94/11. University of Oxford.

Rodrik, Dani. 1989. Credibility of Trade Reform: A Policy Maker's Guide. *The World Economy* 12 (1):1–16.

Rogerson, Chris. 1993. Export-Processing Industrialisation in Mauritius: The Lessons of Success. *Development Southern Africa* 10 (2): 177–98.

Steel, William, and Sam Wangwe. 1991. Comments on Human Capital and Entrepreneurship. In *Economic Reform in Sub-Saharan Africa,* edited by Ajay Chhibber and Stanley Fischer. Washington, D.C.: World Bank.

UNCTAD (United Nations Conference on Trade and Development). 1994. *World Investment Report.* New York: United Nations.

Wood, Adrian. 1994. Give Heckscher and Ohlin a Chance. *Weltwirtschaftliches Archiv* 130 (1):20–49.

Contributors

Robert A. Blewett received his Ph.D. from Virginia Polytechnic Institute. He is professor of economics at St. Lawrence University in Canton, New York. His principal research region is East Africa, where his current research involves the economics of the informal sector, as well as the economics of popular music.

Lisa Daniels, who received her Ph.D. from Michigan State University, is assistant professor in the Department of Economics at Washington College, Maryland. Over the past seven years, she has conducted research on micro and small enterprises in Botswana, Malawi, Zimbabwe, and Kenya for the GEMINI project and has produced numerous articles and reports.

Marcel Fafchamps is assistant professor at Stanford University and holds a Ph.D. from the University of California at Berkeley. He has been an investigator in several projects sponsored by the World Bank and other international organizations; his research area is economic development in Africa.

Michael Farley, associate professor in the Music Department at St. Lawrence University, received his Ph.D. at the University of Iowa. His areas of research include music composition and music as an expression of cultural interaction.

David Himbara, who received his doctoral degree from Queen's University in Canada, is senior lecturer at the University of the Witwatersrand, South Africa. His current research is focused on African political and economic history, and he plans to continue his study of entrepreneurship in Africa. He is the author of *Kenyan Capitalists, the State, and Development* (1994).

Nancy Horn, director of international training at Opportunity International in Elmhurst, Illinois, received her Ph.D. in anthropology from Michigan State University. She has been active in microenterprise development endeavors for over ten years. Her book, *Cultivating Customers: Market Women in Harare, Zimbabwe* (1994), analyzes the culture, urban context, and economics of fresh produce vending. In her future work, she will consider market women's activities as the starting place for research and theory building.

Okechukwu C. Iheduru holds a Ph.D. from the University of Connecticut. He is assistant professor of international relations at Michigan State University. His most recent publications include an article titled "Post-Apartheid South Africa and Its Neighbors: A Maritime Transport Perspective" (1996) and *The Political Economy of International Shipping in Developing Countries* (1996). He is currently writing on the politics of economic empowerment in South Africa.

Mwango Kasengele, who holds a Ph.D. from the University of Glasgow, is an independent development consultant on African affairs, with funding from Japanese Aid to Africa. He has been a university lecturer in both Zambia and the United Kingdom. His current research involves civil service reforms in Africa, with special reference to the Public Service Reform Program in Zambia.

Judith Krieger, a nutritional anthropologist, received her Ph.D. in anthropology from the University of Kentucky. She is currently a research associate at Huxley College of Environmental Studies, Western Washington University. She has worked in Cameroon since 1989, concentrating on women's work, household food security, child growth, and community health.

Janet MacGaffey holds a Ph.D. from Bryn Mawr College and is associate professor of anthropology at Bucknell University. She has written or coauthored books and articles on entrepreneurship, African economic development, and second-economy trade, including *Entrepreneurs and Parasites: The Struggle for Indigenous Capitalism in Zaire* (1987) and *The Real Economy of Zaire* (1991). Her future areas of research will focus on cross-border trade.

Barbara E. McDade, assistant professor of geography at the University of Florida, received her Ph.D. in geography and community and regional planning from the University of Texas at Austin. Her primary research areas are entrepreneurship and economic development in Africa and the African diaspora. She has done fieldwork in Ghana and survey research on black-owned businesses in the United States.

Yvette Monga holds a doctorate in history from the University of Aix-en-Provence and served as a teaching fellow in the Department of History at Harvard University. Her current research interests focus on reevaluating historical interpretations of political and economic development in West Africa, particularly in Cameroon.

Willem Naudé is chair and professor of economics at Potchefstroom University, South Africa, from which he also received his Ph.D. He completed the work for his chapter as a research officer at the Center for the Study of African Economies at the University of Oxford. He has been a visiting professor at Addis Ababa University and an adviser to the United Nations Development Program in Gabon, Côte d'Ivoire, Guinea-Bissau, and Malawi. His research interests are in quantitative development economics, especially with regard to fiscal, spatial, and trade issues.

Mary Johnson Osirim holds a Ph.D. from Harvard University. She is associate professor of sociology and coordinator of Africana Studies at Bryn Mawr College. Her specialty areas include women and development in western and southern Africa and in the English-speaking Caribbean countries, economic sociology, and entrepreneurship. She is currently completing a book on women and African entrepreneurship.

Claire C. Robertson holds a Ph.D. from the University of Wisconsin at Madison. She is associate professor of women's studies and history at Ohio State University. She has done fieldwork in Ghana and Kenya on women entrepreneurs and has published several dozen articles and three books, one of which won the 1985 African Studies Association's Herskovits Award. Her forthcoming book is *"Trouble Showed the Way": Women, Men, and Trade in the Nairobi Area, 1890–1990.*

Anita Spring, professor of anthropology and African Studies at the University of Florida, received her Ph.D. from Cornell University. She has done extensive research and published widely on women in development, medical and social anthropology, gender analysis, farming systems, and environmental resource management. She has done fieldwork in Cameroon, Ethiopia, Kenya, Malawi, Somalia, Swaziland, Zambia, and Zimbabwe.

Recent books include *Agricultural Development and Gender Issues in Malawi* (1995) and *Commercialization of Agriculture and Women Farmers* (forthcoming).

Chikwendu Christian Ukaegbu received his Ph.D. from Northwestern University. He is senior lecturer at the University of Nigeria, Nsukka, and has taught at the University of Wyoming in the Department of Sociology. His research specialty is industrial development and human resources. He recently conducted a study on enterprise survival in the manufacturing sector in Nigeria, and his current research is on ethnicity and politics in Nigeria.

Index

enterprise, in Africa, 251
for microenterprises, 141
for small businesses, 74
sources of, 270
foreign investment in post-apartheid
South Africa, 300
formal sector, 1, 10–11, 15, 19, 21, 51,
96, 104, 135, 219–20, 230, 278–81,
287, 290, 202, 295
Asian clothing factories in
Zambia, 20
barriers to entry, for women, 16–
17
business practices in Nigeria, 22
commerce, under colonialism, 8
contrasted with small- to
medium-sized enterprises, 14
control of scarce resources by, 100
false dichotomy between formal
and informal sectors, 231
loans and tax credits in, 24
MSE entry and, 63
penetration of, by upper-income
Zambian women, 18
public enterprises and, 13
regulations that hinder medium
to small businesses and, 13
stagnation of, in South Africa, 85
state assistance to indigenous
entrepreneurs and, 9
wages and opportunity costs in,
59

GECAMINES (copper mining company
in Zaire), 39, 48
gender
and entrepreneurial activities, 15–
17
differences
in access to critical resources,
111–20
and commodities and profits,
117–19
coping strategies, 120–24
goods sold and profits made by
Kenyan traders, 117–19
among Kenyan vendors in Kutus
Market, 125–26n
and profits, 115–20
and start-up capital, 115–16
and division of labor, 110, 131
food crops grown and, 155–57
in Cameroon, 150, 160
in informal sector of Kenya, 124
in Kenya, 122–24
in rural areas of Zimbabwe, 130
in trade specializations, 43
in Zimbabwe, 278
"gender blackmail," and educational
expenses, 164n
gender-role socialization patterns in
Zimbabwe, 287
Ghana
cane and rattan weavers in, 199–213
as artisan entrepreneurs, 200–202
characteristics of successful, 203–
6
determinants of business success
of, 202
education, 200–202
rural enterprises, characteristics of
success of, 208–9
rural entrepreneurs, 207
urban enterprises, characteristics of
success of, 209–12
urban entrepreneurs, 207–8
Government of National Unity, 69, 309
Grameen Bank, loans to small
businesses, 125

harassment
of entrepreneurs, 18, 40
of "foreign" business people, 225
of informal sector, 24, 29
of Lebanese businessmen in Zaire,
47

as traders in Kenya
  and access to land, 113–14, 117
  child support by, 124
  characteristics of, 111
  duration of businesses of, 121
  education of, 114–15
  hours worked, 123
  income of
    from cash crops, 114
    and profits of, 115–16
  motives to enter trade, 121
  patterns of business growth, 121–22
  reasons for leaving trade, 122
  selling space, legal and illegal, 116
  as suppliers of foodstuffs, 20–21
micro and small enterprises, 66n, 309n
  African Development Bank, 15
  barriers to entry, 56–58
  definition of, 65n, 294–95n
  entry into, 17–20
  entry model, 54–63
    for high- and low-profit industries, 19, 61–63
  factors limiting growth of, 12
  goods and services offered by, in Zimbabwe, 286
  integrationist partnerships in, 79–80
  lack of capital and credit in, 132
  parallelist models of, 79–80
  as sources of income for women, 15
  survival strategies in, 10–13
  sustainability of employment in, 52–53
  women in, 15
    why enter, in Zimbabwe, 278
    in Zimbabwe, 128–42
microenterprises. See micro and small enterprises
microentrepreneurs
  in Kenya, income of, 120
  in Zimbabwe

competition between men and women in, 279, 281–82
educational levels of, 286–88
men, 280
profile of, in Harare and Bulawayo, 286–87
migration, 63, 208, 228, 236
  urban, in Zimbabwe, 132
MSEs. See micro and small enterprises
multinationals, 30, 39–40, 88–89, 143, 185, 190, 238, 249

networks, 15, 28, 44, 73, 96, 233, 279–80
  Asian, 95, 240, 242, 246
  business, 18, 83, 97, 104, 177, 183, 194, 236, 240, 242, 244
  customer, 97, 100
  distribution, 243–44
  financial, 24
  informal, 269
  international, 26
  market, 178
  retail, 236
  social, 23, 25, 160, 169, 171–73, 176–77
    role of, for Duala, 176
  trade, 17, 110, 294
    women's, 130, 134
  traditional, 22
NGOs. See Non-Governmental Organizations
Nigeria
  businesses and disputes over ownership in, 192
  entrepreneurs in
    characteristics of, 186
    delegation of authority by, 190
    secrecy among, 193–94
  managers
    characteristics of, 188
    education of, 186

women—*continued*
    suggestions for improving the
      success of, 293–94
    and trade with South Africa,
      291
    as minors in colonial Zimba-
      bwe, 279
    motives of, to enter trade in Kenya,
      120–21
    and patterns of business growth, in
      Kenya, 121–22
    reasons of, for leaving trading, in
      Kenya, 122
    self-employment of, in Zimbabwe,
      280
    selling space of, legal and illegal,
      116
    status of, in colonial Zimbabwe, 279
    as traders
      access of, to land, in Kenya,
        110, 113–14
      characteristics of, in Kenya, 111
      and child support, in Kenya, 124
      harassment of, in Kenya, 122
      nutritional status of children of,
        in Cameroon, 163
      selling space for, in Kenya,116
    as vendors
      in Cameroon, 157–60
      and inflation in Zimbabwe, 137–
      38
      profit margins of, in Kenya, 126n
    work and dependency load of, 124
women's entrepreneurship, Ten
  Tenets of, 139–41
workshop tailors, 97–98
World Bank, 135, 199, 281, 300
    definition of microenterprises, 294–
    95n
    Regional Program for Enterprise
    Development, 252
    and Zaire, 38

Zaire
    collapse of official economy in, 39
    consequences of economic prob-
      lems in, 38–40
    export commodities in, 41
    GECAMINES (copper mining
      company) and, 39
    harassment of traders in, 46
    and imports from West Africa, 43
    and International Monetary Fund,
      38
    Mariano market, and Angolan civil
      war, 42
    Mariano market (Kinshasa), women
      in, 42
    official and second economies of,
      37–48
    profitability of import trade in, 40
    se débrouillaient in, 40
    strategies to conduct unofficial
      trade in, 45
    trade between East Africa and, 42–
      43
    trade with the Far East, 44
    trade with South Africa, 43–44
    trading trips by entrepreneurs in,
      40–45
    transport problems in, 45
    World Bank and, 38
Zambia
    Asian entrepreneurs in, 94–96
    barriers to Zambian men in, 18,
      132–33
    clothing industry, 93–105
      policy reforms, effect of, on
        women entrepreneurs, 103–4
      effect of *salaula* on, 101–3
      micro and small entrepreneurs in,
        99–101
      policy reforms, by government of,
        103–4
      small-scale women producers in, 97